Perspectives on Kentucky's Past

ARCHITECTURE, ARCHAEOLOGY, AND LANDSCAPE

Julie Riesenweber

General Editor

Kentucky ARCHAEOLOGY

R. BARRY LEWIS

Editor

THE UNIVERSITY PRESS OF KENTUCKY

Copyright © 1996 by The University Press of Kentucky

Scholarly publisher for the Commonwealth,
serving Bellarmine College, Berea College, Centre
College of Kentucky, Eastern Kentucky University,
The Filson Club, Georgetown College, Kentucky
Historical Society, Kentucky State University,
Morehead State University, Murray State University,
Northern Kentucky University, Transylvania University,
University of Kentucky, University of Louisville,
and Western Kentucky University.

Editorial and Sales Offices: The University Press of Kentucky
663 S. Limestone St., Lexington, Kentucky 40508-4008

Library of Congress Cataloging-in Publication Data

Kentucky archaeology / R. Barry Lewis, editor.
    p. cm. — (Perspectives on Kentucky's past)
  Includes bibliographical references (p.) and index.
  ISBN 0-8131-1907-3 (alk. paper)
  1. Kentucky—Antiquities. 2. Indians of North America—Kentucky—Antiquities.
3. Excavations (Archaeology—Kentucky. I. Lewis, R. Barry. II. Series.
F453.K46 1996
976.9'01—dc20   95-32376

This book is printed on acid-free recycled paper meeting
the requirements of the American National Standard
for Permanence of Paper for Printed Library Materials.

Manufactured in the United States of America

To the memory of
William Snyder Webb
1882–1964

CONTENTS

Kentucky's thousands of cultural resources form a tangible record of more than 12,000 years of prehistory and history. They include archaeological sites as well as above-ground structures ranging from individual houses to entire streetscapes of Victorian commercial buildings. These resources combine to form a past and present cultural landscape worthy of preservation.

This publication, the second volume in the Kentucky Heritage Council's Perspectives on Kentucky's Past series, is a product of the council's ongoing effort to make information about the past available to nonarchaeologists. Over the past 160 years, archaeological investigations in Kentucky have recorded more than 15,000 archaeological sites. Ranging from small lithic scatters to large Mississippian towns and from frontier settlements to Civil War earthworks and battlefields to urban industrial complexes, these sites are found throughout the state. Though a great deal has been written about the Native American cultures that lived in what is now Kentucky, most publications are quite technical and were written for other archaeologists. Also, while many people are quite knowledgeable about Kentucky's history, few are aware of the contributions historic archaeologists have made to our understanding of the lives of everyday people during the late eighteenth and nineteenth centuries. *Kentucky Archaeology,* as well as the recently published *Kentuckians before Boone,* goes a long way toward making information concerning Kentucky's past available to a more general audience.

Kentucky Archaeology is an outgrowth of a comprehensive planning process initiated in 1986 by the Kentucky Heritage Council. Recognizing a need to identify what had been learned from over 150 years of archaeological research in Kentucky and to make this information available to other archaeologists, the council contracted with several archaeologists to produce overviews for the Paleoindian, Archaic, Woodland, Mississippi, Fort Ancient, and Historic periods. Each author was instructed to summarize what is known about each period and to identify data gaps in the archaeological record of Kentucky that could be addressed by future archaeological investigations. This project resulted in the publication of the report entitled the *Archaeology of Kentucky: Past Accomplishments and Future Directions,* edited by David Pollack.

When Dr. R. Barry Lewis approached the Heritage Council about editing a volume on Kentucky archaeology aimed at the general public, we saw his proposal as an opportunity to make information on Kentucky's past available to a much wider audience than the above-mentioned publication, which was intended for a much more limited audience (i.e., professional archaeologists).

Dr. Lewis and the other authors of this volume have done an excellent job of characterizing what is known about Kentucky's past and describing the life-ways of the people who lived in what is now Kentucky for thousands of years before Euro-American settlement of the Ohio River Valley. They also have shown that through an examination of archaeological resources dating from the late eighteenth to the early decades of the twentieth century we can learn a great deal about our own heritage.

It is our hope that publications such as this will help dispel the myth that Native American people never lived in Kentucky and that it was just a con-tested hunting area where people camped for only short periods of time. Native Americans lived year-round in what is now Kentucky. They construct-ed houses, planted crops, rejoiced at the birth of new family members, and buried and mourned their dead. In short, Kentucky has a rich and diverse archaeological record that attests to a long history of use by a variety of dif-ferent peoples.

Preservationists have always made decisions about which cultural resources should remain for future generations, but these decisions are becoming more difficult. No longer is preservation a simple matter of saving old buildings from the wrecking ball or restoring them to their original appearance. Preservationists today must not only consider a more compre-hensive and diverse array of properties, but also attempt to unravel the com-plex relationships among them. The Kentucky Heritage Council, The State Historic Preservation Office, encourages study of the commonwealth's archi-tecture, archaeology, and landscape. As a growing number of constituents demand that decisions be weighed in light of many special interests, preser-vation increasingly becomes a public endeavor. The profession must also find ways of communicating information gained through research. By continuing to share insights into the past with others, the Council seeks ultimately to develop the broad support necessary to preserve important archaeological sites and buildings for future generations to admire and study. Cultural resources are a finite resource. Once destroyed they are gone forever. Therefore, we must all become stewards of the past if we are to have a legacy to pass on to future Kentuckians.

David L. Morgan, Executive Director
KENTUCKY HERITAGE COUNCIL
AND STATE HISTORIC PRESERVATION OFFICE
Frankfort, Kentucky

Behind any science—and central to its history—are people, individuals whose questions, ideas, experiences, and personalities informed their relentless search for knowledge. Reading this excellent new synthesis of Kentucky prehistory, I found myself thinking of the stories behind the science, of the wonderful characters who helped lay the base for what has been written here and whose lives and accomplishments contributed so greatly to our appreciation of Kentucky's past.

Imagine having known Constantine Rafinesque, that eccentric spirit whose scientific zeal drove him to cross the mountains in the early years of the nineteenth century to teach at the first trans-Appalachian college. At Transylvania, in Lexington, he pursued his interests in everything from plants, fish, fossils, and shells to the nature of language, following through with observations, systematic study, and numerous publications. By no means intellectually retiring or unambitious, he even wrote a work entitled the "Principal Languages and Primitive Nations of the Whole Earth."

In his *Ancient History, or Annals of Kentucky* (1824), Rafinesque provided the first real documentation of the archaeological resources of Kentucky. Although travel was difficult and many of the areas he visited were far from main roads, his research covered nearly half the state—an enormous personal achievement and a great step forward for the study of Kentucky prehistory. But although a visionary in many ways, Rafinesque was very much a man of his time. His explanation of the origin of the natives of the New World, for example, traced them to Africa by way of Atlantis. The study of New World prehistory has indeed come a long way.

Eventually Rafinesque was eased out of his position at Transylvania College, and he came to be buried in a pauper's grave. We are not sure how this occurred, and it is even unclear if his official portraits are genuine. But this enigmatic individual, with his wide-ranging curiosity about and love of the Bluegrass State, led to what was to become a long line of exceptional personalities who have engaged in a search for "ancient life" in Kentucky.

Rafinesque was followed a quarter of a century later by Ephraim G. Squier and E.H. Davis, who described more comprehensively some of the Kentuckian sites in the Mississippi Valley (1848). The first modern synthesis of Kentucky prehistory was published in 1910 by Bennett H. Young. A comparison of his spartan ideas with the comprehensive detail presented in this volume is itself a lesson in the history of science. After Young came Clarence B. Moore, the "steamboat archaeologist" who conducted the first systematic excavations in the state along the major waterways (1916).

The personal stories of each of these individuals make wonderful reading, but to me the person who led the field of archaeology out of its dark ages was Nels C. Nelson. Nelson's work in the Mammoth Cave region, published in 1917, provided the initial breakthrough in studies of temporal change and cultural process. It was with Nelson that I had my own initial brush with the pioneer period of Kentucky archaeology. It took place in New York City in the 1960s, when I was working on my own Mammoth Cave project in the collections of the American Museum of National History. Walking down one of the dark, office-lined halls, I passed a door marked "N.C. Nelson." The door was slightly ajar, and inside, hunched over the desk, I could see the small figure of a very old man poring over an ancient manuscript.

It shocked me to realize that this was the legendary N.C. Nelson. In my mind, he was part of the distant past of our discipline. I was young and reluctant to disturb him. Since then, I have regretted that hesitation and wished I had seized the opportunity to tell him how deeply I respected his contributions to American archaeology. He died a few years later.

In the 1930s there broke upon the scene of Kentucky archaeology the dynamic duo of Webb and Funkhouser. William G. Webb, physicist, and William D. Funkhouser, zoologist, pursued archaeology as a sideline, with a diligence that resulted in several published field excavations and the first comprehensive review of archaeological resources statewide. These two men gave me, in different ways, my first introduction to the world of field archaeology.

Webb was actively pursuing archaeology when, still in high school, I worked for him in the summer of 1946. I manned a shovel along with John T. Griffin, the friend who had first stimulated my interest in archaeology, and Webb's young professional associate, William G. Haag. We excavated part of an Adena mound near Lexington, and I had no idea the project would be Webb's last fieldwork. Years later, after completing my doctoral work at Yale, I joined the faculty at the University of Kentucky and found Webb, although officially retired, still visiting the museum regularly to work on the collections from his WPA days. Webb was not an easy friend, but he made major contributions to southeastern archaeology not only through his own work but also by giving a start to many young archaeologists who were to become leaders of the discipline.

My experience with William Funkhouser was of a very different nature. In addition to his archaeological work, Funkhouser was dean of the Graduate School and head of the Department of Zoology at the University of Kentucky. A world-renowned expert on the tree-hopping insect Membracidae, he was a dynamic personality—tall, stately, deep-voiced, and forceful in his manner, an excellent public speaker who did a great deal to awaken public interest in Kentucky prehistory. Growing up in Lexington, I knew him to be an important and influential member of the academic community. But by the time I took his introductory zoology class, he was far past his prime as a teacher and researcher. My disappointment matched my overblown anticipation of working with him, and Funkhouser became my first fallen hero.

My years as a student and, later, as a member of the faculty at Kentucky were rich in experiences with other young archaeologists. Two men who continued to work with Webb, and who became great friends of mine, were Charles Snow and William Haag. Beginning with that first summer's fieldwork under Haag, when we also excavated in a Mississippian village, a lifelong friendship grew. In Haag I found a man with a great sense of humor, a deep interest in the human past, and a wide-ranging curiosity, and to this day, I have a deep admiration for him as a scholar, teacher, and truly exceptional human being.

During my years in Kentucky archaeology, my students continued to enrich my life—as they have enriched the lives of their own students. Martha Rolingson, Berle Clay, Lee Hanson, Robert Dunnell, and others taught me as much as I introduced to them and made my years at Kentucky exceptionally satisfying.

This sense of satisfaction is revived as I read this most recent examination of Kentucky prehistory and think about how very far the field has progressed in the past century and a half. The early pioneers of archaeology in Kentucky made these contributions possible. Their stories lie behind the work and, indeed, the personalities of the authors of this volume, who in future years will be looked upon in their turn as inspiring, energetic, and endearing characters in the annals of Kentucky archaeology.

Douglas W. Schwartz, President
SCHOOL OF AMERICAN RESEARCH
Santa Fe, New Mexico

ACKNOWLEDGMENTS

This publication was funded in part by a grant from the Department of the Interior, National Park Service, under the provisions of the National Historic Preservation Act of 1966 and subsequent amendments. This grant was administered by the Kentucky Heritage Council, which serves as the State Historic Preservation Office. Additional funding was provided by a grant from the Commonwealth of Kentucky through the Kentucky Heritage Council under the provisions of KRS 171.381. The opinions expressed herein are not necessarily those of the Department of the Interior, National Park Service, or the Kentucky Heritage Council. Supplementary grants were also provided by the University of Illinois Research Board and the Department of Anthropology, University of Illinois at Urbana-Champaign (UIUC). The continued support of these agencies is gratefully acknowledged.

Charles B. Stout, Staff Archaeologist and Adjunct Assistant Professor, Murray State University, was the art editor and one of the primary artists for this book. He demonstrated that there is little he cannot do with a Macintosh and a flat-bed scanner. He took every line drawing in this book and made it better.

Jimmy A. Railey, who began this project as a Kentucky Heritage Council staff member and ended it as a graduate student at Washington University in St. Louis, drew many of the artifact illustrations. David E. Minor, staff photographer at the UIUC Department of Anthropology, took care of all of the photographs with his usual patience and skill. Dee Robbins, administrative aide, and Janice M. Pankey, transcribing secretary, UIUC, ably handled accounting and personnel problems.

Mary Lucas Powell, director and curator of the Museum of Anthropology, University of Kentucky, facilitated access to the photographic archives for the New Deal–era project records curated at the University of Kentucky.

Paul P. Kreisa, research associate, UIUC, and Susan M. Lewis, operations manager, National Center for Supercomputing Applications, patiently read and commented on the drafts of most chapters.

Finally, my thanks to the anonymous reviewers of the first draft of this book. They made me realize that the book needed to shed the illusion that it was merely a rehash of the Kentucky state preservation plan. They also pointed out that the draft manuscript was too long and wrongly oriented. They were right. Thanks to their advice, a much better book went to press.

R. Barry Lewis

INTRODUCTION

R. Barry Lewis

Kentucky has a rich archaeological heritage. It spans thousands of years, far longer than many people realize. As recently as the 1930s, this heritage was mostly unknown and unexplored, but now archaeologists know much about Kentucky's prehistory and early history. Unfortunately, this information has yet to reach a wide audience.

The objective of this book is to do just that. We, the authors, aim to introduce the reader to the current understanding of Kentucky's archaeology. To achieve this aim, we have tried to strike a balance between *description* of the past and its *interpretation* in human terms. The result is the first modern synthesis of Kentucky archaeology.

Effective synthesis requires emphasis on broad trends at the expense of details. To do this we must omit mention of many interesting aspects of Kentucky archaeology. For the reader who wishes to learn more, we include extensive literature citations and a bibliography of more than 300 items. Not all of our colleagues will agree with the things we emphasize, the sites we discuss, those we omit, or our interpretations of the data. This is inevitable. There isn't even unanimity of opinion among this book's authors on some questions of interpretation. You should expect this of active research areas, such as Kentucky archaeology, in which seemingly simple questions often take decades of hard work to answer definitively.

ORGANIZATION

The scope of this book is from the entry of the first people into Kentucky many thousands of years ago to the beginning of the twentieth century. Chapters 2–7 present the major archaeological developments of these millennia in more or less chronological order. These chapters also follow the same general format. Each describes a time slice of Kentucky's past, which in some cases spans several archaeological periods, in others only one. The topics touched on include typical communities and settlement patterns, major cultural changes, the nature of the economy and subsistence, artifacts, and, where the data permit, the general health and demography of the people. The final sections of each chapter interpret cultural patterns revealed by the archaeology.

More specifically, in chapter 2 Kenneth B. Tankersley, a specialist in the late Pleistocene archaeology of the Midwest, examines the remains of the first inhabitants of Kentucky. These hunter-gatherers entered the region more than 10,000 years ago when glaciers still dominated the northern Midwest and tundra reached as far south as central Illinois and Indiana.

Chapter 3 explores cultural developments and lifeways of the hunters and gatherers who inhabited Kentucky's hardwood forests during the Archaic periods, the millennia immediately after the end of the Ice Age. Richard W. Jefferies, an archaeologist with extensive experience on Archaic sites in Illinois and Kentucky, wrote this chapter.

In chapter 4 Jimmy A. Railey describes cultural changes during the Woodland periods, which follow the end of the Archaic periods in Kentucky's prehistoric chronology. During the Woodland periods, pottery-making became widespread and elaborate burial ceremonialism and mound building became a common part of Woodland ritual life. During the Late Woodland period, the bow and arrow was introduced into Kentucky and true farming began to develop.

In chapter 5 I examine the late prehistory and protohistory of the Mississippi period in western and southern Kentucky. It was a time during which many communities grew up around densely occupied, fortified towns. The Mississippian economy was based on intensive maize agriculture.

Chapter 6, written by William E. Sharp, deals with the same centuries as chapter 5, but focuses on events in the northern and eastern half of Kentucky. Sharp describes the Fort Ancient culture villages, which, like their Mississippian counterparts in western Kentucky, depended on maize agriculture, though the social and political organizations of these two late prehistoric cultures differed in many ways.

Chapter 7 offers an archaeological perspective on the development of Kentucky from the late 1700s up to the early 1900s. It was written by Kim A. McBride and W. Stephen McBride, both of whom are historical archaeologists with extensive field experience in Kentucky and the South.

The rest of the book (chapters 1 and 8) sets the stage, so to speak. Chapter 1, which you are reading now, describes essential background information about Kentucky and archaeology. The concluding chapter, which David Pollack and I wrote, assesses the uncertain future of Kentucky archaeology and what you, the reader, can do to ensure that it does have a future. A glossary of technical terms follows chapter 8.

GEOGRAPHY

Kentucky is a diverse, beautiful place. It ranges from the steep, forested Appalachian Mountains in the east, to gently rolling hills in the middle, and to flat, swampy Mississippi River Valley bottoms in the west. It has some of the most picturesque regions of the Upper South. The social, political, and economic conditions of modern Kentucky are most readily understood within the context of this regional diversity. Kentucky's geography is also very important for interpreting archaeological data. Therefore, even if you know Kentucky well, a brief review of its major geographical regions (fig. 1.1) will be time well spent.

Jackson Purchase

The westernmost region of Kentucky extends from the Tennessee River west to the Mississippi River and from the Ohio River south to the Kentucky-Tennessee state line. It shares a common history, a distinctive environment, and the same underlying geology. The name Jackson Purchase comes from the treaty signed in 1818 after negotiations led by Andrew Jackson. By the terms of this treaty, the Chickasaw relinquished their claims to the western parts of Kentucky and Tennessee (Rennick 1984:151).

In the extreme western corner of the Purchase, along the Mississippi and Ohio river valleys, broad floodplains and steep bluffs support a distinctively southern biota. Cypress swamps, sweetgum-elm forests, and dense stands of cane filled these valleys before extensive clearing began in the late 1800s (Lewis 1974:19–27). Thick loess deposits blanket the bluffs, which are steep-

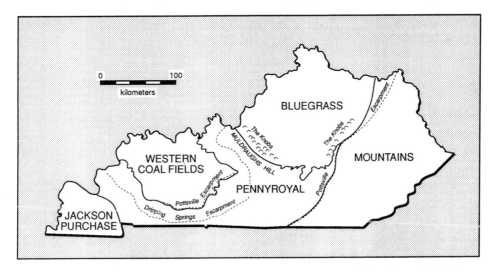

Figure 1.1   Major regions of Kentucky. Adapted from Karan and Mather 1977:110.

est along the Mississippi River Valley. Until the past century, these bluffs were covered by a beech-yellow poplar forest with cane undergrowth. To the east, oak-hickory forests stretch across the central Purchase and the hilly "Breaks of the Tennessee" in Marshall and Calloway counties (Davis 1923:69–80; Lewis 1974:18–21). The lower Tennessee and Cumberland river valleys, which were once in oak-hickory forests, are now the lake bottoms and shorelines of Kentucky and Barkley lakes, massive reservoir impoundments.

Pennyroyal

A rolling plateau called the Pennyroyal dominates west-central Kentucky. It is a karst region, which means that sinkholes and underground streams riddle the underlying limestone formations. Tall-grass prairie was the common native upland cover and hardwood forests filled the stream valleys (Braun 1950:155–56).

Early Euro-American settlers called the Pennyroyal the "Barrens." As Carl Sauer (1927:123–24) shows, the term *barrens* is misleading. It is an artifact of late eighteenth-century English and did not imply that the Pennyroyal was a poor place to settle. It simply meant there were few trees. Consider, for example, John Filson's "Map of Kentucke," published in 1784. It carries this annotation for part of the Pennyroyal: "Here is an extensive Tract, call'd Green River Plains, which produces no Timber, and but little Water; mostly Fertile, and cover'd with excellent Grass and Herbage" (Phillips 1908).

The most rugged Pennyroyal terrain is in the east, especially from the Lake Cumberland area to the Pottsville Escarpment, a low ridge that defines the western border of the Mountains (Karan and Mather 1977:110). The Cumberland River cut a deeply entrenched valley with steep valley walls and narrow floodplains through this part of the Pennyroyal (Sauer 1927:110). The native cover is a mixed forest of beech, yellow poplar, sugar maple, and other deciduous and evergreen trees (Braun 1950:51–52).

Western Coal Field

The Western Coal Field takes its name from the Pennsylvanian coal formations that have long figured prominently in Kentucky's economy. The uplands are "gently rolling to hilly" (Burroughs 1924:3). Surface relief is least in the interior of the Western Coal Field. It is greatest along the southern and eastern margins, where the Western Coal Field encounters the dissected hills of the Clifty Area of the Pennyroyal. Before the development of the coal industry, a beech-maple forest covered the uplands of this region. According to Braun, this forest contained "beech, tuliptree [yellow poplar], and sugar maple, as well as oaks, hickories and other trees" (1950:147).

The northern border of the Western Coal Field is the Ohio River Valley. Its topography and biota closely resemble those described above for the Mississippi and lower Ohio valleys in the Jackson Purchase. The big difference is that many "Mississippi Valley" species, such as bald cypress (*Taxodium distichum*) and pecan (*Carya illinoensis*), become uncommon in the Ohio Valley above the mouth of the Wabash River, which enters the Ohio across from Hopkinsville (Deam 1940:18). The broadest reaches of the valley are in Daviess and Henderson counties near the confluence of the Green and the Ohio rivers and in western Henderson County (Burroughs 1924:5–6). The dissected bluffs that flank the Ohio River are often steep and rise as much as 40–50 meters above the valley floor.

Bluegrass

The Bluegrass was the first extensively settled region of Kentucky. Its distinctive physiography, which is similar to the Nashville Basin in Middle Tennessee, is the result of the large basin of Ordovician limestones that underlies it. The Knobs border the Bluegrass on all sides except the north, where it meets the Ohio River Valley (Davis 1927:4). The major river systems are, from west to east, the Salt, the Kentucky, and the Licking. The valleys of these rivers tend to be deeply entrenched with steep slopes and narrow floodplains (Davis 1927:11).

Before modern settlement, a hardwood forest covered the Bluegrass. The common trees were walnuts, sugar maple, oaks, ash, and beech (Campbell 1985:62–68). Undergrowth was brush, grasses, and cane, the latter of which was abundant only in the central Bluegrass (Campbell 1985:63). Ironically, bluegrass (*Poa pratensis*), the plant that gave its name to this distinctive part of Kentucky, may not have arrived here until the early Historic period (Campbell 1985:56).

The Knobs divide the Pennyroyal and the Mountains from the Bluegrass (Karan and Mather 1977:112). This chain of hills starts near Louisville and curves along Muldraugh's Hill around the southern edge of the Bluegrass. The Knobs' rugged topography supports a diverse forest of oak-hickory, oak-chestnut, and chestnut-beech-yellow poplar communities, with pines common in shaly localities (Braun 1950:136–38).

Mountains

The Mountains, which some call the "Eastern Mountains," is a place of great beauty, narrow rugged valleys, extensive forests, and shallow soil. The Pottsville Escarpment and the Knobs separate it from the Bluegrass and the Pennyroyal. In the extreme southeastern corner of the state, Pine Mountain and the western slopes of the Cumberland Mountains mark Kentucky's highest elevations (Bladen 1973:23). Several rivers also have their headwaters in this region. Sugar maple, basswood, yellow poplar, chestnut, beech, buckeye, northern red oak, and white oak were the common trees of the native forest (Braun 1950:49–54).

The hills are less rugged in the Big Sandy drainage in the northeastern Mountains. The native forests were also different. According to Shaler and Crandall's (1876:12–13) tree census of eight "old forest" stands in the Lower Big Sandy drainage, the dominant trees were several oak species (especially the white oak), beech, hickories, pines, maple, and yellow poplar. Nuttall (1821:29), who descended the Ohio River in 1818, noted that the northern limit of cane undergrowth occurred near the mouth of the Big Sandy River.

HISTORY OF ARCHAEOLOGICAL RESEARCH

A good grounding in regional geography is essential to the understanding of Kentucky archaeology, but the history of archaeological research is nearly as crucial. It provides the context within which the decisions and actions of individual researchers and the impact of events beyond Kentucky become clear, rather than disjointed or divorced from larger trends in American archaeology.

This section describes the development of Kentucky archaeology. By necessity, I draw heavily on Douglas W. Schwartz's *Conceptions of Kentucky Prehistory*, an excellent historical overview published in 1967. To this I add fresh perspectives and new information. The chronological divisions used as topic headings in this section follow Gordon R. Willey and Jeremy A. Sabloff's (1980) treatment of the history of American archaeology.

Speculative Period (Discovery to 1840)

American archaeology up to 1840 was in a period of speculation about the remains that were discovered as the frontier of the country expanded westward (Schwartz 1967; Willey and Sabloff 1980). Kentucky, where archaeology of any kind did not exist until around the 1820s, provides an excellent case in point. Unusual or spectacular places, such as Mammoth Cave, soon attracted the attention of travelers, naturalists, and curiosity seekers. Their reports (e.g., Mitchell 1817) were the first publications on the prehistory of this state.

All archaeological work was of a rudimentary nature in the 1820s, and wild guesses as to the origin and nature of archaeological things were more the norm than the exception. Many people found it easy, if not necessary, to believe that Native Americans—the "Indians"—did not build the mounds that dotted the landscape, that there once existed a "Mound Builder" race that the Indians killed or drove away, and that the Mound Builders or the Indians were possibly Welsh, the Lost Tribes of Israel, or survivors of the lost Atlantean continent. Silverberg (1968) and Willey and Sabloff (1980) describe these and other preposterous ideas that often passed for interpretations of the past during this era of American archaeology.

The person with the best claim to the title of "first Kentucky archaeologist" was a colorful, eccentric field naturalist named Constantine S. Rafinesque (Call 1895). He lived in Kentucky from 1819 to 1825. He is known to history mostly for his contributions in botany, ichthyology, and malacology (Porter 1986:3), and for his unusual personality, which is still the object of controversy (e.g., Boewe et al. 1987; Robbins 1985; Sterling 1978).

Rafinesque's major published contribution to the archaeological literature of Kentucky is ambitiously entitled *Ancient History, or Annals of Kentucky; with a Survey of the Ancient Monuments of North America, and a Tabular View of the Principal Languages and Primitive Nations of the Whole Earth*. He published this slim volume in Frankfort in 1824. It treats world prehistory and early history in 39 pages and is more scholarly posturing than description of facts, a point even Rafinesque (1836:71) concedes. The book's importance lies in an appendix in which he describes the first published approximate locations and dimensions of Kentucky archaeological sites. No one had attempted that before—to describe all of the known archaeological sites in Kentucky. Viewed by modern professional standards, these descriptions are inadequate. Nevertheless, when one considers the time, place, and cultural context within which Rafinesque worked, his compilation is important.

Rafinesque was not an archaeologist in the modern sense of the term. He did not, for example, excavate any of the sites he recorded in his notebooks and described in his publications. His principal archaeological contributions were that he undertook systematic archaeological fieldwork and that he published his results. These publications, although of uneven quality, increased the scientific and public awareness of the archaeological remains of Kentucky and of the Ohio River Valley as a whole.

Classificatory-Descriptive Period (1840–1914)

In the 1840s the focus of American archaeological research began to shift toward description and classification as principal goals (Willey and Sabloff 1980:34). Speculative publications continued to appear throughout this period (e.g., Pickett 1878), as they occasionally do even today. Nevertheless, American archaeology was becoming a scientific discipline and there was less need for conjecture as scholars learned more about the prehistory of the continent.

The first major publication to touch on Kentucky in this new era was Ephraim G. Squier and E.H. Davis's book, *The Ancient Monuments of the Mississippi Valley*, which the Smithsonian Institution published in 1848. Squier and Davis's report is a methodical description of major mound sites in the states bordering the Ohio and Mississippi valleys, replete with mound measurements and detailed site maps (e.g., see fig. 4.19). Ironically enough, Squier and Davis's book also includes Rafinesque's most enduring contribution to American archaeology—all of their information on Kentucky sites, as well as that from several other important sites, is attributed to Rafinesque's unpublished notes and site plans (Call 1895:116–17; Stoltman 1973:119).

During this period, the Kentucky Geological Survey became the primary driving force of archaeological research in this state. The archaeological contributions of Geological Survey staff members usually appeared as minor sections of regional geological or geographical studies (e.g., Linney 1882; Loughridge 1888), but some were also published elsewhere (e.g., Lyon 1859, 1871; Peter 1873). Although none of the staff members had any formal training in archaeology, Frederic W. Putnam, who was employed briefly as an "Ichthylogical [*sic*] Assistant" at the beginning of the Second Geological Survey in 1873 (Jillson 1923:13), soon emerged on the national scene as a major figure in the professionalization of American archaeology (Willey and Sabloff 1980:44–45).

The survey's involvement in archaeology effectively ended in the early 1890s. The major factors that promoted divorcing archaeology from subsequent survey projects were, first, professional archaeologists were being trained by that time; and second, the federal government began to assume an active role in archaeological investigations.

With the creation of the Bureau of Ethnology (later changed to the Bureau of American Ethnology, BAE) in 1879, government archaeologists became involved in investigations in many states (Judd 1967). The first major project of the BAE, as it was called by several generations of archaeologists, was a large-scale survey and excavation of more than 2,000 aboriginal mounds in the eastern United States (Powell 1894:xl–xli). The product was a lengthy report on mounds (Thomas 1894), which proved that there had been no separate Mound Builder race and that the Indians had built the mounds. Although the government archaeologists touched on the western edge of Kentucky during this project (Thomas 1894:279–83), they apparently relied on Kentucky Geological Survey data and publications to plot mound distributions elsewhere in the state (Thomas 1894:plate 20).

Amateur archaeologists also made many valuable contributions to the growth of Kentucky archaeology during this period. Bennett H. Young, a Louisville attorney, amassed a considerable collection of Kentucky artifacts and wrote an important book about the state's prehistory, entitled *The Prehistoric Men of Kentucky* (Young 1910). Another well-known amateur,

Figure 1.2 William Snyder Webb (1882-1964), professor in the departments of physics and anthropology at the University of Kentucky, was the driving force in the beginning of professional archaeological research in Kentucky. Haag 1965:471; reproduced by permission of the Society for American Archaeology.

Clarence B. Moore, excavated many western Kentucky sites in the early decades of this century and promptly reported his findings in well-illustrated volumes (e.g., Moore 1916).

Whatever the source, whether it was survey geologists, BAE archaeologists, or amateur archaeologists, fieldwork and publications of this period remained almost entirely descriptive. Still lacking from American archaeology were tools for measuring time and space in the past. Archaeologists knew that North America had a long prehistory, but they could not estimate adequately the age of sites relative to one another, nor could they delineate changes over time within sites, nor measure similarities and differences between contemporaneous sites in different regions.

Classificatory-Historical Period (1914–1960)

In the decades up to roughly 1940, the necessary temporal and spatial tools were developed, tested, and widely applied in American archaeological research (Willey and Sabloff 1980:83–180). This period also witnessed the expansion of archaeology, or more precisely of anthropology, the traditional parent discipline of archaeology in the United States, into universities and colleges (Meltzer 1985; Patterson 1986:10–14).

Kentucky participated in these national trends lopsidedly, due largely to the biases of William S. Webb, a University of Kentucky physicist who became the major figure in Kentucky archaeology and dominated research until the late 1950s (fig. 1.2). Schwartz (1967) assesses in detail Webb's impact on Kentucky archaeology and only major points need mentioning here. The dedication of this book reflects the extent to which modern Kentucky archaeologists perceive the immense debt owed to Webb.

Webb and his colleague William D. Funkhouser, a professor of zoology at the University of Kentucky, created modern Kentucky archaeology in the late 1920s and early 1930s. They successfully pushed for a department of anthropology and archaeology at the University of Kentucky. It was founded in 1927 with Webb and Funkhouser as the two faculty—in addition to their other academic appointments and at no additional salary (Schwartz 1967:31, 33). The University of Kentucky therefore became home to the second anthropology department in the Midwest (Griffin 1976:5).

The primary stimulus for the creation of this department was to qualify for the grant of a field truck from the National Research Council (Haag 1965:470). Webb and Funkhouser soon put the truck to good use and conducted many small-scale excavations and surveys across the state until the middle 1930s (Funkhouser and Webb 1928, 1929, 1930, 1931, 1935, 1937; Webb and Funkhouser 1929, 1930, 1931, 1932, 1933, 1936). Neither of them had any formal training in archaeology, and in the beginning, they made up for this with simple raw enthusiasm. As Schwartz points out, their field techniques may have been abominable at first, but they improved quickly with experience (1967:47).

The excellent monograph series University of Kentucky Reports in Anthropology and Archaeology is one measure of the extent to which Webb and Funkhouser matured quickly as archaeologists. It was the primary publication outlet for their research (Schwartz 1967:47). It also gave the Kentucky program a degree of visibility outside the state and was undoubtedly a factor in Webb's emergence as a national figure in American archaeology in the middle 1930s.

Webb's archaeological career reached a turning point in 1933 when, besides his University of Kentucky appointments, he accepted the job as the Tennessee Valley Authority's archaeological consultant (Lyon 1982:49). This appointment meant Webb was to control the archaeological investigations associated with several massive dam projects in Tennessee, in Alabama, and eventually, in Kentucky. The job launched him into the national spotlight as an archaeologist and led to many major contributions to archaeology (Haag 1985; Lyon 1982; Schwartz 1967). During the same period, Funkhouser's interest in archaeology gradually lapsed, and after 1940 he was out of the picture altogether (Schwartz 1967:65).

In the late 1930s and early 1940s, Webb directed several major archaeo-logical field projects in Kentucky and elsewhere in the South, all of which were funded by New Deal–era relief agencies (Lyon 1982; Milner and Smith 1986). It was archaeology on a scale previously unknown in the United States. Field crews of 100–150 shovel hands, for example, were not uncom-mon. These projects provided the basis for much of what we know of Kentucky archaeology, and they are referred to time and again throughout this book.

The entry of the United States into World War II brought this era to an end. The publication of descriptive reports on relief agency-sponsored Kentucky excavations occupied Webb's attention throughout the war and into the early 1950s. Unfortunately, the task of analyzing and publishing the results of the New Deal–era projects has yet to be completed. In that sense, Webb's legacy lives on today.

By the time Webb retired in 1957, he had directed more large excavations at Kentucky sites than any archaeologist before or since him. His work also set the stage for the postwar development of several national salvage archae-ology programs (Willey and Sabloff 1980:127), which he had a strong hand in designing (Brew 1968:8; Jennings 1985:282). Through the many publications that resulted from his projects, Webb also made significant contributions to the scientific understanding of the Archaic tradition and the Adena culture in Kentucky and in the Ohio River Valley. His contributions to the understand-ing of the Mississippi period and the Fort Ancient culture, which also could have been substantial, were of less consequence since few of those excava-tions reached the publication stage.

During the last decade or so of Webb's professional life, the focus of American archaeology changed considerably from what it had been at the beginning of World War II. The strong culture historical focus of most New Deal–era archaeology was increasingly criticized. Walter W. Taylor (1967: 73–77), for example, while acknowledging the value of Webb's excavation reports, took him to task in the late 1940s for his rigid trait-list approach to cultural comparisons and classifications. Webb's work after the war also shows little concern with cultural evolutionary theory or with the interrela-tionships of cultural behavior and its social and natural environmental con-texts, all of which began to emerge as important research areas in the early 1950s. For the most part, however, these changes in the discipline occurred too late in Webb's career for him to incorporate them into his thinking and his research.

Explanatory Period (1960–1990s)

In the decades after Webb's retirement, American archaeological research moved beyond the strictly empirical, or natural history, approach that domi-nated Webb's era to a concern with explaining the past in cultural evolutionary terms. The construction of regional chronologies, which once dominated American archaeology, although it was certainly not Webb's forte, was viewed increasingly as merely a necessary step in research, rather than as an end.

In the late 1950s Douglas W. Schwartz assumed the task of keeping alive the strong University of Kentucky tradition of archaeological research. Schwartz directed many federally sponsored archaeological projects in reservoir areas that were slated for construction after World War II. He and his students also analyzed and wrote reports on several New Deal–era projects that had been curated by the Museum of Anthropology at the University of Kentucky since the late 1930s. Some of these reports were published, but others remain as unpublished Master's theses or class term papers (e.g., Young 1962) at the University of Kentucky. Even unpublished, however, the information is far more accessible than that from the as-yet-unanalyzed New Deal–era collections.

Schwartz created the Studies in Anthropology series as the successor to Reports in Anthropology and Archaeology, which issued its last number in the early 1950s. The new series was intended to be broader in scope than its predecessor (Schwartz 1961:vii), but it maintained a strong Kentucky archaeology focus during its brief existence. The series lapsed with Schwartz's departure from Kentucky in the late 1960s. Finally, in a book entitled *Conceptions of Kentucky Prehistory: A Case Study in the History of Archeology*, Schwartz (1967) critically examined the growth of Kentucky archaeology and Webb's role in its development.

Schwartz left Kentucky just as the "cultural resources management" (CRM) era was beginning in American archaeology. As the name implies, cultural resources management is archaeology done specifically to protect and conserve the nation's archaeological and historical resources. The National Historic Preservation Act of 1966 essentially mandated CRM, and additional federal legislation soon supplemented it. As a direct result of this legislation, the scale of Kentucky archaeology increased greatly in the 1960s and remains high in the 1990s.

There are several indicators of the changes wrought by CRM. First, more than 80 percent of the site locations in the state files were recorded since 1966 (Clay 1988b:27). This statistic alone says a great deal about the increased level of archaeological fieldwork in Kentucky.

Second, there are now far more professional archaeologists actively engaged in Kentucky research than at any time in the past. Archaeologists are on the faculty or staff at Murray State University, Northern Kentucky University, University of Kentucky, University of Louisville, and Western Kentucky University. The University of Illinois at Champaign-Urbana, Washington University in St. Louis, and Simon Fraser University in Burnaby, Canada, also have active Kentucky archaeological research programs. Various federal agencies (e.g., the U.S. Forest Service and the U.S.

Army Corps of Engineers) have staff archaeologists in Kentucky. Several state agencies (e.g., the Kentucky Department of Transportation and the Kentucky Heritage Council) also employ archaeologists. Several private Kentucky firms also offer professional archaeological services. The Kentucky Organization of Professional Archaeologists, formed in 1986, now has about 35 active members.

Looking beyond the changes induced by CRM, which are not unique to Kentucky, the most far-reaching effect has been to shift the leadership of Kentucky archaeology from its traditional academic setting to two offices: the Kentucky Heritage Council and the Office of State Archaeology. They define the issues and priorities that will structure Kentucky archaeology in the twenty-first century.

The Kentucky Heritage Council, which is the State Historic Preservation Office, was created in 1966. It advises federal agencies on compliance with Section 106 of the National Historic Preservation Act of 1966. It also supports many programs that promote the preservation and conservation of Kentucky archaeological resources.

The Office of State Archaeology, which is part of the Department of Anthropology at the University of Kentucky, maintains the official Kentucky archaeological site location files. It also issues permits for archaeological investigations on state, county, and municipal lands.

By virtue of the work of these offices, a protective umbrella of federal legislation, and active field archaeologists, much is learned each year about Kentucky's past. Nevertheless, we have only begun to understand the 750 generations of people who lived here before someone first uttered the word "Kentucky."

REGIONAL CHRONOLOGIES

As remarked above, chapters 2–7 are descriptions of the major events, sites, and material culture of Kentucky's past in rough temporal order. This section is an outline of this chronological ordering. It also includes a discussion of several interrelationships of time and space that are crucial to the understanding of a large region such as Kentucky. I begin by describing what chronologies are, how they are constructed, and why they work. Readers who are familiar with the methods of archaeology may wish to skip the next few pages up to the section "The Major Periods of Kentucky Archaeology."

Time and Space in Archaeology

How do archaeologists determine how old things are? Much archaeological research focuses on measuring past time. Measuring time helps archaeologists answer two related questions. First, how old is a given artifact, feature, or association? Second, what is the chronological sequence of the archaeology of a given region? These questions must be answered before detailed interpretations of archaeological patterning are possible.

There are many ways to estimate the age of archaeological materials and the interested reader should consult Fagan (1991) or another method and theory textbook for details. The common methods employed in Kentucky to estimate the age of archaeological materials are cross-dating, stratigraphy, seriation, and radiocarbon dating.

Cross-dating, stratigraphy, and seriation are *relative dating methods*, a term which means that they yield age estimates of relative age (e.g., artifact A is older than artifact B, younger than context X, and the same age as feature Y). Relative dates cannot be anchored to a fixed time scale such as calendar years.

Cross-dating is the process of dating sites by comparisons of similar artifacts. The strength of cross-dating is that it provides a basis for dating sites for which no stratigraphic information exists and sites known only from surface collections (i.e., the collections of artifacts made from the exposed surface of a site). It is also a cheap, fast method for estimating relative site age. For these reasons it is one of the most commonly used relative dating methods.

The analysis of stratigraphy rests on the principle of superposition, which asserts simply that the stuff on the top of any heap was put there last. This principle also implies that the artifacts and features contained in a given stratum or zone of an archaeological site were buried at about the same time. Such simple notions provide a robust basis for inferring the relative ages of artifacts, features, and contexts in a site.

Seriation is a graphical or quantitative method designed to order archaeological materials by similarity, such that the most similar items are close together and the most different items are far apart. The results are comparable to those of cross-dating.

A basic building block of relative dating methods is the *chronological, or historical, artifact type*. The chronological type is a named cluster of artifact characteristics (e.g., the pottery type "Fayette Thick") selected because they are sensitive to temporal and, to a lesser extent, spatial changes. If you have an artifact with attributes that fit within a described type, then the implicit assumption is that it was probably made by someone who lived during the time and in the region associated with that type. Chronological types play an important role in comparing and cross-dating assemblages. Consequently, chapters 2–7 devote much space to their discussion.

The last common dating method in Kentucky, radiocarbon dating, is a *chronometric* technique. Chronometric dating techniques measure the age of archaeological things against some fixed scale, which is commonly our calendar year (e.g., artifact A was made in A.D. 760–70). Radiocarbon dating is based on the known rate of decay of radioactive carbon atoms present in all living things. In the best of conditions, therefore, the archaeologist can take samples of wood, charcoal, leaves, nuts, bone, shell, or even burned-on slop from the side of a cooking pot and find how old they are.

How is dating information used by archaeologists?   Archaeologists use relative and chronometric age estimates to build chronologies. A *chronology* reconstructs the correct order of past human events in a unit of space, generally an archaeological region. The basic units of chronologies are components, phases, and periods. A typical *component* comprises the archaeological remains of one short-lived village. However, since many sites contain evidence of several episodes of site use, individual strata and even excavation levels are often designated as components. Components are the building blocks of phases.

Figure 1.3 shows a portion of the regional chronology for the western Jackson Purchase. This sequence is depicted graphically as two columns of named intervals. The boxes in the right column of figure 1.3 contain the names of phases. You can think of *phases* as detailed descriptions of the human communities of a region during a short interval, for instance one or two centuries. In the example, the sequence begins about 750 B.C. with the O'Bryan Ridge phase and ends with the Jackson phase at A.D. 1700. Phase names are local to the region in which they are defined.

The names in the left column of figure 1.3 are major temporal units called periods. *Periods* are detailed descriptions of contemporaneous phases viewed over many centuries, if not over several millennia. Unlike phases, periods span many regions. Much of the midwestern and southeastern United States share the same archaeological periods as listed in figure 1.3.

Periods and phases divide the natural continuum of prehistory into discrete, well-defined units of time and space. This greatly simplifies the study, comparison, and interpretation of the human past. Indeed, archaeological research would be impossible without the aid of chronologies.

Problems with chronologies.   In eastern United States archaeology, you occasionally find temporal and cultural concepts mixed under one name and, perhaps more confusing, several names applied to the same interval. We have a few examples of this in Kentucky. The Mississippi period, for example, is generally viewed as an interval of late prehistory in western and southern Kentucky that spans A.D. 900 to roughly A.D. 1700. It encompasses the archaeological remains of village farmers of the Mississippian cultural tradition. In the north-central part of the state, archaeologists call somewhat similar farmers the Fort Ancient culture. Since Fort Ancient is defined largely by inferred cultural differences from Mississippian, archaeologists in northern

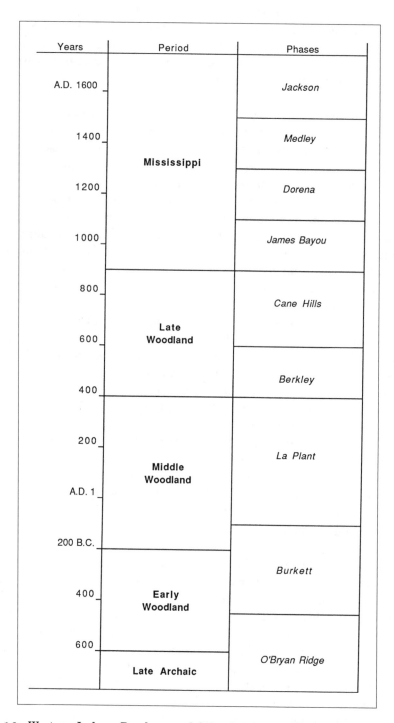

Figure 1.3   Western Jackson Purchase and Cairo Lowland regional chronology.

Kentucky speak of the Late Prehistoric or Fort Ancient period rather than of the Mississippi period.

Archaeologists are aware that this practice confuses their colleagues and the public alike (see Stoltman 1978). Nevertheless, there is no generally accepted solution, nor do all archaeologists agree that the problem warrants attention.

Lest the nonspecialist reader now begin to despair that terms like "Mississippi period," "Fort Ancient," and others are so much gobbledygook, I must add that the distinctions are useful. The terminological problems that arise can be traced back to the need for some conceptual housecleaning by eastern United States archaeologists.

The Major Periods of Kentucky Archaeology

Paleoindian periods.   The Paleoindian periods (fig. 1.4) span the time from the first inhabitants of the Kentucky region around 10,000 B.C. until the end of the Pleistocene Epoch, or Ice Age, about 8,000 B.C. These people were no-

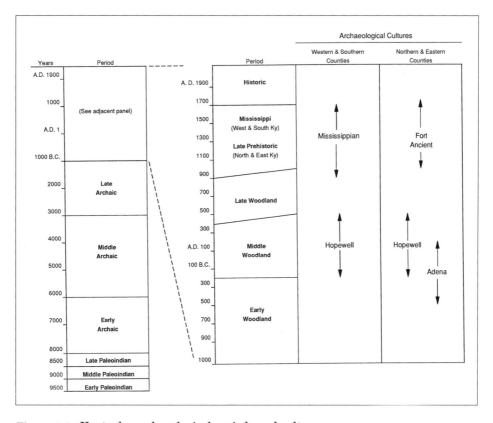

Figure 1.4   Kentucky archaeological periods and cultures.

madic, specialized big-game hunters and gatherers. Most of the big game they hunted was extinct by the end of the Pleistocene.

Archaic periods. There are three Archaic periods: the Early, Middle, and Late. The Early Archaic period spans the first two millennia after the Ice Age, or from roughly 8,000 to 6,000 B.C. The sites of these hunters and gatherers show many cultural effects of the shift toward a temperate environment. Nevertheless, Early Archaic tool assemblages still share many basic similarities with those of their Paleoindian ancestors.

The Middle Archaic period dates from 6,000 to 3,000 B.C. Communities were apparently more settled than in the past. There is evidence of such domesticated plants as squash and gourds in the states surrounding Kentucky, and it is reasonable to assume that these plants were also in use here. Technology became increasingly diversified.

The Late Archaic period, which extends from 3,000 to 1,000 B.C., is the best-known Archaic period in Kentucky, due largely to Webb's interest in the preceramic shell middens of the Green River region. The trend toward food production increased, but it remained only a supplement to hunting and gathering for several more millennia. Regional stylistic traditions of tools and other artifacts can be delineated across Kentucky. Pottery began to be made and used in contemporaneous communities in the southeastern states that border Kentucky.

Woodland periods. There are three Woodland periods: the Early, Middle, and Late. Until recently, most archaeologists (e.g., Griffin 1967) viewed the Early Woodland period (1,000 to 200 B.C.) as a significant period of cultural innovations in which mound ceremonialism, agriculture, and pottery-making were introduced from other parts of North America. Archaeological investigations have now shown that mound building, domesticated plants, and pottery existed in parts of eastern North America before the Early Woodland period. In Kentucky, the Adena culture dominates much of Early and Middle Woodland archaeology. Adena is another of Webb's significant archaeological contributions. During his long career, Webb devoted much of his professional energy to the archaeology of Adena sites and published reports on the excavation of 16 Adena mounds and several syntheses of information about Adena (Schwartz 1967:89–96).

The Middle Woodland (200 B.C. to A.D. 400–500) in the midcontinental United States has become largely synonymous with the Hopewell culture, which archaeologists once viewed as the oldest of two so-called cultural climaxes in North American prehistory, the other being the Mississippi period, which is discussed below (Griffin 1967). Hopewell and other Middle Woodland cultures of the Midwest and Southeast hold interest for many people, if for no other reason than these are the archaeological remains upon which much of the Mound Builder myth was constructed.

The Late Woodland period (A.D. 400 to 900–1000) is the least known archaeological period in Kentucky prehistory. It was a period of great change in the lifeways of the inhabitants of Kentucky. The bow and arrow was probably introduced into the region during the Late Woodland. The drift toward food production finally reached a critical point, and toward the end of the period, fully agricultural communities existed across much of the state.

Mississippi period.   The late prehistory of western and southern Kentucky is largely that of Mississippian farmers. The chiefdoms of this period, which lasted from A.D. 900 to A.D. 1700, had a strong riverine focus, were fully agricultural, and built planned villages and towns that were often fortified. Archaeologists characterize these societies as being of the Mississippian cultural tradition.

Late Prehistoric period.   Fort Ancient villages were still thriving communities when the first settlers appeared in the Ohio River Valley. Although similar in some respects to Mississippian farmers, archaeologists view Fort Ancient as a distinct entity in northern Kentucky and southern Ohio. To divorce this culture from Mississippian cultural connotations, Kentucky archaeologists often place Fort Ancient culture in a Late Prehistoric or Fort Ancient period.

Historic period.   The archaeology of communities for which there is also documentary, or historical, evidence is a relatively specialized area. In Kentucky it finds application only in investigations of sites that were created after about A.D. 1700. Historic period archaeology in Kentucky is largely that of Euro-American settlers, and the temporal divisions of the period emphasize this non–Native American bias.

SUMMARY

To understand Kentucky archaeology, you should first understand Kentucky's geographical diversity. The history of research also provides information that helps to explain the current state of Kentucky archaeology and where it is headed.

The work of Constantine S. Rafinesque, an eccentric field naturalist, is an excellent example of the state of archaeological research in North America before 1848. Although he remains a controversial figure in American natural history, Rafinesque systematically compiled and published invaluable information about many sites during an era when just traveling from one end of Kentucky to the other was an accomplishment.

Between 1848 and 1914 Kentucky Geological Survey geologists conducted most of the archaeological work in Kentucky. Like Rafinesque, their contributions were descriptive, but were far less speculative.

The most representative archaeologist of the era from 1914 to 1960 was William S. Webb, a University of Kentucky physicist who helped to found the first university department of anthropology and archaeology in Kentucky and who almost single-handedly created the basis for modern Kentucky archaeology. After Webb, the strong tradition of research he created continued for another decade under the direction of Douglas W. Schwartz. With the passage of important federal historic preservation legislation in the late 1960s, archaeological leadership passed to state agencies.

Chronologies help archaeologists to interpret the past. Kentucky archaeology's basic chronological framework is outlined in figure 1.4.

<h1 style="text-align:center">2</h1>

ICE AGE
HUNTERS AND GATHERERS

Kenneth B. Tankersley

The first people to inhabit Kentucky were hunters and gatherers who lived at the end of the Ice Age during the Paleoindian periods (approx. 9,500 to 8,000 B.C.). They carried with them a tool kit of Old World derivation. Their archaeological remains and group mobility were unlike those of modern hunter-gatherer bands. Paleoindian bands probably moved their camps many times a year. Their camps were typically small ones, consisting of 20–50 people. Band organization was egalitarian, which means that there were no formal leaders and no social ranking or classes. Except for differences of age, sex, and personal qualities, individuals were considered equals.

There were few Paleoindian hunter-gatherer bands in Kentucky, or anywhere else in the Americas for that matter, and their archaeological sites are small and scattered across the state (fig. 2.1). Unlike later sites, the remains of Paleoindian camps contain no evidence of houses and little refuse or such features as pits and fireplaces. The larger sites are where hunters could watch for game (e.g., ponds or slow-moving streams, stream confluences, shallow river fords, along game trails, at mineral springs) or where there are outcrops of high-quality chert for toolmaking. Sites in these areas were often reused as camps (Tankersley 1989a).

Kentucky's climate at 9,500 B.C. was cooler and more moist than it is today, but a warming trend had begun. During the following 1,500 years, most of the state was an ever-changing mosaic of vegetation. Some areas were patches of open grasslands, while others were dense hardwood forests. Pleistocene big game (megafauna), such as the mammoth, mastodon, bison, ground sloth, horse, musk ox, stag-moose, and peccary, all of which were native to Kentucky during the Ice Age, became extinct or moved north as the glacial ice retreated.

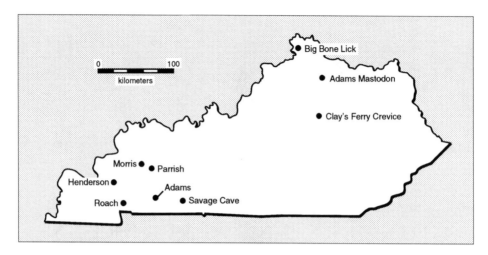

Figure 2.1   Paleoindian sites discussed in the text.

Paleoindian hunter-gatherers responded to these environmental changes in several ways. Settlements shifted from open areas of low relief, such as the Bluegrass and the Pennyroyal regions, to the more rugged, closed terrain of the Mountains. This settlement shift accompanied a significant change in food-getting from specialized big-game hunting to generalized foraging, in which smaller animals, plants, and other forest resources made up the bulk of the diet. Many archaeologists believe that these changes in livelihood were caused by environmental conditions and people killing off the megafauna (Jelinek 1967).

Kentucky Paleoindian sites are divided into three archaeological periods. The Early Paleoindian period (fig. 1.4) ranges from 9,500 to 9,000 B.C., the Middle Paleoindian period from 9,000 to 8,500 B.C., and the Late Paleoindian period from 8,500 to 8,000 B.C. This chapter describes the material culture, subsistence and settlement patterns, and chronology of each period.

EARLY PALEOINDIAN: CLOVIS (9,500–9,000 B.C.)

There are as yet no chronometric dates for Early Paleoindian sites in Kentucky, but artifacts from many Kentucky sites can be cross-dated with Early Paleoindian specimens from radiocarbon-dated contexts in other states. Clovis projectile points (fig. 2.2) are associated with the oldest (ca. 9,500 to 9,000 B.C.) locations.

Tools and Other Artifacts

Kentucky's earliest inhabitants used a distinctive tool kit that was well adapted for the hunting and processing of big game in near-arctic environ-

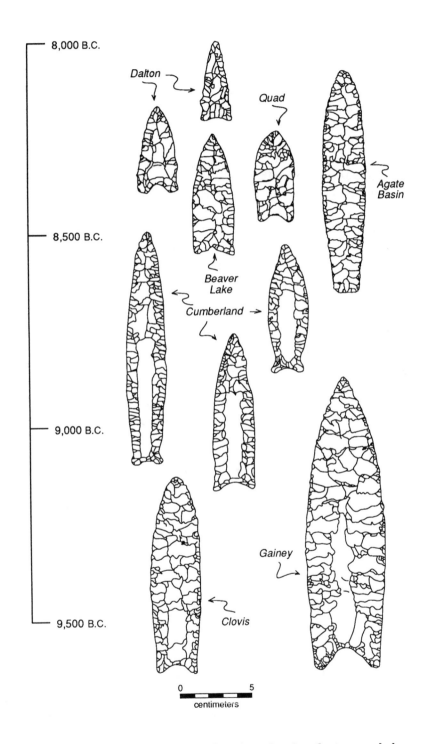

Figure 2.2 Kentucky Paleoindian projectile points showing the temporal changes in this tool type. Adapted from Anderson 1990:165.

ments (Haynes 1982; Jelinek 1971; West 1983). This tool kit originated in Eurasia during the Late Pleistocene, and it changed little as the ancestors of Paleoindian hunters entered North America and gradually spread southward. There are recognizable similarities between the tool kits of Paleoindian hunters in places as far removed as Arizona, Florida, and Kentucky—Pleistocene megafauna were found across the continent.

Specialized hunting requires high mobility by the hunters because large herd animals migrate seasonally. Indeed, specialized hunters had to be at least as mobile as the animals they hunted, but not so much that they "rode the tails" of their migrating prey. One measure of Early Paleoindian mobility is their fluted projectile points, which are often found hundreds of kilometers from where they were made (Tankersley 1989a, 1989b, 1990).

The Early Paleoindian tool kit included a variety of stone, bone, ivory, and antler implements, in addition to items of wood and plant fibers (Saunders, Agogino et al. 1991; Saunders, Haynes et al. 1990; Storck and Tomenchuk 1990). The entire assemblage, however, could be carried in a small purse-like pouch. The tool kit's compact size and light weight are exactly what one would expect of nomadic bands that might pick up their possessions and move camp several times each year, if not each season.

Chipped stone knives and scrapers are the most common tools. They were made from flakes struck from chert nodules and from long blades struck from specially prepared chert cores (Green 1963). Knives and scrapers were necessary for butchering game and processing plant fibers for cordage.

These tools also were used to make other tools. For example, the sharp point of a stone knife or a small spur protruding from the side of a scraper was used to cut long slivers of bone, ivory, or antler that were made into awls and sewing needles. Archaeologists call this the "groove-and-splinter" bone-working technique (Semenov 1964:156–57). Awls and sewing needles, in turn, were essential in the manufacture of baggage, clothing, and shelter. The latter items may have been made from animal hides or from plant materials; regardless, they were both portable and disposable.

The most important Early Paleoindian tool was probably the Clovis Fluted projectile point, which tipped a compound harpoon-like lance. The reconstructed Early Paleoindian lance shown in fig. 2.3 is based on the analysis of hundreds of ground ivory and bone foreshafts from Early Paleoindian sites in North America (Dunbar and Waller 1983; Haynes 1982). These foreshafts are identical with those used in whale hunting by certain Eskimo groups (Lahren and Bonnichsen 1974; McCartney 1971). Like the Eskimo harpoon foreshafts, the ends are beveled and incised to help hold the stone projectile point in its haft. The base of the foreshaft is also about as wide as the flutes in the base of the projectile points. Once hafted, the ears of a fluted point base would protrude from the binding and create barbs similar to those of Eskimo ivory and bone harpoons (Mason 1981).

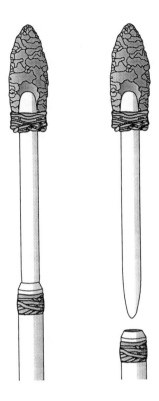

Figure 2.3 The foreshaft and haft of
an Early Paleoindian compound lance.
The foreshaft on the right has been
removed from the shaft to show its
construction. Adapted from Tankersley
1990:290.

Experiments show that fluted points hafted in this manner can penetrate
the thickest and toughest animal hides (Frison 1989). After the projectile
pierces the flesh, the shaft is easily withdrawn, leaving the fluted point-
tipped foreshaft deeply embedded in the prey's body. The compound nature of
the spear allows the hunter to rearm his weapon quickly with another foreshaft and point, and to drive the lance repeatedly into the animal until it
dies.

Early Paleoindians may have made this weapon more effective by con-
necting the lance and foreshaft with strong cord and by employing it in a
manner analogous to a method used by the Bambuti elephant hunters of the
Ituri region of West Africa:

> They use long . . . spears, like harpoons. . . . The spear heads are fixed loosely
> in the shaft, and they are either indented, or provided with barbs like fish-
> hooks, and are attached to the shaft with numerous coils of strong cord. The
> Bambuti . . . approach the elephant from the rear, and having hurled the
> spear at its belly, dart for cover immediately. Maddened with pain, the ele-
> phant stampedes furiously ahead, and the shaft becomes detached from the
> barbed head which sticks fast in the animal's belly, but is trailed along by the
> long coils of cord until finally it gets stuck fast in some shrubbery. The ele-

phant plunges about to free itself, until at last the barbed head comes away, bringing the animal's intestines with it. The elephant may still stagger about for some time, but the Bambuti trail it until it collapses at length from loss of blood. [Schebesta 1933:155]

Whatever strategy that Early Paleoindian hunters used, the compound lance was clearly designed to kill large game efficiently. It took extra time and raw material to make a detachable foreshaft, but the returns, measured in meat, were high.

Beyond compound spears, knives, and scrapers, Early Paleoindian groups had several basic flintknapping tools including two types of hammers: a round hammerstone and a thick cylindrical billet of ivory, antler, bone, or wood. Hammerstones removed thick, short, wide flakes from stone cores. Billets produced thin, long, narrow flakes. Tusk tips and antler tines were used to chip the sharp, serrated cutting edges of stone tools. Unlike the rest of the tool kit, the latter tools were probably thrown away after use.

Subsistence and Settlement Patterns

Early Paleoindian hunters were after big game. Throughout the Americas, their fluted projectile points have been found with the remains of many species of large mammals: mammoth, mastodon, bison, horse, tapir, bear, musk ox, camel, peccary, ground sloth, tapir, bighorn sheep, caribou, elk, antelope, and deer. Small terrestrial and aquatic animals, nuts, berries, and other plant foods have also been found in Early Paleoindian camp sites. The latter resources, however, would have been second choice, or emergency, foods.

Few archaeologists today view Early Paleoindians as strictly big-game hunters. While preserved artifacts suggest an exclusive big-game hunting economy or way of life, other evidence found at sites in other states suggests a mixed foraging strategy in which big-game hunting played an important but not a determinant role. In addition to hunting a variety of animals, Early Paleoindians incorporated carbohydrate-rich plant foods into their diet to counterbalance the nutritional stress and fat depletion that most animals experience seasonally. Early Paleoindians also had access to a wider range of species than was available to subsequent Paleoindian populations. Many of the smaller species provided Early Paleoindians with a source of backup or second choice foods.

The absence of confirmed Paleoindian kill sites in Kentucky may reflect the differences in sediment exposure between Kentucky and the western landscapes rather than markedly different lifeways. Kill sites similar to those discovered at many locales in the western United States are probably present in Kentucky, but are buried deep in the floodplain deposits of the Ohio River or its major tributaries. It would take a big change in erosion patterns or an accident of excavation to expose these sites.

In the western states, Early Paleoindian kill sites were not exposed in quantity until after the 1880s. Massive devegetation and a water table drop across much of the West promoted extensive weathering and erosion—and the discovery of many buried Early Paleoindian sites (Haynes 1990). Comparable changes in the Kentucky landscape might also reveal many early sites. The point is that Early Paleoindian kill sites will eventually be found in Kentucky, just as they have been in several states that border it.

Several possible Paleoindian kill sites are known, but no one has yet identified a direct association between megafauna bones and Paleoindian tools in a Kentucky site. The sites in question, all of which are in the Bluegrass region, include the Clays Ferry Crevice in Fayette County (Vesper and Tanner 1984), the Adams Mastodon site in Harrison County (Duffield and Boisvert 1983), and Big Bone Lick.

Big Bone Lick.   The best known of the possible kill sites is Big Bone Lick in Boone County. These salt spring deposits, which are now part of Big Bone Lick State Park, have been known for nearly 200 years as a source of mastodon bones and the remains of other Pleistocene megafauna. In the early 1800s, President Thomas Jefferson sent Gen. George Rogers Clark to the lick to collect mastodon remains, which were exhibited at the White House (Jillson 1936). Shortly after that, William Goforth, a physician and resident of the community of Big Bone Lick, saw commercial possibilities in mining the lick for fossil bones. He dug around these saline springs and seeps for several years, but never found a complete mammoth skeleton (Jillson 1936). Nevertheless, he did uncover mastodon bones and three fluted Paleoindian projectile points (fig. 2.4 C, E, and H) (Tankersley 1985).

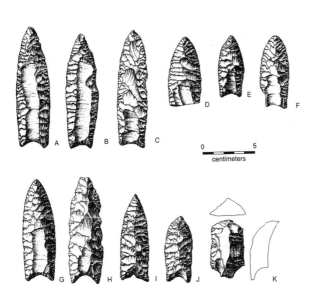

Figure 2.4 Artifacts from Big Bone Lick, Boone County: A-B, Barnes; C-G, Clovis; H, Gainey; I, Beaver Lake; J, Quad; K, profile and cross sections of a Clovis blade tool.

Unfortunately, it cannot be inferred from the account of his excavations that the projectile points were definitely associated with the mastodon bones. Over the decades since Goforth's work at Big Bone Lick, other Clovis points have been found there (see fig. 2.4 C–G), but never in direct association with Pleistocene megafauna (Haynes 1966; Prufer 1960; Tankersley 1985). Paleontologists have excavated portions of the site with the hope of discovering such evidence (e.g., Carr and Shaler 1876; Schultz et al. 1963, 1967), but it continues to elude them (Tankersley 1987).

While definite evidence of Early Paleoindian kill sites has not been forthcoming in Kentucky, many campsites have been discovered. They are restricted to areas that once attracted game (e.g., salt springs, marshes, sinkhole ponds, shallow river crossings, sandy terraces), hilltops and bluffs that overlook game areas, and the source locales of chert, the raw material of many Paleoindian tools. The scientifically examined Paleoindian camps, most of which are in the western Pennyroyal, include the Adams, Parrish, and Savage Cave sites.

Adams.   The Adams site overlooks the North Fork of the Little River in Christian County. It is a single-component Clovis site spread along the circumference of a large sinkhole (Gramly and Yahnig 1991; Sanders 1983, 1988, 1990; Sanders and Maynard 1979; Smith and Freeman 1991). Today, a conduit (possibly a cave) drains the sinkhole, which was probably filled with water during the Late Pleistocene. The scatter of artifacts on the sinkhole perimeter is probably associated with the edge of an old sinkhole pond or marsh.

The artifact assemblage displays remarkable temporal uniformity (Sanders 1983, 1988, 1990). Artifacts include tons of manufacturing debitage; hundreds of broken fluted point preforms; broken or exhausted fluted points; a large assemblage of unifacial tools; and large blade cores (fig. 2.5). The large quantity of fluted point preforms and unifacial tools shows that the Adams site was both a workshop and habitation. The massive bulk of chipped stone found at Adams suggests that the cultural deposit resulted from intermittent occupations. Clovis peoples were attracted to the site because of the sinkhole pond and the high-quality chert that occurs nearby. They collected this chert and then worked it into preforms and tools at the site.

Parrish.   The Parrish site is on a sandy terrace at the confluence of several creeks in Hopkins County. The discovery in 1938 of one Clovis and two Cumberland points (fig. 2.6 A–C) at this site prompted its excavation by Webb (1951). Four fluted points and 280 unifacially worked tools, including many end scrapers, were found during this excavation (Rolingson and Schwartz 1966). The significance of these finds, however, is obscured by the remains of a Late Archaic occupation that covered and partly disturbed the

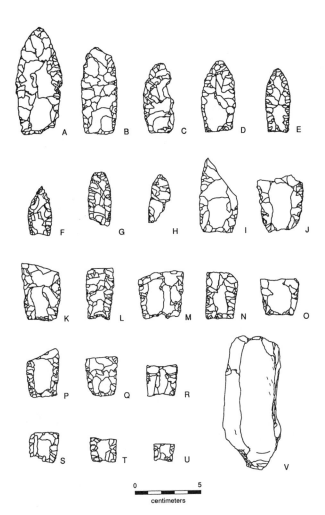

Figure 2.5 Adams site
artifacts: A-U, Clovis
projectile points; V,
Clovis polyhedral core.

remains of the Paleoindian camp (Rolingson 1964). The excavations did not
yield datable Early Paleoindian deposits or the remains of extinct megafauna. Nevertheless, based on cross-dating of the artifacts, Webb (1951) argued
that an Early Paleoindian occupation was present at Parrish.

The results of the Parrish excavation are controversial. Haag (1942a)
noted that Parrish was the first excavated site in the eastern United States
to produce a quantity of Early Paleoindian material. Martin et al. (1947), on
the other hand, argued that the apparent association between the Late
Archaic midden and the Early Paleoindian artifacts shows that Parrish was
much later than Early Paleoindian sites in the West. They also felt that the
Parrish subsistence pattern was more generalized foraging than big-game

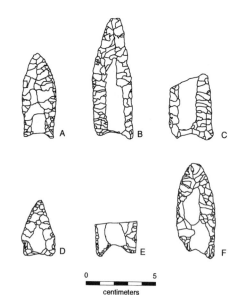

Figure 2.6 Paleoindian arti-
facts from other Pennyroyal
sites: A-D, Parrish site (A,
Clovis; B-C, Cumberland; D,
Reworked fluted point); E-F,
Savage Cave site (E, Gainey; F,
Clovis).

hunting. Thompson (1954) reinforced Martin's interpretations by asserting that the assemblage represents a technological transition between Paleoindian and Archaic lifeways. The current interpretation of the Parrish site is that the assemblage actually represents multiple components (i.e., Early Paleoindian, Late Archaic, and traces of other occupations), and not a single transitional Paleoindian-Archaic occupation (Tankersley 1989b).

Savage Cave.   This site includes the area around the entrance of a limestone cave in Logan County. During the 1960s, Savage Cave received considerable, but largely unwarranted, attention as an example of a Paleolithic or "Early Man" site in the United States (Carstens 1980). The claim of a Paleolithic occupation was based on the report of an assemblage of crude chipped stone tools, with an apparent absence of projectile points, which had been found there in a stratum capped by Late Pleistocene sediments (Cambron 1974). Subsequent research demonstrated that the presumed Paleolithic tools were not human artifacts.

The evidence of an "Early Man" occupation was based on the discovery of Paleoindian projectile points and the remains of extinct Pleistocene fauna (Guilday and Parmalee 1979). Fourteen Paleoindian projectile points (e.g., fig. 2.6 E–F) have been reported from Savage Cave. Nevertheless, as in the Big Bone Lick case, there is no demonstrable link between the artifacts and the Late Pleistocene fossils (Schenian 1988a). All that can be said with confidence is that Paleoindian groups visited Savage Cave.

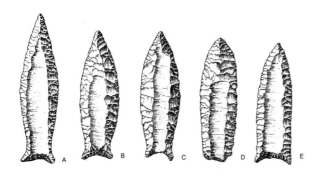

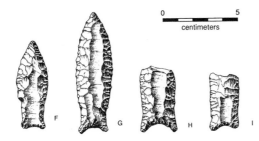

Figure 2.7 Cumberland projectile points surface collected from Kentucky sites: A, Hardin County; B, D-E, Boyle County; C, Harrison County; F, Owen County; G-H, Hart County; I, Site 15Pu208 in Pulaski County.

MIDDLE PALEOINDIAN (9,000–8,500 B.C.)

Middle Paleoindian assemblages show an increase in stylistic diversity when compared to the Clovis tool kit. The two basic types of Middle Paleoindian projectile points are called Gainey and Cumberland (see fig. 2.2). Gainey points have deeper and more rounded basal concavities than do Clovis points. They are best known from sites in the northeast and Great Lakes (Curran 1984; Deller and Ellis 1988; Simmons et al. 1984; Storck and Tomenchuk 1990). In contrast, Cumberland points (fig. 2.7) are more common in the mid-south and southeastern states. Middle Paleoindian points have not been found in dated contexts in Kentucky, but elsewhere they are found in components deposited between 9,000 and 8,500 B.C. (Haynes et al. 1984).

Tools and Other Artifacts

By comparison with the preceding period, the Middle Paleoindian tool kit exhibits a number of differences (fig. 2.8). For example, prismatic blades and polyhedral blade cores are absent. The core and blade technology was replaced by the technique called bipolar lithic reduction. This technological change occurred as toolmakers began to use poorer quality stone for their tools. Spurred end scrapers are the most abundant Middle Paleoindian tool. Limaces, or slug-shaped side scrapers, are also common.

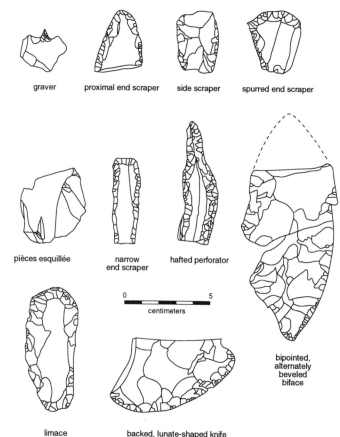

graver   proximal end scraper   side scraper   spurred end scraper

pièces esquillée   narrow end scraper   hafted perforator

0   5
centimeters

bipointed, alternately beveled biface

Figure 2.8
Paleoindian tool types.
Adapted from
Tankersley et al. 1993.

limace   backed, lunate-shaped knife

Subsistence and Settlement Patterns

Widespread vegetational changes marked the Middle Paleoindian period (Jacobson and Grimm 1988). The geographic extent and abundance of trees and grasses changed continuously (Webb 1988), and it is unlikely that vegetation stability existed anywhere in Kentucky. Concurrent with these vegetational changes, animal assemblages were reorganized, their ranges shifted, and some species became extinct. Although it is unlikely that environmental changes pushed all of the big-game species into extinction (Guilday 1982; Lundelius et al. 1983), their populations were reduced substantially (Grayson 1987).

The changes in plants and animals also affected the Middle Paleoindian settlement pattern. In Kentucky, a mixed foraging strategy probably developed that emphasized the hunting of both large and small game. Archaeologically, the effects of this strategy can be traced in the wider distribution of Middle Paleoindian than of Clovis artifacts. The Henderson site in western Kentucky is a good example of the kind of campsite left by these hunter-gatherers.

Henderson. The Henderson site is in Lyon County at the confluence of Eddy Creek and the Cumberland River. It sits on a small terrace wedged between a bluff and a narrow section of the Eddy Creek floodplain. To the south of the site, there was a shallow river ford before Lake Barkley flooded the area. After local collectors reported finding seven Middle and Late Paleoindian projectile points in the general area of this site (Rolingson 1964), it was excavated in the early 1960s. These excavations did not uncover intact Late Paleoindian features, but they did find parts of three Cumberland points (Rolingson and Schwartz 1966). The associated unifacial tools, including 33 end scrapers and 63 flake tools, are typical of Middle Paleoindian assemblages.

The presence of broken points, scrapers, and knives suggests that the site was used to process meat and hides procured from the immediate vicinity. The shallow stream crossing just south of the site would have provided ample opportunities to ambush game. The large quantity of Middle Paleoindian artifacts suggests that the site was either occupied by a single large group or intermittently used by several smaller groups.

LATE PALEOINDIAN (8,500–8,000 B.C.)

Late Paleoindian site assemblages contain unfluted lanceolate projectile points. There are two basic types of Late Paleoindian projectile points— Lanceolate Plano and Dalton Cluster points (see fig. 2.2) (Justice 1987). Lanceolate Plano points are best known from radiocarbon-dated deposits on the Plains. Dalton Cluster points, on the other hand, have been found in cave and rockshelter deposits in the midwestern and southeastern states. Both projectile point forms are associated with radiocarbon-dated contexts that fall between 8,500 and 8,000 B.C. (Frison and Stanford 1982; Goodyear 1982). Examples of these types have not yet been found in dated contexts in Kentucky.

Tools and Other Artifacts

The Late Paleoindian tool kit is more diverse than comparable Early and Middle Paleoindian kits (Deller and Ellis 1988). Late Paleoindians manufactured a variety of bifacial and unifacial tools (see fig. 2.8), such as large, bipointed, alternately beveled bifaces; backed bifaces; proximal end and side scrapers; asymmetrical end scrapers; narrow end scrapers; hafted perforators; and backed and snapped unifaces (Ellis and Deller 1988). Many of these

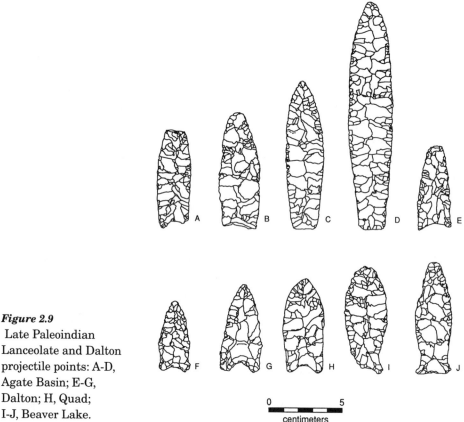

Figure 2.9
Late Paleoindian
Lanceolate and Dalton
projectile points: A-D,
Agate Basin; E-G,
Dalton; H, Quad;
I-J, Beaver Lake.

differences are undoubtedly related to changes that occurred in Kentucky's vegetation and fauna at the end of the Pleistocene. For example, tusk-bearing animals such as mammoths and mastodons became extinct. As a result, ivory implements such as the foreshaft disappear from the Paleoindian tool kit. The fluted projectile point also vanishes from the archaeological record along with the ivory foreshaft. Chipped stone knives and scrapers are smaller than their Early Paleoindian counterparts, possibly reflecting the processing of smaller game. Some of these tools were hafted to bone or wooden handles.

Late Paleoindian projectile points are stylistically diverse (fig. 2.9). Some are long and narrow, and others are short and wide. Some have wide, flaring, basal ears, and others lack ears altogether. Some have resharpened sides, and others have resharpened tips. Despite their variety, their primary function was the same as that of fluted projectile points—to kill game.

Subsistence and Settlement Patterns

The environmental changes that occurred around 8,500 B.C. were among the most profound and rapid of the past 18,000 years (COHMAP Members 1988; Jacobson et al. 1987; Webb 1987, 1988; Webb et al. 1987). The Ice Age was over and the Pleistocene big game went with it; most megafauna were extinct by 8,500 B.C. (Mead and Meltzer 1984; Meltzer and Mead 1983; Semken 1983, 1988). The geographical patterns of North American forests and grasslands changed rapidly to adjust to new climatic conditions (Lundelius et al. 1983).

To adapt to these changed conditions, Late Paleoindian hunter-gatherers became generalized foragers whose survival depended on the use of a variety of resources. Unlike the Pleistocene megafauna, which were often concentrated in herds, Late Paleoindian food animals, such as the whitetail deer, bear, and turkey, were dispersed throughout the forests. Since resources were more evenly spread, hunter-gatherer bands did not move as often or as far as their Early and Middle Paleoindian ancestors did.

Late Paleoindian bands expanded into every region of Kentucky. Areas that were sparsely populated by Early Paleoindians, such as the Mountains, were part of the Late Paleoindian settlement pattern. Likewise, Late Paleoindians were the first people to use rockshelters on a regular basis. The Roach and Morris sites in western Kentucky are good examples of excavated Late Paleoindian campsites.

Roach.   This multicomponent site is on a small terrace of the Ewes Branch floodplain in Trigg County, less than 20 km southwest of the Henderson site. The Paleoindian assemblage consists of 13 projectile points, 115 end or side scrapers, and 52 flake tools, including gravers and knives (Rolingson 1964; Rolingson and Schwartz 1966). There appear to be several projectile point styles in this assemblage, but they are all probably classifiable to the Dalton type cluster (see Justice 1987).

Like the Middle Paleoindian Henderson site, Roach displays a large assemblage of tools used for the processing of meat and hides. The stylistic heterogeneity of the Dalton points found at Roach suggests that the deposit represents several intermittent occupations by Late Paleoindians.

Morris.   Morris is situated on a terrace about 3 m above the Sugar Creek floodplain in Hopkins County. This location was one of the highest spots between the swampy Sugar Creek floodplain and a major bison trail about 3 km from the site. Artifacts found during excavation in the early 1940s suggest that the site was intermittently occupied for more than 10,000 years. The Paleoindian assemblage, which dates somewhere between 9,000 and 8,000 B.C. includes 27 projectile points, 253 end or side scrapers, and 54 flake tools (Rolingson and Schwartz 1966). All these artifacts, except two possible Cumberland points, are typical of a Dalton assemblage. This is a large Late Paleoindian assemblage, comparable in size to that of well-known northeastern sites such as Bull Brook in Massachusetts (Byers 1954) and Shoop in Pennsylvania (Witthoft 1952).

High ground, wetlands, and close proximity to an important game trail likely attracted Late Paleoindians to this site. The wetland provided access to a variety of aquatic plant and animal resources, and the game trail provided opportunities to kill large animals passing through the area. The Dalton point style diversity and the more than 300 unifacial knives and scrapers found at Morris suggest that it was used repeatedly by several Late Paleoindian groups.

PALEOINDIAN LIFE IN KENTUCKY

Many questions remain unanswered about Paleoindian hunter-gatherers in Kentucky. For example, no one knows exactly when Paleoindians first entered this state, but it is unlikely that they arrived before 10,000 B.C. Also, although the ancestors of these people can be traced back to Siberia, researchers do not know which parts of North America they crossed to reach Kentucky. We can be confident that Kentucky was colonized by waves of Paleoindian groups. Clovis was the first archaeological culture to appear in this state, but we do not know what other cultures might have migrated into Kentucky, nor do we know what cultures might have developed here.

Kentucky Paleoindian occupations are identified by distinctive chipped stone tools, particularly projectile points. Worn flake ridges on some of these artifacts suggest that they were carried together, side by side, in a bag or pouch. Use-wear studies of the knives and scrapers show that plant fibers and animal skins were obtained and processed, possibly to make sacks, clothing, shelter, or traps. Well-preserved sites have yielded ivory, bone, and antler tools. Although it is safe to assume that organic raw materials were used by the Paleoindian inhabitants of Kentucky, we do not know the extent to which they were used nor do we know how they were employed.

Early and Middle Paleoindians narrowed their preferences to a few large game animals, but their survival depended on a mixed foraging strategy. In other words, these groups occasionally had to obtain small terrestrial game, aquatic animals, and plant foods. In contrast, Late Paleoindian groups relied more on these less desirable resources because the larger game animals had become extinct. The question of why the megafauna became extinct remains unanswered. Were these animals unable to respond to the rapidly changing environment, were they simply hunted into extinction, or was it a combination of both pressures?

Paleoindian sites occur over a wide area, but they are concentrated in specific topographic settings and microenvironments. These areas include terraces or floodplains near the confluences of major streams or their tributaries (e.g., Henderson, Roach, Parrish); the margins of bogs and ponds, saline springs, or major game trails (e.g., Morris, the Adams Mastodon site, Clays Ferry Crevice, Big Bone Lick); and areas that display these features in combination with abundant masses of high-quality lithic material (e.g., Adams, Savage Cave).

Nearly all of the documented Paleoindian sites are in areas where game could have been obtained, processed, or monitored. Early Paleoindians in Kentucky avoided rugged terrain except for areas that contained high-quality lithic materials or provided a view of a mountain gap. The exploitation of these areas by Middle and Late Paleoindians may be related to the shift in their subsistence strategy from specialized hunting to a generalized foraging pattern.

Paleoindian groups did not live in isolation. Indeed, contact between groups occupying neighboring areas would have been necessary to maintain an open exchange of information, raw material, and marriage partners. Archaeologically, our only indication of Paleoindian exchange is the presence of artifacts manufactured from so-called exotic lithic raw materials. Although groups may have collected all of their own local lithic material, the bulk of exotic stone was probably obtained through exchange networks. In Kentucky, most of the Paleoindian artifacts made from exotic lithic material have been recovered in areas associated with predictably high game resources, such as salt licks. Exotic lithic artifacts have not been recovered at quarry and workshop sites. This suggests that intergroup contact and social interaction were confined to specific hunting areas.

Although we can use distinctive lithic raw materials as a rough measure of social interaction, we know nothing about the populations that were directly involved in the exchange systems. The low density of artifacts spread across the Kentucky landscape suggests that Paleoindian populations were sparse and scattered. We do not, however, have any direct demographic data. This situation may be the result of Paleoindian mortuary practices. Perhaps Paleoindians cremated most of their dead or left them to decompose on the ground.

Although rarely found, Early and Middle Paleoindian burials tend to contain only one or two individuals. Late Paleoindian inhumations, on the other hand, can almost be classified as cemeteries (Morse 1975). This change suggests an increase in the relative frequency of Late Paleoindian burials and a general increase in their archaeological visibility. This trend may be related to an increase in population or to a decrease in mobility, or to both factors.

Where Paleoindian graves have been discovered elsewhere in North America, they usually consist of a very decomposed skeleton, covered in red ochre, and associated with a cache of exquisitely knapped bifaces made from exotic cherts. These burial goods usually represent a single tool kit and may be the dead person's possessions.

SUMMARY

Early Paleoindian groups were comprised of specialized hunters, who were ultimately descended from Old World progenitors. Their livelihood was made possible by the existence of large game animals that thrived in the diverse mosaic of Late Pleistocene vegetation that covered much of Kentucky. When the environment changed radically, however, the large game became extinct and Paleoindian groups had to change their way of life.

Kentucky's archaeological record reflects those changes in Paleoindian livelihood. Early, Middle, and Late Paleoindian subsistence activities varied in their use of the landscape and lithic resources. As specialized hunters, Early and Middle Paleoindians used a narrower portion of the landscape. Consequently, their sites are limited to areas that attracted and concentrated game, areas where game could be monitored, and areas that provided the raw materials needed to manufacture tools used in the procurement and processing of game. Many of their tools were transported over great distances because specialized hunting involves a high degree of mobility.

With extinction of the megafauna, Late Paleoindians developed generalized hunting and foraging activities that were successful almost everywhere in Kentucky. Late Paleoindians concentrated on using the best of smaller game and plant resources. In doing so, these hunter-gatherers dispersed across the landscape. More of their tools were manufactured from locally available materials because their economy involved less mobility than that of their predecessors. As long as the Paleoindian population density remained low, generalized foraging withstood environmental change. It was this livelihood that created the basic pattern of continuity visible archaeologically between the Late Paleoindian and Early Archaic periods.

HUNTERS AND GATHERERS
AFTER THE ICE AGE

Richard W. Jefferies

For thousands of years, Kentucky and its inhabitants felt the effects of the end of the Ice Age. The landscape and the lifeways of hunter-gatherers changed greatly. Between 8,000 and 1,000 B.C., the number and average size of hunter-gatherer bands increased. The forests and streams and the animals that lived in them gradually approached the conditions that would be described thousands of years later in the first written accounts of Kentucky.

Kentucky's climate was not constant during these millennia. A warm, dry period, called the *Hypsithermal climatic interval,* influenced the lives of hunter-gatherers across the midcontinent between 7,000 and 3,000 B.C.

The 7,000 years of prehistory between 8,000 and 1,000 B.C. span the archaeological record of the *Archaic cultural tradition.* The Archaic tradition concept was first introduced into the archaeological literature by William Ritchie (1932) to describe a preceramic assemblage he had excavated at the Lamoka Lake site in New York State. The term soon entered general use to describe the archaeological remains of post-Pleistocene, New World hunter-gatherers who did not make or use pottery (Stoltman 1978:708). Later, Willey and Phillips further defined the Archaic as the "stage of migratory hunting and gathering cultures continuing into environmental conditions approximating those of the present" (1958:107). They characterized Archaic groups as subsisting on many kinds of plants and animals, and proposed that the specialized gathering and processing of wild plant seeds may have led to the development of gardening among Archaic groups (Willey and Phillips 1958:110).

Archaeologists divide the Archaic cultural tradition into Early, Middle, and Late periods based on temporal, technological, social, subsistence, and settlement criteria (fig. 1.4). The Early Archaic period ranges from 8,000 to 6,000 B.C.; the Middle Archaic extends from 6,000 to 3,000 B.C.; and the Late Archaic spans 3,000 to 1,000 B.C. This chapter describes the major features of each period.

EARLY ARCHAIC (8,000–6,000 B.C.)

This period encompasses the major technological and social changes among hunter-gatherers that followed the retreat of the glaciers at the end of the Pleistocene Epoch.

Tools and Other Artifacts

Much of the dating of Early Archaic sites rests on general changes in projectile point styles that can be traced in the stratigraphy of deeply stratified Archaic sites. Among the most important of these sites are the Longworth-Gick site in Kentucky (Collins 1979); St. Albans in West Virginia (Broyles 1971), Modoc Rock Shelter (Fowler 1959; Styles et al. 1983) and Koster (Brown and Vierra 1983) in Illinois; Rose Island and Ice House Bottom in Tennessee (Chapman 1975, 1976, 1977), and several sites in the North Carolina piedmont (Coe 1964). The stylistic changes seen in the cultural stratigraphy of these sites (fig. 3.1) provide the basis for cross-dating Early Archaic components over much of eastern North America. The reader is referred to Noel D. Justice's (1987) excellent book for details about the projectile points that figure importantly in cross-dating Kentucky's Archaic sites.

Compared to the Late Paleoindian period, the biggest change in projectile points is the introduction of notched bases (e.g., compare figs. 2.9 and 3.2). In most other respects, Early Archaic tool kits closely resemble those of the Late Paleoindian period. This technological continuity suggests that many aspects of Late Paleoindian life in Kentucky changed slowly over several thousands of years after the end of the Pleistocene.

Subsistence

Early Archaic bands were small, and they hunted and gathered over large territories, much like their Paleoindian predecessors. The widespread distribution of corner and basal notched points, such as the Kirk and LeCroy types (fig. 3.2 A–D, P–Q), the presence of tools made from nonlocal materials, and the general absence of middens, features, and burials in Early Archaic sites suggest that most camps were used only for a short time. Comparatively few tools associated with collecting or preparing plant foods are found at Early Archaic sites, reflecting the continued importance of animals as food (Dragoo 1976:11). Aquatic foods, such as fish and mussels, were apparently not important.

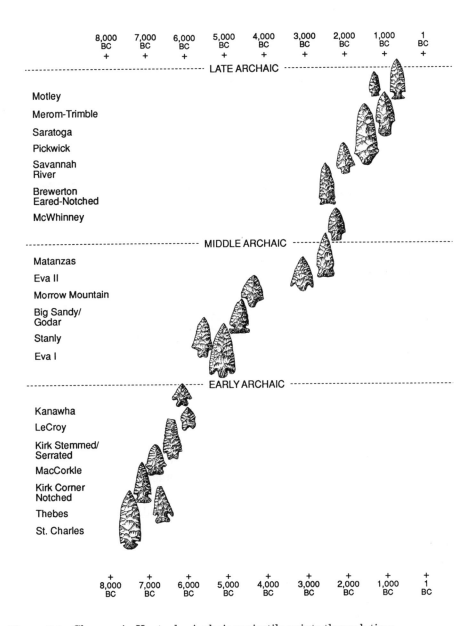

Figure 3.1 Changes in Kentucky Archaic projectile points through time.

Settlement Patterns

Most of the detailed information about the Early Archaic comes from stratified sites in the Ohio Valley and the Mountains regions (fig. 3.3), but stratified deposits are not limited to those regions. They are found everywhere in the state where the remains of camps could be sealed below alluvium, cov-

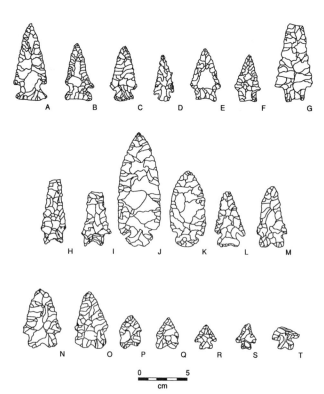

Figure 3.2. Early
Archaic projectile points:
A-D, Kirk Corner
Notched; E-F, Kirk
Stemmed; G-I, Kirk
Serrated; J-K, Dovetail;
L, Thebes Diagonal
Notched; M-O,
MacCorkle; P-Q, LeCroy;
R-T, Kanawha. Adapted
from Jefferies 1988: fig. 2.

ered by slope wash at the base of hills, or buried in rockshelters (e.g., the
Morrisroe site on the lower Tennessee River [Nance 1986a]). The stratified
sites in the Ohio Valley and the Mountains are important because they are
well preserved and because they have been excavated. Examples include the
Longworth-Gick site in Louisville and Cloudsplitter and Deep Shelter in the
Daniel Boone National Forest.

Longworth-Gick is located on a low floodplain ridge near the Falls of the
Ohio River at Louisville. Hunter-gatherer bands camped seasonally along
this ridge during the Early Archaic period, and Ohio River floods periodically
covered the remains of their camps with alluvium. Over time, Ohio River
alluvium successively capped the remains of at least eight Early Archaic
camps in the locality called the Longworth-Gick site. These eight components
and the "sterile" alluvium lenses that separate them extend nearly 7 m (21
ft) below the modern ground surface (Collins 1979).

Archaeologists divide the stratigraphy of the Longworth-Gick site into a
series of superimposed zones. The oldest Early Archaic zone, which occurred
between 7,500 and 6,500 B.C., contained small Kirk projectile points. Larger
Kirk points were found in an overlying midden zone, which is dated to 6,490

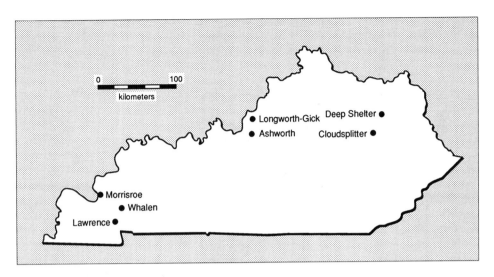

Figure 3.3   Major Early and Middle Archaic sites discussed in the text.

B.C. The uppermost Early Archaic zone, dated to about 6,470 B.C., contained an assemblage with LeCroy and Kanawha Bifurcate Base projectile points (Collins and Driskell 1979:1024–38).

These stratigraphic zones are the remains of Early Archaic camps that took place between late summer and winter when floods were unlikely (Collins and Driskell 1979:1024–26). The most intense period of site use, as reflected by the number of charcoal-filled pits and burned areas, occurred in the Kirk and the Bifurcate Base zones (Collins 1979:581–82). Analysis of the remains of these Early Archaic camps revealed that artifact diversity increased through time and plant food use intensified at the expense of hunting (Collins 1979:582).

Unfortunately, little direct evidence was found of the kinds of plants and animals eaten by the Early Archaic inhabitants of Longworth-Gick. Hickory nuts were probably an important resource, along with many other nuts, wild seeds, fruits, and roots. Only one animal bone fragment was found at the site, so little can be said about which animal foods were preferred (Duffield 1979:table 9.35; Lannie 1979:986).

East of Longworth-Gick, across the Bluegrass, the rockshelters that overlook the Red River and nearby drainages in the Mountains have been the focus of archaeological investigations for more than 60 years (Funkhouser and Webb 1929, 1930; Webb and Funkhouser 1936). Recent work by Cowan et al. (1981) shows that some of these shelters contain the remains of Early Archaic camps.

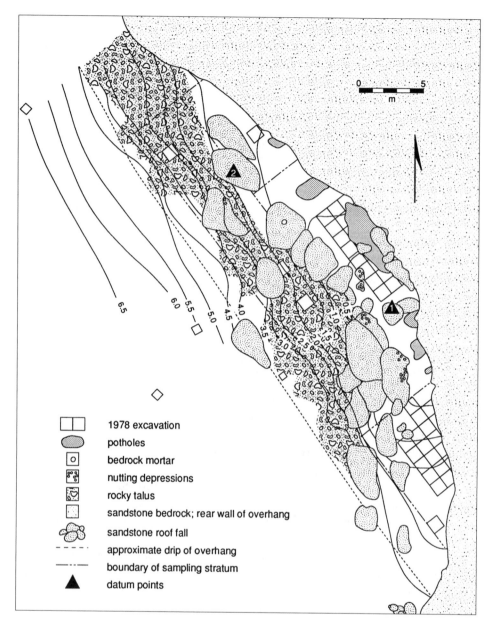

Figure 3.4 The Cloudsplitter rockshelter floor showing excavated areas and features. Adapted from Cowan et al. 1981: fig. 2.

Cloudsplitter rockshelter in Menifee County is a small shelter that could have housed a small group, perhaps two or three families (fig. 3.4). Around 7,000 B.C., Early Archaic hunters and gatherers occupied the shelter briefly in the fall as part of their seasonal round of deer hunting and nut collecting

(Cowan et al. 1981:74). The remains of their camps consist of a few post molds and hearths, as well as projectile points of the Kirk and LeCroy Bifurcate Base types.

The Cloudsplitter inhabitants lived in a climate cooler and wetter than modern conditions. Plant remains found in the archaeological deposit and pollen collected from the shelter's sediments show lingering effects of the Late Pleistocene environment. Although deciduous trees were present locally, boreal forest trees such as hemlock and spruce still grew in the upper elevations of the Mountains. The animals, however, were similar to those found in the area in modern times. The Early Archaic deposit contains the bones of whitetail deer, elk, beavers, birds, and turtles eaten by the people who lived in the shelter (Cowan et al. 1981:73–74).

In what is now Cave Run Reservoir on the Licking River in Rowan County, the lower levels of Deep Shelter also contained the remains of several Early Archaic occupations (Dorwin et al. 1970:132). These camps, which contain assemblages with Kirk, LeCroy, and St. Albans Side Notched type projectile points, were used between 6,000 and 7,000 B.C. The diversity of plants and animals in the locality around Deep Shelter attracted Early Archaic hunter-gatherers to camp there (Dorwin et al. 1970:133). None of the nearby Cave Run Reservoir open sites yielded Early Archaic material, suggesting that rockshelters were the preferred location for long-term or repeated occupations (Dorwin et al. 1970:137).

As noted above, most Early Archaic sites are the remains of small, temporary camps that offer only a limited glimpse of the lives of these hunter-gatherers. Several studies along the lower Tennessee-Cumberland valleys in the western Pennyroyal illustrate the ephemeral, short-term nature of these Early Archaic camps. At the Morrisroe site on the Tennessee River some 18 km upstream from its confluence with the Ohio River, archaeologists from Simon Fraser University exposed a late Early Archaic midden that contained few remains compared to such sites as Longworth-Gick and Cloudsplitter. The assemblage of this small camp includes Kirk Stemmed and Kirk Serrated points and it dates between 6,500 and 6,000 B.C. (Nance 1986a). Morrisroe repeats the general pattern of Early Archaic site use noted earlier by Rolingson and Schwartz (1966) in their study of Paleoindian and Early Archaic occupations in this part of Kentucky.

In the mountains of southeastern Kentucky, Early Archaic camps have long been known to have existed in the region's narrow valleys and bluffs. Recently, however, Early Archaic sites were also found in Floyd County on mountain ridges and level side benches. The presence of middens and features in these sites, which contain Kirk, LeCroy, and Pine Tree (Kirk-like) projectile points, suggests a relatively intense Early Archaic occupation of this part of southeastern Kentucky (Rossen 1985:14). Comparable mountaintop sites are reported in Boone County, West Virginia (Wilkins 1977). The

Early Archaic mountaintop sites in these regions are interpreted as fall camps associated with food gathering in the early Holocene deciduous forests that capped the mountains (Wilkins 1977:3–8).

Burials

Early Archaic burials are rare in Kentucky, but these hunter-gatherers probably treated their dead with as much care and compassion as did later groups. The scarcity of burials is due partly to the highly mobile way of life. Any given camp would be used for a few weeks or part of a season and then the band would move on. Most burials are, therefore, of one or a few individuals. Cemeteries, in the sense that we think of them, did not exist. The scarcity of burials is also due to how few Early Archaic bands there were in Kentucky relative to, for instance, the Fort Ancient villagers of the Late Prehistoric period.

The best example of Early Archaic treatment of the dead comes from the Lawrence site in the Trigg County uplands east of the Cumberland River. Excavations revealed a large, 17 cm thick Early Archaic midden that accumulated from a series of brief camps (Mocas 1977). The main diagnostic Early Archaic artifacts in the midden were several Kirk-like projectile points (Mocas 1977:124–27).

Feature 72 at Lawrence contained the skeletal remains of two adult males and their associated grave goods (Mocas 1985). The individuals were between 22 and 28 years old at death. They were buried in flexed positions, which means that the legs were tucked against the trunk of the body. Both burials contained necklaces of domesticated dog canine teeth and beaver incisors. A cache of flaked stone tools, including projectile points, drills, and scrapers, accompanied one burial. These tools are similar to other Archaic implements found at this site, but they are larger and less modified and resharpened (Mocas 1985:82–89). The cache and the condition of the tools in it suggest that it was intended for the buried individual's use in the afterlife.

Another example of the Early Archaic treatment of the dead is seen at the Ashworth site, a Bullitt County rockshelter located on a tributary of the Salt River south of Louisville (DiBlasi 1981). The flexed burial of an individual who met a violent death was found near the shelter's rear wall. The only artifact found with this individual was an Early Archaic projectile point embedded in its spine (in a thoracic vertebra) (DiBlasi 1981). This shelter also contained the remains of an Early Archaic camp, the assemblage of which included Ashworth Corner Notched (Kirk-like) and Kirk projectile points, bone needles, a bone bead, and an antler flaker.

MIDDLE ARCHAIC (6,000–3,000 B.C.)

Around 7,000 B.C., the midcontinent climate gradually became warmer and drier than modern conditions in the same region. This warm, dry spell, which climatologists call the Hypsithermal climatic interval, lasted thousands of years. It affected plants, animals, and people in Kentucky and elsewhere across the midcontinent. Fossil pollen, or microscopic plant spores, provides the clearest picture of these effects. Pollen samples from the Old Field Swamp peat deposit in southeastern Missouri indicate major vegetation changes in the lower Mississippi Valley and eastward into Kentucky between 7,000 and 1,000 B.C. Old Field Swamp was at its driest around 5,000 B.C., when the pollen shows that the dense bottomland forest had become a savanna-like grassland. After 3,000 B.C., the climate changed again, this time toward moist conditions and the forest reclaimed the region around the swamp (King and Allen 1977).

By 6,000 B.C., regionally distinct archaeological cultures also began to develop throughout the eastern United States. Differences between these cultures, which were caused partially by adapting to local environmental conditions, were manifested in a variety of technological, settlement, subsistence, and social characteristics. Since the Kentucky Middle Archaic is poorly known, most detailed information about these regionally distinct cultures comes from excavations in adjacent states. Important comparative sites include Eva (Lewis and Lewis 1961) and Ice House Bottom (Chapman 1977) in Tennessee, Black Earth (Jefferies and Lynch 1983) and Modoc Rock Shelter (Fowler 1959; Styles et al. 1983) in southern Illinois, Doerschuk (Coe 1964) in the North Carolina piedmont, Gregg Shoals (Tippitt and Marquardt 1984) along the Savannah River in Georgia, and the Walnut and Poplar sites (Bense 1987:379) in Mississippi. Several Middle Archaic phases have been identified at these sites, based on the occurrence of morphologically distinct projectile point types (fig. 3.5). Broadly similar phases can be identified by cross-dating known Kentucky Middle Archaic sites.

Tools and Other Artifacts

One of the most distinctive Middle Archaic characteristics is the development of regional projectile point styles (Cook 1976; Fowler 1959; Lewis and Lewis 1961; Nance 1986b). Middle Archaic occupations in eastern and central Kentucky, for example, are typically identified by the presence of Morrow Mountain, Matanzas, and Big Sandy II points (fig. 3.5 A–B, F–L), which have been found in dated deposits elsewhere. In western Kentucky, typical Middle Archaic types include Eva (fig. 3.5 C–E), Cypress Creek, and Big Sandy points.

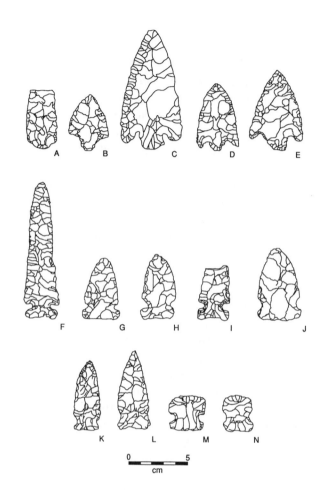

Figure 3.5 Middle Archaic projectile points and scrapers: A-B, Morrow Mountain II; C-E, Eva; F-J, Big Sandy II-Godar; K-L, Matanzas; M-N, side-notched end scrapers. Adapted from Jefferies 1988: fig. 4.

The similarity of projectile point styles within a region reflects the exchange of information and ideas among groups of people who were adapting to broadly similar environmental conditions. Societies sharing similar projectile point styles appear to have shared other cultural characteristics as well, such as the way that they built their houses, the kinds of food that they preferred, and the way they organized their activities over the landscape.

Regional differences in Middle Archaic assemblages reflect differences in the way hunter-gatherer groups adapted to distinct environments. These demands are readily seen in the variety of specialized tools that first appear in the Middle Archaic. For example, new groundstone implements such as axes, pitted anvils, grinding stones, and pestles (fig. 3.6) come into common use to exploit and process a wide range of plant foods. Another device, the spear-thrower or atlatl (figs. 3.7–3.9), made hunting more effective by extending the spear's killing range.

Figure 3.6 Middle Archaic groundstone tools: A-B, grooved axes; C, pestle; D-F, pitted stones. Reproduced with permission of the William S. Webb Museum of Anthropology, University of Kentucky, negatives 5505 and 6019.

Subsistence

Across the midcontinent, Middle Archaic subsistence was based on a wide variety of animals and plants (Fowler 1959; Jefferies and Lynch 1983; Styles et al. 1983). Whitetail deer and wild turkey were the most important game. Hickory and other nuts were important plant foods, and starchy seeds, greens, and sap were also eaten.

Many details about Middle Archaic subsistence in Kentucky can be inferred from investigations at Eva, one of the best-documented Archaic sites in northern Tennessee (Lewis and Lewis 1961). This large floodplain site, located in what is now Kentucky Lake, consisted of two major Middle Archaic components in an extensive midden with many human burials, features, and the remains of a possible structure. Whitetail deer was the most important game animal in the Middle Archaic components, but opossum, raccoon, and bear were also hunted. Comparisons between the two components show that the use of shellfish, fish, and birds increased throughout the Middle Archaic. River mussels, in particular, grew in dietary importance.

Settlement Patterns

The reduction of forests and the increase of grasslands during the Hypsithermal affected human settlements in Kentucky (Conaty 1985; Janzen 1977; Jefferies 1983; Nance 1985) and elsewhere in the Midwest (Brown and Vierra 1983; Cook 1976; Fowler 1959). In many areas, the ephemeral nature of most early Middle Archaic occupations suggests high group mobility, not unlike that of Early Archaic bands. This is particularly true of eastern and central Kentucky, where Middle Archaic settlement patterns are similar to those of the Early Archaic.

Middle Archaic sites, for example, are rarely reported in the Pennyroyal, and archaeologists infer that few people lived there. In Christian County, Sanders and Maynard (1979:272) attribute the sparse population density of this part of the Pennyroyal to the impact of the Hypsithermal, which would have promoted the spread of upland grasslands at the expense of forests and changed many resources that bands had once exploited in the region.

In the Bluegrass, small Middle Archaic sites have been found along Gunpowder Creek in Boone County (Sussenbach 1986). Based on the small assemblages, the lack of artifact concentrations, and low tool diversity, most

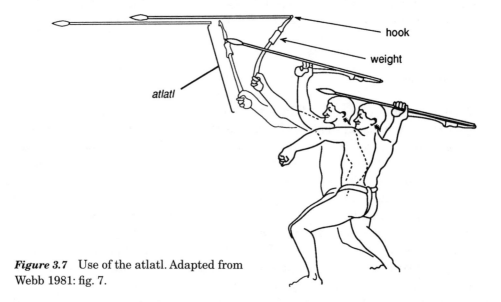

Figure 3.7 Use of the atlatl. Adapted from Webb 1981: fig. 7.

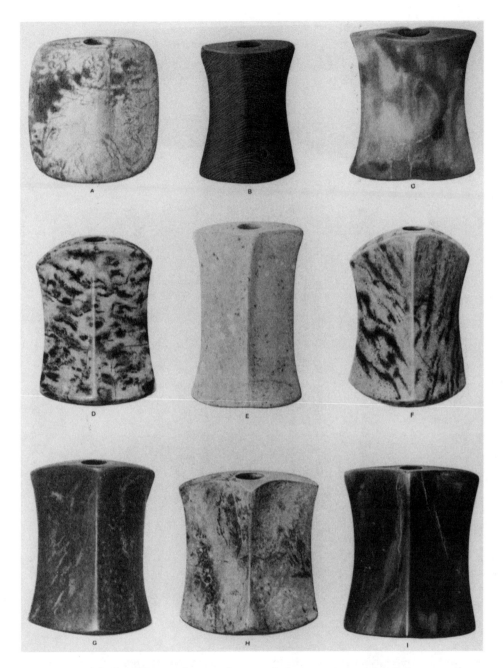

Figure 3.8 Atlatl weights, or bannerstones, acted as counterweights to increase the throwing power of atlatls. These weights are from the Indian Knoll site in Ohio County. Moore 1916: plate 10; reproduced by permission of the Library, Academy of Natural Sciences of Philadelphia.

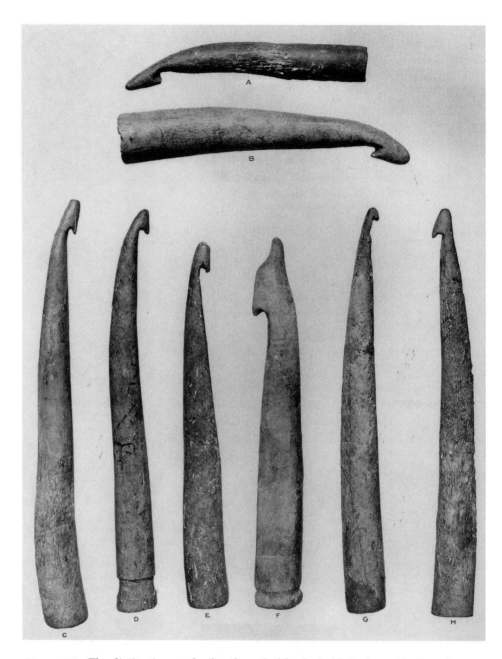

Figure 3.9 The distinctive notch of antler atlatl hooks held the base of a throwing spear. Moore 1916: fig. 10; reproduced by permission of the Library, Academy of Natural Sciences of Philadelphia.

of these sites are interpreted as seasonal hunting and processing camps (Edging 1987:40–46). Two other Gunpowder Creek sites, which show evidence of more intensive use, may have been base camps. Edging (1987) suggests that localities like Gunpowder Creek were used by hunters and gatherers from large Ohio Valley base camps. They probably lived at these sites seasonally while they collected food to supplement the resources available in the river valley. Similar ephemeral, short-term camps are reported from Grant and Owen counties (Rolingson 1968). They have also been found on ancient point bars and floodplain ridges in the Ohio River Valley in Jefferson County below Louisville (Collins and Driskell 1979:1035–36).

Intensively occupied Middle Archaic sites have been discovered and, in a few instances, excavated in the lower Tennessee-Cumberland valleys and in the Ohio River Valley. Some of these Middle Archaic sites were base camps used on a long-term or year-round basis (Nance 1987). For example, at the Morrisroe site in the lower Tennessee Valley, the remains of small, temporary Early Archaic camps were capped by two large Middle Archaic base camps between 6,200 and 3,600 B.C. The oldest Middle Archaic component, which occurred between 6,000 and 5,500 B.C., was the biggest and most intensive occupation. Cypress Creek and Eva projectile points are common in the assemblage (Nance 1986b), which also contained many other stone tools, including two milling stones with residues of what may be plant resins. Burned clay and fired areas marked the probable locations of hearths and fires. The midden also contains many hickory nut and walnut shells and the bones of fish, deer, turtles, snakes, waterfowl, and other birds. The remains of this camp were capped, in turn, by a late Middle Archaic occupation that took place around 3,500 B.C. The assemblage contained side-notched and stemmed projectile points.

Long-term, intensively occupied components are also known from the lower levels of sites such as Reid, Hornung, and Miller in the Ohio River Valley near Louisville. Archaeologists disagree whether these sites, which date between 4,000 and 3,000 B.C., should be considered Late Archaic (Granger 1983; Janzen 1977) or late Middle Archaic (Collins and Driskell 1979:1030) components, the latter of which is the view taken here.

The Jefferson County late Middle Archaic sites are situated with easy access to at least two diverse habitats (e.g., the Ohio Valley, the outer Bluegrass, and the Knobs). Janzen (1977:140–41) proposes that the environmental diversity of the river valley in the Falls of the Ohio locality allowed Archaic groups to select sites where they could live most, if not all, of the year. Sites with comparable assemblages are present in western Kentucky, southern Indiana, southern and central Illinois, and eastern Missouri (Cook 1976; Fowler 1959; Jefferies and Lynch 1983; Miller 1941). Projectile points and engraved bone pins from sites in the latter regions are similar to those found at many late Middle Archaic sites in Jefferson County and adjacent regions (Granger 1988:fig. 12; Janzen 1977:137).

Burials

As with the Early Archaic period, relatively little is known about how Middle Archaic groups disposed of their dead. Excavation of the KYANG site in Jefferson County revealed 32 burials associated with the late Middle Archaic Old Clarkesville phase component, which is dated to around 3,100 B.C. (Granger 1988). Burials, consisting of 1 male, 5 females, 13 juveniles, and 13 adults of undetermined gender, were placed in flexed positions in deep bowl-shaped pits. Some graves contained one individual and others contained two. Grave goods associated with the burials include engraved bone pins; wolf, deer, and bear tooth necklaces; red ochre; groundstone pendants and beads; a deer antler atlatl hook; and a variety of chert tools (Granger 1988:175).

Additional information on Middle Archaic burial practices comes from the Black Earth site, located a short distance north of the Ohio River in southern Illinois. More than 150 Middle Archaic burials, some of which contained artifacts resembling those at the KYANG site, were excavated at the site. The kinds and distribution of grave goods suggest that there were few social differences among these people except for distinctions based on age and gender (Jefferies and Lynch 1983).

LATE ARCHAIC (3,000–1,000 B.C.)

After the climate moderated around 3,000 B.C., Archaic settlements were more dispersed than they had been during the Middle Archaic. In many parts of Kentucky, the size, number, and distribution of Late Archaic sites suggest that there were basic changes in hunter-gatherer band social organization and the use of the landscape (Conaty 1985; Fowler 1959; Jefferies 1983; Nance 1985, 1986a). Late Archaic societies were still egalitarian, but evidence of increased social complexity (e.g., social inequality) is present at some sites, especially the large Green River shell mounds (Rothschild 1979; Webb 1946; Winters 1968). Some burials also contain exotic grave goods made from Great Lakes copper and marine shells, suggesting special treatment of high-status individuals (Winters 1968).

Tools and Other Artifacts

The Late Archaic tool kit consisted of a wide range of flaked stone (fig. 3.10), groundstone, and bone tools (fig. 3.11) used for specialized tasks, as well as tools made from such materials as wood, which are not preserved. Typical

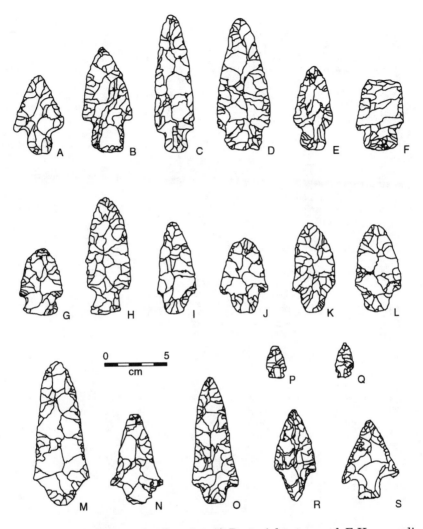

Figure 3.10   Late Archaic projectile points: A-D, straight stemmed; E-H, expanding stemmed; I-L, contracting stemmed; M-O, Ledbetter; P-Q, Merom-Trimble; R, Gary; S, Wade. Adapted from Jefferies 1988: figs. 5 and 6; specimen R adapted from Justice 1987: fig. 41, a; specimen S adapted from Justice 1987: fig. 39, e).

projectile points had large straight, expanding, and contracting stems, but smaller stemmed and side-notched types were also common. Some tool changes were functional; others were stylistic and reflected culturally different ideas about the ideal appearance of a tool. The presence of artifacts made from nonlocal raw materials shows that long-distance trade networks in central North America existed as early as 3,000 B.C. (Goad 1980).

Figure 3.11 Bone and antler artifacts excavated from the Late Archaic Indian Knoll site in Ohio County by C.B. Moore in 1916. Similar tools and implements are found in many Middle and Late Archaic sites. Moore 1916: fig. 8; reproduced by permission of the Library, Academy of Natural Sciences of Philadelphia.

Subsistence

The staple diet was whitetail deer and hickory nuts, supplemented by small mammals, birds, fish, seeds, fruits, and nuts. River mussels were an important food in some regions (Marquardt and Watson 1983). Certain starchy

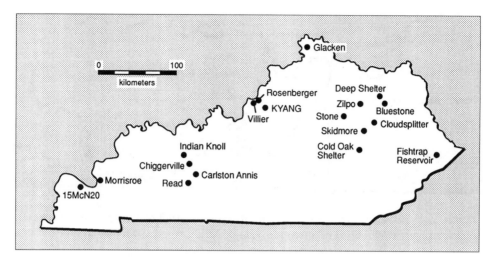

Figure 3.12   Major Late Archaic sites discussed in the text.

seeds, such as goosefoot, marsh elder, and knotweed, also were used widely for food (Cowan 1985b:229–30). The occasional presence of native and tropical cultivated plants (e.g., maygrass, goosefoot, squash, and gourds) suggests that some groups experimented with gardening (Chomko and Crawford 1978; Cowan et al. 1981; Watson 1985).

Settlement Patterns

Late Archaic sites are more numerous than Middle Archaic ones, but in many areas they are small and represent relatively short-term occupations (fig. 3.12). Exceptions include the large, deep shell middens along the Green River. Differences between Middle and Late Archaic sites reflect steady population increases, social organization changes, and adaptation to local environmental conditions.

Much more is known about the archaeology of the Late Archaic period than about any of the preceding periods in Kentucky prehistory. The following sections draw selectively from this wealth of information to illustrate general points about Kentucky Late Archaic life.

The Green River Shell Mounds. The Late Archaic sites of the Green River Valley are some of the most thoroughly investigated archaeological sites in eastern North America. They were also among the first Kentucky sites to be systematically excavated (e.g., Moore 1916; Nelson 1917). Nevertheless, it was not until William S. Webb's work along the Green River during the late 1930s and early 1940s that the "Shell Mound Archaic," as he called it, was

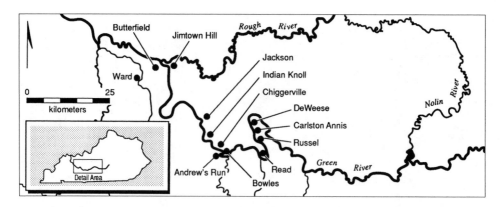

Figure 3.13 "Shell Mound Area" Archaic sites investigated by New Deal era archae-ologists under Webb's general direction. Adapted from Webb 1974: facing p. 119.

defined in print. The terms *shell mound* and *shell midden* refer to the dense concentrations of river mussel shell found in many of these sites.

Between 1937 and 1941, during the most intensive period of the shell mound investigations, Webb directed excavations at the Carlston Annis, Read, Chiggerville, Indian Knoll, Jackson Bluff, Jimtown Hill, Baker or Andrew's Run, Butterfield, Barrett, and Ward sites (fig. 3.13) (Rolingson 1967; Webb 1946, 1950a, 1950b, 1974; Webb and Haag 1939, 1940, 1947a). These excavations yielded thousands of artifacts and much information about Archaic culture, and contributed to the development of the Archaic tradition concept in the archaeology of eastern North America.

Nearly 50 prehistoric shell mounds are known along the Green River and its tributaries in the Western Coal Field and Pennyroyal. The middens at many of these sites accumulated gradually throughout prehistory (Rolingson 1967:418–19), but the most extensive excavated remains are those of Late Archaic camps dating between roughly 3,200 and 1,400 B.C. (Hockensmith et al. 1985).

The shell mound excavations revealed specially prepared clay floors, hearths, tool caches, and burials (Hockensmith et al. 1985). Flexed burials, often containing a variety of grave goods, were common at some sites (figs. 3.14–3.15). Some burials contained artifacts made from nonlocal raw materials obtained by trade (Goad 1980; Winters 1968). Variations in the treatment of the dead reflect social distinctions in Late Archaic society (Rothschild 1979; Winters 1968).

Subsistence. Many of the Green River shell middens are components of the Indian Knoll phase (Rolingson 1967:409–10), and date between 2,500 and 1,500 B.C. This phase is limited to the middle Green River region, and it

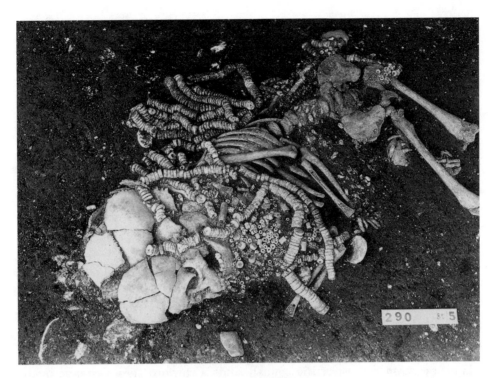

Figure 3.14   Late Archaic Carlston Annis burial showing shell beads. Reproduced by permission of the William S. Webb Museum of Anthropology, University of Kentucky, negative 5335.

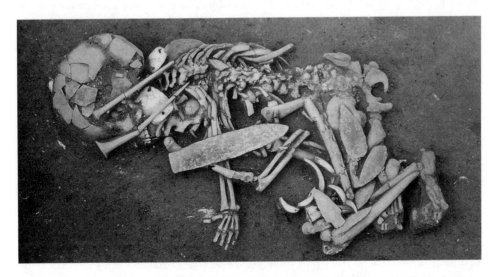

Figure 3.15   Late Archaic Indian Knoll burial showing chert bifaces, shell pendants, bone pins, and animal teeth. Reproduced by permission of the William S. Webb Museum of Anthropology, University of Kentucky, negative 3759.

includes many of the sites Webb excavated. Components share the following features: a diversified economy, seasonal encampments, a variety of stemmed projectile points, and elaborate grave goods associated with a few burials.

These hunter-gatherers used at least 73 kinds of plants (Crawford 1982), but most of the plant remains in the Green River shell mounds are from fewer than 10 species. Hickory nut shells comprise about one-half of the identified plant remains at most sites. Acorn and walnut shells and small quantities of blackberry, grape, honey locust, persimmon, grass, and knotweed seeds account for much of the remainder.

Squash rinds have been found at a few Indian Knoll phase sites (e.g., Marquardt and Watson 1983). These rinds could be examples of early domesticated species or local wild ones. If they represent an early domesticate, Late Archaic groups were beginning to experiment with gardening. Except for a possible sunflower seed from Carlston Annis, no other cultivated or domesticated plants have been found in these middens (Crawford 1982:207–8).

Enough is known about the nature of plant gathering in the Indian Knoll phase to suggest the direction of shifts in Late Archaic subsistence practices. The lowest excavation levels at Carlston Annis, for example, contain few plant remains, most of which are hickory nut shells. In the upper levels, however, acorn shells were more common than hickory nut shells; the upper levels also contained most of the squash rinds. Crawford sees a change in the Late Archaic settlement system reflected in these changes in plant utilization. The inhabitants of the oldest camp at Carlston Annis, represented by the lowest excavation levels, gathered plants from the immediate vicinity and processed them at the shell mound. Later, in the camps represented by the upper excavation levels, foragers gathered and processed most of their nuts and other plants away from the shell mounds, probably on the wooded slopes and uplands that flank the river valley (Crawford 1982:209).

Settlements. The basic archaeological characteristics of the Green River shell mound assemblages were defined by Webb (1974:236–40) at the Indian Knoll site in Ohio County. The common projectile points have stemmed or notched bases. The discovery of many atlatl parts (hooks, weights, and handles) (figs. 3.7–3.9) in Indian Knoll phase sites underscores the importance of the atlatl, or spear-thrower, as an Archaic hunting weapon. Grooved axes, bell-shaped pestles (fig. 3.6, C), steatite bowls, and stemmed scrapers are also common artifacts (Rolingson 1967:410).

Most of the excavated Indian Knoll phase shell middens were base camps occupied for several seasons of the year (Rolingson 1967). Other short-term camps probably lie in the uplands beyond the Green River Valley and its tributaries. Winters (1974) identifies several possible Indian Knoll phase site types, including settlements, base camps, transient camps, and hunting camps. *Settlements* covered 2–3 acres (.8–1.2 hectares) and were occupied during the winter. These sites contain the remains of permanent houses and many storage pits and burials. *Base camps* were comparable in size to settlements, but were occupied only during the summer and contained no houses, many projectile points, and few storage pits or domestic implements. *Transient camps* were occupied in the spring and fall when groups were on the move between settlements and base camps. Smaller hunting, fishing, and gathering camps also were used throughout the year (Winters 1969:137).

Toolmaking and tool maintenance and the processing of food and other raw materials were more important tasks at settlements and base camps than at transient or hunting camps (Winters 1974:xvii). Other activities, such as fishing and woodworking, were seldom done at hunting camps. According to Winters's (1974:xvi) site type criteria, the Read, Chiggerville, and Ward sites were settlements; Carlston Annis, Indian Knoll, and Barrett were base camps; the Butterfield site was a transient camp; and Kirkland was a hunting camp.

Burials, Political Organization, and Trade

Thousands of burials, most of which probably date to the Indian Knoll phase (Rolingson 1967:414), have been excavated in the Green River shell mounds. Some of these individuals were buried with ornaments, tools, and other artifacts placed in their graves. Grave associations include strings of shell or stone beads (fig. 3.14); conch shell gorgets and pendants; turtle shell cups and rattles; atlatl parts; copper artifacts; lumps of red ocher; bone hair pins, and conch shell cups. Archaeologists have used the differential treatment of these burials to explore Late Archaic social differences (Rothschild 1979; Thiel 1972; Winters 1968). Other researchers have used copper and marine shell artifacts from the graves to investigate Late Archaic trade networks (Goad 1980).

Late Archaic hunter-gatherers have traditionally been described as egalitarian societies in which few status distinctions were made. Rothschild's (1979) analysis of Indian Knoll burials suggests, however, that different status levels may have existed in these societies. One social level included males and children buried with a variety of artifact types. Another level comprised only adults who were buried with a single kind of artifact, the nature of which may reflect activities in which the deceased individual participated (Rothschild 1979:671).

The Indian Knoll burials suggest an egalitarian society in which status was based on gender and in which social differences were minimal (Rothschild 1979:672). In general, the distribution of utilitarian objects in the graves was based on the age of the deceased, not the dead person's gender.

This suggests that everyday objects found in a grave were the personal possessions of the deceased (Rothschild 1979:671).

The association of copper and marine shell artifacts with a few Indian
Knoll burials may also reflect the participation of some individuals in long-
distance trade networks. Goad (1980:11) proposes that the copper and
marine shell artifacts at Indian Knoll phase sites reflect the strategic location of the Green River region at the interface of a northern region involved
in the exchange of Great Lakes copper and a southern region that provided
marine shell from the southern Atlantic and Gulf coasts. Some Late Archaic
residents of Indian Knoll and other nearby sites may have served as middlemen in the exchange of these materials between these two distant regions.

Health. The Indian Knoll phase skeletons have been an important source of
information about the health of Late Archaic populations in the midcontinent
(e.g., Blakely 1971; Cassidy 1972, 1980, 1984; Johnston and Snow 1961).
These studies show that the Indian Knoll people were quite healthy, but they
suffered when food ran short, as it sometimes did during bad years. Many
people had arthritis, and its effects are readily seen in the degeneration of
joints in the arms and legs of skeletons. Dental caries were uncommon and
occurred mostly in adults. Most teeth also show a high degree of wear, which
was the primary cause of abscesses and tooth loss. As expected in an egalitarian society, men and women experienced similar diseases, and everyone suffered from essentially the same physical stresses (Cassidy 1984:324–26).

The Bluegrass Late Archaic. Late Archaic settlements throughout the
Bluegrass were generally small base camps along the narrow floodplains of
entrenched rivers and streams, smaller floodplain and upland sites, and rockshelters. Most were short-term occupations that left behind evidence of few
activities other than hunting, game butchering, and toolmaking. The general
absence of large, intensively occupied Late Archaic sites in the Bluegrass may
reflect a nearly uniform distribution of plant and animal resources across this
region. Such a resource distribution would have provided many suitable site
locations (Turnbow et al. 1983:29) and little incentive to reuse them.

The Stone site in Clark County is an example of a small Bluegrass campsite. The assemblage contained scrapers, spokeshaves or notches, and gravers
made from modified flakes; cores; unmodified debitage; bifaces; hammerstones; and contracted- and straight-stem projectile points. Food preparation
and processing pits, a circular or oval structure, and two possible lean-tos
composed the major archaeological features of this camp (Turnbow et al.
1983:411).

Evidence of a more substantial terminal Late Archaic occupation in the
Bluegrass comes from the Zilpo site on the Licking River floodplain in Bath
County (Rolingson and Rodeffer 1968). Rolingson and Rodeffer defined two

distinct components at Zilpo, an upper zone containing Cogswell (or Gary) points and Johnson Plain potsherds and a lower zone containing Cave Run (or Saratoga) points (1968:35–39). Both point types are similar to specimens dated to the Late Archaic–Early Woodland periods in other parts of eastern Kentucky. The limited range of tool types and the small number of features found at Zilpo suggest that it was an intermittently occupied camp.

Central Ohio Valley Late Archaic.   Much of what is known about central Ohio Valley Archaic adaptations is based on research conducted in southwest Ohio (Vickery 1980). The oldest widely recognized Late Archaic complex is the Central Ohio Valley Archaic, which dates to 2,750–1,750 B.C. Diagnostic artifacts include McWhinney Heavy Stemmed projectile points and hafted end scrapers; scrapers; atlatl hooks and weights; bell-shaped pestles; and grooved axes. The distribution of McWhinney points includes southwestern Ohio, northern Kentucky, and southeastern Indiana (Vickery 1980:35-36). There are no excavated Kentucky components of this complex.

The Maple Creek phase (ca. 1,750–1,000 B.C.) is a terminal Late Archaic phase in the central Ohio Valley. The definition of this phase is based on work at the Maple Creek site on the Ohio River in Clermont County, Ohio. This intensively occupied base camp contained living floors, pit features, and many kinds of artifacts (Vickery 1980). Floral and faunal remains suggest that the site was occupied during the summer, the fall, and possibly the winter.

Diagnostic artifacts associated with Maple Creek components include McWhinney, Merom Expanding Stem, and Trimble Side Notched projectile points. These types are also associated with terminal Late Archaic Riverton culture sites along the Wabash River in Illinois (Winters 1969). A chipped stone microtool industry is also thought to be a diagnostic Maple Creek trait.

Little is known about the geographical extent of the Maple Creek phase. Maple Creek components, as reflected by the occurrences of Merom-Trimble points, are found north into south-central Ohio and to the east and west along the Ohio River (Vickery 1980:30). The presence of Merom-Trimble projectile points in parts of north-central Kentucky may also reflect a Maple Creek presence south of the Ohio River.

Archaeological investigations at the Glacken site in Boone County near Big Bone Lick revealed a dense concentration of Late Archaic artifacts, a disturbed midden deposit, and 12 features (Boisvert 1982a). The pit features, most of which appear to have been used in food preparation, resemble those excavated by Vickery (1980) at the Maple Creek site in southern Ohio. Analysis of faunal remains indicates that Glacken was occupied during the fall and winter between 2,100 and 1,000 B.C. (Boisvert 1982b:7–8). Prehistoric activities performed at Glacken appear to be comparable to those identified at other central Ohio Valley Late Archaic sites, despite its unique location near the salt springs (Boisvert, personal communication, 1989).

Falls of the Ohio.   The Ohio River Valley at Louisville was covered by dense forests by the beginning of the Late Archaic period. Numerous floodplain sloughs and oxbow lakes offered a diverse, reliable food supply for Late Archaic hunters and gatherers (Collins and Driskell 1979:1036). The Falls of the Ohio locality was so attractive that the number of sites increased sharply in the Late Archaic period.

Large Late Archaic middens of earth or shell comprise about one-third of all floodplain sites that can be dated from surface evidence. Late Archaic sites are also located in the interior lowlands, and some of those sites have large, deep middens. In 1979, the 46 known upland sites in the Falls locality were small open sites; a few rockshelters and caves also contained evidence of Late Archaic occupations. Generally speaking, floodplain, interior lowland, and upland habitats were exploited intensively by Late Archaic hunters and gatherers (Collins and Driskell 1979:1030).

Important excavated Late Archaic sites on the Ohio River floodplain include the Rosenberger and Villier locations in Jefferson County (Collins and Driskell 1979:1026), both of which Granger (1988:fig. 1) includes in his Lone Hill phase, dating between 2,400 and 1,200 B.C. Rosenberger was a large, multicomponent site with nearly 400 features, including large and small circular pits, burned areas, debris scatters, artifact caches, and more than 200 burials (Driskell 1979:801–3). Although most features cannot be definitely associated with a specific archaeological period, many are probably attributable to the intensive Late Archaic occupation. The assemblage contains projectile points of McWhinney, Merom-Trimble, and Brewerton-like types, atlatl weights and three-quarter grooved axes, all of which are typical of a Late Archaic base camp occupied between 2,300 and 1,000 B.C. (Collins and Driskell 1979:1026).

Analysis of plant and animal remains, as well as of the chemical composition of some of the human bone, indicates that the site's inhabitants were generalized hunter-gatherers (Lannie 1979:1002-6). Most of their food came from hickory nuts, walnuts, acorns, whitetail deer, fish, small mammals, and wild turkey (Duffield 1979: table 9.35).

At Rosenberger, the most distinctive and widest variety of burial goods were associated with young adults and middle-aged adults. For example, the grave of two young adult males contained bifaces, projectile points, bone fishhooks, atlatl parts, a net weight, and a grooved axe. Grave goods were usually not found with older adults. The distribution of grave goods at Rosenberger differs from the typical pattern of Late Archaic Indian Knoll burials, where some individuals of all ages were accompanied by an assortment of burial objects (Driskell 1979:773). Utilitarian objects comprised 98 percent of the Rosenberger grave goods, and ornaments and ceremonial items are less common than at Indian Knoll (Driskell 1979:774).

The Villier site was a seasonally or intermittently occupied campsite during much of the Late Archaic period (Robinson and Smith 1979). The Villier assemblage contained more Merom-Trimble projectile points than have been recovered from Rosenberger and other Late Archaic sites in the region. The presence of the Merom-Trimble points suggests cultural ties with terminal Late Archaic Riverton culture and Maple Creek phase groups across the Ohio River.

Elsewhere in the Falls locality, Granger (1986) has defined the Lone Hill phase, which dates between 2,400 and 1,200 B.C. Investigation of the multicomponent KYANG site, which is on a knoll overlooking a former marsh and sluggish stream in Jefferson County, exposed nine burials and their associated artifacts. A cache of three stemmed Rowlett projectile points was found with one burial. This projectile point type and other stemmed bifaces are commonly associated with Lone Hill occupations (Granger 1986).

The Eastern Mountains Late Archaic.   Archaeological evidence of substantial, long-term Late Archaic occupations is found throughout the Mountains, especially in rockshelters (fig. 3.16) and along narrow valleys. The most detailed information comes from the Daniel Boone National Forest,

Figure 3.16   Hooton Hollow rockshelter in Menifee County. Reproduced by permission of the William S. Webb Museum of Anthropology, University of Kentucky, negative 4356.

which stretches along the western edge of the Mountains region, and the impoundment areas of reservoirs.

Skidmore Phase.   The Skidmore phase, which lasted from 2,400 to 1,650 B.C. (Turnbow and Jobe 1981:468–71), is centered in Rowan, Menifee, and Powell counties. Components are characterized by projectile points with contracted to straight stems and long ovate blades, chert adzes, and grinding stones. Base camps, such as the Skidmore and Bluestone sites, are concentrated in the region's narrow river valleys. They contain diverse artifact assemblages, large middens, and earth ovens and roasting pits with large quantities of fire-cracked rock—all of which are typical of long-term occupations. Rockshelters and other upland sites were mostly limited activity, short-term camps. Floodplain and upland sites usually contain similar artifacts, but these assemblages have less debitage and fire-cracked rock and lower artifact diversity than the floodplain base camps.

At the Skidmore site on the Red River Gorge floodplain in Powell County, archaeologists found the remains of two Late Archaic base camps capped by one that contains Archaic/Woodland artifacts. The Late Archaic assemblages contain large quantities of debitage and fire-cracked rock, many kinds of projectile points and cutting and perforating implements, and numerous ground-stone tools, such as grooved axes, pitted stones, and pestles (Cowan 1985b:236). The oldest camp, which probably occurred between 3,000 and 2,000 B.C., left a 20–25 cm thick midden with many artifacts, fire-cracked rock concentrations, and earth ovens (Cowan 1976). Late Archaic hunter-gatherers made another base camp at Skidmore between 2,000 and 1,000 B.C., and Early Woodland groups also lived there and left behind undecorated, limestone-tempered potsherds (Cowan 1976:71) and other debris comparable to the assemblages of the Late Archaic camps. Differences between the distribution of features in the two Late Archaic middens at Skidmore may reflect changes in Late Archaic technology. In the oldest Late Archaic camp at Skidmore, food was cooked in earth ovens. In the succeeding base camp, the inhabitants cooked on fires built on sandstone hearths (Cowan 1976:71–72).

Another example of a Skidmore phase base camp is the Bluestone site complex in Rowan County. This dense Late Archaic midden, which is dated to about 2,500–2,100 B.C., contained 42 features including pits, chipping stations, pitted or groundstone features, and hearths (Brooks et al. 1979: 108–20). The most common diagnostic artifact in the assemblage was a stubby, stemmed projectile point that resembles some Skidmore site specimens (Brooks et al. 1979:71) and projectile points of the Cogswell and Cave Run types.

The Skidmore and Bluestone base camps offer important evidence that the seasonal movements of Archaic hunter-gatherer bands in this general region emphasized the use of floodplain resources. Before these sites were excavated, Marquardt (1970) and Dorwin et al. (1970) argued that bands moved seasonally between rockshelters and open lowland sites. They hypothesized that floodplain sites reflected brief occupations during which a band hunted and collected floodplain food resources (Marquardt 1970:85). The base camp excavations, however, show that the floodplain sites were important in the seasonal round of local hunter-gatherers.

But what of the rockshelters? Late Archaic seasonal use of rockshelters has been documented in excavations at Cloudsplitter in the Red River Gorge region of Menifee County (Cowan et al. 1981) and at Deep Shelter in Rowan County (Dorwin et al. 1970). Cloudsplitter shows little evidence of use during the Middle Archaic period, but people settled there again between 2,500 and 1,000 B.C. By the beginning of the Late Archaic period, this locality was covered in a mixed oak, hickory, and chestnut forest. Late Archaic groups living in the Gorge visited the shelter and collected chestnuts and hickory nuts for food. They left behind an assemblage that contains projectile points of the McWhinney Stemmed and Merom-Trimble Notched types (Cowan et al. 1981). A squash rind, found in a rockshelter level dated to about 1,800 B.C., also shows that squash was being grown by some of eastern Kentucky's Late Archaic residents (Cowan et al. 1981:74–75).

Slone Phase.   In Pike County, which occupies the southeasternmost corner of Kentucky, the Slone phase offers a glimpse of Late Archaic occupations younger than those of the Skidmore phase. Slone, which dates to around 1,900 B.C. (Dunnell 1972:92), was defined from archaeological investigations in the Fishtrap Reservoir on the Levisa Fork of the Big Sandy River. It is one of three Late Archaic phases originally proposed by Dunnell (1972) for this region, but the other two phases, Thacker and Sim's Creek, are now considered part of the Woodland periods.

Slone sites were seasonally occupied floodplain settlements. They do not contain evidence of substantial structures, and the artifact assemblages are sparse (Dunnell 1972:27–32). The main focus of the diet was hunting and nut collecting; there is no evidence of cultivated plants in the Fishtrap Lake sites. Nuts were prepared using pestles, manos, and nutting stones, then cooked in large sandstone-filled earth ovens (Dunnell 1972:27–32). Typical assemblages include five-holed pestles, chipped stone axes, bifacially asymmetrical knives, a variety of stemmed projectile points, and siderite (ironstone) flaked stone tools (fig. 3.17). The preference for siderite tools is the only attribute shared by all Slone components.

Cogswell Phase.   This phase includes the latest Late Archaic and the earliest Early Woodland sites in the Mountains. It dates between 1,500 and 800

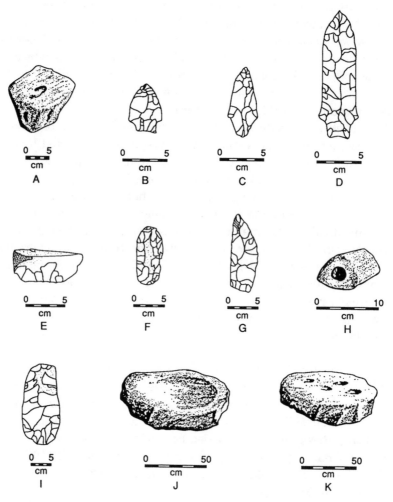

Figure 3.17 Slone phase artifacts: A, pestle; B-D, projectile points; E, chopper; F-G, cutting tools; H, atlatl weight; I, axe; J, metate; K, nutting stone. Adapted from Dunnell 1972: fig. 7.

B.C. and includes settlements found throughout the major drainages of eastern Kentucky. Components are distinguished by the presence of Cogswell contracting stem projectile points made from Haney and Paoli cherts (Ison 1988:215). These Late Archaic groups lived by hunting, gathering, and the cultivation of a variety of plants.

One of the most thoroughly documented Cogswell phase sites is the Cold Oak Shelter in Lee County (Ison 1988). The Cogswell component at this site is the remains of a camp that dates to the very end of the Late Archaic period (around 1,000 B.C.). As is true in some rockshelters, the dry shelter environment preserved many fragile plant and animal remains that usually decompose quickly in open sites (e.g., twisted fiber strands, basket fragments, wooden artifacts). The plant food remains include charred and uncharred hickory nuts, acorn and chestnut shells, and sunflower, goosefoot, marsh elder, knotweed, and possibly maygrass seeds. Although the list of plants includes many edible species, nut fragments are the most common food remain in this and other Cogswell phase sites. The remains of whitetail deer, turkey, squirrel, black bear, box turtle, fish, crayfish, and mussels were also found (Ison 1988:211).

The absence of hickory nut husks, chestnut burrs, and acorn caps suggests that initial preparation of nuts occurred where the nuts were gathered rather than at the shelter (Ison 1988:217). Interestingly, the importance of thin-shelled acorns and chestnuts, based on shell weight, exceeded that of hickory nut by a ratio of 7 to 1 at the Cold Oak Shelter. Thin-shelled nuts are usually underrepresented in most sites because they are easy to break and hard to preserve (Lopinot 1984). Their presence at Cold Oak probably reflects the excellent preservation conditions found in the shelter. It also hints at the kinds of biases that can be present in dietary reconstructions based on plant remains from open-air sites.

Projectile points of the Cogswell contracting stem type are diagnostic artifacts of the Cogswell phase. Wade projectile points are also found in the assemblages. Cogswell phase stone toolmakers preferred using Haney and Paoli cherts from the Newman geological formation to make their tools. This preference for distinctive raw materials gives archaeologists insight into the movement of Cogswell phase groups over the eastern Kentucky landscape. For example, a Cogswell point of Paoli chert was found at a rockshelter in Perry County in southeastern Kentucky. The location lies outside the Cogswell phase core area and beyond the source region for Paoli chert (Ison 1988:215); it must have been traded or carried into southeastern Kentucky by Cogswell hunters.

The Lower Tennessee-Cumberland Valleys.   It was once believed that some lower Tennessee-Cumberland Late Archaic floodplain sites were semisedentary occupations (e.g., Coe and Fischer 1959:22), but the absence of heavy grinding tools, features, and burials at these sites argues against this interpretation. Many of these floodplain sites were briefly occupied by foragers who exploited both valley and upland resources (Nance 1977:14). This is a significant change from Middle Archaic settlement patterns in this region.

These settlement changes are especially clear at Morrisroe, a multicomponent site in Livingston County. The Middle Archaic occupation at Morrisroe was a stable base camp that *was* occupied on a more-or-less permanent basis. Toward the beginning of the Late Archaic period (after about 3,500 B.C.), however, the use of this site became short-term and sporadic (Nance 1986a:12).

Middle to Late Archaic settlement changes comparable to those noted at Morrisroe are also reported for other regions of the Midwest and Southeast (e.g., Brown and Vierra 1983; Cook 1976; Fowler 1959; Janzen 1977; Jefferies 1983). The changes are at least partially due to the impact of the warmer, drier Hypsithermal interval (King and Allen 1977). Middle Archaic groups responded to the climatic changes by altering their exploitation strategies, resulting in the intensive use of localities with diverse, abundant, and reliable subsistence resources. These resources were commonly found in the major river valleys and near swamps and lakes. As the impact of the Hypsithermal lessened, the distribution of critical subsistence resources increased. The more dispersed settlement patterns associated with the Late Archaic in many areas reflect a cultural response to these changing conditions.

Western Kentucky Late Archaic assemblages include a variety of stemmed projectile points. Straight-stemmed types are most common, comprising 60 percent to 80 percent of the points in some terminal Late Archaic assemblages. Ledbetter-Pickwick and Adena-like projectile points also occur at some sites (Nance 1986a, 1986b).

Hickory nuts were one of the main Late Archaic plant foods. Walnuts and acorns were also eaten, as were grapes and the fruits of hawthorn and honey locust (Wymer 1987). There is little direct information about Late Archaic game animals in this part of Kentucky, due partially to the poor bone preservation of the excavated sites and partially to the few analyzed archaeological faunal collections from sites in this region. At the Eva site in northern Tennessee, the Late Archaic remains show that deer was the most important game animal, but other mammals such as the opossum, raccoon, and bear were also hunted. River mussels, which had been an important food during the Middle Archaic occupations at Eva, were no longer gathered. The Eva site foragers may have had no choice, since increased precipitation may have flooded the shoals and killed the mussel beds, or the river channel may have shifted and rendered the mussel beds inaccessible to the site's inhabitants (Lewis and Lewis 1961:20–21).

A comparison of artifacts from Late Archaic sites in the Crooked Creek locality of the Land Between the Lakes National Recreation Area suggests that upland and floodplain sites away from the major valleys were also used differently (Nance 1977). Upland sites were used for hunting and related activities. Few plant processing tools are found at those sites, suggesting that any upland plant foods used by Late Archaic groups required little preparation before they were eaten or carried to another area. Upland site toolmaking consisted of making general purpose flake tools from locally available cherts. Some projectile points were made from nonlocal material, providing insights into the movement of these Late Archaic groups over the landscape and the role of tool curation behavior in shaping the character of upland site assemblages (Nance 1977:13). Floodplain sites in the Crooked Creek drainage were used for a wide range of tasks; some of these sites were base camps from which Late Archaic groups exploited both floodplain and upland resources (Nance 1977:13).

Beyond the mouths of the Tennessee and Cumberland rivers, important Late Archaic evidence comes from Site 15McN20, located on an alluvial ridge near the Ohio River in McCracken County. It is one of the few excavated sites in the lower Ohio Valley that contains Late Archaic material that is not mixed with the remains of later or younger occupations (Butler et al. 1981:122).

The Late Archaic deposit at 15McN20 extended to a depth of 90 cm below surface; test excavations produced large quantities of chert debitage and fire-cracked rock, carbonized plant remains, Late Archaic straight-stemmed projectile points similar to the Saratoga Type Cluster (Winters 1967:25), and a smaller projectile point resembling the Trimble Side Notched type. Most of the flaked stone artifacts were made of chert collected from nearby gravel bars. The processing of cobbles from these gravel bars was a major Late Archaic activity at 15McN20 (Butler et al. 1981:60–71).

DISCUSSION

Archaic peoples inhabited all parts of the state, but the ways in which they exploited the natural resources and the intensity with which they exploited them varied across Kentucky and through time. They also interacted with, or were part of, groups living in nearby areas of the Southeast and Midwest and shared ideas, beliefs, and material goods with them. Evidence of the communication and interaction between these groups is often difficult to find, but it does exist.

This chapter shows that most of what is known about Kentucky's Archaic cultures comes from relatively few sites. Most of these sites are deeply stratified and contain cultural deposits that are separated from those of preceding and subsequent occupations. These unmixed deposits provide encapsulated collections of artifacts, features, and paleoenvironmental data that give a glimpse of the technology, subsistence practices, social organization, and other aspects of Archaic cultures.

Much of what is known about Archaic groups is also based on the distribution of diagnostic projectile points and a few other artifact types that can been confidently dated to the Archaic periods. Little is known about how these prehistoric social groups were organized, the extent of their annual range, how they exploited natural resources, how different groups interacted with each other, or what role these people had in the development of horticulture.

Nevertheless, archaeologists have a general idea of what life was like during these 7,000 years of prehistory. Changes in the ways Archaic people adapted to the environment can be best seen in terms of several trends that transcended the Archaic periods. The rest of this chapter examines these trends.

Population

Population density increased during the Archaic periods. A rough estimate of the magnitude of this increase can be obtained by calculating the number of Early, Middle, and Late Archaic components per century (table 3.1). Since not all of the state's Archaic components are recorded, these data are at best only a relative measure of this trend. The rightmost column of table 3.1 suggests that around 20 Early Archaic components were created each century. Archaeologically, the remains of these occupations are contained in small surface scatters of a few diagnostic Early Archaic artifacts, reflecting the small size of the groups that inhabited the sites and the short intervals during which these sites were used.

The number of components decreased sharply during the Middle Archaic period to about eight sites per century. This decrease may reflect a general reduction in Middle Archaic population density in Kentucky, but more likely it indicates a change in the distribution in people over the landscape, with more people living in fewer sites. This apparent decrease in site frequency may also reflect a methodological problem—it is difficult to identify Middle Archaic sites from surface remains. Whatever the explanation, evidence from several Ohio Valley sites suggests that groups became more sedentary during the Middle Archaic. They established long-term, possibly multiseasonal camps near extensive lowland wet areas, such as swamps and lakes. This may have been one of several cultural responses to the warmer, drier conditions of the Hypsithermal, about which more will be said in the next section.

During the Late Archaic, the number of components increased sharply, rising to 36 sites per century. This figure is nearly double the Early Archaic rate and more than four times the Middle Archaic rate. The increase in site frequency may be due to the dispersal of groups after the end of the Hypsithermal, but evidence for numerous Late Archaic sites, some of which are quite large, in several parts of the state argues for population increase as well.

Sedentism

Evidence in the form of low artifact densities, few features, and little, if any, midden accumulation suggests that Early Archaic groups were highly mobile hunters who did not stay in one place very long. Stone tools made from nonlo-

Table 3.1   EARLY, MIDDLE, AND LATE ARCHAIC COMPONENTS
             PER 100 YEARS

Archaeological period	Range (years B.C.)	Duration in years	No. of components	Components/ 100 yrs
Early Archaic	8,000-6,000	2,000	404	20.2
Middle Archaic	6,000-3,000	3,000	249	8.3
Late Archaic	3,000-1,000	2,000	722	36.1
Totals	8,000-1,000	7,000	1,375	19.6

cal raw materials reinforce the interpretation that these groups traveled widely and made new tools from suitable raw materials found during their travels.

Evidence of increased sedentism is more common during the Middle Archaic, especially, as noted in the preceding section, at sites next to wet areas. Many of these sites contain thick midden deposits, numerous features, burials, and a variety of tools, all of which are typical of permanent camps. Some archaeologists maintain that this trend toward permanent occupations can be at least partially explained by the drier conditions of the Hypsithermal. Although Middle Archaic groups undoubtedly continued to exploit the uplands, the more reliable food resources of the wet areas made them attractive places to live.

The nature and distribution of Late Archaic sites differ somewhat from sites of the Middle Archaic, but sedentary communities were definitely taking hold. The assemblages of many small Late Archaic sites show that these camps were used for a variety of extractive tasks by groups from larger base camps in the same or nearby regions.

Dietary Importance of Plant Foods

A variety of plant foods became important in the diet during the Archaic periods. Early Archaic assemblages contain few groundstone tools, generally associated with plant food processing, and most archaeologists infer that Early Archaic bands in Kentucky did not depend on plant foods as much as their descendants did. The abundance of plant remains, grinding stones, grinding slabs, and pestles in Middle and Late Archaic assemblages reflects the increased importance of plant foods. Nuts and oily seeds (e.g., hickory nuts, sunflower, marsh elder) were important foods throughout the Middle and Late Archaic periods. During the Late Archaic, starchy weed seeds (e.g., goosefoot, maygrass, knotweed) began to play a more important role in the diet. Late Archaic groups eventually cultivated some of these plants and laid the foundation for the development of horticulture during the Woodland period.

Social Complexity

Archaic groups were egalitarian, which means that most social distinctions were based on age and gender. Inherited statuses and statuses that set some individuals apart socially from others were not important in Archaic life. Evidence for increased social complexity during the Archaic periods comes largely from the analysis of burials and the artifacts associated with them. Given the limited available evidence, little can be said about the social organization of Early Archaic groups other than to note that they were small and consisted of individuals related by kinship.

More is known about Middle Archaic social organization because of the excavation of several sites that contained numerous burials. Middle Archaic groups also appear to have been largely egalitarian. Distinctions in burial practices are largely attributable to differences of age and gender. Leadership roles were probably filled by individuals having the appropriate personal abilities, rather than by inheritance.

Late Archaic groups were also essentially egalitarian. Some Late Archaic burials were accompanied by exotic artifacts made from marine shell and copper, an association that some archaeologists interpret as symbolic of high social status (Winters 1968).

Interaction and Exchange

Little evidence of Early Archaic interaction and exchange has been found in Kentucky. Projectile points made from nonlocal cherts probably reflect the extent of Early Archaic group movements over the landscape. These groups undoubtedly encountered similar bands during their annual round, but the nature of that interaction is unknown.

Some Middle Archaic sites offer considerably more evidence for interregional exchange and interaction. Carved and engraved bone pins found at Middle Archaic sites in Kentucky, Illinois, Indiana, and Missouri are virtually identical in form and decoration (Breitburg 1982). These pins were carved in distinctive shapes and decorated by a variety of engraved geometric designs, such as zig-zags and diamonds (fig. 3.11; e.g., the leftmost specimen and the pin in the middle of the top row). The distribution of identical artifacts over most of the midcontinent strongly suggests that groups who made and used these pins interacted on a fairly regular basis. Unfortunately, how, why, and when they interacted is not yet known.

Interregional exchange appears to have been more common during the Late Archaic than during the Middle Archaic. Late Archaic exchange also involved more than one region (the Atlantic or Gulf coasts and the Great Lakes), suggesting greater economic complexity than during the Middle Archaic period.

Most evidence of Late Archaic exchange consists of objects of nonlocal raw materials found with burials. For example, the copper artifacts associated with nine burials at three Late Archaic Green River shell middens (Barrett, Carlston Annis, and Indian Knoll) (Winters 1968:table 10) reflect some kind of trading between west-central Kentucky groups and bands that lived north of the Ohio River. Likewise, the presence of artifacts made of marine shells from the southern Atlantic or Gulf of Mexico coasts is evidence of interaction between Green River groups and those living to the south. Although more common than copper artifacts, Late Archaic marine shell items are found only in graves in Kentucky.

Both copper and marine shell could be obtained directly, but this cannot adequately explain their presence on Kentucky Late Archaic sites. Goad (1980) proposes that some Late Archaic individuals in the Green River region served as middlemen for the southern marine shell trade network and for the northern copper trade network. Accumulated copper and shell artifacts became incorporated in the sociopolitical sphere as indicators of personal status among the people who lived near the Green River shell mounds (Goad 1980:12).

Technology

One of the most notable areas of Archaic cultural change is technology. Highly mobile Early Archaic groups apparently maintained a simple inventory of portable equipment, the preserved parts of which consist largely of flaked stone items. Tools and implements made from perishable materials such as wood, leather, and fiber were undoubtedly part of the tool inventory, but their remains are poorly represented in the archaeological record. Other than the hearths and shallow basin pits preserved at some sites, few examples of Early Archaic processing facilities are known.

Middle Archaic tools and implements are more diverse than those of the Early Archaic. In part, the diversity reflects an increasing familiarity with the surrounding environment, its resources, and the means to exploit those resources efficiently. Many kinds of Middle Archaic groundstone tools are associated with the gathering and processing of plants, and the increased importance of these tools has been interpreted by many archaeologists as reflecting the growing significance of plant foods in the Middle Archaic diet. Other artifacts represent parts of compound tools made from different materials. For example, Middle Archaic assemblages contain examples of the atlatl (figs. 3.7–3.9). Often, the atlatl weight was ground stone, the hook and handle were bone or antler, and the spear point was flaked stone. The shaft that connected these parts was of wood, which is usually not preserved in the archaeological record.

Some sites provide evidence of Middle Archaic pit storage technology. The morphological attributes of some pits suggest that subsurface storage became more important in Middle Archaic camps than it was during the Early Archaic.

Much of the evidence of increased technological complexity during the Middle Archaic period may be associated with trends toward greater sedentism and reduced group mobility. Many of the technological requirements of the highly mobile Early Archaic life-style were no longer maintained as groups spent more of their annual cycle in fewer locations. The establishment of multiseasonal base camps made the expenditure of the time and energy required to produce less portable tools and facilities more practical.

The trend toward increasing technological complexity continued through the Late Archaic, as evidenced by the diversity of tool kits and the common use of a variety of raw materials to make tools. The use of starchy seeds probably required changes in food processing techniques. This may have involved different cooking techniques and new kinds of containers. Differences noted in Late Archaic assemblages, and site characteristics in Kentucky and other parts of the Midcontinent, reflect specialized adaptations to regionally distinct environments. These cultural differences take on greater significance during the Woodland periods, which are discussed in the next chapter.

SUMMARY

The Archaic cultural tradition endured for 7,000 years, which is approximately one-half of North American prehistory, as currently defined. The Early, Middle, and Late Archaic periods encompass the archaeological record of these hunter-gatherers.

Early Archaic (8,000–6,000 B.C.) hunter-gatherers ranged over Kentucky to find the seasonally available plants and animals on which they depended. The general absence of middens, burials, and other archaeological features and the few artifacts that compose most sites, suggest that these foragers lived in small, highly mobile bands. The lifeways and tool kits of Kentucky's Early Archaic groups resembled in many ways those of their Paleoindian ancestors except for the animals they hunted and the plants they collected.

Regionally distinct cultures developed during the Middle Archaic period (6,000–3,000 B.C.), and the differences between these cultures reflect the adaptations of groups to local environmental conditions across Kentucky. Sites dating to the first half of the Middle Archaic period are generally marked by light scatters of flaked stone artifacts, suggesting that life was not substantially different from that of the Early Archaic period. By 4,500 B.C., however, some of these hunter-gatherers were living most of the year at one location, recognizable archaeologically by thick middens, burials, and other features and by evidence of the increased importance of plant foods in the diet. The preferred locations for these camps were in valleys that offered more abundant, diverse, and reliable food sources than the drier upland settings did. Hunter-gatherers used upland sites less often, where they exploited a narrower range of seasonally available resources. Changes in the seasonal cycle and the occupation of sites located in diverse environmental settings may reflect adaptations to the drier, warmer Hypsithermal conditions.

Late Archaic (3,000–1,000 B.C.) sites are more numerous than those of the Early or Middle Archaic periods. The abundance of these sites reflects both a general population increase and changes in the ways that prehistoric groups lived. Some Kentucky Late Archaic sites, particularly those along the Green River, developed a more complex form of social organization than earlier Archaic groups had, and they acquired copper and marine shell artifacts through long-distance trade networks. Deer meat, hickory nuts, and acorns were staple Late Archaic foods, just as they had been for earlier Archaic groups, but starchy weed seeds also became an important part of the diet. The presence of squash and gourd seeds at Kentucky sites suggests that Late Archaic people were beginning to experiment with plant cultivation.

The Archaic periods span millennia of considerable environmental changes in North America and cultural changes in human groups. The Early Archaic way of life resembled that of Paleoindian hunters. By the Late Archaic period, however, groups were exploring new technologies and social behavior that would be more fully developed in the succeeding Woodland periods.

4

WOODLAND CULTIVATORS

Jimmy A. Railey

The millennia from 1,000 B.C. to A.D. 900–1000 span several periods and well-defined archaeological cultures of the Woodland tradition. The term *Woodland* came into wide use in the 1930s in the eastern United States to describe prehistoric groups who made pottery, constructed burial mounds, and lived by hunting, gathering, and gardening (Stoltman 1978). Archaic complexes, it was thought, lacked these traits. More recent prehistoric cultures, such as Mississippian and Fort Ancient, differed from those of the Woodland periods in pottery styles and technology, platform mounds, and true agriculture.

This chapter examines the Woodland tradition archaeology of Kentucky, viewed primarily within the framework of its three periods—Early, Middle, and Late. Following common practice, Early Woodland (1,000–200 B.C.) brackets the time after the introduction and first widespread use of pottery until the beginning of the Hopewell "florescence." Middle Woodland (200 B.C.–A.D. 500) is nearly synonymous with the archaeology of Hopewell and Hopewellian groups. Late Woodland (A.D. 500–1000) spans the centuries between the end of Hopewell and the beginning of the Mississippian and Fort Ancient traditions.

Several archaeological cultures, notably Adena and Hopewell, crosscut the Woodland periods. The concept of the Adena culture was one of William S. Webb's principal contributions to eastern United States archaeology. From its inception, however, it has been treated as a primarily Early Woodland phenomenon, and the authors of major textbooks (e.g., Jennings 1989:230–33) continue to view it as such. Nevertheless, as will be shown in this chapter, it is probably more a Middle Woodland culture than an Early Woodland one.

The Hopewell culture, which is nearly a synonym for the Middle Woodland period in the minds of many archaeologists, rests on a firmer foun-

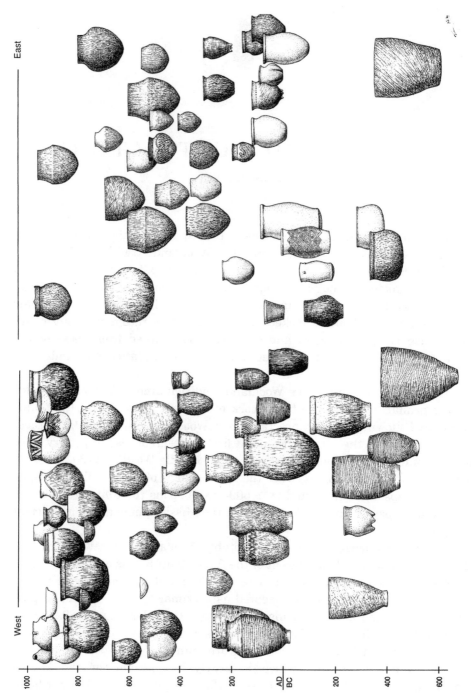

Figure 4.1 Generalized chronology of Woodland pottery vessels in Kentucky.

dation than Adena. For decades, Hopewell was viewed as one of the two climaxes of cultural development in the prehistoric East (Griffin 1967), the other so-called climax being the Mississippian tradition of late prehistory. Cultural climaxes aside, there can be no question that the Hopewell culture represents one of the most fascinating archaeological manifestations in North America.

EARLY WOODLAND (1,000–200 B.C.)

Tools and Other Artifacts

The Early Woodland period is distinguished from the Late Archaic by several criteria, the most archaeologically apparent of which is the presence of ceramics in assemblages. The first pottery was made in eastern and possibly central Kentucky by 1,000–800 B.C., and it reached the western part of the state around 500 B.C. (Seeman 1986:564). As measured by the presence of potsherds, the beginning of the Early Woodland period varies, therefore, by as much 500 years from one end of Kentucky to the other.

Early Woodland pottery of western and southern Kentucky is part of a widespread southeastern pottery tradition (Brown 1986; Haag 1939; Walthall and Jenkins 1976). The earliest pots are typically conoidal or flowerpot-shaped vessels with narrow, flat bases (fig. 4.1). The exteriors of these pots commonly exhibit cordmarking, fabric impressions, or cord-wrapped dowel impressions. On the oldest vessels, cordmarking or fabric impressions may also be found on the interior walls.

The oldest pots in central and eastern Kentucky are typically thick-walled cordmarked, plain, or fabric-impressed vessels tempered with coarse grit and rocks. These pots, of a type known as Fayette Thick (Griffin 1943), share similarities of form and decoration with early ceramics in the Northeast and the Midwest. Fayette Thick vessels were barrel-shaped jars and large, deep, basin-shaped jars or cauldrons (fig. 4.1: 400 B.C. vessels).

Other distinctive changes in technology include the presence of notched and stemmed projectile points similar to the Kramer, Wade, Savannah River, Gary, Turkeytail, Greeneville, Camp Creek, and Nolichucky types, examples of which are illustrated by Justice (1987). Most of these types are found across the midcontinent during the Early Woodland period. Adena Stemmed points (fig. 4.2, bottom row) became common after about 500 B.C.

The oldest scraps of textiles and twined fabrics in Kentucky also date to this period. Along the western edge of the Mountains in Menifee County, textiles, cordage, grass beds, and a wooden cradleboard, all of which could date to the Early Woodland period, were found in the dry sediments of Newt Kash Hollow Rockshelter (fig. 4.3) (Webb and Funkhouser 1936). Textile scraps (fig. 4.4), slippers, dessicated human feces, and other perishable Late Archaic and

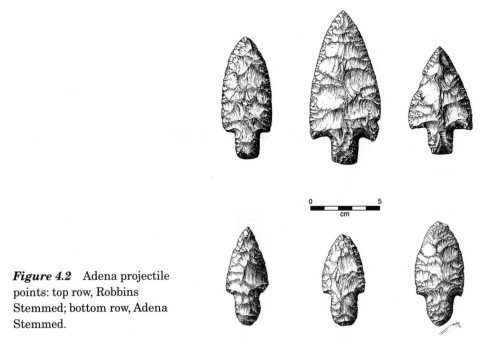

Figure 4.2 Adena projectile
points: top row, Robbins
Stemmed; bottom row, Adena
Stemmed.

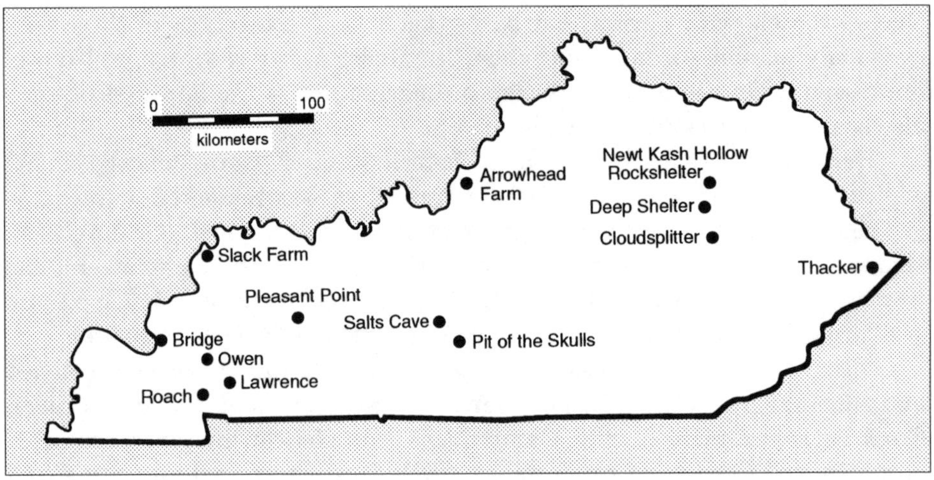

Figure 4.3 Early Woodland sites discussed in the text.

Early Woodland artifacts have also been found in Salts Cave in Hart County
in the Pennyroyal region (Watson 1969, 1974:235–37). These materials,
which are preserved only in the dry environments of caves and rockshelters,
add a wealth of detail to our understanding of the lives of the Woodland
inhabitants of Kentucky.

Figure 4.4 Prehistoric fabric found in Salts Cave. The largest specimen measures approximately 20 cm wide. Aboriginal exploration of this cave occurred primarily during the Early Woodland period. Young 1910:303; reprinted by permission of The Filson Club, Louisville, Kentucky.

Subsistence

Hunting and gathering, supplemented by gardening, were the mainstay of the Early Woodland subsistence pattern. A variety of animals were consumed, including whitetail deer, small mammals, box turtles, fish, and birds.

Nuts were gathered in abundance and stored for year-round consumption. Early Woodland gardeners grew squash and gourds and cultivated several weedy indigenous plants for their edible seeds. Cultivated plants included sunflower, maygrass, goosefoot, sumpweed, giant ragweed, and possibly erect knotweed (Cowan 1985b:207–17).

At Salts Cave, dried feces and the intestinal contents of a well-preserved mummy provide an excellent "snapshot" of Early Woodland diet. Seeds, including sunflower, goosefoot, amaranth, knotweed, and maygrass, composed much of the diet (Yarnell 1974). Early cave explorers also ate squash, nuts, greens, fleshy fruits, and medicinal herbs (Schoenwetter 1974:56).

Settlement Patterns

Early Woodland settlement patterns are generally similar to those of the Late Archaic. Base camps or villages are marked by thick middens and occur primarily in the major river valleys. In other regions, the Bluegrass for example, populations were dispersed among small, frequently shifting camps and settlements in the rolling uplands.

One important difference from the Late Archaic period is the appearance of specialized ritual sites located away from the settlements. These sites were "sacred grounds," where people assembled for group ceremonies or to bury their dead. At the beginning of the Early Woodland period, ritual sites were isolated, nonmound mortuaries marked by one or a few burials or cremations. The graves were often associated with offerings that ranged from a few artifacts to large caches of bifacial blades or other materials. Beginning around 500–400 B.C., burial mounds and earthen and palisaded enclosures began to be constructed in some parts of Kentucky.

One critical factor in these settlement shifts may have been territorial circumscription. As population density increased during the Woodland periods, the territories within which individual groups hunted, gathered, and gardened grew smaller, or more circumscribed, and competition for prime lands increased. It became necessary for groups to establish conspicuous symbols of their territorial claims (Railey 1991; Seeman 1986). Specialized ritual facilities may have been one solution to this problem. As resting places for ancestors, mortuary sites were instrumental in focusing a group's territorial consciousness and undoubtedly occupied a prominent place in its traditions. Thus, whether constructed as isolated sites or elements of a consolidated settlement, ritual facilities were perpetual, unifying symbols of group solidarity, territorial rights, and mythological heritage.

Crab Orchard Culture. Archaeological assemblages described as the Crab Orchard complex (Butler and Jefferies 1986; Maxwell 1951; Muller 1986) span the Early Woodland and part of the Middle Woodland in western Kentucky. Some of these sites are called "Baumer" in the older Ohio Valley archaeological literature. The earliest Crab Orchard pottery is the conoidal, flat-based jar. Adena Stemmed (fig. 4.2) and Turkeytail (Justice 1987:173–79) points are the most common projectile point types associated with this pottery. Cultural influences from the South can be seen in the presence of pinched, incised, and punctated pottery of the Alexander Series in Tennessee-Cumberland sites and in the Western Coal Field (Rolingson 1967:390–91; Rolingson and Schwartz 1966:43–46).

Large, intensively occupied, early Crab Orchard sites are concentrated in the Ohio Valley, where the rich floodplain environment encouraged sedentary settlements. Many of these settlements (e.g., the Bridge site at the mouth of the Cumberland River in Livingston County [Nance 1985] and the Slack Farm site in Union County [Pollack and Munson 1989]) have thick middens and were occupied for centuries (fig. 4.3). The people who lived in these camps hunted whitetail deer and gathered nuts and other foods from the valley forests. Reliable harvests of fish and waterfowl were also possible in the floodplain streams, lakes, and sloughs.

Comparable sites that are related to the Crab Orchard complex, such as Lawrence (Mocas 1977), Owen (Allen 1976), and Pleasant Point (Myers 1981), are found along the Ohio River's many tributaries. Like the Ohio Valley sites, these were aggregated Early Woodland settlements that were occupied on a year-round or extended seasonal basis. They were also probably used in much the same way as those in the Ohio Valley.

Bluegrass Settlement Patterns. The narrow floodplains of the major rivers in the Bluegrass were generally ill-suited to habitation during prehistory, and Early Woodland groups tended to settle on the region's rolling ridgetops, attracted there by a variety of rich resources, including productive soils and many springs. Consolidated settlements in the Bluegrass did not occur until later Woodland times.

In contrast, the Ohio River floodplain, which forms the northern boundary of the Bluegrass, offered prehistoric peoples ample bottomlands and more concentrated resources. Despite the important environmental differences between these localities, Early Woodland settlements and cultural expressions are essentially similar along the Ohio and in the Bluegrass uplands. Although the Ohio River floodplain had supported major Archaic settlements (Boisvert 1986; Driskell and Allen 1976; Vickery 1980), there is little evidence that such settlements continued after around 800 B.C. Thus Early Woodland settlement patterns in the region were not simply a response to local environmental conditions, but followed widespread social patterns that encouraged settlement dispersal.

Seeman (1986) proposes that Early Woodland social groups in the middle Ohio Valley were smaller than their Late Archaic predecessors and lived in more constricted territories. He also argues that Early Woodland mortuary rituals assumed many important functions that had once been carried out in Late Archaic base camps. With the dispersion into smaller Early Woodland communities, the integration of society required a new setting, so native peoples began constructing mortuary mounds and ritual enclosures. Seeman's scenario may indeed explain the apparent disappearance of large base camps along the middle Ohio River by the end of the Late Archaic. It does not, however, account for the apparent absence of Late Archaic and Early Woodland base camps in the Bluegrass uplands. Available evidence suggests that few, if any, major changes took place in Bluegrass settlement systems from Late Archaic to Early Woodland times.

In the Falls of the Ohio locality on the western edge of the Bluegrass, Early Woodland life also shows little change from that of the Late Archaic (Collins and Driskell 1979). In this locality, however, substantial base camps are found in both periods, and population densities apparently remained relatively high. Population densities were sparse, however, in the neighboring dissected uplands of the western Bluegrass (Driskell et al. 1984; Sorensen et al. 1980).

Early Woodland in the Mountains. Early Woodland groups in the Mountains often used rockshelters, perhaps more so than at any other time in the region's prehistory. This pattern is common across the region. Although most researchers view rockshelters as temporary or seasonal camps, the heavy midden accumulations and wide range of artifacts found in many Mountains rockshelters suggest sustained occupations, some of which may have been more-or-less year-round. A general pattern of settlement dispersal and the rise of horticulture may have contributed to this trend. Ison (1989) suggests that hillside cultivation was the most viable option for Woodland gardeners in the Mountains, and this factor may have encouraged long-term occupation of rockshelters with easy access to hillside garden plots.

In the Daniel Boone National Forest, substantial bottomland base camps that had existed during the Late Archaic period were gradually abandoned during the Early Woodland as preferred campsites shifted more to rockshelters (Cowan 1985b:238). This trend correlates with the intensification of gardening and the increased utilization of seeds from weedy plants that thrive in disturbed environments. The earliest large storage pits in the Mountains are found in Early Woodland rockshelter deposits; their presence emphasizes the increased importance of food production in this period.

Resource utilization was also increasingly localized at this time; for example, the quantity of Bluegrass cherts in Early Woodland assemblages drops considerably from what it had been in Late Archaic sites. This pattern was apparently brought about by the breaking up of large bands into smaller social groups by Early Woodland times, and a consequent reduction in each group's territory (Cowan 1985a, 1985b). This pattern is also consistent with Seeman's (1986) explanation of the apparent abandonment of Late Archaic base camps and the rise of Adena mound building in the middle Ohio Valley.

In chapter 4, Jefferies described the Late Archaic/Early Woodland Cogswell phase in the Mountains region. The Cogswell settlement pattern emphasized base camps, but the occupations at these camps were apparently not as intensive as those of their Late Archaic ancestors. Early Woodland peoples continued this shift away from the lowland base camps, and the utilization of rockshelters increased sharply. Newt Kash Hollow (Webb and Funkhouser 1936) and Cloudsplitter (Cowan 1985a, 1985b; Cowan et al. 1981) are examples of intensive Early Woodland rockshelter occupations in Menifee County.

The intensive Cogswell phase component at Newt Kash Hollow contained thick, coarsely tempered potsherds and Adena Stemmed and other stemmed and corner-notched projectile points (cf. Webb and Funkhouser 1936:125). As noted earlier, the dry shelter environment preserved many otherwise perishable Early Woodland artifacts. The plant remains from this site have also figured prominently in major research efforts on the development of prehistoric food production in Eastern North America (e.g., Asch and Asch 1977; Fowler 1971). These remains include seeds of sunflower, goosefoot, marsh elder (sumpweed), giant ragweed, and canary grass (maygrass) as well as hickory and walnut shell fragments (Jones 1936), all of which were gathered or cultivated by the rockshelter inhabitants.

The thick ash lenses and large storage pits of the Early Woodland component at Cloudsplitter rockshelter (fig. 3.4) were deposited between 850 and 450 B.C. The Early Woodland occupants of the shelter exploited many kinds of seeds, including sunflower, sumpweed, maygrass, and erect knotweed. This plant use pattern contrasts strongly with that of the Late Archaic inhabitants of Cloudsplitter, who depended heavily on nuts and used few cultivated plants other than squash.

In the Big Sandy drainage, Early Woodland camps and villages tend to be concentrated in the narrow valleys, wherever groups could find suitable stretches of bottomland. Many rockshelters were used heavily, as were some small mountaintop sites. Pottery-making appears to have entered this part of the Mountains by 900 B.C. or slightly later. This inference is based on finds of thick, quartz-tempered sherds that resemble Watts Bar Cordmarked and Swannanoa ceramics, which date between 900–500 B.C. in the southern Appalachians (Lafferty 1978:138–42).

In Pike County in the easternmost Mountains, the Early Woodland is represented by the Thacker phase (Dunnell 1972). The settlements of this phase are small (e.g., the Thacker site occupation covered an area 35 m in diameter), and earth ovens are the only features found on (Dunnell 1972).

Components are distinguished by quartz-tempered ceramics and Adena and other stemmed projectile points. Dunnell (1972:86) suggests that the quartz-tempered ceramics are related to the Watts Bar Cordmarked type mentioned above. Thacker phase groundstone artifacts include bowls, hammerstones, nutting stones, and gorgets.

Burials

There is relatively little information about Early Woodland treatment of the dead. At the Arrowhead Farm site near Louisville, a bundle burial was found in association with a refuse-filled pit, potsherds, and a burned area interpreted as a funeral fire. This occupation may have been a small camp or a specialized mortuary site. A similar example comes from the Roach site, a small seasonal camp on the Tennessee River. Although Roach lacks direct evidence of human burials, excavations revealed five drilled rectangular bar gorgets clustered near a large fire pit (Rolingson and Schwartz 1966:43–46). Gorgets of any kind are rarely found outside of graves, so the fire pit may have been a crematory basin.

Early Woodland peoples used caves for a variety of reasons, including as specialized mortuary facilities. One such location is the Pit of the Skulls site in Barren County, where several human skulls and a pelvis were found (Hemberger 1985). These individuals had been dismembered and placed in the deep cave pit in which they were discovered. One skull exhibits cranial deformation of the kind seen when infants are carried in cradle boards. Similar cranial deformation is reported for Adena skeletons (cf. Neumann 1942), and suggests an Early or Middle Woodland date for this feature.

Broken and butchered human bones were also found in the Salts Cave vestibule in Hart County. Given their condition, the remains were first interpreted as evidence of cannibalism (Duffield 1974:131; Robbins 1974:161–62). However, these bones and those from the Pit of the Skulls, which show similar breakage patterns, can also be explained as mortuary ritual that did not necessarily involve cannibalism (e.g., Seeman 1986:568).

MIDDLE WOODLAND (200 B.C.–A.D.500)

Throughout much of the Eastern Woodlands during the Middle Woodland period, there was a proliferation of burial mounds, earthen enclosures, distinctive new styles of decorated pottery, and interregional exchange of ritual items. Many of these developments took place within an widespread exchange network known as the Hopewell Interaction Sphere (Caldwell 1964; Struever 1964), in which native peoples traded goods and ideas. This network and the general Hopewellian phenomenon have received considerable attention from archaeologists (e.g., Brose and Greber 1979; Caldwell and

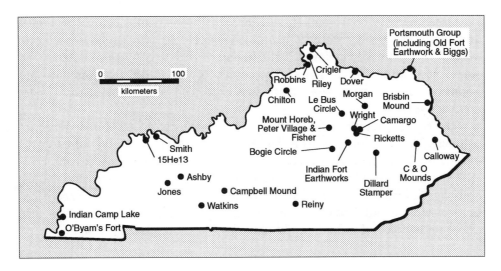

Figure 4.5   Middle Woodland sites discussed in the text.

Hall 1964; Chapman 1980:70–77; Prufer 1964; Seeman 1979b; Struever 1964, 1968; Struever and Houart 1972).

The Middle Woodland period spans many centuries, and distinctive cultural changes are evident over the course of this time span. For ease of discussion, I have subdivided this period into two subunits, the early Middle Woodland (200 B.C.–A.D. 250) and the late Middle Woodland (A.D. 250–500). Middle woodland sites in Kentucky are identified in figure 4.5.

Tools and Other Artifacts

Early Middle Woodland pottery includes conoidal and barrel-shaped jars (fig. 4.1). Vessels in the Bluegrass and eastern Kentucky are usually undecorated and have outflaring, thickened rims. Cordmarked, cord-wrapped dowel, and fabric-impressed vessels are more common in western and southern Kentucky. Across the state, one also finds check stamped and simple stamped jars, surface treatments that are more common in states to the south. Some sherds bear Hopewellian decorative modes, which are typically noded and zoned designs executed by incising, punctating, dentate stamping, or rocker stamping.

During the late Middle Woodland, most pottery vessels were cordmarked jars, except in the southeastern corner of Kentucky where plain surfaced jars were common (fig. 4.1). Simple stamped, check stamped, complicated stamped, brushed, scratched, and unzoned rocker stamped vessels also occur in small frequencies. Hopewellian and southeastern stamped pottery were no longer made after about A.D. 500–600, but cordmarked wares continued with little change into the Late Woodland period.

Other aspects of technology also changed stylistically. Adena Stemmed and other stemmed projectile points, for example, are common in early Middle Woodland assemblages, but these gave way to notched and expanded stem types after A.D. 1. Throughout much of the state, the common late Middle Woodland projectile points are expanded stem and shallow side-notched types.

The ceremonial life of Middle Woodland peoples is reflected in a variety of artifacts. These include, for example, stone gorgets, stone or clay tablets with incised designs, stone pipes, bars or hemispheres of barite and galena, crescent-shaped mica objects, copper bracelets and rings, copper and shell beads, and clay figurines. Certain symbolic themes, especially stylized representations of raptors and raptor-like birds such as vultures, crows, and ravens, also are commonly found in Middle Woodland artifacts and pottery designs.

Subsistence

Middle Woodland subsistence was based on hunting, gathering, and gardening. At least nine plants—squash, gourd, maize, sunflower, maygrass, erect knotweed, little barley, certain varieties of goosefoot, and sumpweed—are known or are presumed to have been cultivated in the midcontinent. Maize, maygrass, erect knotweed, little barley, and goosefoot seeds are high in carbohydrates, and the oily seeds of sunflower and sumpweed are rich in protein.

Maize is unknown from Middle Woodland sites in Kentucky, and its cultivation can only be tentatively assumed. The importance of maize in Middle Woodland subsistence has been debated for at least three decades. Years ago, maize was reported from excavated Middle Woodland components in several eastern states, but with few exceptions (e.g., Chapman and Crites 1987) these discoveries are now discredited. Bone chemistry analyses and other archaeological studies demonstrate that maize could have been only a minor and sporadic element in prehistoric diets in the midcontinent until the end of the Late Woodland period.

Settlement Patterns and Mound Building

The Middle Woodland period is nearly synonymous with burial mounds in the minds of many archaeologists. Although many have been destroyed, these mounds are still present in many regions. Most of the excavated burial mounds in the Bluegrass and eastern Kentucky were constructed during early Middle Woodland times. To judge from the absence of large habitation sites, early Middle Woodland groups in central and eastern Kentucky probably lived in small, scattered settlements with ritual spaces such as burial mounds and earthen enclosures serving as focal points of group ritual and social integration. In western and southern Kentucky, most groups resided in central base camps or villages, which often contain thick middens. Early Middle Woodland burial mounds are largely unknown from these regions.

During the late Middle Woodland, settlement systems changed in some parts of the state. Large nucleated settlements emerged in the Bluegrass and eastern Kentucky. In western and southern Kentucky, on the other hand, there are few large late Middle Woodland villages or camps.

Burial mound building declined during late Middle Woodland times in central and eastern Kentucky, and in some areas, mounds began to be built in or near the village rather than isolated from it. In contrast, most of the excavated western Kentucky mortuary mounds appear to have been built near villages or in isolated locations during the late Middle Woodland. Stone mounds and the use of stone in earthen burial mounds also became common during the late Middle Woodland period.

The Adena and Hopewell cultures dominate Early Woodland and Middle Woodland archaeology, so it is best to begin our survey of Kentucky Middle Woodland sites by examining Adena and its relationship with Hopewell.

The Adena Culture and the Middle Woodland Period in Central Kentucky. Hundreds of burial mounds, circular enclosures, and other earthworks were constructed in the Bluegrass and northeastern Kentucky between 500 B.C. and A.D. 200 (i.e., during the late Early Woodland and early Middle Woodland periods). In Ohio, Greenman's (1932) investigation of similar mounds led to the first synthesis of the Adena culture. Greenman presented Adena as the less-elaborate predecessor of Hopewell, a view that persists widely to this day. William S. Webb was influenced strongly by Greenman's Adena research. He excavated many Kentucky Woodland mounds in the 1930s and early 1940s and greatly extended the archaeological understanding of this culture (Webb and Baby 1957; Webb and Snow

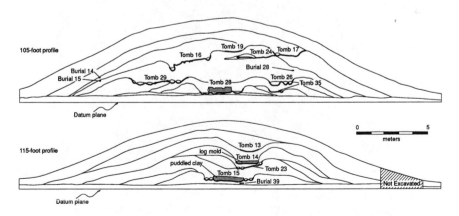

Figure 4.6 Stratigraphic profile of the Robbins Mound in Boone County. Adapted from Webb and Elliot 1942: fig. 7.

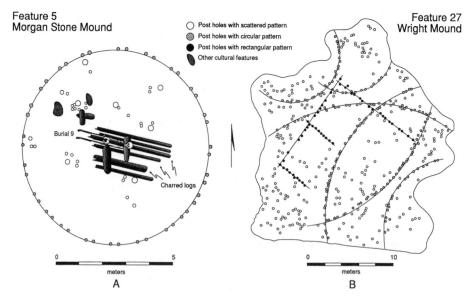

Figure 4.7   Adena submound structures: A, Morgan Stone Mound in Bath County; B, Wright Mound in Montgomery County. Adapted from Webb 1940: fig. 22; 1941b: fig. 14.

Figure 4.8   Excavated Adena log tomb at the Wright Mound in Montgomery County. Reproduced by permission of the William S. Webb Museum of Anthropology, University of Kentucky, negative 2263.

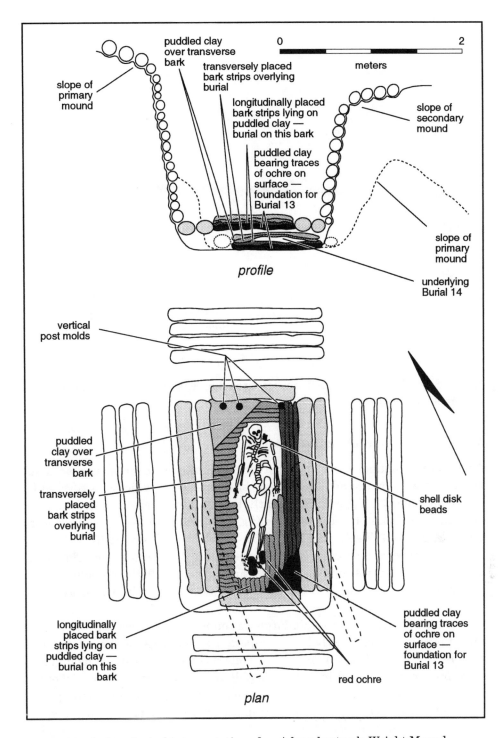

Figure 4.9 Archaeological interpretation of an Adena log tomb, Wright Mound, Montgomery County. Adapted from Webb 1940: fig. 20.

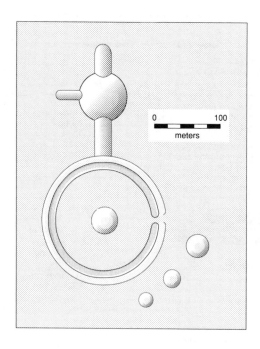

Figure 4.10   An Adena "sacred circle" enclosure with associated mounds in Montgomery County. Adapted from Squier and Davis 1848: plate 32).

1945). Since Webb's time, Adena research has cast much new light on this archaeological culture.

Burial Mounds and Other Earthworks

Adena burial mounds were not constructed all at once. Each mound accumulated gradually by the addition of new burials, each of which was covered by an earthen mantle (fig. 4.6). Frequently, the remains of circular structures or enclosures lie beneath these mounds (fig. 4.7). Some of these structures were quite large, and Webb (1941a:252–53; Webb and Snow 1945) originally believed they were domiciles. It is now clear that Webb was wrong. They were either charnel houses used in burial ritual (Seeman 1986) or roofless ritual enclosures not necessarily associated with mortuary activities (Clay 1986, 1987).

Adena mounds often contain large log tombs or cysts (figs. 4.8–4.9). These burial facilities were used both as temporary receptacles for the dead and as final resting places (Brown 1979). The skeletons found in a single mound also were prepared for burial in any of the following ways: cremations, defleshed skeletons, bundle burials (the disarticulated bones of a skeleton wrapped or "bundled" together), and extended inhumations (i.e., the manner in which the dead are treated in modern U.S. society).

Many ditched earthworks, including both large, oval enclosures and smaller circular ones, are also believed to be Adena features (fig. 4.10). The

Figure 4.11 Kentucky Adena artifacts: A-C, groundstone gorgets; D, copper gorget; E, chert celt; F, chipped limestone hoe; G, groundstone tubular pipes; H, copper bracelets with preserved fabric adhering to middle specimen; I, copper finger ring; J, stone elbow pipe; K, bone comb; L, cut animal jaw, showing possible method of insertion in skull with incisor teeth removed; M, disk shell beads; N, engraved stone tablets; O, mica crescents used as headdress ornaments; P, reconstructed vessel forms; Q, projectile points and ceremonial knife forms.

Figure 4.12 Preserved textiles from Adena mounds: A, preserved fabric adhering to copper bracelet from the Wright Mound; B, textile sheath on copper dagger from the Drake Mound in FayetteCounty. Reproduced by permission of the William S. Webb Museum of Anthropology, University of Kentucky, negatives 2312 and 4132.

A

B

stockaded enclosure at the Mt. Horeb site in Fayette County (Webb 1941b), for example, resembles the structures found beneath many Adena burial mounds, and both earthen enclosures and submound structures may have served similar functions. Other so-called sacred circles include LeBus Circle in Bourbon County, Bogie Circles in Madison County, Indian Fort Earthworks in Clark County, and Camargo Earthworks in Montgomery County.

Artifacts

Most of what is known about Adena tools and other artifacts comes from the excavation of burial mounds. The distinctive artifacts associated with Adena graves include stone gorgets, tubular pipes, elbow and platform pipes, stone balls, celts, hoes, simple and engraved tablets, hammerstones, galena and barite artifacts; bone and shell tools and objects; copper bracelets, rings, and

A   B

Figure 4.13 Adena ceramic vessels: A, Adena Plain (24 cm high); B, Montgomery Incised. Both vessels are from the Morgan Stone Mound in Bath County. Reproduced by permission of the William S. Webb Museum of Anthropology, University of Kentucky, negatives 1802 and 4125.

beads; mica crescents, Adena and Robbins type projectile points (fig. 4.2), and textile fragments (figs. 4.11–4.12). The raw materials for many of these items were obtained by trade from distant sources.

Ceramic vessels are not often found in direct association with Adena burials, but potsherds are common in mound fill and near mounds. Although Webb interpreted these sherds as chance inclusions in mound fill, it now appears that preparing food, feasting, and, consequently, breaking pots were part of graveside rituals (Clay 1983).

The most common pot was a limestone or sandstone tempered jar of the type called Adena Plain (fig. 4.13, A) (Haag 1940:75–79, 1942b:341–42). Montgomery Incised (fig. 4.13, B), a decorated Adena Plain variety, is known from a few sites. A few cordmarked, simple stamped, and check stamped sherds are also present in some mounds.

Although the pottery type called Fayette Thick has traditionally been viewed as an Adena artifact (e.g., Webb and Snow 1945:27, 242–43), Fayette Thick sherds are rare at Adena sites and may not have been associated with Adena mound building (Clay 1980).

Adena Society

Burial mounds, "sacred circles," ditched earthworks, and other enclosures have always been a fundamental part of the distinctive nature of Adena. For a long time, archaeologists could not satisfactorily explain why Adena groups built these earthworks. One widely held interpretation viewed the mounds and earthworks as the products of a complex society supported by maize agriculture, and possibly influenced by the civilizations of Mexico (e.g., Willey 1966:268). It is now known that the groups who built the Adena mounds and earthworks were much simpler societies than originally believed, and the distinctive elements of their culture are indigenous and not the product of Mexican influences.

The major factors that led archaeologists to revise their understanding of Adena culture are, first, the absence of large Adena village sites, and second, the lack of good evidence that maize was of any economic importance to them. Adena groups resided in small, dispersed settlements, and they lived by hunting, gathering, and gardening. Recent analyses of Adena skeletons (e.g., Milner and Jefferies 1987; Shyrock 1987) also suggest that men and women were treated equally in death and, implicitly, equally in life. Many researchers (e.g., Clay 1991; Mainfort 1989; Shyrock 1987) continue to debate the question of the complexity of Adena society.

Regardless of the complexity of Adena societies, important social relationships were probably defined by kinship. Rituals connected with the burial of the dead in mounds and the use of other ceremonial sites drew together the people of widely scattered camps and villages. Even though they lived apart, these rituals continually reaffirmed their identity as one group (Seeman 1986:574). The imposing and highly visible mounds and other earthworks may have also symbolically defined group territories (Railey 1991).

Adena Chronology and Cultural Relationships

For a long time, Adena was considered the forerunner of the Middle Woodland Hopewell culture in the Ohio Valley (Mills 1902:452–79). Adena was treated as an Early Woodland culture with a time span of 1,000 B.C.–A.D. 1 (e.g., Dragoo 1963:292–93; Willey 1966:268). Today, however, it is generally agreed that Adena is a post-500 B.C. phenomenon (Clay 1980; Griffin 1974:xvi, 1978a:62; Seeman 1986:566; Stoltman 1978:718). Viewed from Kentucky, the relationship between Adena and Hopewell is more a cultural than a chronological problem.

Dragoo's (1963) excavation of the Cresap Mound in northern West Virginia resolved the major chronological questions about the development of Adena. Based primarily upon the Cresap findings, Dragoo defined two phases, here called Early and Late Adena, respectively. Early Adena mounds are relatively small. Late Adena mounds are larger and more complex, have submound structures or log tombs, and contain evidence of elaborate burial ritual. Reel-shaped gorgets, incised tablets, copper bracelets, mica crescents, and other ritual artifacts are also more common and more skillfully crafted in

Figure 4.14 Platform pipe from the Crigler Mound in Boone County. The light-colored portions of the pipe are a plaster reconstruction of the original form. Reproduced by permission of the William S. Webb Museum of Anthropology, University of Kentucky, negative 5717.

Late Adena sites. Among domestic artifacts, Dragoo suggests that Fayette Thick pots and narrow-bladed Adena Stemmed points tend to be found in Early Adena sites and Adena Plain jars and broad-bladed Robbins points are present in Late Adena components (fig. 4.2).

In Kentucky, Early Adena sites include the Fisher Mound (Webb and Haag 1947b) and the large oval enclosure at Peter Village, both of which are in Fayette County. Peter Village has been of particular importance in recent assessments of the nature and dating of Adena. The first large oval enclosure built at Peter Village was a stockade; it was later replaced by a 2 m deep ditch (Clay 1985a, 1988a). Large quantities of barite/galena debris and artifacts have been found inside the enclosure and a natural outcrop of this mineral lies nearby. Based on his analysis of the occupation debris from this site, Clay infers that Peter Village was occupied first by peoples who made Fayette Thick vessels, and again later by an unrelated group who made Adena Plain pottery. He also speculates that this site was mostly a barite/galena processing center and not really an Adena "village."

Clay suggests that the early (350–200 B.C.) occupation at Peter Village should not be considered Adena at all, since the nature of the site and its assemblage, particularly the distinctive Fayette Thick "cauldron" vessel form, have not been found at other Adena sites in the region (Clay 1988a). Furthermore, he speculates that it was only during the early component that the site functioned as an enclosure, or at least a palisaded one; later "Adena" groups reused the site for other purposes.

Clay's findings at Peter Village suggest that the excavated Adena mounds in Kentucky, with the possible exception of Fisher, were constructed after 200 B.C. Of greater significance is the further implication that Adena, or at least Late Adena, is properly viewed as a Middle Woodland culture. Adena mound building must also overlap significantly with the rise of the great Hopewell centers of southern Ohio and Hopewellian complexes in the Midwest and Southeast.

Other lines of evidence support this interpretation. First, several corner-notched and expanded-stem projectile points and blades found with Adena burials at the Crigler (Webb and Snow 1943:528–29), Ricketts (Webb and Funkhouser 1940:221–22), and Dover (Webb and Snow 1959:60–61) sites are similar to Middle Woodland forms. This similarity suggests that some Ohio Hopewell and some Kentucky Adena mounds were contemporaneous. Second, there is the platform pipe (fig. 4.14) from the Crigler Mound in Boone County. This pipe was found in the original humus beneath the Crigler Mound (Webb and Snow 1943:530). It is classifiable as a Hopewell-17 type (Seeman 1977), which dates between A.D. 50 and 200. Its presence implies contemporaneity with Ohio Hopewell sites.

Finally, other Hopewellian elements in Kentucky Adena sites include the remains of a square-to-rectangular structure, possibly a charnel house, at the Riley Mound in Boone County (Webb 1943), and the presence of sand-tempered, stamped ceramics with podal supports at the larger Wright Mound (Haag 1940) and the Camargo Earthworks (Fenton and Jefferies 1989), both of which are in Montgomery County. Although they are rejected by Seeman (1986:566–67), the radiocarbon dates of A.D. 50–210 for Wright Mound samples are temporally consistent with the presence of the stamped sherds, which are generally unknown in pre-Hopewellian contexts in the middle Ohio Valley.

An important point to be derived from this examination of mounds and chronology is that Adena should be viewed as an early regional expression of Hopewell rather than as its predecessor.

The End of Adena

Around A.D. 300 nucleated villages began to be built along the middle Ohio Valley and possibly in the Bluegrass. The construction of large burial mounds declined sharply. Middle Woodland assemblages also changed. Adena, Robbins, and similar projectile point types gave way to a weak-shouldered, expanded-stem projectile point. Cordmarked vessels are the most common pottery, and globular jars replace the barrel-shaped Adena vessels. Small amounts of decorated Hopewell ware are found at some sites, along with sand-tempered stamped and cordmarked Connestee pottery from eastern

Tennessee (Keel 1976:247–55) and limestone-tempered, check stamped ceramics, but these types disappear from Kentucky sites after A.D. 500.

What caused these changes? No one can say for sure. Some anthropologists suggest that large-scale trade networks, involving the sorts of exotic items found in Adena sites, are unstable because they tend to fuel more and more demand for these items. In traditional, small-scale societies, this demand can become increasingly difficult to meet (e.g., Earle 1991:97). Often the result is inflation and overextension of the entire exchange system, which can eventually lead to its collapse. This, in turn, can lead to increasing hostilities and warfare. The establishment of nucleated villages may have been a defensive measure related to increased conflict caused by the breakdown of the Hopewellian exchange network.

Whatever the causes, the establishment of nucleated villages had important economic consequences and implications for the expression of ritual life. Villages became the focus of ritual activities, and in this sense they were like the large base camps of Late Archaic times. They also assumed many socially integrating functions formerly ascribed to burial mounds and enclosures, and this may explain the dramatic reduction in mound building at the end of the Middle Woodland (Railey 1991).

Mound building did not cease, and some groups in the Bluegrass continued to build mortuary facilities. Nonetheless, the scale of mound construction diminished considerably, and there was a general shift to the use of stone in mound construction (Kellar 1960). The best-known example of a late Middle Woodland stone mound is the Chilton site, an isolated series of stone burial mounds along a broad ridge in Henry County (Funkhouser and Webb 1937). The assemblage from this site includes stone and bone gorgets, copper, galena, a Copena-like stone elbow pipe, and two expanded stem projectile points.

Middle Woodland in Southern and Western Kentucky.   As noted in the preceding section on the Early Woodland period, the Crab Orchard culture in Western Kentucky spans part of the Early and Middle Woodland periods. Intensively occupied villages and base camps, such as Indian Camp Lake in Carlisle County (Kreisa and Stout 1991), were the main types of settlements during the early Middle Woodland (fig. 4.5). After 100 B.C. Crab Orchard assemblages began to look conservative by comparison with the Adena and Hopewellian cultural changes underway in nearby regions. There is little evidence of the strong trend toward gardening and participation in the Hopewell Interaction Sphere that is found among other Middle Woodland groups, such as those of the Illinois River Valley. One possible exception to this generalization is O'Byam's Fort (fig. 4.15), a "tuning fork-shaped" earthwork near the town of Hickman in Fulton County (Carstens 1982:29–37; Loughridge 1888; Mainfort and Carstens 1987). This site, which lies on the periphery of the

Crab Orchard region as it is usually defined, dates between A.D. 1 and 300 (Mainfort and Carstens 1987:60). It is the only large, earthen Woodland enclosure known in this region. Given its size and apparent uniqueness, it may have been the ritual focus of several communities in much the same way as were many Middle Woodland earthworks of the Ohio Valley.

Muller (1986:115–17) suggests that the natural bounty of the Ohio Valley inhibited the adoption of horticulture, which would have been, at best, a labor-intensive alternative to hunting and gathering. This, in turn, may have curbed the development of social ranking in Crab Orchard society and the ritual trappings that accompany it. Muller also observes that in southern Illinois, Crab Orchard mortuary patterns follow those of the preceding Middle and Late Archaic periods—burials, occasionally accompanied by modest grave goods, were interred in pit graves within the village or camp.

Along the Ohio River in the Western Coalfield, late Crab Orchard sites do contain a few decorated potsherds and other evidence of limited participation in the Hopewellian Interaction Sphere. In southern Illinois, these traits appear in the Crab Orchard region around 100 B.C. (Butler and Jefferies 1986:528).

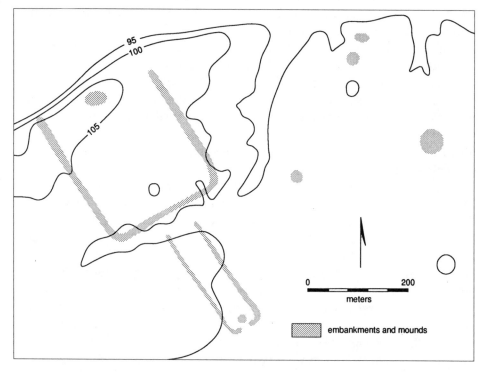

Figure 4.15 The O'Byam's Fort earthwork and mounds in Fulton County. This is the only known large Woodland enclosure in western Kentucky. Adapted from Mainfort and Carstens 1987: fig. 1.

Noded Crab Orchard jars and sherds of a Hopewell ware type, Havana Zoned Dentate, are reported from the Smith site and Site 15He13, both of which are in Henderson County (Hoffman 1966; Marquardt 1971). The Smith site also contained burials with Hopewellian grave goods (Hoffman 1966:28; Muller 1986:119–20). The presence of Hopewellian items at these and other Crab Orchard sites in this region contrasts with the absence of such materials downriver. It remains to be seen whether this difference represents more extensive interaction with Hopewellian groups in the Wabash drainage and other regions, differences in the way contact with other regions was regulated, or merely the lack of information about Middle Woodland burials and their associated grave goods in sites further downriver.

In the Ohio Valley near the mouth of the Wabash River, late Middle Woodland ceramics of the Mann phase (A.D. 250–500) show many Hopewell decorative elements. The most prominent site of this phase is the large earthwork at the Mann site in Posey County, Indiana (Kellar 1979). Another notable component is Rutherford Mound, located down the Ohio River in Hardin County, Illinois (Fowler 1957). Few Mann phase components have been identified on the Kentucky side of the Ohio River, and none has been systematically investigated.

Decorated vessels show a variety of treatments: complicated stamping, simple stamping, check stamping, rocker stamping, rocker-dentate stamping, Hopewell crosshatched rims, red filming, trailing or wide-line incising, punctations, and brushing. Most Mann phase pots, however, are cordmarked and undecorated.

To the south, in the Green River drainage of the Western Coalfield and the Pennyroyal, Archaic shell middens, with their well-drained, moundlike surfaces, were favored settlement locations for Woodland peoples. Middle Woodland artifacts from these sites include cordmarked and plain pots; a few check stamped, simple stamped, and complicated stamped sherds; and corner-notched and weak-shouldered, expanded-stem points (Rolingson 1967; Watson 1985:119; Webb 1946:360–62, 1950a:343–44; Webb and Haag 1939: 25–27, 1940:100–101, 1947a:37–38).

Mound excavations at the Ashby site in Muhlenberg County and the Jones Mound in Hopkins County suggest that Green River groups were not isolated from Middle Woodland developments. The Ashby site comprised two small mounds (Hoffman 1965; Rolingson 1967:319–21) and possibly a small settlement or mortuary camp near the mounds. Mound A measured 21 m in diameter and was approximately 1.5 m in height. In its center was a circular depression of white clay, surrounded by a rectangular darkened area that might have marked the remains of a charnel house. Upright sandstone slabs stood on the north and west edges of the dark area. Artifacts found within the circular depression include two stone gorgets, a mica sheet, a piece of barite/galena, two miniature copper celts, and two copper awls. Mound B measured about 15 m in diameter and contained a "thin layer of whitish earth" and a hearth. Mound B artifacts include a cordmarked jar, which had been shattered upon a mound surface, projectile points, and three caches of flint debris and sandstone pebbles. No burials were found in either mound.

The Jones Mound measured 18 m by 12 m and stood 1.2 m high (Purrington 1966; Rolingson 1967:321). It contained three subfloor rectangular burial pits, each of which held extended burials. These pits had been initially covered over by two small elongated mounds enclosed by a circular earthwork. Subsequent mound construction stages covered the small mounds and the circular enclosure. Three more burials, which are possibly intrusive, were found in the third mound stage. The Jones Mound assemblage includes cordmarked jars and a few rocker stamped sherds.

Little is known about the settlement systems of which the Ashby and Jones Mound mortuary facilities were a part. They may have been ritual facilities that linked a series of dispersed communities similar to those of Adena groups to the east. The Jones Mound circular enclosure has many Adena counterparts, and contemporaneity between the Jones Mound and some Adena sites cannot be ruled out.

Hopewellian interaction also left its mark on the karst uplands of the Pennyroyal, but domestic life apparently continued with little change. Settlement patterns appear to have been similar to those of the Early Woodland—there were camps and villages in the river bottoms, the rolling uplands, and the many caves and rockshelters that dot the region. Most domestic pots are cordmarked jars; a few check stamped and simple stamped sherds are also present. Early Middle Woodland projectile points are mostly Adena Stemmed and Copena Triangular (Justice 1987:207–8) types; expanded stem and weakly side notched forms became common after about A.D. 250.

The Watkins Mound site is the most prominent late Middle Woodland site complex in the Pennyroyal (Dowell 1979; Ray 1967; Seeman 1979a:290). It is located along an upland stream in Logan County and consists of two burial mounds surrounded by a sprawling village. The larger of the two mounds was excavated by amateur archaeologists in the 1960s. The excavation exposed 36 burials, 19 of which were in crude stone-lined graves. There are hints of possible social differentiation among the burials—some stone burial crypts are more elaborate than others, and the amount of grave goods with individual interments varies as well. Domestic and ritual artifacts (fig. 4.16) were associated with 27 of the Watkins burials. Among these artifacts are expanded stem projectile points, one Copena Triangular point, a cache of 23 triangular bifaces, a cache of 36 flake bladelets, three ceramic elbow pipes, two mica scraps, five rectangular gorgets, and an incised vessel with tetrapodal supports (fig. 4.17).

Another Hopewellian mortuary site, which was vandalized and destroyed before much could be learned about it, was the Campbell Mound in Warren County (Dowell 1979). Located on a bluff spur overlooking the Barren River, this mound contained four conch shell gorgets (one of which bears an elabo-

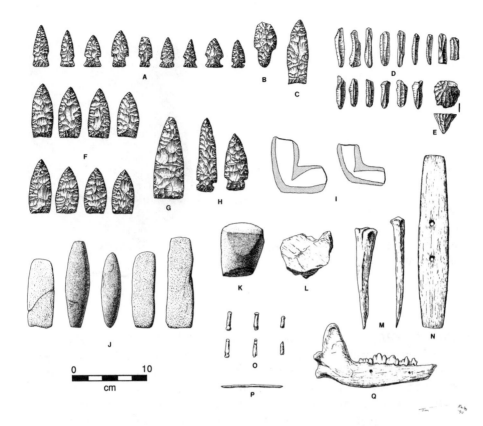

Figure 4.16 Selected artifacts from the Watkins Mound in Logan County: A, expanded stem and side-notched projectile points; B, Adena stemmed projectile point; C, Copena lanceolate projectile point; D, flake bladelets; E, bladelet core; F-H, bifacial blades; I, interior profiles of ceramic elbow pipes; J, groundstone gorgets; K, greenstone celt; L, mica; M, bone awls; N, bone gorget; O, bone beads from bracelets; P, bone pin; Q, wolf mandible. Adapted from Dowell 1979.

rate engraved design), four celts, one expanded stem projectile point, and pieces of cut mica.

In the easternmost Pennyroyal, along the upper Cumberland River, there also are indications of Middle Woodland base camps and villages, but only two Woodland mound sites have been recorded in the region, and neither has been excavated. The Reiny site in Russell County was excavated in the late 1940s and is now covered by Lake Cumberland. It contained a thick midden, which suggests that the early Middle Woodland settlement there was a substantial one. The assemblage shows connections with Crab Orchard groups to the northwest and with sites in Tennessee. There are many sherds of thick, conoidal vessels with flat, cordmarked bases. There are also a few plain, check stamped, simple stamped, and cord-wrapped dowel-impressed sherds. Projectile points include 20 lanceolate or triangular specimens and two weak-shouldered, expanded-stem points.

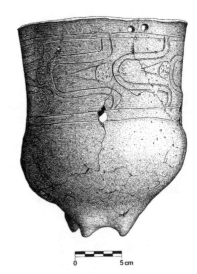

Figure 4.17 Incised vessel with podal supports from Watkins Mound. From Pollack et al. 1985.

Middle Woodland in the Mountains. Middle Woodland burial mounds and enclosures similar to those described earlier for the Bluegrass are present in the lower Big Sandy drainage of northeastern Kentucky. The environment of this part of the Mountains differs greatly from the gently rolling Bluegrass uplands, and Middle Woodland camps and villages tend to be concentrated in the narrow valleys wherever suitable stretches of bottomland occur. The numerous rockshelters of the lower Big Sandy drainage were also heavily used.

The Calloway site in the Tug Fork drainage of Martin County is a good example of the small, dispersed Middle Woodland camps of the lower Big Sandy (Niquette and Boedy 1986; Niquette et al. 1987). Calloway consists of scattered small rock ovens, hearths, and a few associated artifacts. Carbonized plant remains found in the archaeological features include nutshells, maygrass, goosefoot, and grape seeds (Fritz 1986). Calloway was occupied sometime between 250 B.C. and A.D. 200 (Niquette and Boedy 1986:104–5).

The best-known Adena site in the region is the C & O Mounds in Johnson County (Webb 1942). Excavations there revealed several overlapping circular structures under both mounds and numerous log tombs and crematory basins within the various mound stages (Webb 1942:317). Both mounds appear to be Late Adena mortuary facilities (Johnson 1982:789). The C & O Mounds assemblage included expanded center gorgets, copper bracelets, mica fragments, and Robbins Stemmed points. Most ceramic vessels were plain, but the sherds of a few incised, simple stamped, cordmarked, and check stamped pots were also found (Haag 1942b).

An impressive array of Middle Woodland earthworks is found at the Portsmouth Group (fig. 4.18) at the mouth of the Scioto River. These earthworks extend along both banks of the Ohio River in Greenup County, Kentucky, and Scioto County, Ohio. The group includes several geometric

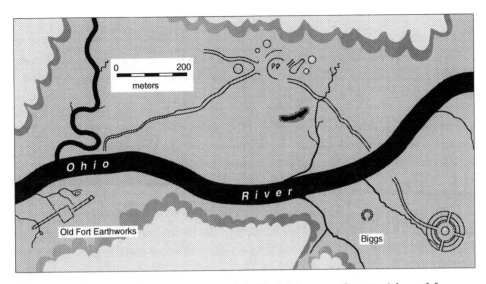

Figure 4.18   The Portsmouth Group earthworks in Greenup County. Adapted from Squier and Davis 1848: plate 27.

enclosures, embankment lines or "causeways," and burial mounds. Two of the Kentucky components of the Portsmouth Group—the Old Fort Earthwork and the Biggs site—have been archaeologically investigated.

Limited excavations at the Old Fort Earthwork (figs. 4.18–4.19) revealed an assemblage of Adena Plain ceramics and two boatstones, all of which sug-

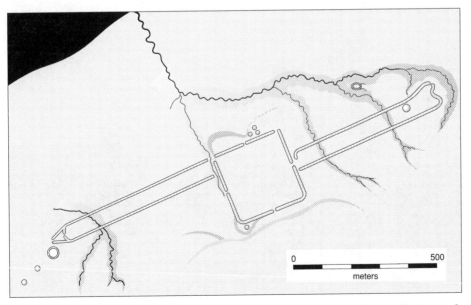

Figure 4.19   The Old Fort Earthwork in Greenup County. Adapted from Squier and Davis 1848: plate 28.

gest Adena affinities at this very Hopewell-looking site (Henderson et al. 1988:77–79).

The Biggs site (figs. 4.18 and 4.20) is a burial mound enclosed by a circular ditched earthwork (Hardesty 1964). Excavation of the mound revealed a central cremation on a clay platform and an associated fire basin. Among the few artifacts found in the mound were unusual hematite and quartz-tempered ceramics, a tubular pipe, four celts, and a piece of mica. A maize kernel was also reported from Middle Woodland context at this site, but subsequent analysis showed that the specimen is modern and was an accidental inclusion in the archaeological deposit (Jack Rossen, personal communication 1986).

The Adena-like artifacts from the Old Fort Earthworks and Biggs suggest early Middle Woodland construction dates and underscore the significant overlap between Adena and Hopewell. Despite intensive archaeological activity in this area, there is no evidence for any contemporaneous villages near these sites, which is consistent with the pattern noted earlier between monumental earthen architecture and dispersed settlement during early Middle Woodland times.

The only excavated mound that appears to be a late Middle Woodland construction in the lower Big Sandy drainage is the Brisbin Mound in Boyd County (Aument 1985, 1986; Brisbin 1976). This mound is a small, stone-and-earth mortuary facility located on an upland ridge overlooking the Big Sandy Valley. It contained a single, stone-lined crypt with cremated human

Figure 4.20 The Biggs site in Greenup County. Reproduced by permission of the William S. Webb Museum of Anthropology, University of Kentucky, negative 3192.

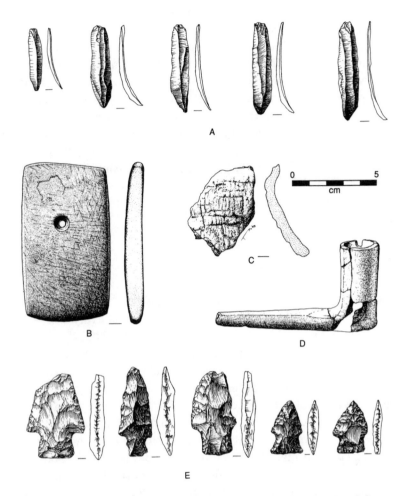

Figure 4.21 Middle Woodland artifacts from the Brisbin Mound in Boyd County: A, flake bladelets; B, groundstone gorget; C, fabric impressed sherd; D, ceramic elbow pipe; E, projectile points. Adapted from Aument 1985: figs. 4 and 5.

skeletal remains and two artifact caches. The assemblage consisted of typical Middle Woodland artifacts such as lamellar bladelets and expanded-stem projectile points. Other artifacts include an unusual ceramic elbow pipe with a long, contracting stem, a copper awl, a net or fabric-impressed sherd from a miniature vessel, and a few straight-stemmed projectile points (fig. 4.21).

Sites such as Brisbin and the many other stone and earthen mounds recorded in its vicinity suggest a concentration of Woodland mound building activity near the confluence of the Big Sandy and Ohio rivers. Most of these sites are isolated mortuary facilities. All of the recorded habitation sites (e.g., Hamilton et al. 1983; Maslowski 1984; Railey and Walters 1985) appear to have been small settlements. This pattern suggests, as seen elsewhere in

Kentucky, a pattern of dispersed communities in which social ties were reinforced through ritual activities focused on mortuary sites.

Elsewhere in the Eastern Mountains, sites similar to the large Adena burial mounds of the Bluegrass are unknown. Most prehistoric sites are found in the region's many rockshelters. Middle Woodland use of rockshelters ranged from short-term camps that left few traces to extended, possibly semi-sedentary, occupations with thick middens and rich assemblages.

Middle Woodland peoples sometimes used rockshelters for mortuary ritual purposes. The Dillard Stamper Shelter #1 in Wolfe County is a good example (Funkhouser and Webb 1930:266–75). This site contained a cremated burial associated with a cache of 14 triangular and ovate bifaces, a chipped stone celt, two pieces of polished sandstone, several antler flaking tools, and two Robbins-like blades.

LATE WOODLAND (A.D. 500–1000)

By the beginning of the Late Woodland period, earthwork construction and the long-distance exchange of goods had declined sharply. For a long time, archaeologists believed that these and other Late Woodland cultural changes were caused by the collapse of the Hopewell Interaction Sphere. The possible significance of the Hopewell Interaction Sphere is less certain now, and archaeologists are exploring other explanations.

Braun (1977; 1986; Braun and Plog 1982), for example, argues that the decline in earthwork construction and the trade of ritual items shows that the interaction between groups in neighboring regions was stabilizing. In other words, cultural mechanisms like the Hopewell Interaction Sphere simply became unnecessary in late Middle Woodland times and the "decline" was simply part of an evolutionary transition. Muller (1986:128–29, 146–47), on the other hand, sees the decline as a major disruption associated with the increasingly localized focus of Late Woodland village economies. Whether Braun or Muller is correct, the Hopewellian "decline" and the cultural changes that archaeologists associate with the Late Woodland period are still major research issues in eastern North American prehistory.

The following sections describe the major features of the Late Woodland period in Kentucky. For ease of discussion, the period is divided into sub-units—the early Late Woodland (A.D. 500–800) and the terminal Late Woodland, which began at A.D. 800. Late Woodland ended at A.D. 900 in western and southern Kentucky and A.D. 1000 in central and eastern Kentucky.

Tools and Other Artifacts

In most areas, the big difference between late Middle Woodland and early Late Woodland assemblages is the absence from the latter of decorated Hopewellian ceramics and nonlocal goods placed with the dead. The thread of local cultural continuity was strong, and throughout most of Kentucky, early Late Woodland cooking pots are cordmarked jars, much like their late Middle Woodland predecessors. Other tools also remained essentially unchanged.

During the terminal Late Woodland, however, there began to emerge strong regional differences in ceramic styles, subsistence, and settlement patterns. The centuries from A.D. 800 to 1000 also witnessed some of the most significant cultural changes of the Woodland tradition, some of which were uniform and widespread, others sporadic and localized.

One widespread technological change that occurred around A.D. 700–800 was the introduction of the bow and arrow. Its presence in Kentucky is marked archaeologically by small, light, triangular arrow points in assemblages. In the Mountains and much of the Bluegrass, triangular points are immediately preceded by thin, corner notched points of the Jacks Reef type (Ritchie 1961:26–27), which may also have been used as arrow points (Seeman 1992).

Unlike the uniform spread of the bow and arrow, terminal Late Woodland pots tend to differ stylistically from one region to the next, a pattern that reflects the increasingly local focus of trade and interaction. In the lower Ohio Valley and extreme western Kentucky, terminal Late Woodland vessels and their decoration foreshadow the rich ceramic diversity of the Mississippian tradition.

Subsistence

Horticulture intensified during the Late Woodland period, but gardening was still only a supplement to hunting and gathering in most Kentucky regions. Basically, the same plants cultivated during the Middle Woodland were in native gardens throughout most of the Late Woodland period. Between A.D. 800 and 900, maize-based horticulture became the mainstay of prehistoric economies in western Kentucky. As demonstrated in the next chapter, the emergence of maize as a staple crop soon changed the course of cultural development in Kentucky.

Although the bow and arrow represented a significant advance in hunting and warfare technology, it had little effect on the hunter's choice of prey. Preferred game continued to be the whitetail deer, raccoons, and other forest mammals that had commanded the attention of hunters since the end of the Pleistocene Epoch. The real gains provided by the bow and arrow were when and how hunters hunted. The bow was a more efficient hunting tool than the atlatl-propelled spear. Its design also made it an excellent ambush weapon that could be used with moderate success by solitary hunters.

Settlement Patterns

By A.D. 300 Woodland peoples in some parts of Kentucky in adjacent regions lived in nucleated villages. One common pattern was a circular village with a

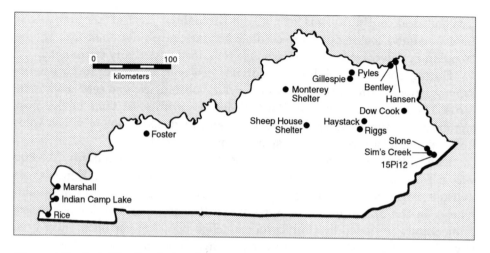

Figure 4.22 Late Woodland sites discussed in the text.

central public space around which were grouped the houses, work areas, and accumulated garbage of the village's inhabitants (Cobb and Faulkner 1978:54–96; Esarey et al. 1984; Railey 1984; Winters 1967:52–60). Another pattern involved villages set along bluff edges and river banks and enclosed by earthen embankments on the landward side (Dancey 1988; Shott 1989).

The development of circular villages and the general trend toward larger, more aggregated settlements in some Kentucky regions (fig. 4.22) may have resulted from growing population densities and smaller, more circumscribed territories. Smaller territories also encouraged the intensification of food production, as competition for natural resources intensified.

Elsewhere in the state, conditions favored dispersed settlements, such as in rockshelters and small open camps. In the lower Ohio Valley, there was even a shift away from the large settlements of the Middle Woodland period toward more dispersed communities during early Late Woodland times (Muller 1986:148).

Terminal Late Woodland settlement patterns are complex. In the middle Ohio Valley, many long-inhabited, large villages were abandoned by A.D. 750 (Church 1987; Shott 1989). Along the lower Ohio Valley, most communities were small hamlets and farmsteads throughout the Late Woodland period (Muller 1986:165–66). Around the mouth of the Ohio River and along the Mississippi Valley, Late Woodland communities included a range of settlement sizes from small camps to large villages, some of which contained mounds and plazas (Kreisa 1988; Sussenbach and Lewis 1987).

Western Kentucky Late Woodland. Early Late Woodland communities in the Jackson Purchase and lower Ohio Valley did not differ greatly from their

Middle Woodland ancestors. Between A.D. 600 and 900, however, many cultural aspects changed in a direction that can best be described as the increased Mississippianization of society. In the Mississippi Valley, Cane Hills phase (A.D. 600–900) sites are mostly small ones, a pattern Muller (1986) also identifies in the lower Ohio Valley. The big difference between the Ohio Valley and Mississippi Valley sites is that some large Cane Hills sites, such as Indian Camp Lake and Marshall, have thick middens and other evidence of sustained occupation by many people (Kreisa and Stout 1991). One site, Rice in Fulton County, was large (15 ha) and contained three mounds, a possible plaza, and a large midden (Kreisa and Stout 1991:136). This site suggests the beginnings of a hierarchical settlement system during the Cane Hills phase—a pattern that became much more pervasive in the subsequent Mississippi period. Other Cane Hills phase indicators of impending Mississippianization include new vessel forms—pans, funnels, stumpware (a thick funnel with feet), and hooded bottles (fig. 4.1). Plain and red-filmed pottery gradually became more popular relative to cordmarked vessels (Kreisa 1987a; Sussenbach and Lewis 1987:109–10). By A.D. 850–900, maize-based horticulture became the mainstay of the economy in this area.

The picture in the lower Ohio Valley of southern Illinois and the adjacent part of Kentucky is broadly similar to that just described for the Mississippi Valley. The settlement pattern of Lewis phase (A.D. 600–900) sites differed considerably from that of the Middle Woodland period. Where Crab Orchard settlements had been aggregated, floodplain-oriented communities, Lewis sites are small and distributed across the same kinds of floodplain landforms that were preferred by later Mississippian groups (Muller 1978:279).

The Lewis phase floodplain settlements were permanent, or at least multiseasonal communities. Each village contained numerous cylindrical storage pits and rectangular houses, some of which were larger than 50 m² in area (Cole et al. 1951:167; Muller 1986:133). Subsistence was based on hunting, gathering, and gardening. Unlike their late Cane Hills phase neighbors in the Mississippi Valley, maize does not appear to have been a Lewis phase crop (Muller 1986:130–50). Most Lewis pots were cordmarked jars with elongated, pointed bases. Expanded-stem points were common during the early Lewis phase, but small arrow points dominate later assemblages.

Small stone burial mounds and hilltop stone enclosures were constructed in the lower Ohio Valley uplands of southern Illinois during the Lewis phase (Muller 1986:134–35, 150–53). These features offer the first good evidence of specialized ceremonial sites in this region. Similar stone mounds are known in the adjacent portions of Kentucky, but none have been investigated.

During the very short Douglas phase (A.D. 900–950), the material culture and lifeways of the inhabitants of the lower Ohio Valley became Mississippianized (Muller 1986:159–62). These changes are particularly

Figure 4.23 Yankeetown phase ceramics. Redmond 1990: fig. 3-25; used by permission of the author; drawing by Rachel Freyman.

noticeable in the pottery. The typical vessel is a plain surfaced, or perhaps red-filmed or incised, globular jar.

Farther up the Ohio Valley, fundamental social and economic changes were also felt during the terminal Late Woodland (or Emergent Mississippi period) Yankeetown phase (A.D. 700–1000) (Redmond 1990). Typical Yankeetown habitation sites, which are identified by the presence of jars and bowls with distinctive decorations (fig. 4.23), are generally 1 ha or less in area (Muller 1986:165–66; Seeman and Munson 1980:55). Floodplain sites are numerous and seem to reflect a dispersed pattern of small, sedentary hamlets. Hunting camps are also scattered throughout the region (Seeman and Munson 1980).

In Kentucky, most Yankeetown sites are found from Hancock to Union counties on the Ohio River floodplain or along the valley bluffs (Marquardt 1971; Ottesen 1981; Turnbow et al. 1980). Large, bell-shaped pits are a common feature at Yankeetown sites and may be associated with increased production of maize at this time. Recent excavations at the Foster site in Daviess County (Sussenbach 1992) uncovered a bell-shaped pit containing maize, along with domesticated goosefoot, maygrass, little barley, and several wild plant foods. Many sites with Yankeetown components were inhabited for a long time, which makes it difficult to distinguish details about their internal organization archaeologically.

In summary, small, dispersed terminal Late Woodland settlements exist-ed throughout the lower Ohio Valley. Similar settlements thrived in the Mississippi Valley, but large planned villages also developed there in Late Woodland times. The various factors that governed this interregional pattern are not well understood. The population density may have been lower in the Ohio Valley than in the Mississippi Valley, and the Ohio Valley groups may have lived in small, dispersed settlements to maximize their use of rich agri-cultural soils. The picture is complicated greatly by the lack of good subsis-tence data from terminal Late Woodland sites in the lower Ohio Valley. Comparative data from the contemporary Dillinger phase in southern Illinois suggest that maize horticulture was still a supplement to hunting and gath-ering even toward the end of the Late Woodland period (Jefferies and Butler 1982:1496–1500; Muller 1986:157). Whatever the subsistence base of the lower Ohio Valley villages, chiefdom-level societies did not emerge until the Mississippi period.

The Newtown Complex in Central and Northeastern Kentucky. The Newtown complex (Griffin 1956; Seeman 1980) comprises late Middle Woodland and early Late Woodland sites in the Bluegrass and northeastern Kentucky. Most Newtown sites are located in the middle Ohio Valley between the mouth of the Miami River and the Ohio's confluence with the Kanawha. These sites are identifiable archaeologically by the presence of jars with thickened angular shoulders (fig. 4.24, G).

Several Newtown villages in the rolling uplands of Mason County pro-vide examples of a general trend toward nucleated settlements in the Bluegrass around A.D. 300–500. The Pyles (Collins 1980; Railey 1984) and Gillespie sites (Railey 1985a) are circular villages with central plazas (fig. 4.24 H); both sites cover roughly 1.3 ha. The circular village plan foreshad-ows the layout of many Fort Ancient sites in this region.

In northeastern Kentucky, substantial Newtown occupations are present at the Bentley and Hansen sites, both of which are located along the Ohio River in Greenup County across from the mouth of the Scioto River (Ahler 1987, 1988; Henderson and Pollack 1985) and at Site 15Gp183 located near the mouth of Tygarts Creek. The Newtown occupations at Bentley and Hansen were substantial settlements between A.D. 300 and 600. At Bentley, Newtown features included the remains of houses in the central portion of the site and a line of rock-filled earth ovens along the terrace edge. The exca-vated portion of the Hansen component, which may represent only the east-ern end of a large settlement, contained three oval houses, refuse-filled pits, and rock ovens (Ahler 1987). Hansen also yielded evidence of a mixed hunt-ing, foraging, and gardening economy. The Hansen villagers grew squash, marsh elder, goosefoot, knotweed, and maygrass (Lopinot 1988).

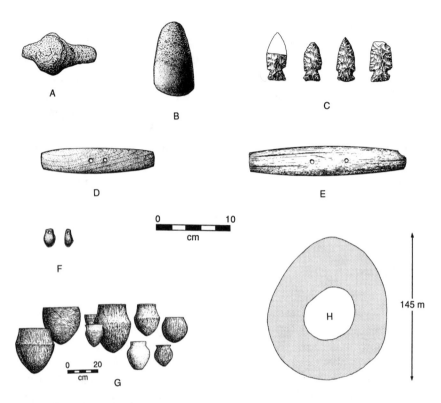

Figure 4.24 Newtown complex artifacts and features: A, expanded center stone; B, pecked and ground celt; C, expanded stem projectile points; D, slate gorget; E, bone gorget; F, drilled elk incisors; G, reconstructed ceramic vessel forms; H, circular midden and plaza of the Pyles village site

In the interior Bluegrass, away from the middle Ohio Valley, there are few excavated Woodland sites that postdate roughly A.D. 250. Villages appear to have been established in some parts of the central Bluegrass, but the settlement patterns show considerable local variation. Rockshelters were occupied in some localities, and Newtown-like assemblages have been identified at the Monterey Rockshelter (Railey 1985a) in Owen County on the lower Kentucky River, and at the Sheep House Shelter in the Silver Creek drainage of Madison County (MacDonald 1986).

By terminal Late Woodland times (ca. A.D. 700–1000), Newtown villages in central and northeastern Kentucky appear to have been abandoned, and a more dispersed settlement pattern, similar to that of Adena-Hopewell times, returned. Recent excavations at the Grayson site in Carter County (Ledbetter and O'Steen 1992) revealed a small terminal Late Woodland habitation. The small size of this site is similar to contemporary habitations in Ohio (e.g., Church 1987; Seeman 1992) and West Virginia (e.g., Niquette and

Hughes 1991; Shott 1989). Unlike their Adena and Hopewell forebearers, however, terminal Late Woodland peoples in the middle Ohio Valley did not build massive burial mounds or other public works.

Late Woodland in the Southeastern Mountains.   In the Daniel Boone National Forest along the western edge of the Mountains, there is little archaeological evidence of aggregated bottomland settlements during the late Middle Woodland and early Late Woodland periods. In Powell County, the Haystack and Rogers rockshelters have occupations that are contemporaneous with Newtown sites to the north (Cowan 1975, 1978, 1979a, 1979b). Expanded-stem points and Newtown cordmarked ceramics are reported from both shelters, and radiocarbon dates from Rogers fall between A.D. 400 and 750. These sites also contain well-preserved organic materials including plants, leather, and dried feces. Subsistence activities appear to have changed little from the Early Woodland pattern of hunting, gathering, and gardening. The economy was based on the utilization of a wide spectrum of plants, including black walnut, goosefoot, maygrass, sumpweed, sunflowers, squash, gourds, and various fruits and berries.

To the east in Pike County, Dunnell's (1966) Sim's Creek phase, which follows the Thacker phase, roughly brackets the Middle and Late Woodland periods. Sim's Creek phase sites are small settlements similar to those of the Thacker phase. The Sim's Creek site (type site of the Sim's Creek phase) was a base camp or small village that contained five houses, many earth ovens, and several pits. The assemblage is characterized by cordmarked and plain ceramics, and crude, side-notched points. The economy appears to have been based on hunting and gathering. The only direct evidence for gardening activities is one sunflower seed.

Other Sim's Creek phase sites are primarily seasonal camps or small hamlets. Two of these, Slone and Site 15Pi12, both of which are in Pike County, contained at least one earth oven; the Slone component also yielded storage pits and cache pits filled with groundstone tools. The small size of most Sim's Creek camps is exemplified by the component at Slone, which measured only 25 m in diameter.

In the Big Sandy drainage in Lawrence County, late Middle Woodland and Late Woodland settlements are generally similar to those of the Sims' Creek phase to the south. The Dow Cook site (fig. 4.25) is a good example of the Woodland settlements in this region (Niquette and Kerr 1989). The Dow Cook midden, most of which accumulated during the Middle and Late Woodland occupations, approaches 45 cm thick. The Late Woodland assemblage consists mostly of cordmarked vessels, expanded-stem and notched points, and Middle Woodland traits, such as mica scraps, flake bladelets, and bladelet cores.

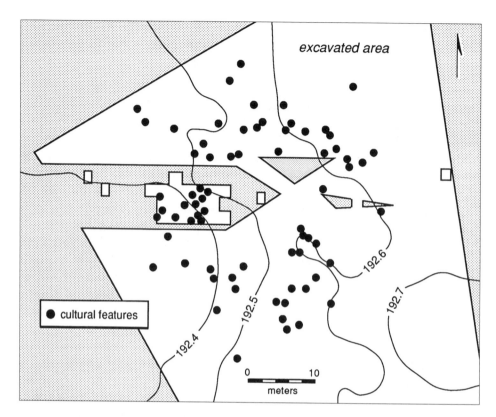

Figure 4.25 Distribution of features at the Dow Cook site in Lawrence County. Adapted from Niquette and Kerr 1989: fig. 11.

The site's Middle to Late Woodland inhabitants lived by hunting, foraging, and gardening. Nuts and blueberries were gathered in the nearby uplands. Maygrass, knotweed, sunflowers, sumpweed, squash, and gourds grew in gardens in nearby clearings. Maygrass was apparently cultivated intensively; it comprised 67 per cent of all identified seeds at the Dow Cook site (Wymer 1989).

This circular Middle to Late Woodland settlement covered about 2,000 m². Niquette and Kerr (1989) argue that the "doughnut ring" shape of the Dow Cook site plan resulted from recent plowing of the site. Alternatively, the settlement may have been structured around an open plaza, as were the contemporaneous villages of Pyles and Gillespie in Mason County. The major difference between these sites and the Dow Cook settlement is that Pyles and Gillespie each cover an area roughly seven times larger than Dow Cook.

After about A.D. 750, Big Sandy region groups apparently lived in small, dispersed habitation sites. Terminal Late Woodland occupations are distinguished primarily by Jacks Reef Corner Notched and stemless triangular arrow points. Terminal Late Woodland ceramics are poorly known in the region, but they may have been cordmarked vessels with collared and castellated rims (cf. Seeman 1980).

DISCUSSION

The Introduction and Spread of Pottery

Archaeologists use the first appearance of pottery as a convenient marker for the beginning of the Woodland tradition throughout most of the Eastern Woodlands. Available evidence suggests that the earliest ceramic vessels in eastern Kentucky date to around 1,000–800 B.C., and around 600–300 B.C. toward the west. Nevertheless, we have little direct evidence of this early pottery in Kentucky. The dating of its appearance is based mainly on information from surrounding states.

The earliest pots in the Southeast are the fiber-tempered vessels of Florida and coastal Georgia, which date to about 2,500 B.C. Within a millennium, technologically similar vessels were being made across the coastal plain in the southern states as far north as southern Tennessee. We do not know why it took so long for this technology to be introduced into Kentucky. Reid (1983, 1984) argues that climatic conditions in the central Eastern Woodlands during the Late Archaic may not have favored the consistent preservation of the soft, fiber-tempered wares, so that the apparent chronological lag in the spread of ceramic technology is due to the vagaries of the archaeological record. If Reid's argument is correct, then it is possible that fiber-tempered pottery really was a part of Late Archaic assemblages in Kentucky.

Regardless of the precise dating of the introduction of pottery technology into Kentucky, this innovation was not accompanied by profound cultural changes (e.g., Dragoo 1976:16; Stoltman 1978:711). Life continued much as it had before.

Several lines of evidence suggest that horticulture intensified somewhat at roughly the same time that ceramics were introduced in Kentucky and surrounding areas (cf. Cowan 1985a, 1985b; Watson 1985; Yarnell and Black 1985). The use of this pottery may have led to important changes in the cooking of some hard-textured foods (cf. Braun 1983). Before the coming of ceramic vessels, the boiling of nuts and other foods was presumably done by the process called "stone boiling," in which a basket or skin full of water is heated by hot stones that are pulled from a fire and dropped in it. Some foods used by Woodland groups needed to be cooked longer than stone boiling could do efficiently. Pots set on hot coals may have solved this problem.

Subsistence Trends and the Rise of Horticulture

The archaeological record contains much information about what people ate in the past. In Kentucky, the relative abundance of well-preserved organic remains from dry caves, rockshelters, and open habitation sites has figured prominently in the reconstruction of prehistoric subsistence trends (e.g., Cowan 1985b; Watson 1985). These data are crucial to the resolution of several enduring archaeological questions.

For example, as recently as the 1980s, some archaeologists argued that maize cultivation was an important component in the development of Hopewell (e.g., Chapman 1980:71–77). The direct evidence provided by archaeobotanical data and bone chemistry studies does not support this argument. Comparative evidence suggests instead that Adena-Hopewell subsistence patterns did not differ significantly from those of other Woodland tradition groups.

Although hunting and gathering were of great economic importance during the Woodland periods, the importance of native cultivated crops, such as goosefoot, sumpweed, maygrass, sunflower, little barley, and possibly giant ragweed, increased. Nevertheless, the prevailing image of Woodland subsistence is that of societies in which horticulture was a supplement to hunting and gathering. The nature and scale of Woodland horticulture is also commonly distinguished from Mississippian and Fort Ancient field agriculture (e.g., Watson 1989). Other researchers (Fritz 1990; Smith 1989) question the utility of this distinction and suggest that many Woodland groups in the Eastern Woodlands practiced a field agriculture based on native grain crops as important staples well before maize-based farming began at the end of the Late Woodland.

Horticultural and nonhorticultural Woodland groups may have also coexisted in Kentucky, a situation documented ethnographically elsewhere in the world (e.g., Hart and Hart 1986; Milton 1984; Peterson 1978). Nevertheless, this possibility seems unlikely because some of the best data on Early Woodland horticulture in Kentucky comes from uplands located far from large floodplains (e.g., Cowan 1985a, 1985b; Ison 1988; Watson 1974). Furthermore, Ison (1989) argues that horticulture in the Mountains region was carried out on hillsides, and this contradicts any image of a persisting hunting-gathering tradition among "marginal" upland groups.

Although the degree and intensity of Woodland farming remains debatable, there is good evidence for a widespread shift toward intensive, maize-based horticulture at the end of the Late Woodland period. From the strict functional perspective, full-scale agriculture did not emerge in Kentucky until around A.D. 900 because no economic need existed that would have sustained its development. Hunting, foraging, and a modest amount of horticulture provided a stable economic base that endured in the rich Kentucky environment for millennia.

Late Woodland culture was in a state of flux, which culminated in the widespread adoption of maize-based agriculture and the establishment of chiefdom-level societies. Whether they are called terminal Late Woodland or Emergent Mississippian, occupations dating between A.D. 800 and 1000 have been intensively investigated in some parts of the Midwest (e.g., Bareis and Porter 1984), but this research has only begun in Kentucky. The beginning of maize agriculture was only one component of the processes that led to the development of complex Mississippian chiefdoms in western and southern Kentucky, and to the very different Fort Ancient villages of northern and eastern Kentucky. Maize agriculture apparently emerged along different regional pathways, involved different maize varieties (Fritz 1990), and is associated with different kinds of cultural development (e.g., Mississippian versus Fort Ancient).

Settlement Patterns and Sociopolitical Dynamics

To summarize Woodland settlement trends, Early and early Middle Woodland peoples in central and eastern Kentucky lived in small, dispersed homesteads or hamlets and conducted much of their social and ritual life at ceremonial centers where burial mounds or large earthen enclosures were built. After about A.D. 300, nucleated villages appear across many parts of central and eastern Kentucky, accompanied by a dramatic curtailment of mound and earthwork construction. The village became the focus of social and ceremonial life, as well as subsistence and economic activities. Finally, by A.D. 700, village life was apparently abandoned and people dispersed once again into small homesteads or hamlets. For reasons that are still unclear, large ceremonial centers did not reappear at this time.

In contrast to their contemporaries to the east, Early and early Middle Woodland peoples in western and southern Kentucky lived as least part of the year in large base camps or villages, some of which were occupied for long periods. Settlement patterns for these areas are unclear between A.D. 300 and 700, but there may have been a shift toward more dispersed camps and more burial mound building—again, the opposite of what we see in central and eastern Kentucky. By terminal Late Woodland times (A.D. 700–1000), dispersed settlement appears the rule here as elsewhere, but hierarchical settlement systems began to develop along the Mississippi River.

The patterns of Woodland settlement aggregation and dispersal reflect the operation of many different forces on the decisions made by Woodland groups, and they cannot be accounted for by only one or a few causes. Some of the settlement shifts appear to reflect changes in village organization. For example, the circular village with a central plaza that characterizes the Pyles and Gillespie sites in Mason County may mark major social and political changes in some Woodland villages. Some anthropologists suggest that, with greater social complexity, settlements tend to show more organized planning (Hodder 1982:124–25), and this may be the case with sites such as Pyles and Gillespie.

Significantly, however, there is little evidence to suggest that village aggregation resulted in social and political changes during Late Woodland times. Societies appear to have remained at a kin-based level of organization, with decentralized political authority. Aggregation, however, is often unstable in small-scale societies that lack a centralized authority mechanism capable of settling disputes (Johnson and Earle 1987; Kent 1989; Tuzin 1976). This persistent absence of centralized authority is underscored by the widespread disintegration of village societies and the reemergence of dispersed settlement patterns in many areas during terminal Woodland times (e.g., Church 1987; Cobb and Faulkner 1978:130; Lewis and Kneberg 1946:36–37). It is unclear whether this trend reflects a relaxing of external threats from warfare, a progressive straining of internal social relations, or elements of both factors. What is clear is that there was a perpetual tug-of-war between the forces of aggregation and dispersal during the Woodland periods.

Ideological Meanings of Mounds and Middle Woodland Iconography

Woodland burial mounds and other earthworks have received considerable attention since the beginning of archaeological inquiry in eastern North America (e.g., Braun 1977; Brown 1979; Mainfort 1989; Seeman 1979a; Shyrock 1987; Struever 1968). Few researchers have examined the possible ideological implications of the burial mounds and the rich assemblages found within them. For example, the symbolism of Middle Woodland mortuary assemblages has received only sporadic attention (e.g., Cowan 1990; Hall 1979).

The widespread distribution of Middle Woodland iconography probably reflects historical factors at least as much as broad changes in social conditions. Useful ethnographic analogs may be found in places such as Melanesia and other places where the spread of particular cults resulted in widespread distinctive forms of ceremonial activity, ritual architecture, and iconography that were usually changed to suit local conditions (Tuzin 1980). A similar kind of cult may have spread throughout eastern North America during Middle Woodland times, accompanied by the spread of distinctive Hopewellian artifacts (Prufer 1964).

Certain recurrent ideas exemplify this Hopewellian cult. For example, the multistage burial programs and assemblages found in many Woodland mortuary contexts transmit a significant symbolic message. Elaborate processing of the dead reflects a common concern, found among many traditional societies, about the spiritual status of the deceased immediately after their death (Barber 1988). The dead are perceived as potentially dangerous to the living, and great care must be taken to deal properly with the body to ensure the deceased's safe passage to the afterworld—and the safety of those left behind. Such concerns may account for some aspects of Middle Woodland mortuary ritual.

Others have suggested that the involvement of the dead in the activities of the living is an ideological characteristic of horticultural economies (e.g., Campbell 1959:125–29; Charles 1985; Charles and Buikstra 1983; Goldstein 1976; Hodder 1982:104; Saxe 1970). In this sense, fertility, death, and rebirth are connected with the agricultural cycle and territorial claims, which are typically intensified with the rise of horticulture and are legitimized through lineal ties with dead ancestors. Fertility, death, and rebirth may have also been central themes in the act of moundbuilding itself—the heaping of fresh layers of earth symbolizing both burial and renewal.

Hawks and other raptorial birds also figured prominently in Woodland iconography and ideas about death and rebirth. For many traditional societies, these and other animals consumed the flesh of the dead and carried the spirit to a new life (Barber 1988:171–74; Bell 1928:84; Habenstein and Lamers 1963:83). The widespread occurrence of the raptorial bird motif in Middle Woodland times suggests that Adena and Hopewellian groups may have shared this set of beliefs.

The Hopewell Collapse and Its Aftermath

Gordon Willey (1985) identified the Hopewellian-to-Mississippian transition as one the major continuing problems of American archaeology. Given its position between the major "climaxes" of the Middle Woodland and Mississippian periods, the Late Woodland period has often been viewed as an interval of cultural decline and stagnation in the Eastern Woodlands. One of the major remaining questions about the Late Woodland period concerns the end of the Hopewellian cult and its ritual trappings. Braun (1977, 1986; Braun and Plog 1982) argues that the Hopewellian "decline" reflects increasing social interaction among Late Woodland groups; he reasons that ritual exchange involving exotic items loses its effectiveness when interaction between different social groups becomes regularized.

Although this may be true for some areas, it does not fully account for the appearance of planned, nucleated villages in many parts of the east between A.D. 300 and 500. Contrary to Braun's argument, evidence from the middle Ohio Valley suggests a more inward focus among many Late Woodland societies relative to their Hopewellian predecessors. This introversion is also consistent with the evidence of increased warfare as the Hopewell Interaction Sphere disintegrated (Dragoo 1976:19; Ford 1974:402–3; Prufer 1964; Tainter 1977). In sum, the Hopewellian decline in the middle Ohio Valley appears to be less of an evolutionary transition and more of a full-scale breakdown of long-distance relationships.

SUMMARY

Several notable technological changes occurred during the Early Woodland period (1,000–200 B.C.), the most visible of which was the introduction of pottery. The most significant subsistence trend involved the utilization of seeds from weedy annuals and a general intensification of horticulture. Specialized nonmound mortuary facilities, such as cemeteries and burial caves, and other ritual facilities appear; the construction of burial mounds may have begun toward the end of the period.

The Middle Woodland period (200 B.C.–A.D. 500) witnessed a dramatic elaboration of ritual life and long-distance exchange networks, all evidenced in the archaeological record by a proliferation of burial mounds, earthen enclosures, and nonlocal artifacts. Some groups participated in these changes more than others. This is reflected in the archaeological record by the regional and temporal variation in mound-building and settlement patterns.

Ceramic decoration was diverse and sometimes elaborate. Most vessels, however, were undecorated. Like mound building and ritual paraphernalia, decorated Middle Woodland ceramics do not occur everywhere in Kentucky. Middle Woodland pottery vessels also experienced significant morphological changes over time, such as a progressive thinning of vessel walls and a gradual change from flat-base conoidal and vase-shaped jars to more globular and subconical forms.

Around A.D. 250, there were widespread changes in settlement and ritual expression, but these trends apparently proceeded in opposite directions in different parts of the state. For example, in western Kentucky, nucleated base camps and villages of the Crab Orchard complex apparently fragmented into small, dispersed habitations, whereas in the Bluegrass and northeastern Kentucky scattered Adena communities coalesced into the large, planned villages found in Newtown and related complexes.

Mound building and long-distance exchange sharply diminished by the beginning of the Late Woodland period around A.D. 500, but domestic assemblages remained essentially identical to those of late Middle Woodland times. Horticulture continued its rise to prominence within some local subsistence economies, but foraging and hunting remained at least as important as gardening. Maize became a common element in the diet after about A.D. 850, although its importance varied regionally. The continued intensification of horticulture was probably tied to general population increases that, in turn, effected subtle changes in territory size, settlement, social organization, and other archaeologically visible patterns.

Toward the end of the Late Woodland period, the pace of cultural change quickened throughout most of Kentucky. The bow and arrow was introduced around A.D. 800, and ceramic decoration became more diverse in some regions. Important settlement pattern changes also occurred, but these trends followed different trajectories across the state. In the eastern half of Kentucky, many nucleated villages were abandoned, but Mississippi River groups along the far western edge of the state established communities that laid the foundations for the Mississippian towns that followed.

5

MISSISSIPPIAN FARMERS

R. Barry Lewis

Between A.D. 900 and 1700, many prehistoric groups in the southeastern United States shared an agricultural economy based on the cultivation of maize, beans, squash, and other crops. Although they spoke many different languages, these groups also shared numerous symbols, decorative motifs, and styles (Brown 1985) that link them together archaeologically in the Mississippian cultural tradition. The centuries during which these societies thrived is called the Mississippi period.

By A.D. 900 agriculture, a Mississippian hallmark, surpassed hunting and gathering as the primary economic base of prehistoric societies in the Mississippi Valley of western Kentucky (Sussenbach 1993). A.D. 1700 also marks a major cultural event–the beginning of a continuous Euro-American presence in the Illinois Country, in the Mississippi Valley, and, within decades, in the Ohio Valley. The archaeological evidence of Mississippian social groups in Kentucky ceases by A.D. 1500–1700.

Mississippian societies differed considerably from those of the Archaic and Woodland periods. In formal anthropological terms, Mississippian groups were "ranked societies" (Fried 1967) or "chiefdoms" (Service 1971). Only a few individuals could fill some leadership and other special-privilege statuses and roles in Mississippian society. Only a few could be chiefs, war leaders, or shamans. Some of these statuses and social roles were inherited, and they were passed down within one family or clan for generations.

The settlements of the Mississippian chiefdoms formed a hierarchy of different kinds of sites, the most archaeologically visible of which were planned towns with centrally located plazas flanked by buildings set on platform mounds. The towns were the social, political, and religious centers of Mississippian society (Lewis and Stout 1992; Stout and Lewis 1993). Their

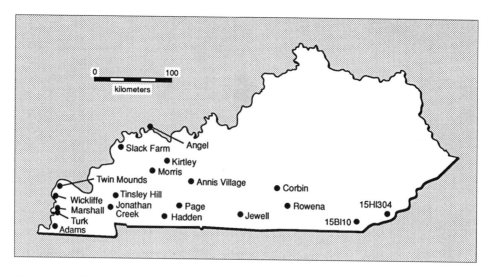

Figure 5.1   Mississippian sites discussed in the text.

remains also are among the largest, most complex archaeological sites in Kentucky (Clay 1981:74).

Mississippian sites are concentrated in southern and western Kentucky (fig. 5.1). Contemporaneous groups, which archaeologists call the Fort Ancient culture, lived in the Bluegrass and parts of the Mountains. Among the general similarities shared by the Mississippian and Fort Ancient cultures were nucleated villages with public spaces and defensive fortifications and a mixed economy that emphasized agriculture. William Sharp examines Fort Ancient archaeology in chapter 6.

To describe effectively the rich Mississippian archaeology of Kentucky, this chapter examines the Mississippi period in two parts–early Mississippi (A.D. 900–1300) and late Mississippi (A.D. 1300–1700). The final section interprets major cultural patterns of this period.

EARLY MISSISSIPPI PERIOD (A.D. 900–1300)

Jackson Purchase Towns and Villages

Many cultural changes that are widely characterized as Mississippian (as defined by Griffin 1985), including the major elements of a regional settlement hierarchy, were present along the Mississippi River in Kentucky by the end of the Late Woodland period (see chap. 4).

The Marshall site, a large village site on the Mississippi Valley bluffs in northwestern Carlisle County, offers the best available information about early Mississippi period components, especially the James Bayou phase (A.D. 900–1100) (Sussenbach 1993; Sussenbach and Lewis 1987).

The houses of the James Bayou phase village at Marshall were usually set in shallow basins dug into the ground. Like most early Mississippian sites of this region, none of the house floors had interior hearths (Lewis 1990b). House walls were constructed by setting poles in narrow trench-like footings or by digging a separate hole for each wall pole. Although there is evidence for mounds and other earthworks (Sussenbach and Lewis 1987) at Marshall, the nature and age of those features are largely unknown.

The Marshall site inhabitants lived by agriculture, hunting, and gathering. Maize was a very important crop, as could be seen by the discovery of maize cupules, kernels, and glumes in houses, pits, and throughout the village midden. Hickory nuts, pigweed, smartweed (knotweed), and the American lotus were common gathered plant foods (Woodard 1987). Whitetail deer, fish, and turtles provided most of the meat (Kreisa 1987b).

Pottery technology improved during the Mississippi period. Early Mississippian potters made many more kinds of pots than their Late Woodland ancestors and their products show greater technological skill. Nevertheless, all pots were made by the coiling method or by mass modeling from a lump of clay. The potter's wheel and true glazes were unknown throughout prehistory in the Americas.

In the oldest Mississippian villages of the Mississippi Valley, most domestic pots were plain or cordmarked jars and bowls of the types Baytown Plain and Mulberry Creek Cordmarked. Other vessels were red-filmed bowls; large shallow fabric-impressed bowls called pans or saltpans; and fired clay funnels of the type Wickliffe Thick. Fired clay "grog" and, increasingly, pulverized mussel shells were mixed into the pottery clay to help control shrinkage. Shell-tempered pottery eventually became so widely used across the Midwest and the Southeast during the Mississippi period that archaeologists now treat it as a crude "index fossil" for the Mississippian culture.

Artifacts other than potsherds are often sparse on Mississippian sites, and early sites like Marshall are no exception. The chipped stone assemblage is dominated by fragments of large chert hoes and flakes struck from hoes bits to resharpen them. Projectile points, bifaces, scrapers, gravers, picks, and other tools are present but rare.

Marshall is unusual in that it is one of the few large James Bayou communities for which there are excavated data. Unlike most other major James Bayou settlements, which were continuously occupied throughout much of the Mississippi period, Marshall is well preserved because it was abandoned during the Dorena phase (A.D. 1100–1300). A new community, called the Turk site, was founded on the next bluff spur, a few hundred meters south of Marshall.

By A.D. 1100 aboriginal towns existed throughout western Kentucky and southeastern Missouri (Lewis 1991). The basic plan of these large communities was an open plaza bordered by platform and burial mounds, which was in turn surrounded by houses, granaries, and work areas–the real living space of the town. Most towns were built in commanding, highly visible locations along bluffs, terraces, and prominent natural levees of the major river valleys (Lewis and Stout 1992; Stout and Lewis 1993). In most other ways, the settlement system and economic organization of these Dorena phase (A.D. 1100–1300) communities were comparable to those of the James Bayou phase. The impression of cultural continuity, however, may also reflect simply how little we understand these early Mississippi period communities.

The Turk site is a good example of a Dorena phase town. Turk (fig. 5.2) covers about 2.5 ha of a dissected bluffcrest of the Mississippi Valley in northeastern Carlisle County (Edging 1985). It is a compact site relative to other towns in the region. Its small size is simply a function of available building room on the ridge upon which it is built rather than evidence of an early Mississippi period cultural preference for small towns. The site's center is dominated by the characteristic Mississippian mound-and-plaza arrangement of public space. In the late 1800s several smaller mounds could be identified outside the area bordering the plaza (Loughridge 1888:183–84), but they have long since been destroyed.

The major site occupation at Turk began during the Dorena phase and continued into the early Medley phase (Lewis 1990a, 1991). The village midden near the plaza is 0.5–1 m thick and contains a complex jumble of wall-

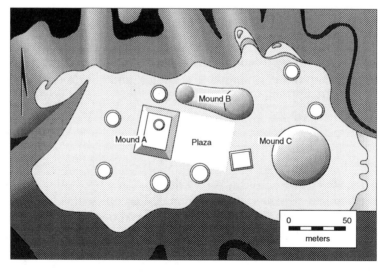

Figure 5.2   The Turk site in Carlisle County.

trench house remains, refuse-filled pits, post pits, fire basins, and burials. As at the neighboring Marshall site, maize was ubiquitous in the midden, and it was clearly the Turk community's most important staple crop. Gathered plant foods were hickory nuts, goosefoot, marsh elder, and persimmons (Edging 1985). Whitetail deer, raccoon, and wild turkey were staple game animals (Kruger 1985).

The Dorena phase assemblage at Turk is dominated by plain jars and bowls. Wickliffe Thick funnels, fabric-impressed saltpans, red-filmed bowls, and flanged bowls with incised rims are also present. Clay grog-tempered pottery of the types Baytown Plain and Mulberry Creek Cordmarked is rare at Turk (Lewis 1985:20–27).

As at Marshall, the nonceramic artifacts at Turk are mostly hoe fragments and bit resharpening flakes. Other common stone implements are adzes, abraders, projectile points, and flake tools (Stelle 1985).

In northern Ballard County, the Wickliffe town site (fig. 5.3) was both contemporaneous with the Turk site and constructed in a similar ridge-top setting. Wickliffe was long known to Kentucky citizens as a tourist attrac-

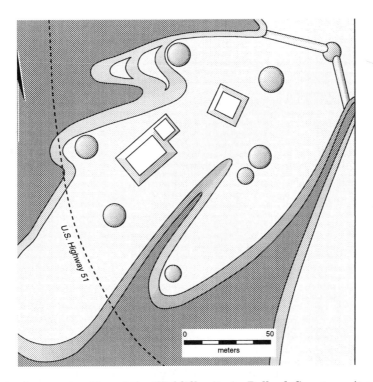

Figure 5.3 A reconstruction of the Wickliffe site in Ballard County as it appeared about 100 years ago. The dotted line marks the present path of U.S. Highway 51/62 across the site.

tion called Ancient Buried City. Developed in the 1930s by two wealthy amateur archaeologists, Fain and Blanche King, Ancient Buried City gave countless school groups and the public a glimpse of the past in the form of a museum built around open excavations protected from the elements by frame shelters.

In 1983 Ancient Buried City was converted into the Wickliffe Mounds Research Center, a Murray State University archaeological museum and research and field methods training facility (Wesler 1985, 1989, 1991; Wesler and Neusius 1987). Although sorely damaged many decades ago by the construction of U.S. Hwy 51/62 and by the Kings' enthusiastic, but untrained and poorly documented excavations, this site has, over the past 60 years, probably communicated a greater sense of Kentucky's past to more people than any other single place or person has.

Fundamental Mississippian developmental changes similar to those documented in the Mississippi Valley have also been found in the eastern Jackson Purchase region and the lower Ohio Valley. In the Tennessee-Cumberland valleys, the Jonathan Creek phase, as described by Clay (1979:119–20), is comparable in culture and time to the James Bayou and early Dorena phases.

Jonathan Creek phase sites range from the Jonathan Creek site, a large fortified village (Clay 1979; Webb 1952), to the Dedmon site, an isolated farmstead (Allen 1976). The Jonathan Creek site was located less than 2 km from the left bank of the Tennessee River in Marshall County (fig. 5.4). The location is a good one for a village, and it was used during the Late Woodland period and throughout most of the Mississippi period.

The Mississippian community at Jonathan Creek surrounded a central plaza flanked by several platform mounds. Excavation of the southern edge of this community in the early 1940s exposed many houses, pits, burials, hearths, and at least eight stockade lines, which encircled the town at one time or another. Some, if not most, of the stockades were built during the Jonathan Creek phase. The houses also show the same gradual shift from walls made of individually set posts to walls set in trenches that occurred across this region in the early Mississippi period.

The economic base of Jonathan Creek phase communities was probably maize agriculture, hunting, and gathering, but this inference is based on sketchy data. The Jonathan Creek site excavations provide few details, in part because archaeologists did not rigorously collect this kind of information in the 1940s, and in part because the Jonathan Creek excavations have yet to be completely analyzed. At Dedmon, a Jonathan Creek phase farmstead, whitetail deer, raccoons, and wild turkeys were important game animals (Allen 1976:160), but the excavators found no direct evidence of cultivated plant foods (Allen 1976:166).

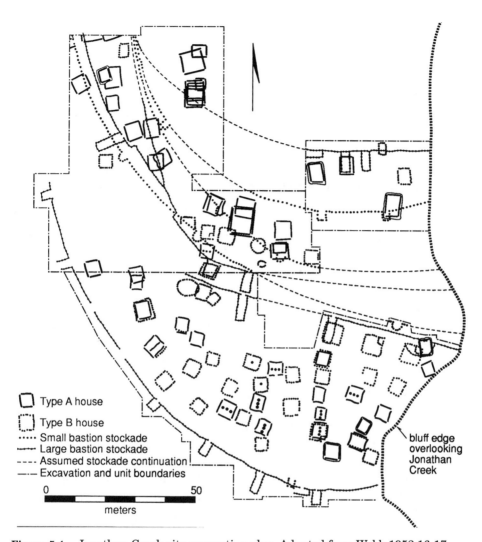

Figure 5.4. Jonathan Creek site excavation plan. Adapted from Webb 1952:16-17.

Most Jonathan Creek phase vessels were undecorated, shell-tempered jars, bowls, and pans (Clay 1963a:113–22). Shell-tempered cordmarked jars and red-filmed vessels are present in small quantities at some sites.

Western Coalfield Towns and Villages

The centerpiece of Mississippian research in the Ohio Valley between Union and Breckinridge counties lies across the river in Indiana. It is the Angel site, a very large (ca. 40 ha) town site in Vanderburgh and Warrick counties near Evansville (Black 1967). The Angel town and ceremonial center figured prominently in the prehistoric developments of the Ohio Valley. Given the site's location just upstream from the confluence of the Green and Ohio rivers, Angel also must have been an important factor in the late prehistory of the Green River drainage in west-central Kentucky.

Several investigators (e.g., Green and Munson 1978; Hilgeman 1992; Honerkamp 1975; Power 1976) have described and refined the Angel phase, which is intended to bracket the existence of this prehistoric town and its satellite communities. Since Angel was occupied for a very long time—at least A.D. 1100–1450—the Angel phase is more a chronicle of the Mississippi period in the Ohio Valley than a true archaeological phase.

Almost all Angel phase pottery is undecorated, shell-tempered utilitarian wares. Red filming and negative painting were the principal decorative techniques (Hilgeman 1992). Shell-tempered cordmarked pots and fabric-impressed pans are minor wares, and incised sherds are very rare (Kellar 1967:468).

Angel phase nonceramic artifacts include almost the full range of known Mississippi period tools, implements, and ornaments (Kellar 1967:433–63). Small, triangular projectile points are common, followed by abraders, scrapers, perforators, groundstone celts, and flake knives, in roughly that order of abundance.

The typical Angel house had a hip roof and walls set in narrow trenches (Black 1967:497–98). Some houses were constructed with their floors in shallow basins, but this architectural feature does not appear to have been as common in this part of the Ohio Valley as it was in the Tennessee-Cumberland or Mississippi valleys.

The economy was, as in other Mississippian communities throughout the Mid-South, based largely on agriculture, hunting, and gathering. They grew maize, beans, pumpkins, and other plants. Whitetail deer, squirrels, raccoons, and wild turkeys were common game animals (Kellar 1967:481–83).

To the south of the Ohio Valley, in the Green River drainage, the Kirtley, Morris, and Annis Mound sites offer a good picture of early Mississippian developments between A.D. 1000 and 1300. Kirtley, in the Cypress Creek uplands of McLean County, was a small village of 6–8 houses that may have been occupied for several decades. The houses were of wall-trench construction and several large, shallow "midden pits," tentatively interpreted as trash-filled, house wall plaster pits, were found near them (Rolingson 1961:47).

Most of the Kirtley pottery vessels are undecorated, shell-tempered household wares. The assemblage also contains small quantities of shell-tempered, fabric-impressed pans, red-filmed vessels, cordmarked jars, and a few sherds of a shell-tempered, check stamped ware (Lewis 1990b:table 6; Rolingson 1961:53–54). Nonceramic artifacts include projectile points, scrapers, drills, and knives, three full-grooved axes, a celt, and several other groundstone implements (Rolingson 1961:48–53). The full-grooved axes and some of the other artifacts are probably artifacts from an older pre-Mississippian camp.

The Morris site in Hopkins County (fig. 5.1) was a bigger Mississippian community than Kirtley, but it also dates around A.D. 1000–1300. It was a fortified village of about 12 houses arranged around a small plaza or public space (fig. 5.5) (Rolingson and Schwartz 1966:64–126). On at least two occasions, the villagers built a defensive stockade, complete with bastions, around their community (Rolingson and Schwartz 1966:78–79).

Most of the Morris houses were of wall-trench construction and the floors contain postmolds and small pits (Rolingson and Schwartz 1966:71–76), some of which appear to have been hearths. Most of the Morris site pottery vessels are shell-tempered, undecorated jars, bowls, and pans. Nonceramic artifacts include triangular projectile points, picks, adzes, small stone and pottery disks, a hoe, a discoidal, pottery trowels, and bone awls (Rolingson and Schwartz 1966:79–83).

Annis Village, the last Western Coalfield site to be discussed, is located in the Big Bend of the Green River in north-central Butler County (Lewis 1988a). It resembles the Morris site except for the presence of a large platform mound (Young 1962). The mound, which measured roughly 30 m long, 25 m wide, and about 4 m high (Young 1962:6–7), was situated on the banks of the Green River at one end of the village plaza. The plaza itself was flanked by the remains of at least 12 houses (Lewis 1988a:30). On several occasions during its existence, the village was enclosed by a stockade. One of these stockades may have even been constructed across the northern edge of the primary stage of the platform mound, effectively cutting it off from the rest of the village (Young 1962:21a–24).

Excavation of the platform mound showed that it had been built in several stages. The first stage was marked by the remains of a large house, apparently a dwelling, that showed extensive evidence of remodeling and repair (Young 1962:98–106). Outside the house was a large deposit of domestic refuse. In the next construction stage, the remains of the house were leveled and more dirt was added to the mound. Upon this fresh base, two large buildings with interior hearths were constructed. The absence of garbage and other household debris in and around these buildings suggests that they were not dwellings, but served some nondomestic role. In the final mound level, the remains of the two buildings were cleared away, more dirt was added to the mound, and a new building was constructed on its top. Like the first building, it was repaired or at least remodeled several times, but there was little evidence of domestic debris in or around the building.

The Mississippian pottery from the platform mound excavation is predominantly an undecorated shell-tempered utility ware. In general, however,

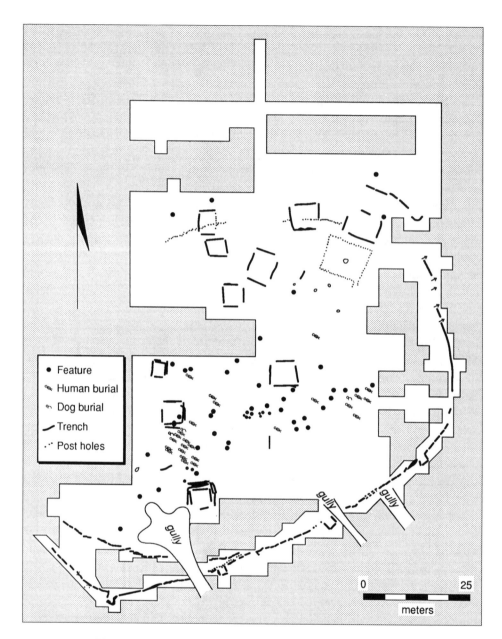

Figure 5.5. The Morris site in Hopkins County. Adapted from Rolingson and Schwartz 1966:68.

the pottery resembles that described above for other Western Coalfield sites. Although many Woodland and a few late Mississippi period sherds were also found at Annis Village (Lewis 1990a:table 6; Young 1962:55–79a), analysis of the ceramics suggests that the main occupation of this site began around A.D. 800–900 and continued to about A.D. 1300.

Mississippian sites such as Kirtley, Morris, and Annis Village were once viewed as frontier settlements of agricultural groups from the major river valleys, such as the Ohio (e.g., Hanson 1960:36–38; Rolingson 1961:58). Mississippian peoples, in general, were thought to have been aggressive colonists who carried the seeds of their culture throughout the midcontinent, and these fortified settlements had much of the "outpost" about them.

The image of Mississippian colonists in the Green and other Kentucky valleys tends to vanish upon close inspection. Most, but by no means all, villages were occupied for many years, as can be seen in the evidence of house repair and rebuilding. Annis Village, in particular, endured long enough for the main platform mound to be rejuvenated several times. The "military fire base"-like impression created by the presence of stockade lines is more illusion than reality. The stockades typically lack evidence of continuous maintenance. They were, therefore, probably not a constant village feature, but were constructed when the villagers felt threatened. These are all characteristics of sedentary villagers in a familiar environment, not colonists carving out a new life in a hostile land.

One other site, although something of an enigma, also reinforces the interpretation of Mississippian culture as a gradual development rather than as a sudden intrusion in river drainages like the Green. This is the Page site, located near the Mud River in Logan County. Page was once the most extensive mound complex in Kentucky. When it was investigated by Webb and Funkhouser in the late 1920s, the site contained at least 67 recognizable mounds. Many more had apparently been destroyed.

Webb and Funkhouser excavated 18 mounds at Page and discovered that most were the remains of cist-type burial facilities. Only one mound they excavated, Mound 3, was a platform mound that had been built in several stages (Webb and Funkhouser 1930:181–87), much like the Annis Village mound described above. Several other Page mounds, which Webb and Funkhouser did not investigate, may also be non-mortuary features.

The archaeological significance of the Page site centers on the mortuary cists. Comparable late prehistoric sites are unknown in Kentucky. The cists themselves are unusual enough to warrant quoting Webb and Funkhouser's (1930:147–50) descriptions of one of them:

> [Mound 48] was ovoid in shape and measured sixty feet in length north and south, forty feet in width east and west and seven feet in height....The removal of the earth from the sides of the mound at once revealed a heavy, well built wall of rock which had been constructed entirely around the central area. This wall enclosed a rectangular pit fifteen feet in length, six feet in width and five feet in depth in inside measurements [fig. 5.6]. This pit was

almost completely filled with human bones, charcoal and ashes. Thousands of fragments of human bones in all stages of burning were taken from this pit together with bushels of charcoal. The inside walls of the pit showed evidences of terrific heat, the inside edges of the rocks having been cracked and blackened while the clay in the interstices had been burned to brick....It would be a mere conjecture to attempt to estimate the number of individuals represented in these cremations. A rough count in the field of one bone which could be most quickly and easily recognized–namely, the head of the femur–showed one hundred and eighty-two examples of the right femur....The bones seemed to be in three distinct layers, each layer about a foot thick and separated by a few inches of small flat stones and earth. It would appear that the pit had thus served on three different occasions as a place of cremation of a large number of individuals. [Webb and Funkhouser 1930:147–49]

It is difficult, if not impossible, to interpret the Page mortuary complex without knowing the cultural context within which it existed. Unfortunately, this is precisely the information we lack from Page. No houses, middens, or other domestic contexts have been excavated there. Even the age of the complex is hard to estimate with precision since the burial cists yielded few cross-data-

Figure 5.6   Rock-lined crematory pit after excavation at the Page site. It measures approximately 5 m long, 2 m wide, and 1.8 m deep. Webb and Funkhouser 1930:148.

ble artifacts. Most of the Page site potsherds came from the fill of the platform mound, Mound 3. All of the roughly 300 sherds from this mound were
limestone-tempered, and all but four were plain; of the remaining sherds, one
specimen was cordmarked and one was check stamped. Allen infers that the
absence of shell-tempered pottery from the site collections "might indicate
that the mounds were constructed prior to the availability of significant
amounts of shell tempered pottery in whatever village debris area was being
used for mound fill" (1977:13) and tentatively assigns the major occupation of
the site to the early Mississippi period. Whatever its age, the mere presence
of the Page mound complex shows that much remains to be learned about
Mississippian life in this part of western Kentucky.

Pennyroyal

Most information about the early Mississippi period in the Pennyroyal comes
from excavations at Corbin, a large village, and at Hadden, a mortuary site.
One other large village, Jewell in Barren County, was occupied during most
of the Mississippi period. It will be described in the section on the late
Mississippi period, below.

Corbin was a fortified town located in a wide bend of the Green River
Valley in Adair County (Duffield 1967:4). It covered about 2 ha, included at
least three mounds and a shallow midden, and existed between roughly A.D.
1000 and 1200. None of the mounds were erected over burials or burial facilities; all of them appear to have been built as substructure mounds or for
other purposes (Fryman 1968:12–15, 23–26). Mound B, situated near the center of the site, was an unusual earth cap over a rough, square-shaped, rock
platform that measured 7.2 m on each side (Duffield 1967:16; Fryman
1968:26–33). The limestone and sandstone rocks of the platform had been
placed so that their flattest surfaces were turned upwards. Nevertheless,
Duffield (1967:18), one of the excavators, argues that the rock pavement
would have been too uneven to make a good floor. Beneath the platform were
the remains of a circular building that measured about 5 m in diameter, a 12-
m-long wall trench that may have been the footings for the wall of a building,
and several burned areas (Fryman 1968:38–39).

The village plan, house architecture, stockade lines, and other major features of the Corbin community are all part of the familiar Mississippian pattern. The big differences between this village and those from farther west in
Kentucky are found in the artifacts. Consider, for example, that more than
28,000 artifacts were recovered during the 1967 field season at Corbin
(Fryman 1968:63). In western Kentucky, or even the lower Green Valley, all
but a few of these artifacts would be potsherds. At Corbin, however, over
20,000 artifacts are classified as "flint detritus" (Fryman 1968:63), and there
are only 835 potsherds (Fryman 1968:135). This difference may reflect

resource access patterns in part, but there is probably more to this problem than simply that.

The nonceramic artifacts include 161 projectile points, 108 of which are small, triangular specimens (Fryman 1968:75). There are also drills, knives, reamers, 12 categories of scrapers, anvils, discoidals, and debitage, among other classes of debris. Given the tool diversity, forms, and other characteristics of the Corbin stone tools, at least part of the Mississippian assemblage probably includes artifacts from Late Archaic and Early Woodland components at Corbin.

The Corbin site pottery is also unusual. Most sherds are a shell-tempered, check stamped type called Wolf Creek Check Stamped. Shell-tempered, plain jars and bowls, which were the most common pottery vessels at Mississippian sites in extreme western Kentucky, make up only 9 percent of the entire Corbin collection. Most of the remaining sherds are shell-tempered cordmarked specimens of the type McKee Island Cordmarked.

Comparable pottery assemblages are unknown among Kentucky sites, but this is undoubtedly a reflection of how little archaeological work has been done in southern Kentucky rather than this site's cultural uniqueness. Nevertheless, it is clear that the cultural ties of the Mississippian inhabitants of the Corbin site were closer to the Southeast (possibly eastern Tennessee and the Carolinas, where shell-tempered, check stamped types are more common) than to the Mississippian complexes of western Kentucky (Fryman 1968:158).

Hadden is a small Late Woodland and early Mississippi period mortuary complex on a hilltop overlooking the Whippoorwill Valley in Todd County. At Hadden (and at other southern Kentucky sites like it), there are only a few small mounds, each of which contains one or a few stone-lined mortuary cists (Allen 1977:11). One of these cists has been excavated. It was a stone slab-lined crematory that measured approximately 1.6 m long, 1 m wide, and 70 cm deep (Long 1961:79–91, 1974). The pottery from the fill of the mound that covered this cist suggests an early Mississippi period date for the site. The assemblage includes coarse and fine shell-tempered, plain utility wares of the types Mississippi Plain and Bell Plain; and red-filmed, check stamped, and cordmarked sherds of the types Old Town Red, Wolf Creek Check Stamped, and McKee Island Cordmarked (Long 1961:18–28).

The Corbin site shows that early Mississippi period communities were nearly as complex and just as enduring in the river valleys of the Pennyroyal as in the major valleys of the Mid-South. But other aspects of Mississippian settlement in the Pennyroyal are largely unknown. Few Mississippian sites have been excavated in this region. Sites like Hadden suggest that burial customs and ritual in the Pennyroyal and southern Western Coal Field differed from those of the Jackson Purchase, where features such as crematory cists are unknown.

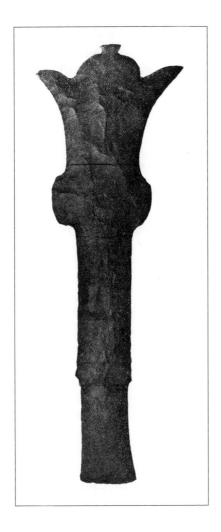

Figure 5.7 Chipped stone mace (38 cm long) from a Mississippian site in Edmonson County. Young 1910:189; reprinted by permission of The Filson Club, Louisville, Kentucky.

The Edmonson County stone mace (fig. 5.7) also exemplifies our ignorance of Mississippian developments in the Pennyroyal. This artifact was found more than a century ago near Chameleon Springs (Webb and Funkhouser 1932:109). A few comparable maces, all of which share a form associated with the Mississippian "Southern Cult," are known from sites in Missouri, Oklahoma, and Georgia. The presence of this exotic artifact suggests that there is much we do not understand about the Mississippi period in major parts of Kentucky.

Summary

Mississippian communities developed across western and southern Kentucky between A.D. 900 and 1300. It was once believed that these developments were the result of migrations or invasions of Mississippian peoples from a distant heartland, into regions inhabited by Late Woodland groups. However, we now believe that these developments were largely indigenous, cumulative products of the casual movements of people and the exchange of ideas and technology. The factors that led to these developments are discussed in greater length at the end of this chapter.

LATE MISSISSIPPI PERIOD (A.D. 1300–1700)

The centuries between A.D. 1300 and 1700 witnessed both the greatest development and the end of Mississippian culture in Kentucky. The basic settlement system and village economy of Mississippian communities remained stable, without major changes from early Mississippi period conditions, until between A.D. 1500 and 1700, at which time these societies collapsed (Lewis 1990a, 1990b, 1990c).

Mississippi Valley

In the Mississippi Valley of western Kentucky and adjacent parts of Missouri and Illinois, some towns that had probably been occupied continuously since the Late Woodland period were abandoned during the Medley phase (A.D. 1300–1500), and other towns emerged to prominence in the same general region.

Why some towns died and others, even nearby ones, apparently thrived, is as yet unexplained. It may have been simply part of a general pattern of town growth–a village would become important for religious, economic, or political reasons; it would adopt the trappings of power and prestige (e.g., large plazas and platform mounds; more inhabitants); and dominate its neighbors until its place was usurped by another community that repeated the cycle.

Mass extinctions of Mississippian communities occurred during the Jackson phase (A.D. 1500–1700) (Lewis 1990a, 1990b). The end of Mississippian culture across Kentucky was apparently due more to unique or catastrophic causes, such as introduced European diseases, than to general developmental cycles.

The Adams site is a representative Medley phase town in Fulton County (Lewis 1986, 1990b; Stout 1989). This large (7.25 ha) Mississippian town is located on a creek that drains into the Mississippi Valley (fig. 5.8). It consists of a central mound group, plaza, and two distinct village segments, one located to the east of the central plaza and the other situated southwest of the main platform mound. These public and private spaces, which cover the remains of a large Late Woodland village, were the main town features

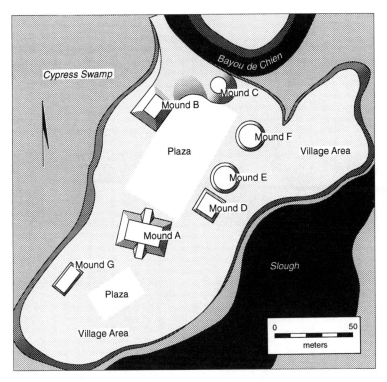

Figure 5.8   The Adams site in Fulton County. Stout 1985.

during the Dorena (A.D. 1100–1300) and Medley (A.D. 1300–1500) phases (Lewis 1990b).

Thick village middens blanket the site around the plazas and mound group. Due to the spatial limits of the terrace upon which this town was constructed, the middens are packed densely with the remains of wall-trench houses, pits, fire basins, and other features. Nevertheless, at any given time, houses or house groups stood as much as 25–30 m apart in the residential areas of the site (Stout 1989:94).

The Adams villagers hunted whitetail deer, raccoons, and wild turkeys and ate many kinds of turtles and fish. They grew maize, beans, squash, and gourds in fields near the town and gathered persimmons, hickory nuts, and the starchy or oily seeds of several wild plants in the forest and patches of waste ground.

Most household vessels were shell-tempered jars, bowls, and plates of the types Mississippi Plain and Bell Plain. Decorated vessels (fig. 5.9) are common relative to older Mississippian assemblages, but the sherds of these vessels seldom account for more than 3–5 per cent of Medley components.

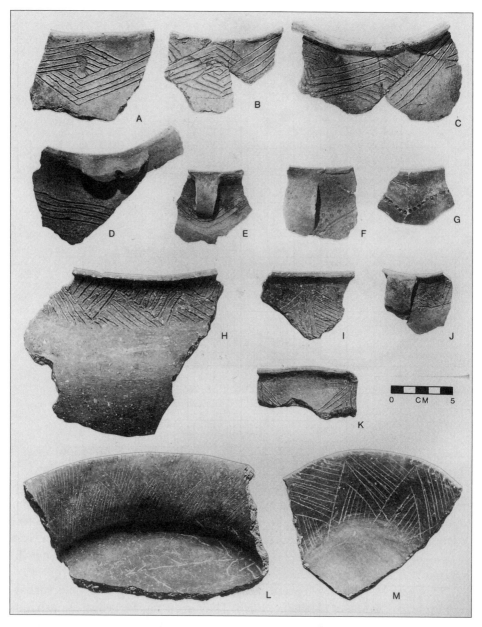

Figure 5.9 Late Mississippi period pottery types from Mississippi Valley sites: A-C, Matthews Incised, *var. Beckwith*; D-E, Matthews Incised, *var. Matthews*; F-G, Matthews Incised, *var. Manly*; H, J, Barton Incised, *var. Barton*; I, K, Barton Incised, *var. Kent*; L-M, O'Byam Incised, *var. O'Byam*. Lewis 1990a: fig. 3-6.

Nonpottery artifacts include hoes and hoe bit resharpening flakes, projectile points, sandstone abraders, metates, adze fragments, bone awls, pottery ear-spools and pins, and drills. Chert for making stone tools is a scarce resource in the Lower Mississippi Valley, and small chipped stone tools were some-times made from recycled hoes.

Along the Mississippi Valley, the Jackson phase (A.D. 1500–1700) brackets the centuries during which many eastern North America native groups became extinct, were decimated, or were otherwise culturally and biologically affected by their first contacts with the people and the diseases of the Old World (cf. Milner 1980; Ramenofsky 1987). Towns, villages, and hamlets were abandoned as the inhabitants died of the combined effects of diseases, starva-tion, and exposure. In the Jackson Purchase, the distinctive late prehistoric ceramic technology essentially ceased and left no stylistic successors.

In western Kentucky, the end probably came during the 1500s. Travelers' accounts and other historical information from the late 1600s suggest that the aboriginal population density of this region had been low for some time (Lewis 1986). Jackson phase components have been identified at Adams, Sassafras Ridge and Twin Mounds in Kentucky, and at Callahan-Thompson, Hess, and the Story Mound site across the Mississippi River in Mississippi County, Missouri (Lewis 1988b, 1989, 1990a). These components span the ter-minal episode of prehistoric aboriginal occupations in the region, which may have lasted for less than a century.

Jackson phase assemblages, about which little is yet known, are general-ly similar to those of the Medley phase except for a few artifacts, such as astragalus dice, "Nodena" points, and disk pipes, that provide useful temporal markers for this phase (Lewis 1988b, 1990a, 1990b). It is, of course, also pos-sible that European artifacts may be found in Jackson phase components. Nevertheless, this possibility appears unlikely since western Kentucky lies well outside the routes of the sixteenth-century Spanish expeditions in the Southeast.

Tennessee-Cumberland Valleys and Western Pennyroyal

The Tinsley Hill phase (A.D. 1300–1450) spans the last centuries of Mississippian presence in the Tennessee-Cumberland and lower Ohio Valleys (Butler 1991). Several Tinsley Hill components have been excavated, includ-ing the Tinsley Hill and Rodgers sites in the Cumberland Valley, and Birmingham, Goheen, Roach, and possibly Jonathan Creek in the Tennessee Valley (Clay 1979).

The settlement system and economy of Tinsley Hill phase communities differed little from older Mississippi settlements in this region. Tinsley Hill, a large village, covered 7 ha of the Cumberland Valley and adjacent bluffs near

Figure 5.10   Conch shell (*Busycon perversum*) gorget with the engraved figure of a ball game player. It was found in an aboriginal grave on the Cumberland Valley bluffs near Eddyville, Lyon County, around 1900. Taken from Holmes 1904.

the mouth of Eddy Creek (Clay 1961, 1963b, 1963c; Schwartz 1961; Schwartz and Sloan 1958). Excavations in the village midden revealed Jonathan Creek and Tinsley Hill phase occupations stratigraphically separated by soil that had washed off the slopes of a nearby bluff (Clay 1979).

Most Tinsley Hill phase pottery is Mississippi Plain or Bell Plain, the region's ubiquitous Mississippi period utility wares. Incised jars and plates of the types Matthews Incised and O'Byam Incised, *var. Stewart* are also present (Clay 1979:123), but as in the Medley phase, decorated pots account for only a small part of the assemblage.

The estimated A.D. 1450 ending date of the Tinsley Hill phase is probably not an accurate estimate of the collapse of Mississippian societies in this region. Numerous late Mississippi period artifacts (e.g., figs. 5.10–5.11) have been looted from Tennessee-Cumberland sites by relic hunters for the past 150 years, but little is known about the context or associations of these artifacts. There are also a few artifacts, such as ground astragalus dice from

Figure 5.11 Mississippian bottles from the Jackson Purchase: A, bottle bearing modeled or appliqued forearm bones and hand motifs, Hickman County; B, negative painted bottle with an annular ring base from Trigg County; C, bulbous-leg tetrapod bottle from Trigg County. All specimens are about one-fifth actual size. Young 1910:136; reprinted by permission of The Filson Club, Louisville, Kentucky.

Tinsley Hill (Clay 1961:63) and the Stone site in the Tennessee part of the Barkley Reservoir (Coe and Fischer 1959), that are present in sixteenth-century contexts elsewhere in the Mid-South (Lewis 1988b, 1990c). However, early European artifacts have not been reported from this region.

Western Coal Field

As noted above, the Angel phase spans most of the Mississippi period in the Ohio Valley along the northern edge of the Coal Field. It is followed by the Caborn-Welborn phase (A.D. 1400–1700), which centers on late Mississippi period and protohistoric villages around the confluence of the Wabash and Ohio rivers (Green and Munson 1978:294). Although the Caborn-Welborn phase is far more temporally and spatially circumscribed than the Angel phase, its precise relationship to the Angel phase has yet to be worked out. Nevertheless, Caborn-Welborn clearly developed from local roots (e.g., strong continuity is easily demonstrated between the domestic pottery of the Angel and Caborn-Welborn phases). The end of Caborn-Welborn communities in the Western Coal Field is not known with any great certainty. The problem is complicated by the general lack of eighteenth-century historical accounts from this part of the Ohio Valley.

The Caborn-Welborn settlement pattern was more dispersed than that of the Angel phase (Green and Munson 1978:294). The Angel phase settlement pattern was dominated by one very large community, the Angel site, which was located more or less at the hub of a network of small villages, hamlets, and farmsteads (Green and Munson 1978:294). In the Caborn-Welborn pattern, several large villages shared the social, economic, and political roles formerly held by the Angel site. The lower levels of the settlement hierarchy appear to have changed little from the Angel phase.

The strongest continuity between the Caborn-Welborn and Angel phases is found in the undecorated utilitarian pottery. Decorated pottery is slightly more common in Caborn-Welborn sites, and it differs in some respects from decorated Angel phase wares. In particular, fine-line and trailed incising and punctations are common Caborn-Welborn decorative techniques. These decorated Caborn-Welborn vessels have been favorably compared to northern Midwest (Oneota), eastern Tennessee (Dallas phase), and Lower Mississippi Valley pottery of roughly the same age (Green and Munson 1978:300–302). Too much can be made of these differences in the decorated pottery, because it is not unexpected that pottery from the southernmost tip of Indiana would show more similarity to pottery of the Mississippi Valley and the South than does pottery from the rest of Indiana. It is also true that several motifs are shared between Angel phase negative painted plates and incised Caborn-Welborn jars; detailed analysis may reveal additional similarities.

Caborn-Welborn nonceramic artifacts are basically the same as those of the Angel phase, but with some interesting additions. End scrapers, which are common on many Oneota and late Fort Ancient sites in Ohio and central Kentucky, are also common Caborn-Welborn artifacts. Diagnostic Mississippi Valley late Mississippi period artifacts such as willow leaf-shaped Nodena points and disk pipes (Williams 1980) have also been found at Caborn-Welborn sites.

A total of 23 Caborn-Welborn sites have been identified in Kentucky, all of which are located in the northern Western Coalfield. One of these sites, Slack Farm near Uniontown in Union County, has been partly excavated; the investigation of this site has yielded new information about the nature of Kentucky Caborn-Welborn components. A monograph describing the archaeological investigations at Slack Farm is in preparation (David Pollack, personal communication, 1992).

Other data also suggest a significant Caborn-Welborn phase presence in the Western Coalfield. At the Smithsonian Institution, for example, there is a collection of Mississippian artifacts (catalog nos. 447779–808) from aboriginal graves at Grundy Hill (apparently the Grundy Hill site reported by Webb and Funkhouser [1932:382]) that includes a disk pipe, Barton Incised sherds, and an astragalus die, all of which are associated with late Mississippi period contexts in other parts of the Mid-South.

Lyon (1871:401–03) described a mound on Lost Creek near Morganfield in Union County that "was erected over a stone pavement and contained a burial pit five feet deep filled with skeletons. The mound also showed a large number of intrusive burials of which some were apparently quite recent since in one were found copper bells" (Webb and Funkhouser 1932:382). The site is interesting from several perspectives. First, it provides an Ohio Valley region example of a type of mortuary facility that occurs across south-central Kentucky (e.g., the Page and Hadden sites). Second, there are few reported aboriginal graves with possible Euro-American grave goods from western Kentucky, and at least the intrusive burials in this mound may date to the Caborn-Welborn phase, if not to the Historic period.

Southern and Eastern Pennyroyal

Only two major late Mississippi period sites, Jewell and Rowena, have been excavated in the southern and eastern Pennyroyal. Jewell is located along the Barren River in Barren County. Although it began in the early Mississippi period, the village spanned from A.D. 1000 to 1450 or possibly to A.D. 1550 (Hanson 1970:51–63).

Originally, Jewell had at least three mounds, but only one was still visible when the site was excavated in the early 1960s. As at older Mississippian sites in the Pennyroyal, such as Corbin and Annis Village, the remaining platform mound at Jewell had been constructed in several stages, each of which was capped by one or two buildings (Hanson 1970:22).

There was no delineable plaza in the village and no evidence that it was ever enclosed by a stockade (Hanson 1970:21). As often seen in long-lived Mississippian sites, builders reused old house locations for new constructions. The resulting superimposed house patterns show that average house size became larger over time (Hanson 1970:12). This suggests either that the average family size grew during the early Mississippi period or the organization of household space changed gradually.

Nonceramic Jewell site artifacts include small, triangular projectile points, knives, drills, scrapers, anvils, celts, a chert hoe, and a pick. The pottery assemblage shows a high frequency of Wolf Creek Check Stamped sherds, but the list of types and their relative proportions are much more like contemporaneous western Kentucky assemblages than like those of older sites such as Corbin. The common utility ware was the coarse shell-tempered plain jars, bowls, and pans of the type Mississippi Plain. Small quantities of fine shell-tempered bowls, fabric-impressed pans, and shell-tempered cord-marked, negative painted, and incised sherds were also found (Hanson 1970; Lewis 1990b:table 6).

To the east of Jewell, there are few large Mississippian sites in the Cumberland drainage of the eastern Pennyroyal. The Rowena site, in fact, is the easternmost large Mississippian site to be excavated in Kentucky. This site is characterized as a "small regional center . . . located near a good river crossing on a major [historically documented] trail" (Weinland 1980:134). It consisted of three mounds and an associated village on the second terrace of the Cumberland River in Russell County (Weinland 1980). Excavation of one of the platform mounds revealed that it had been erected in 3–4 stages, each of which had been capped by a large building with walls measuring greater than 8 m on a side. Few details are known about the village area associated with this mound.

More than half the Rowena site potsherds are Mississippi Plain utility wares, followed by McKee Island Cordmarked, Dallas Cordmarked, Dallas Decorated (which shares many general similarities with Matthews Incised from western Kentucky), and Wolf Creek Check Stamped, in that order of frequency (Weinland 1980:97–117). The assemblage is broadly similar to that described from the Jewell site, the differences probably reflecting the length of time the two sites were occupied more than anything else. The Rowena assemblage shows its geographical distance from the Mississippian communities of the Western Coalfield and Jackson Purchase.

MISSISSIPPIAN SITES IN THE BLUEGRASS AND THE MOUNTAINS

Mississippian sites are both sparse and incompletely known in the remainder of Kentucky. This reflects, in part, the archaeological distinction made between the Mississippian and Fort Ancient cultures. Fort Ancient sites are present across most of northern and eastern Kentucky during the Mississippi period. Parts of these regions have the shortest growing seasons and the coldest average temperatures in the state (Karan and Mather 1977:120–21), facts that may have affected the spread of Mississippian farmers into these regions. It would be foolish to draw inferences about Mississippian settlement patterns from climatic data alone, but the relationship between Mississippian and Fort Ancient settlement patterns has yet to be fully explained.

The entrenched stream valleys and narrow floodplains of the Bluegrass and the Mountains apparently offered little to Mississippian groups. Evidence of Mississippian occupations is limited to the Louisville area of the western Bluegrass and the extreme southeastern corner of the state.

For years there was no consensus among archaeologists that Mississippian cultural tradition sites were present in the Falls of the Ohio locality at Louisville (cf. Granger et al. 1981; Kellar 1973). Several Mississippian sites on the Indiana side of the Ohio River have been excavated (Guernsey 1939, 1942), but few details about these sites are available. Griffin's assessment sums up many researchers' feelings about the late prehistory of this region: "The Louisville area seems to have been the eastern border of Mississippian sites but no significant analysis of any of the material–which apparently represents important settlements–has been published" (1978b:551).

In the southeastern Mountains, Pisgah phase sites are present in Harlan, Letcher, and Perry counties (Niquette and Henderson 1984:54;

Figure 5.12   Yellow pine figurine of a man found in a dry cave or rockshelter near Pineville, Bell County, in 1869. It measures 65 cm high and is 23 cm wide at the base. Pepper 1928: plates 1-2; courtesy of the National Museum of the American Indian, Smithsonian Institution.

Schock 1977). Pisgah spans most of the Mississippi period in the southern Appalachian Mountains (Dickens 1976), but only a few Kentucky components have been identified. Site 15Hl304 in Harlan County was a small late Mississippi period hamlet of possibly two houses constructed on a low floodplain knoll. Excavation of one of these houses revealed a square structure that measured about 5 m on each side. It was set in a shallow basin and contained no interior features. Radiocarbon age estimates suggest that the house dates to between A.D. 1300 and 1400 (Lewis 1990b).

The last Mountains location to be described, Site 15Bl10, is also Kentucky's most unusual Mississippian site, partly because it is made entirely of wood and partly because it is in New York City. The Heye Foundation–Museum of the American Indian contains this "site," a yellow pine human figure found in the mid-1800s by L. Farmer in a dry cave or rockshelter near Pineville, Bell County (Young 1910:268–69). The figurine represents a seated or kneeling man whose hands rest on the outside of each thigh (fig. 5.12). Fine details of facial and other features of this figurine are obliterated, but Young (1910:269) reports that one ear was pierced as though for jewelry. The figurine's pose, the placement of the hands, its size, and other features strongly resemble Wilbanks phase (A.D. 1200–1450) stone figures from Etowah, a Mississippian site in northern Georgia (Brown 1985:plates 140–41). No other large wooden artifacts are known in Kentucky.

DISCUSSION

Chronology

Regional chronological sequences provide the means to an end. Local spatial and temporal relationships and developments must be well understood before archaeologists can address other research questions. Therefore, it is useful to begin the examination of Kentucky Mississippian trends by reviewing the major chronological issues.

Maize agriculture is one of the fundamental cultural changes associated with the Mississippian tradition, and it is convenient to mark the beginning of the Mississippi period at A.D. 900, by which time this important economic development was well underway. There is no reason to believe, however, that this and other important cultural changes of the Mississippian tradition sprang up suddenly and fully developed across Kentucky. Such an image is fostered by archaeologists' use of stage-like periods and phases in which the afternoon of December 31, A.D. 899 was still the Late Woodland and the following dawn ushered in a brand new period. The Mississippian cultural tradition did not arise anywhere as a monolithic bundle of economic, social, political, or religious traits. Rather, the earliest recognizable form of the tradition emerged gradually from close interaction among groups across much of the East, and it continued to develop and change throughout the period.

By A.D. 1700 Euro-American colonists began to spread throughout the Mississippi Valley. They soon entered the midcontinent, but there is remarkably little ethnohistorical information about native communities of western and southern Kentucky–the core of the Mississippian part of the state. It is likely that most Kentucky communities of the Mississippian cultural tradition were probably abandoned sometime between A.D. 1500 and 1700 due to diseases and other indirect effects of the presence of Europeans in the Southeast. Consequently, almost all of the Kentucky Mississippian communities lie beyond the pale of written history.

Based on the dubious value of negative evidence, some archaeologists argue that much of Kentucky and adjacent states was abandoned by native populations sometime after A.D. 1300, but well before the earliest possible arrival of Europeans or their diseases in the midcontinent. Like the "Mississippian heartland" notion, it is an idea that has deep roots in the literature and can be traced for more than a century back in American history and archaeological thought. The available Kentucky data do not support this hypothesis. There does not appear to have been a significant depopulation of western and southern Kentucky until at least the 1500s and the beginning of the European presence on this continent.

Social and Political Organization

Most archaeologists view Mississippian societies as typical examples of chiefdoms in which leadership roles were ascribed, society was ranked, and the power of chiefs could be great but was usually not absolute. For a long time it was believed that the power of the chief was maintained by the essential role that he or she played in the control of resources and their redistribution within society. It has since been discovered that the redistributive function of the chief, as traditionally conceived, may have been neither as significant nor as widespread as once thought (Kreisa 1990:26–29).

Social status differences existed among the members of Kentucky Mississippian societies, but they were not extreme. The elite may have enjoyed the right of access to some areas of towns, and possibly to some resources, that were denied to other villagers. Nevertheless, no status differences have come to light that are as striking as the elaborate grave offerings and mass human sacrifices revealed, for example, at the Cahokia site in the American Bottom of southwestern Illinois (Fowler 1989:144–50). This may reflect real differences between Illinois and Kentucky Mississippian societies, or it may merely be the case that research on Kentucky Mississippian sites has not focused on contexts within which elaborate graves are likely to be found.

The politics of kinship are fundamental to understanding the organization of many Mississippian communities, including those of Kentucky. The kinship ties of the "elite" members of society, the relationship between members of the dominant family or families, the principal town, and the bones of revered ancestors contained in a town's temple, charnel house, or mortuary cist defined a Mississippian community in social terms. In this sense, these prehistoric towns and villages were profoundly different from the Euro-American settlements that eventually replaced them.

Nevertheless, the social definition of a Mississippian community becomes a slippery concept when one considers a truly unusual site such as Page in Logan County. The scientific understanding of Page is limited to Webb and Funkhouser's (1930) description of the excavation of a platform mound and numerous slab-lined, bone-filled mortuary cists there in the late 1920s. Very likely, the Page cists were processing facilities for the deceased individuals of the village. Although he does not address the Page case, Clay (1984:140–44) gives a similar interpretation to the "stone box" graves commonly found in Mississippian contexts across Kentucky. He also notes that social distinctions are identifiable in the treatment of some of the Mississippian dead in western Kentucky.

In many prehistoric societies of the Midwest and Mid-South, the manner in which the dead were handled suggests that infants and small children were seldom afforded the same social status as full members of the community into which they were born. Allen's (1984) analysis of human skeletal remains at the Adams town site in Fulton County revealed that infants and small children were often buried in house floors, wall trenches, or in the town middens. The remains of adults and juveniles are less common in these contexts, and most individuals above a certain age were probably buried in designated cemetery areas, such as have been found at Mississippian sites elsewhere in Kentucky. The latter pattern, that of separating in death the adults and juveniles from the infants, was a common Mississippian practice. A good example is at the Wickliffe town site in Ballard County, where the Mound C and Mound D burials exhibit a strong age bias.

Exchange and Interaction

For many decades it was believed that western Kentucky and the neighboring regions of adjacent states formed a "Mississippian heartland," the point of origin for the Mississippian cultural tradition. Mississippian culture was thought to have diffused outward from this region and eventually to have dominated the final centuries of prehistory in the East. Portions of the "Mississippian heartland" hypothesis were recently laid to rest by Smith (1984), but its legacy lives on in many published interpretations of late prehistoric developments in Kentucky. These interpretations invoke migrations of Mississippian groups into a given region as the primary cause of late prehistoric cultural changes. It is an idea that recalls Frederick Jackson Turner's (1920) "frontier hypothesis" for the opening of the American West. Just as many aspects of our understanding of the West changed with the passing of the frontier hypothesis, the image of Mississippian migrants is vanishing with the heartland hypothesis.

If invading hordes of Mississippian colonists can no longer be depended upon to account for the spread of this cultural tradition, what other mecha-

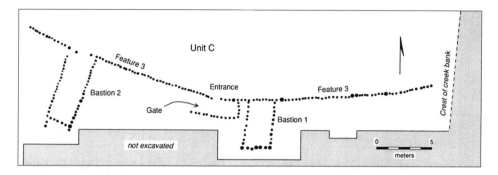

Figure 5.13   Palisade line at Jonathan Creek showing apron-type gate and bastions.
Adapted from Webb 1952:23.

nism exists? The most robust answer is simply the sustained interaction, on
many different levels, that, when taken together, formed a regional social
web of communities.

Mississippian interaction and trade did have a spatial focus. The western
and southern Kentucky communities share their greatest similarities of technology, decorative motifs and styles, village layout, mortuary treatment, and
other features with contemporaneous societies in the Tennessee-Cumberland
drainages of Tennessee and northern Alabama. There were also strong ties to
the major Mississippian towns, such as Kincaid and Angel in the Ohio Valley.
Towns and villages in the lower Mississippi Valley of Tennessee, Arkansas,
and Mississippi, on the other hand, appear to have had less impact on the
course of events and the lifeways of Kentucky Mississippian groups, except
along the extreme western border of the state. Even there, the cultural ties to
the Tennessee-Cumberland drainages remained strong.

Warfare is an apparently inevitable form of social interaction, and it was
certainly a part of Mississippian life. The most abundant archaeological evidence of Mississippian warfare is the remains of defensive fortifications.
Large villages and towns were often enclosed by wooden stockades at least
once, if not several times, during their existence. These fortifications range
from simple palisades to the deeply bastioned works with covered, apron-type
gates found at Jonathan Creek (fig. 5.13).

But warfare against whom? Defense against whom? Back when the
Mississippian heartland hypothesis was viable, the answer was fairly simple–invaders seeking to expand their territories. The answer still is a simple
one, although perhaps less romantic–fighting with one's neighbors.
Territorial expansion does not appear to have been a significant motive for
war. If anything, conflict may have been stimulated more by the desire or
ambition of individuals to acquire prestige in their communities than by the
intent to acquire territory, captives, or other resources.

Settlement Patterns

One of the most distinctive changes from the Late Woodland period is the increase in the diversity and organizational complexity of settlements. For example, only villages and farmsteads can be identified during the Late Woodland period in extreme western Kentucky, but by the late Mississippi period communities were organized in three delineable levels and five types of sites that ranged in size and complexity from towns to farmsteads (Kreisa 1990:131–39).

The Mississippi period settlement system was hierarchical (Peebles 1974; Phillips et al. 1951; Smith 1978). At the apex of this hierarchy were the large towns, such as the Adams site in Fulton County, which contained central plazas, mound complexes, and many inhabitants. At the hierarchy's base were the considerably smaller, less archaeologically visible, but far more abundant hamlets and farmsteads. In between, there is little agreement among archaeologists as to the exact nature and complexity of the settlement levels that separated the top and bottom of this hierarchy (e.g., Fowler 1978; Muller 1978; Price 1978; Smith 1978). Nevertheless, the fundamental differences between levels tend to be viewed as a gross gradient of decreased site size, decreased resident population size, fewer platform mounds and other earthworks, fewer public spaces, and increased site type abundance from the top of the hierarchy to its base.

Research in Kentucky has shown that the traditional hierarchical model is not universally true of Mississippian settlements. Kreisa (1988, 1990) demonstrates that the western Kentucky Mississippian settlement system combined aspects of both hierarchical and heterarchical frameworks. Kreisa (1990:146–47) describes it as a "dualistic" system in which food production and other essential economic activities took place in all sites, whether they were towns or hamlets; elite members of society coordinated and controlled the design, construction, and maintenance of the mound and plaza complex that formed the distinctive core of towns and villages; the chief dealt primarily with issues and policies that affected society as a whole, and decisions concerning the day-to-day functioning of individual communities remained at the local level.

Viewed archaeologically, towns are the most impressive Mississippian settlements. They are the largest sites, contain the greatest concentrations of mounds and other earthworks, and are the most difficult to investigate. In extreme western Kentucky, towns were often occupied for hundreds of years, if not for the entire Mississippi period. Typically, these settlements also rest on the remains of Late Woodland villages. It is not yet understood, however, why some Mississippian towns were abandoned during the period while towns only a few kilometers away were unaffected.

Farther to the east, in the Western Coalfield and the Pennyroyal, Mississippian towns and villages may not have endured as long as the towns along the Mississippi, lower Ohio, and Tennessee-Cumberland valleys. The difference appears to be on the order of communities lasting at most one or two centuries, while in the Jackson Purchase comparable communities might endure for more than half of a millennium. The village middens of the Western Coalfield and Pennyroyal sites are thinner; there is less evidence of house-basin reuse; the assemblages span a shorter interval of prehistory; and settlements usually contain fewer mounds and earthworks than sites in the major river valley towns. These and other differences suggest that several Mississippian settlement systems existed across Kentucky. The cultural implications of these different settlement systems are poorly understood by archaeologists.

Economy

The development of maize agriculture is a hallmark of the Mississippian cultural tradition. Viewed archaeologically, the evidence of the Late Woodland/Mississippi period economic shift from a mixed hunting, gathering, horticulture strategy to a strong emphasis on maize agriculture is striking (Sussenbach 1993). Where occupations older than A.D. 900 tend to yield few if any preserved fragments of maize, younger occupations have fragments of maize in every examined soil sample.

Although agriculture and the principal cultivated plants–maize, beans, squash, and gourds–were of overwhelming economic importance, older crops, gathered foods, and game continued to be important in the Mississippian diet. In extreme western Kentucky, gathered plant foods included hickory nuts, persimmons, and the seeds of goosefoot, erect knotweed, and maygrass (Dunavan 1985). Common game animals were whitetail deer, wild turkeys, turtles, and fish.

Tools and Technology

Mississippian tools, containers, ornaments, and other objects differ considerably from those of older periods. Many of these differences are merely stylistic. Other fundamental differences reflect the major economic and social changes of the Mississippian tradition and, sometimes, the local availability of certain raw materials.

Mississippian assemblages also differ from region to region. The Mississippi Valley and lower Ohio Valley towns and villages typically have very sparse stone tool assemblages and extensive evidence of the recycling of old, broken, or unusable tools into new implements. These communities are in regions where usable chert sources are scarce, except for the nearly ubiquitous deposits of small chert gravel and cobbles. Chert for tools larger than projectile points had to come from the Tennessee-Cumberland valleys and from southern Illinois. Contemporaneous sites elsewhere in Kentucky enjoyed ready access to extensive local chert sources. The assemblages at sites in the latter regions are more diverse and show much less evidence of stone tool recycling.

Pottery technology also changed much during the period. Until about A.D. 1300, the surface finishes of utilitarian vessels in western Kentucky, where the data are the most complete, tend to be plain, fabric-impressed, or red-filmed. Common vessels were globular jars, hemispherical bowls, flanged-rim bowls, hooded bottles, and pans. Incised vessels are rare. Between A.D. 1300 and the end of the Mississippian presence, incised jars, bowls, and plates become common and red-filming diminishes in popularity. Decorated pots, however, never account for more than 3–5 percent of the total vessel assemblage.

The final artifacts to be discussed, those of sixteenth-century European manufacture, have never been reported from sites in Kentucky, but they have been found in Mississippian contexts in Missouri and Tennessee. Although it is unlikely that the sixteenth-century Spanish explorers entered the Kentucky region, there is no reason a priori why trade goods, cast-off gear, and other material evidence of their presence could not have found its way into Kentucky Mississippian sites. The only glimpse that we have yet of artifacts that may date to this century is Lyon's (1871) Union County report of copper bells found with burials that were intrusive into a mound. Unfortunately, all we have is Lyon's account; the bells, which could be easily dated, cannot be found today. Were they Clarksdale style bells (Brain 1975), similar to those found in sixteenth-century contexts at the late Mississippian sites of Campbell in southeastern Missouri and Parkin in northeastern Arkansas (Morse 1981:69–70), a new chapter would be opened in Kentucky archaeology.

Nutrition and Health

Little is known about the general health of Kentucky Mississippian populations. The most informative research is based on analyses of human skeletons from burials. For example, Lewellyn (1964) compared data for 127 Mississippi period individuals from the Tinsley Hill cemetery in Lyon County with information for 22 individuals from the Long site, located across the state in Russell County. His results show that the Tinsley Hill site inhabitants were a heterogeneous population in which effects such as enamel hypoplasia and dental caries were common (Lewellyn 1964:30, 38–39). The

Long site population, on the other hand, was a homogeneous one that exhibited fewer caries, but significantly more occlusal wear. Lewellyn (1964:38) infers that these conditions may reflect the greater dependence upon maize agriculture by the Tinsley Hill site inhabitants.

SUMMARY

The fabric of society experienced fundamental changes in the final 800 years of Kentucky prehistory. From these political, social, and economic changes emerged larger scale societies than had previously existed in the midcontinent. These societies were part of a developmental web that spanned much of the East and the South.

The core of the Mississippian tradition was the agriculturally based chiefdom. Settlement was dualistic, with one or a few major towns as the leading or principal communities and a heterarchy of smaller sites in which most people lived. The power of chiefs does not appear to have been absolute. Viewed in that light, the Kentucky Mississippian societies may have been qualitatively different from the powerful and tightly controlled Mississippian chiefdoms of the American Bottom region of Illinois.

The Mississippi tradition did not emerge full-blown in A.D. 900. It also did not develop in a single heartland, nor was it the product of diffusion from prehistoric states in Mesoamerica. It was an indigenous, essentially pansoutheastern development out of local Late Woodland cultures.

The Mississippi period effectively marks the end of the aboriginal archaeological record in western and southern Kentucky. By the beginning of extensive Euro-American colonization in the late 1700s, the Mississippian towns and villages of Kentucky had apparently long been abandoned.

6

FORT ANCIENT FARMERS

William E. Sharp

The late prehistoric groups of north-central and northeastern Kentucky are known archaeologically as the Fort Ancient tradition (fig. 6.1). Fort Ancient sites are also present in adjacent regions of southeastern Indiana, southern Ohio, and western West Virginia (Griffin 1966). These groups shared with other late prehistoric people of eastern North America an agricultural economy based on the cultivation of maize, beans, and squash. Hunting, fishing, and gathering of wild plant food resources continued to be important aspects of Fort Ancient subsistence.

The Fort Ancient and Mississippian traditions were contemporaneous. Material culture was similar, but subtle differences in the styles and decorations of pottery and in stone and bone tools distinguish Fort Ancient and Mississippian assemblages. Material culture differences are more pronounced early in the sequence, suggesting that the two traditions developed from somewhat different Late Woodland patterns.

Like many contemporaneous Mississippian sites, by A.D. 1200 Fort Ancient villages often contained a central plaza ringed by houses; palisades also enclosed some villages. The most important distinction between Fort Ancient and Mississippian traditions is the absence of platform mounds at Fort Ancient sites. Such mounds, when found at Mississippian sites, are interpreted as the focus of community social, political, and religious activity (Lewis, chapt. 5). The implication is that Fort Ancient and Mississippian farmers were organized into groups in a different manner.

Fort Ancient culture thrived in the middle Ohio Valley until after European exploration of North America was well underway, as shown by the number of European trade items found in late Fort Ancient sites. It has been difficult, however, to establish a definite link between the Fort Ancient archaeological culture and historically documented Native American peoples.

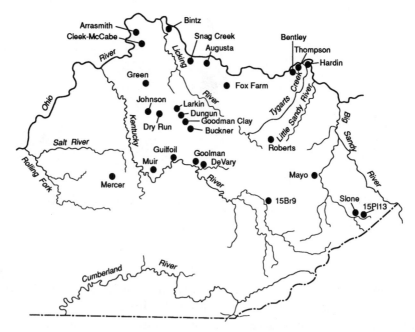

Figure 6.1   Eastern Kentucky showing Fort Ancient sites discussed in the text.

This chapter examines Fort Ancient chronology in three parts—early Fort Ancient (A.D. 1000–1200), middle Fort Ancient (A.D. 1200–1400), and late Fort Ancient (A.D. 1400–1750). The discussion of each part also examines important Fort Ancient chronological trends and archaeological phases (Dunnell 1961, 1972; Henderson et al. 1992; Turnbow and Sharp 1988) and their implications. The final section examines selected aspects of Fort Ancient culture.

FORT ANCIENT BEFORE A.D. 1200

Early Fort Ancient phases include Osborne in the Inner Bluegrass (Turnbow and Sharp 1988) and Croghan on the Ohio River in Greenup County (Henderson et al. 1992). Representative early sites include Muir, Dry Run, Thompson, and possibly Dungun and Goodman Clay (fig. 6.1).

Muir, the best-documented Osborne phase component, is a hamlet occupied between A.D. 1000 and 1100 in central Jessamine County. It consisted of several households scattered along a broad ridge crest near Jessamine Creek. The site plan differs from the compact site form of many later Fort Ancient villages.

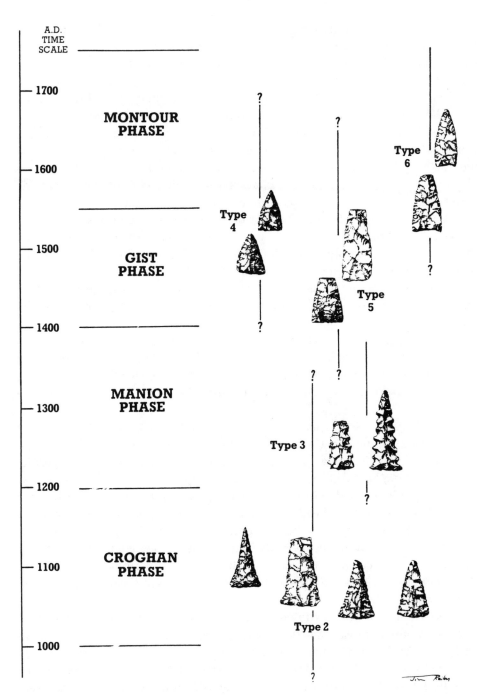

Figure 6.2 Stylistic developments in Fort Ancient triangular point morphology, Henderson and Turnbow 1987:215.

Each household at Muir was defined archaeologically by the remains of a house surrounded by refuse-filled pits and burned patches of soil; bare areas that contained few features and artifacts separated each household. The rectangular houses were small, had single-set post walls, and were set in 30–50 cm deep basins. The house floors usually contained small, probably centrally located hearths. These houses were used for sleeping and storage.

Most of the ceramic vessels at Muir were limestone-tempered Jessamine Cordmarked jars. The rims of these jars often have thick strap or loop handles with castellations on the rim above the handle. Handles and the occasional use of shell as temper are characteristics that distinguish Jessamine series pottery from earlier Late Woodland pottery. Small McAfee Plain "pinchpot" molded bowls were the only other vessel form identified.

Other Osborne phase artifacts are clay earspools, clay elbow pipes, clay discoidals, sandstone pipes, and long, narrow "Type 2" triangular projectile points (fig. 6.2). Local chert sources, which included many Kentucky River chert cobbles, supplied most of the raw material for flaked stone tools. Bone tools include reamers, awls, and other perforating and hide working implements.

The Osborne villagers at Muir depended heavily on large game, especially whitetail deer, elk, bear, and wild turkey. Other animals found at the Muir site are beaver, raccoon, gray fox, dog, gray squirrel, woodchuck, otter, bobcat, and opossum. Fish and mussels contributed little to the diet (Breitburg 1988).

The villagers also raised corn and beans and may have cultivated erect knotweed and sunflowers (Rossen 1988). Corn was found in all archaeological features and was probably an important part of the diet. Unlike older prehistoric economies, Fort Ancient groups did not depend heavily on wild nuts or the starchy-oily seeds of native cultivated plants (Rossen and Edging 1987).

Burials have not yet been found on any Osborne phase site, and mortuary facilities appear to have been separate from the villages, as they were during most of the Woodland periods (Clay 1985a; Railey, chap. 4). Two isolated Bourbon County stone mounds, Goodman Clay and Dungun (Clay 1984) used between A.D. 1000–1200, may be early Fort Ancient (i.e., Osborne phase) burial sites.

The Thompson site, situated on a long, low rise in the Ohio Valley of Greenup County across from the mouth of the Scioto River, also contains an early Fort Ancient component, in this case one of the Croghan phase, which dates between A.D. 1000 and 1200 (Henderson and Turnbow 1987). The assemblage resembles that of contemporaneous Baum phase sites in the central Scioto Valley of Ohio. Most vessels were grit-tempered, cordmarked jars, the rims of which bear strap or loop handles or U-shaped lugs (fig. 6.3).

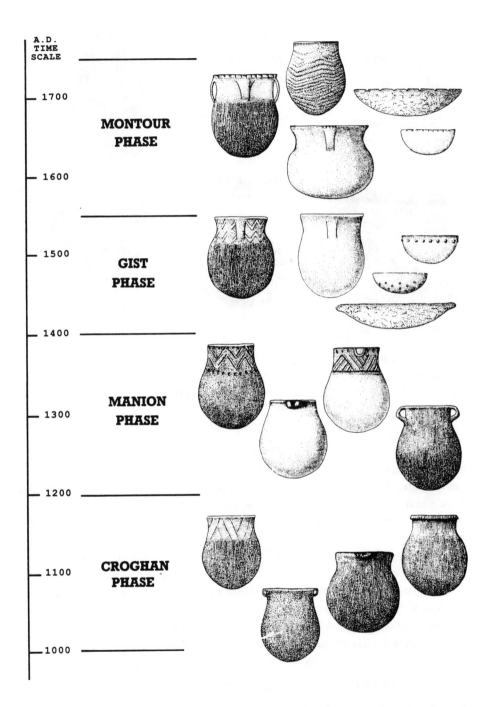

Figure 6.3 Fort Ancient pottery form and stylistic developments, based on investigations at six northeastern Kentucky sites. Henderson and Turnbow 1987:212.

Figure 6.4   Baum Cordmarked Incised rims and appendages from the Croghan component at the Thompson site: A-B, wedge-shape rim strips, thicker at the base than at the lip; C-D, line-filled triangle incised motif; E-F, semicircular lugs.

Wedge-shaped, cordmarked rim strips are common on Croghan jars (fig. 6.4). Type 2 triangular points (fig. 6.2) were the only point type associated with the Croghan component. Food remains, like those at Muir, are mostly large game and corn. No burials or house remains were excavated at the Thompson site.

To summarize, the Osborne and Croghan phases provide evidence of the increased importance of agriculture and sedentary village life in central and northeastern Kentucky between A.D. 1000 and 1200. Archaeological investigations of Kentucky components also show that Fort Ancient was an indigenous development and not the result of replacement of local Woodland groups by Mississippian migrations, as proposed by Prufer and Shane (1970).

MIDDLE FORT ANCIENT (A.D. 1200–1400)

Even though only one phase, Manion in Mason County (Henderson et al. 1992), is defined for Middle Fort Ancient, information on Fort Ancient sites dating between A.D. 1200 and 1400, is well documented. Important Middle

Fort Ancient components include Arrasmith, Buckner, Cleek-McCabe, Fox Farm, Green, Guilfoil, Johnson, and Mercer Village (fig. 6.1).

Between A.D. 1200 and 1400, Fort Ancient villages were often either a ring of 20–30 houses and household refuse around a plaza, or a line of houses that followed the natural trend of a ridge or river terrace. The former pattern can be readily identified in the map of the two circular village and plaza patterns at the Buckner site in Bourbon County (fig. 6.5). Guilfoil, an average thirteenth-century circular village in Fayette County, measures 100 by 125 m (Fassler 1987). This and comparable villages probably had populations of 100–300 individuals.

The houses at Buckner were rectangular and larger than the older Osborne phase houses in the same region. Built in shallow basins with a cen-

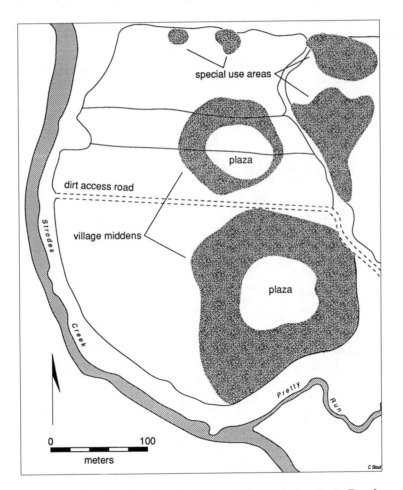

Figure 6.5 The surface distribution of midden at the Buckner site in Bourbon County reveals the location of two circular village and plaza patterns.

tral fire hearth, some houses had walls made by setting posts in trenches. Pits and other evidence for domestic activity are present to the side or behind the houses, and burials are located in front of the houses toward the plaza.

Some circular villages have burials near the houses and small burial mounds on the plaza edge (Henderson et al. 1992). This inclusion of mortuary activity and facilities into a domestic setting is a radical change from older patterns.

Cleek-McCabe, a middle Fort Ancient circular village in Boone County, contains two mounds located on opposite sides of the midden ring. One of these mounds, which was excavated in the 1930s, contained the remains of 21 individuals and many rock concentrations, burned areas, prepared clay hearths, and post molds (Goodell 1971). Beneath the mound were found the remains of several large rectangular buildings that contained fired areas, a prepared clay hearth, limestone slab platforms, and burials (fig. 6.6). These structures covered the remains of yet another building, a circular one measuring 13 m in diameter (Rafferty 1974). These structures may have been charnel houses. The construction sequence and overlap of the structures also

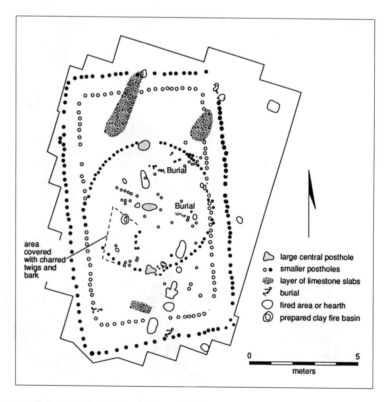

Figure 6.6 Submound structures beneath the Cleek-McCabe mound in Boone County. Adapted from Rafferty 1974:122.

show that the location of the circular building directly influenced where the other structures and, ultimately, the mound were built. This suggests that each building and the mound were linked together either by ritual or by the association with the place covered by the mound. It also implies that the mound marked the end of a ritual cycle that had begun decades earlier with the construction of the circular building.

Another important middle Fort Ancient site is Fox Farm, a large (10–16 ha), complex village situated on a broad ridge about 10 km south of the Ohio River and 2.5 km south of the Licking River in Mason County (Turnbow 1992). The site contains evidence of a long Fort Ancient occupation, which is preserved in an 80-cm-thick midden. The earliest occupation at the site is a Manion phase component.

Typical Manion phase vessels were shell- or limestone-tempered, cord-marked jars with lugged rims or rims with thick strap or loop handles (figs.

Figure 6.7 Manion phase jar sherds from the Fox Farm site: A-F, Fox Farm Cordmarked rims and appendages; G-I, incised and punctated rims and body sherds.

6.3, 6.7 A–F). The necks of some jars were decorated with wide-line incised or punctated designs (fig. 6.7 G–I). As during early Fort Ancient, there are a number of regional ceramic styles in the Bluegrass and along the Ohio River during this time, but all show a general similarity and all assemblages are dominated by jars.

Nonceramic Manion phase artifacts include serrated Type 3 and nonserrated Type 5 triangular projectile points (fig. 6.2), sandstone discoidals, elbow pipes, celts, grooved abraders, crudely chipped limestone disks, bone tools, and bone and shell beads.

Farming was an important source of food for middle Fort Ancient villagers (Rossen 1987, 1992). The Fox Farm Manion component was especially rich in corn kernels and cobs and domestic beans. Whitetail deer, elk, bear, and turkey continued to be the most important game animals (Breitburg 1992, Tune 1987).

In summary, by A.D. 1200 Fort Ancient groups in Kentucky were true village farmers. It is clear, however, that hunting continued to be an important part of their economy. Some differences in social status within these communities may be reflected in who got buried in mounds and who was interred in front of their house. The number and spatial distribution of sites and the similar, but distinctive regional material culture suggest that each village was relatively autonomous.

FORT ANCIENT AFTER A.D. 1400

Around A.D. 1400, the forms and styles of domestic pottery in the central Ohio Valley became more homogeneous. Village size increased, but the number of villages decreased. Burial mounds disappeared from the archaeological record. Burials were placed near houses, in what appear to be family cemetery areas. Often stone slabs cover the tops of graves. Villagers continued to rely heavily on corn and large game animals, much like their predecessors (Breitburg 1992; Rossen 1992). Native American and, later, Euro-American items on Fort Ancient sites after A.D. 1400 indicate increased extraregional Fort Ancient exchange.

Archaeologists call these trends the Madisonville horizon. An archaeological *horizon* is some cultural complex or other bundle of cultural objects or ideas that spreads rapidly over a large area but does not last long. The Madisonville horizon does precisely that; it marks widespread trends in the central Ohio Valley in the final centuries before the beginning of sustained contact with Europeans.

Along the Ohio River in northeastern Kentucky, the Madisonville horizon includes two archaeological phases—Gist (A.D. 1400–1550) and Montour (A.D. 1550–1750) (Henderson et al. 1992). Madisonville horizon sites include

Figure 6.8 Madisonville Cordmarked jar from the Hardin Village site in Greenup County. This specimen measures 15 cm high. Reproduced by permission of the William S. Webb Museum of Anthropology, University of Kentucky, negative 4177.

Augusta (Hale 1981), Bentley, Bintz, DeVary, Goolman, Hardin, Larkin, Snag Creek (fig. 6.1), and others. All are large villages, except for Goolman and DeVary, which are small winter hunting camps (Turnbow et al. 1983).

During the early part of the Madisonville horizon, the typical cord-marked jars of earlier Fort Ancient sites were replaced by globular, shell-tempered cordmarked and plain jars of the Madisonville series (fig. 6.8). These jars usually have smoothed necks and thin strap handles along the rims (fig. 6.9). Decoration, which was more common early in the horizon, includes curvilinear and rectilinear patterns incised on the smooth neck area of jars (fig. 6.9).

Hemispherical bowls also became common, accounting for about 25–40 percent of assemblages (Henderson et al. 1992). Bowl decoration was usually confined to notching the lip of the bowl; occasionally, a notched or beaded horizontal strip of clay was added just below the rim. Bowls also may have tab handles or small effigy figurines on the rim.

Other introduced Madisonville horizon vessel forms include large, shallow bowls called saltpans. These vessels were used throughout most of the horizon. Later in the horizon, a perforated vessel called a colander occured at a limited number of sites.

Madisonville horizon triangular projectile points are exclusively Types 4, 5, and 6 (fig. 6.2). Bifacial end scrapers are another distinctive artifact found frequently on later horizon sites (Railey 1992). Functional and ornamental artifacts made of bone, antler, or shell are common.

The Madisonville horizon, as remarked above, brings the archaeology of some Fort Ancient communities into the historic era. The Hardin Village site (Hanson 1966) is a well-described representative component. Hardin Village was occupied between A.D. 1500 and the early 1600s (Hanson 1966; Pollack

Figure 6.9   Madisonville Cordmarked: A-C, jar handles; D-F, decorated sherds.

and Henderson 1983). It covers about 4.5 ha of the first terrace of the Ohio River in northeastern Greenup County. Excavation of about 10 percent of the site in 1939 uncovered the remains of 301 graves, 189 refuse-filled pits, 45 burned soil areas, and 6 houses.

The houses were large, rectangular buildings that ranged in size from 6 by 17 m to 9 by 22 m. Similar houses are known from contemporaneous sites in the same general region (e.g., Bentley, which is described below, and the Buffalo site [Hanson 1975] in West Virginia). They differ greatly, however, from older Fort Ancient houses.

The size and design of the Hardin Village buildings resemble small Iroquoian longhouses (e.g., Heidenreich 1978:376–77). Longhouses were bark mat-covered, multiple-family dwellings. The fireplaces that dotted the length of a longhouse were shared by two or more families, who would cook, eat, live, and store their food and personal belongings in their share of the longhouse space. Flimsy partitions sometimes divided a building into individual family cubicles. Hardin Village houses were probably similar multiple-family dwellings.

The Hardin Village pottery was mostly Madisonville series cordmarked or plain vessels. Other fired clay artifacts were pottery disks, sherd scrapers, pestles, pipes, effigies, anvils, balls, rattles, spoons, pendants, and ear plugs. Distinctive nonceramic artifacts were small triangular projectile points, bifacial end scrapers, disk pipes, bone and shell beads, and shell gorgets (fig.

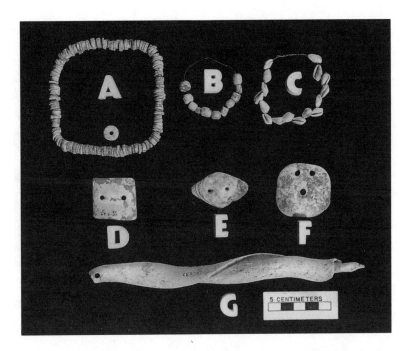

Figure 6.10 Shell artifacts from the Hardin Village site: A, disk beads; B, barrel-shaped beads; C, marginella beads; D-F, gorgets; G; conch columella pendant. Hanson 1966:154. Reprinted from Lee H. Hanson Jr., *The Hardin Village Site*, copyright © 1966 by the University of Kentucky Press, by permission of the publisher.

6.10). The shell gorgets consist of engraved Citico-style rattlesnakes, crosses, and masks (fig. 6.11), as well as round, rectangular, and diamond-shaped plain specimens.

A few Euro-American copper or brass objects were also acquired through trade and reworked into ornaments by native craftsmen (fig. 6.12). No Euro-American tools or other utilitarian items were found at Hardin Village, which suggests that the villagers did not have direct contact with Old World colonists.

Mention of metals and the possibility of European contacts brings us into the early Historic period. Researchers have long questioned whether there is a firm relationship between prehistoric Fort Ancient culture and historically recorded Native American groups (Griffin 1966; Hanson 1966; Henderson et al. 1986). Thus far, the only investigated Kentucky site that bears on this question is Bentley.

The Bentley site, also known as Lower Shawneetown, lies 13 km downstream from Hardin Village (fig. 6.1). It covers 1.2 ha of the second terrace of the Ohio River directly across from the former mouth of the Scioto River in southern Ohio. Excavation of a small part of the Fort Ancient component in

Figure 6.11   Citico-style engraved rattlesnake gorget, shell mask gorget, and shell beads from a burial at Hardin Village. Reproduced by permission of the William S. Webb Museum of Anthropology, University of Kentucky, negative 4158.

Figure 6.12   Madisonville Cordmarked jar, brass/copper tubes and beads, and shell beads from a Hardin Village burial. The jar stands 16 cm tall. Reproduced by permission of the William S. Webb Museum of Anthropology, University of Kentucky, negative 4157.

the late 1930s revealed clusters of "smudge pits" filled with carbonized corn, refuse-filled pits, rock piles, post molds, and the remains of one structure (Pollack and Henderson 1983, 1984). This rectangular building, which measured 9 by 15 m, was similar in size and shape to the Hardin Village longhouses described above.

The Bentley assemblage contained Madisonville cordmarked, plain, and grooved-paddle jars, small triangular projectile points, bifacial end scrapers, disk-type and other pipes, and Euro-American trade items. Few bone tools or shell ornaments were recovered. Euro-American trade goods were found with Fort Ancient burials as well as in features and village midden. These are not reworked Euro-American objects, as were found at Hardin Village. The Bentley site non-native artifacts include rifle parts, domestic implements (fig. 6.13), and ornaments.

Bentley is probably the remains of an eighteenth-century Shawnee village called Lower Shawneetown (Henderson et al. 1986; Pollack and Henderson 1984). In 1751 about 1,200 people lived at Lower Shawneetown, and it was one of the major villages on the Ohio River from the mid-1730s to 1758 (Henderson et al. 1986). Besides the Shawnee, the villagers included members of the Five Nations Iroquois and Canadian Iroquois from near Montreal, Delaware from the Atlantic Seaboard, and other Native American groups. A few French or English traders also lived full- or part-time at this village. Although the village layout of Lower Shawneetown is unknown, the estimated population size and historic accounts suggest that the village probably covered a large area on both sides of the Ohio River.

Not all Madisonville sites were villages. As remarked at the beginning of this section, late Fort Ancient winter hunting camps have also been excavated at the Goolman and DeVary sites, both of which are located in a small sheltered valley in eastern Clark County (Turnbow et al. 1983; Turnbow and Jobe 1984).

The Goolman site contained three small houses with an associated assemblage of hunting and hide-processing tools. The largest structure was a 4 by 5 m rectangular communal building with walls defined by large, deeply set posts placed about 1 m apart. The floor and hearth area contained abundant household refuse, suggesting it was intensively used.

To either side of the large building were two smaller oval structures, each of which was 2.5–3 m wide and 4–5 m long. Inside these buildings, which were probably sleeping quarters, were centrally located hearths and a few artifacts.

Sherds of Madisonville series plain and cordmarked jars with thin strap handles were found in and around the houses. Most of the Goolman site projectile points are Type 5 and 6 (fig. 6.2) triangular specimens.

In keeping with the characterization of the site as a winter hunting camp, few plant remains, most of which were wood charcoal and nutshells,

Figure 6.11   Euro-American artifacts from the Bentley site: A-E, rifle parts; F, brass/copper kettle ear; G, iron scissor fragment; H, clasp knife with a pistol grip handle. Pollack and Henderson 1984:15.

were found at Goolman. Whitetail deer were the most common game; analysis of tooth eruption patterns shows that most of the Goolman deer were taken between November and February.

In summary, the Madisonville horizon brings the archaeology of the Bluegrass and Ohio River Valley into the Historic period. Despite the fact that much is known, much remains to be learned about this dynamic period of Kentucky prehistory and protohistory.

FORT ANCIENT IN THE MOUNTAINS

Fort Ancient in the Mountains is restricted to the Kentucky and Big Sandy drainages. A single phase, Woodside (Dunnell 1972), has been proposed to encompass Fort Ancient in the Mountains region. Representative components include Mayo (Dunnell 1961, 1983; Purrington 1967), Roberts, Slone, 15Br9, and 15Pi13 (fig. 6.1).

There were at least two types of Woodside sites—villages and camps. The relationship between these two site types is unclear. Perhaps the latter represent hunting camps associated with the villages. Villages were the year-round settlements of corn farmers who supplemented their diet by hunting, fishing, and gathering of wild plants (Dunnell 1972). Each village consisted of several houses arranged around an open plaza. Stockades surrounded many villages, and villagers threw their refuse and buried some of their dead between the houses and the stockade wall. Firepits and storage pits were dug near the houses.

Woodside camps may have been hunting camps associated with the villages. Some of these camps (e.g., Site 15Pi7) were so transitory that they left behind no recognizable hearths, pits, houses, or other archaeological features. Debitage or stone toolmaking debris, projectile points, cutting tools, and scraping tools are more abundant at camps than are pottery and animal bone and shells. This is different from village assemblages, in which the latter are common.

The Slone site on the Levisa Fork in Pike County (fig. 6.1) was a stockaded circular village. The stockade, which had been rebuilt three times, enclosed an area 62–76 m in diameter. Inside it were at least 12 rectangular houses that ranged in size from 6 by 7 m to 7 by 12 m. Most contained centrally located hearths, and many had small attached porticos or covered cooking areas on the side that faced the plaza. Near each house were hearths, basins, earth ovens, and rock- or potsherd-lined storage pits. Burials, often covered by stone slabs, were placed between the houses and the village wall.

Most of the Slone site pots were shell-tempered plain, cordmarked, or exterior roughened jars with strap handles. The only other vessel form was the saltpan. Other distinctive artifacts are small triangular projectile points (some of which appear similar to Railey's [1992] Types 4–6 [fig. 6.2]), stone disks, elbow pipes, and bone and antler tools. Ornaments include bone, stone, and shell beads; pendants made of turkey digit bones; perforated animal teeth; imitation teeth or claws made of cannel coal and sandstone; small diamond-shaped marine shell gorgets, and conch columella ear plugs. A single radiocarbon date from Slone suggests that it was occupied in the 1400s.

Fort Ancient occupations are also found in rockshelters. The William S. Webb Memorial Rockshelter site (Cowan and Wilson 1977) in Menifee County is a good example. Unlike many other rockshelters, which contain several different components, this small dry shelter was apparently used only as a temporary camp by Fort Ancient groups (Cowan and Wilson 1977). Excavations revealed a compact living floor with several hearths and pits. The assemblage included one Madisonville Cordmarked vessel, small triangular projectile points, flake tools, debitage, a grinding slab, fiber cordage, cut cane, and several corn kernels and husks.

In summary, less is known about Fort Ancient chronology in the Mountains than in the Bluegrass and Ohio Valley. Older Mountains region sites than Slone are present, and later sites probably are too. With a few exceptions (e.g., projectile point morphology [Dunnell 1972] and the relative frequency of knot-roughened pottery [Cowan 1975, 1976]), Mountains region Fort Ancient material culture resembles that reported from contemporaneous Bluegrass and Ohio Valley sites.

DISCUSSION

The preceding pages describe the nature of the Fort Ancient tradition in Kentucky. The following discussion extracts from these descriptions a general view of Fort Ancient society as it existed in the central Ohio Valley from A.D. 1000 to 1700 and examines its relationships to similar cultural manifestations in eastern North America.

The Fort Ancient culture occupied the geographic area that had been the center of the Adena and Ohio Hopewell cultural developments during the Early and Middle Woodland periods. These cultures share broad developmental similarities with Fort Ancient, and information from sites such as Muir suggests that Fort Ancient is mostly an indigenous development.

Economy

Agriculture was the main food source, and corn, beans, and squash were the important crops. Hunting, fishing, and gathering supplemented the diet. Fort Ancient hunting focused on large game animals such as whitetail deer, elk, and bear. This pattern differs from the Mississippian pattern, which emphasized whitetail deer, raccoons, wild turkeys, and fish (Smith 1986).

Muir and other sites show that corn and domestic beans were important parts of the Fort Ancient diet by A.D. 1000. Furthermore, studies of prehistoric health (Cassidy 1980; Perzigian et al. 1984), assessments of the dietary contribution of corn (Broida 1983, 1984), and analyses of Fort Ancient plant remains (Rossen and Edging 1987; Wagner 1983, 1984, 1987) demonstrate unequivocally that corn was important economically throughout the late prehistoric period. A corn-based agricultural economy continued to be an integral part of Fort Ancient life until these native populations were killed or displaced during the Historic period.

Although Fort Ancient groups may have been as dependent on corn as Mississippian societies were (Rossen and Edging 1987), if not more so, the pattern of Fort Ancient corn production differed in important respects. Fort Ancient agriculture is best characterized as a shifting field strategy that was based on low labor input and was extensive rather than intensive in nature. Field locations were not fixed, and concepts of land ownership and tenure were probably never firmly developed.

Settlement Patterns

Fort Ancient villages often contained a central plaza or public area surrounded by concentric mortuary, residential, and refuse zones. Some villages also were palisaded. Other communities showed less planning in their layout. For example, the early Fort Ancient Muir site consisted of structures spaced randomly along a broad ridge. Similarly, most late Fort Ancient sites, while generally very large, lack obvious internal village structure.

The presence of winter hunting camps associated with the Madisonville horizon suggests that the seasonal settlement system, called the Miami-Potawatomi pattern (Fitting and Cleland 1969), had long been present in the Fort Ancient area. In the Miami-Potawatomi system, some inhabitants of large, permanent villages would disperse in the fall to live in small winter hunting territories. These small groups, usually extended families, would return to the main village in the early spring to help ready the fields for planting.

Many Fort Ancient villages were periodically moved, probably every 10–30 years, depending upon the exhaustion of available agricultural land resources, game and firewood depletion, and general village deterioration. Some sites appear to have been reoccupied, but other abandoned villages may have later served as agricultural fields. This contrasts with the Mississippian settlement pattern, which was associated with large sites along the major river valleys that were occupied more intensively and for much longer.

Social Organization

Burial practices illustrate the lack of a Fort Ancient elite class in early Fort Ancient communities. Before A.D. 1400, burial mounds were occasionally associated with villages of houses set around a small plaza. Burials could be either in the mound or on the plaza edge in front of the house. Placement in one or the other may indicate low-level social distinctions. On the other hand, the absence of special treatment for individuals, either by position in the mound or by possessions placed with the body, suggests a low level of social stratification.

At Madisonville horizon Fort Ancient sites (i.e., those that were occupied after A.D. 1400), burials often occur in groups or clusters throughout the village. These burial clusters may be the graves of related individuals (Pollack et al. 1987). Grave goods associated with some Madisonville horizon burials also suggest status differences existed. The distribution of burials with grave goods, however, appears to be random, with grave goods placed with individuals belonging to many different groups rather than concentrated in one or two burial clusters. Such a distribution of grave goods within villages show that most status positions in Madisonville society continued to be based on individual achievement rather than through inheritance.

Early historical accounts of Native American groups in the Northeast and Great Lakes regions describe patterns of social and political integration based on age, kin relations, and clan membership that are similar to late Madisonville horizon patterns described here. These patterns are often called leagues or confederacies and include many groups, such as the Illinois, Miami, Huron, Neutral, Shawnee, and many others, in addition to the Five Nations or League of the Iroquois.

Exchange and Interaction

Warfare, trade, and eventually Euro-American contacts changed Fort Ancient culture. Warfare's importance as a developmental factor is difficult to assess (Graybill 1981), but it must have been a common part of late prehistoric life. Fort Ancient skeletons often bear the evidence of mortal wounds. Scalped individuals, for example, have been found at Fox Farm (Robbins and Neumann 1972) and the Larkin site (Pollack et al. 1987).

Trade with regions beyond the Fort Ancient area was also an important activity. Items of nonlocal origin occur on Fort Ancient sites throughout the late prehistoric period, and the scale of interregional exchange increased over time. Exotic, or at least nonlocal, trade items are especially common in Madisonville horizon components.

The most visible trade items are the marine shell beads and simple shell gorgets found in early and middle Fort Ancient assemblages. Spatulate celts and Mississippian-like ceramics also are occasionally found in southwestern Ohio Fort Ancient sites (Cowan 1987), which suggests interaction with Mississippian groups further down the Ohio Valley. However, interregional trade volume was light until about A.D. 1400.

The Fort Ancient area's location on the western side of the Appalachian Mountains between the Atlantic seaboard and the Great Lakes may have been strategically situated for north-south trade after about A.D. 1400. Regardless of the factor or factors that motivated it, trade increased around A.D. 1400–1450. This coincided with the creation of larger Fort Ancient villages. Late Fort Ancient trade artifacts include shell masks and Citico-style gorgets, which probably came from eastern Tennessee, and catlinite disk pipes and ceramics from the Great Lakes region.

Despite the occurrence of early Euro-American trade goods at several Fort Ancient sites in Kentucky and surrounding states, attempts to establish specific connections between the Fort Ancient culture and historically documented groups have not been entirely satisfactory. The dimensions of this problem were examined above in the discussion of the Bentley site.

The central Ohio Valley was one of the last areas of Eastern North America to be explored by Europeans. The first historical accounts of this region were not written until the eighteenth century, and by that time few native groups lived in the Ohio Valley (Hunter 1978). The early Euro-American artifacts in Fort Ancient sites and, centuries later, the sparse population density reported throughout Kentucky by the earliest travel narratives suggest that Fort Ancient groups were affected indirectly by the presence of Euro-Americans along the Atlantic seaboard as much as 200 years before the first Euro-Americans arrived in the central Ohio Valley.

The most important indirect effect of the European presence was the diseases they carried with them from the Old World. The common cold, smallpox, chicken pox, influenza, measles, and other diseases penetrated the mid-continent with disastrous effects long before the first "Long Hunter" crossed the Appalachians into the Ohio River drainage.

Other factors besides disease were also at work in the abandonment of much of the central Ohio Valley by the end of the seventeenth century. After sustained contacts began between Euro-American traders and Native Americans on the Atlantic and Gulf coasts and the Great Lakes, many native groups adjusted their way of life to improve trading opportunities. Native American participation in the trade required the acquisition of furs or deer skins. Increased competition for these commodities led to fierce struggles far in advance of European exploration or settlement and are probably at least partially responsible for the disruption of Fort Ancient culture.

Unlike the Mississippian parts of Kentucky, the Fort Ancient tradition can be linked to at least one Native American group whose name is known to history. In the 1700s the Shawnee had the clearest claim to the central Ohio Valley as their ancestral homeland, and some late Fort Ancient sites were probably occupied by the Shawnee. Nevertheless, as with all direct historical links between named ethnic groups and the archaeological record, this tie cannot be pushed back in time very far.

SUMMARY

Early Fort Ancient sites represent a transition to village life based on the cultivation of corn, beans, and squash. Early Fort Ancient villages were not as nucleated, as planned, or as permanent as later sites. By A.D. 1000 triangular projectile points had largely replaced earlier styles, a change that undoubtedly marked the widespread adoption of the bow and arrow as the preferred hunting weapon. Cooking pots and other vessels, however, still resembled their Late Woodland counterparts, except for shell tempering, handles, and some decorative motifs.

By A.D. 1200 substantial nucleated villages were being built in central and eastern Kentucky. Often consisting of houses arranged around a plaza, these communities had 100–300 inhabitants. Some villages were fortified. Some, perhaps the ones that were occupied the longest, also had burial mounds in the plaza or near the village. The relatively even distribution of A.D. 1200–1400 Fort Ancient sites across northeastern Kentucky suggests considerable village autonomy. Ceramic trends initiated during earlier Fort Ancient times continued. The use of shell as a tempering agent increased in popularity, as did vessels with thick handles, lug appendages, and incised decoration. The jar continued to be the most common vessel form. Serrated triangular points and chipped limestone disks are often found on Kentucky sites dating between A.D. 1200 and 1400.

Late Fort Ancient or Madisonville horizon sites can be distinguished from older Fort Ancient sites by differences in settlement organization, mortuary patterns, material culture, and increased interregional exchange. Most communities are nucleated, but often, either because of long, intense occupations or changing patterns of community organization, many Kentucky Madisonville sites lack identifiable plazas. There also seem to be fewer late Fort Ancient sites than middle Fort Ancient sites in Kentucky, but in general, the late sites are larger in size. The use of burial mounds ceased by the beginning of the Madisonville horizon, and extended burials covered by stone slabs became common. Regional ceramic series were replaced by the Madisonville series, and pans, colanders, and bowls were common in assemblages for the first time. Catlinite disk pipes, engraved marine shell gorgets, and shell mask gorgets provide evidence of greatly expanded trade networks. Small amounts of historic trade items are present on very late Madisonville horizon sites.

FROM COLONIZATION
TO THE TWENTIETH CENTURY

Kim A. McBride and W. Stephen McBride

In the middle 1770s Euro-Americans built their first settlements in Kentucky. This is noteworthy for several reasons. First, the archaeological record of the eighteenth century is dominated by the remains of Old World settlers, most of whom were from Europe and Africa. Some Native American groups still claimed land in Kentucky, but their campsites and villages, which previously dominated the archaeology of Kentucky, ceased to exist during this period. Second, the information contained in diaries, probate records, land deeds, marriage registers, oral histories, and other documents created by these new settlers enriches and supplements the archaeological record, blending the traditional materials of history and archaeology.

This chapter describes Kentucky archaeology from the mid-1700s to the early 1900s. A brief introductory section outlines the types of sites most commonly excavated. This is followed by a detailed overview of Kentucky's historical development, drawing from many of the larger excavation projects conducted around the state.

THE HISTORICAL ARCHAEOLOGY DATABASE

Frontier Archaeology

If any part of the United States is known for its frontier heritage, it is Kentucky. The exploits of Daniel Boone, James Harrod, and Simon Kenton are part of each child's heritage. Settlers passing through the Cumberland Gap or fighting off Native American raids at their stations are images that have entered our national folklore and have formed an important part of Kentuckians' state pride.

Although some aspects of frontier life, particularly warfare between the invading settlers and Native Americans, are well documented, actual daily living conditions are not well understood. Archaeology can provide the key for understanding these and other conditions. The big problem is finding the frontier sites. As shown by O'Malley's work at Bluegrass frontier stations and Carstens's continuing search for Fort Jefferson in the Jackson Purchase, frontier sites can be difficult to locate.

The most extensive frontier site studies have been O'Malley's (1987b) examination of Inner Bluegrass stations, her excavations at Fort Boonesborough on the Kentucky River (O'Malley 1989), and her work at the town of Washington in Mason County (O'Malley 1988). This work is beginning to provide new information about frontier life, especially architecture, material culture, and foodways. For example, archaeology and associated historical research at early stations and frontier towns have demonstrated great variation in the number of artifacts present on these sites (O'Malley, personal communication 1991). These data will provide the basis for reconstructions of early trade routes and analyses of the economies of these early settlements.

Rural Plantations and Farmsteads

Many Kentucky plantation sites are complex, being composed of such special function structures as slave quarters, smokehouses, springhouses, animal pens, and the like. Larger plantations and farms also often contained multiple dwellings, like slave cabins or quarters, overseer's houses, and tenant houses. Some of Kentucky's plantation sites are today located in or near urban areas such as Farmington or Locust Grove in Louisville, or Ashland in Lexington, but they retain enough acreage to preserve the remains of many outbuildings and work areas. Archaeological work at these sites has often focused on locating these outbuildings, or locating and excavating secondary domestic buildings. The results provide information on the spatial layout of these types of sites.

Few small and middle-sized farm sites are as complex as the plantations, especially in the number of dwellings and such support structures as mills or blacksmith shops. Nevertheless, the farms are more representative than the plantations of the way of life of most of the population, and in that sense, they are of equal, if not greater importance. Excavations at farms in Jefferson County (O'Malley 1987a), Meade County (Otto and Gilbert 1982, 1984), and Floyd County (Esarey 1993b; Huser 1993) support historical research from the 1930s that suggested farm families often spent less of their income on consumer items than did other types of families (Nourse 1934).

Other studies of farms (e.g., Fiegel 1989) demonstrate that archaeological collections provide a wealth of information on the origin of purchased items, which in Kentucky refers primarily to Ohio Valley and East Coast markets.

Although rural lifeways are still relatively important in Kentucky, the process of moving off the farm has been a significant one in Kentucky, especially during the twentieth century. For many people, this process has involved wage labor in the mining or lumbering industries. Archaeological investigations at these sites, such as Schenian's (1988b) work at Onionville, a small late nineteenth- and early twentieth-century coal community, provide a glimpse into this transition.

Cities

Archaeology in and of cities is a rapidly growing research area in the United States. The intensity of occupation and the rich documentary records common for urban sites make them ideal subjects for historical archaeology. Much archaeological work is also taking place in cities because large redevelopment projects, which often uncover archaeological deposits, are common. Within Kentucky, large archaeological excavations have occurred in Louisville, Lexington, Covington, and Frankfort. Most of these projects have focused on residential sites, but governmental and industrial locations have also been investigated. They have demonstrated the intensity of land use common to urban areas, the high density of artifacts on urban sites, and the pattern of reuse and filling that characterizes land of high value. The archaeological collections from these sites form an important data base for comparison to rural sites.

Industry

In Kentucky, a variety of industrial and manufacturing sites have been investigated archaeologically. These include grist mills, potteries, a glass factory, and nitre mines. The first known example of historical archaeology in the state was done on a manufacturing site. This was Webb and Funkhouser's (1936) investigation of a nitre mine in Menifee County.

Another important industry that archaeologists are studying in Kentucky is milling. Milling was once critical to Kentucky's economy, and water-powered grist and flour mills were once ubiquitous across the state. Few of these mills remain today, and their appearance and operation are being forgotten. Several Kentucky mills have been examined archaeologically, including the Shaker Mills at Pleasant Hill, Mercer County (Janzen 1981), David Ward's Mill (Granger 1984) and Fisher's Mill in Jefferson County (McBride et al. 1988), and Wellman's Mill in Lawrence County (Niquette and Donham 1985).

Military Sites

Military site excavations are generally focused on forts and encampments, but battlefields are also beginning to receive attention (e.g., Braley 1987;

Scott and Fox 1987). Issues addressed by archaeologists include camp housing and layout, equipment provisioning, food provisioning and foraging, social stratification, fort architecture and construction, troop deployment, and the location of individual battlefield engagements (Braley 1987; Parrington 1980; Poirer 1976; Rutsch and Peters 1977; Scott and Fox 1987; Wright 1982).

Carstens's research on the Revolutionary War site of Fort Jefferson in Ballard County stands essentially alone among pre–Civil War military (as opposed to militia or settler sites) archaeology projects in Kentucky. Civil War sites have, by comparison, received considerable attention. Union Army earthen fortifications near Covington, Glasgow, and Cumberland Gap have been investigated, as have the Union Army machine shop, hospital, convalescent camp, and headquarters at Camp Nelson, Jessamine County (Harper et al. 1981; McBride and Sharp 1991; Schock 1978a, 1978b, 1987; Walker 1975).

Much less work has been conducted at Confederate sites in Kentucky. One of the few such projects has been the field survey and mapping of a Confederate mortar battery in Cumberland Gap National Park (Walker 1975). This battery consisted of a 40 m long earthwork with three rock-lined mortar pits. The pits were 2–3 m across and 1.5 m deep. Preliminary survey and/or metal detecting has also been conducted at several battlefield sites, such as recent work at Perryville by R. Berle Clay (personal communication 1992).

FROM COLONIZATION TO THE TWENTIETH CENTURY

Exploration and Early Settlement (1749–1810)

By 1749 British traders were at the Native American village of Lower Shawneetown on the Ohio River (fig. 7.1), the archaeology of which Sharp describes in the preceding chapter (see also Henderson et al. 1986:50). The location of trading houses at this site is unknown. Traders also may have been living at other Kentucky villages, but we do not yet have evidence of their presence, nor have the remains of any trading houses been excavated.

In 1749, an expedition under Céloron de Blainville explored the Ohio Valley to take formal possession of it for France. British traders encountered by this expedition were warned to leave the area controlled by the French (Alvord 1920:227). Tensions sparked by this and other British and French encounters in the Ohio Valley finally resulted in the French and Indian War.

Between 1754 and 1758 the French controlled trade in the Ohio Valley and visited Lower Shawneetown and other villages (Henderson et al. 1986:52). Their fortunes soon turned, however, and after the British captured Fort Duquesne (site of the present city of Pittsburgh, Pennsylvania) in 1758, the French abandoned much of the Ohio Valley. Many Native American vil-

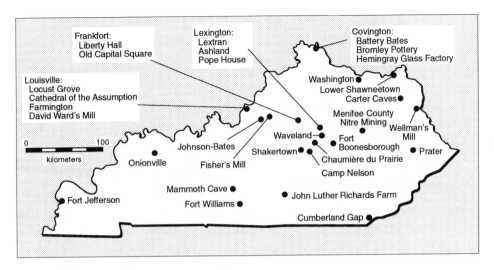

Frankfort:
Liberty Hall
Old Capital Square

Lexington:
Lextran
Ashland
Pope House

Covington:
Battery Bates
Bromley Pottery
Hemingray Glass Factory

Louisville:
Locust Grove
Cathedral of the Assumption
Farmington
David Ward's Mill

Washington
Lower Shawneetown
Carter Caves

Menifee County
Nitre Mining
Wellman's Mill

Waveland
Fort Boonesborough
Johnson-Bates
Shakertown
Prater
Chaumière du Prairie
Onionville
Fisher's Mill
Camp Nelson

0 100
kilometers

Mammoth Cave
Fort Williams
John Luther Richards Farm
Fort Jefferson
Cumberland Gap

Figure 7.1 Historical sites discussed in the text.

lages that had allied themselves with the French, including Lower Shawneetown, also were abandoned at this time.

By the late 1760s hunters from the East were making long sojourns into Kentucky. These "Long Hunters," hailing from Virginia, Pennsylvania, and North Carolina, entered Kentucky through the Cumberland Gap or from the Ohio River and stayed in Kentucky for months or even years at a time. Some of the more famous of these hunters were Elisha Walden, Benjamin Cutbird, Simon Kenton, James Harrod, Kasper Manslar, Squire Boone, and Daniel Boone (Rice 1975:28).

The exploration and trail blazing of the Long Hunters were very important to the later settlement of Kentucky. Many hunters examined land conditions for themselves or others, including land speculators, in the anticipation of future settlement. Their reports to land companies and speculators fueled the interest of settlers to move to Kentucky.

Following the battle of Point Pleasant in 1774 and the Treaty of Pittsburgh in 1775, Lord Dunmore approved settlement south of the Ohio River and west of the Kanawha River. Settlers and speculators quickly moved into the Bluegrass region, which was by that time well known from the accounts of the Long Hunters. They came from the southeast through the mountains by way of Cumberland Gap and Pound Gap, or from the northeast down the Ohio and Kentucky rivers. Settlers from the Piedmont, western North Carolina, and western Virginia entered primarily through the gaps, and those from Pennsylvania, western Maryland, and western Virginia generally came down the Ohio River.

The first Euro-American settlements in Kentucky were founded at Harrodstown, now Harrodsburg, in March 1775 (it was platted in 1774), and at Boonesborough in April 1775. Other settlements soon followed. By 1780 there were three clusters of settlements in Kentucky—one at the Falls of the Ohio and Beargrass Creek; one north of the Kentucky River, which took in the Lexington area and the southern fork of the Licking River; and the Harrodstown, Danville, and Logan's Fort cluster south of the Kentucky River (Rice 1975:120).

Early settlers had reason to fear attacks by Native Americans, so they initially settled in or around forts or "stations." Unlike the temporary camps of the early explorers and Long Hunters, none of which have been located by archaeologists, these permanent settlements are providing archaeologists with useful information about life on the frontier. The stations ranged from a single fortified cabin or blockhouse to what was almost a fortified town, comprised of several cabins enclosed by a stockade (O'Malley 1987b:26–28). The larger stations seem to have been inhabited by several families. Some settlers may also have lived in cabins outside the stations when there was less threat of raids (Chinn 1975:101; Ellis et al. 1985:5–7; Rohrbough 1978:29).

O'Malley (1987b) has examined many Bluegrass frontier stations. Although her study was primarily based on historical documents, she also surveyed archaeologically 61 of 158 known Bluegrass stations. Test excavations at four station sites yielded information about their sizes and layouts, and such eighteenth-century artifacts as creamware and pearlware dish sherds. Although of a preliminary nature, O'Malley's work promises that, over the next few decades, archaeology will offer a fresh perspective on life at these early settlements.

An example of the fruitfulness of more detailed research is O'Malley's additional work at Fort Boonesborough. Although historical records gave the general location of this fort, one of the fundamental places of Kentucky frontier history, its precise location was unknown until recently. O'Malley (1989) found the site with the aid of traditional archaeological survey methods and the analysis of historical records. Further excavations exposed possible cabin remains, a pit or hearth filled with ash and animal bones, and several postmolds. These features, and the middle to late eighteenth-century, white salt-glazed stoneware, creamware, and gunflints found at the site suggest that Fort Boonesborough has finally been discovered. Most of this site, however, has yet to be excavated.

The early Kentuckians picked an inauspicious time to establish their settlements. The Revolutionary War was beginning and many Native American groups in the Ohio Valley, particularly the Shawnee, were allied with the British. This gave the Shawnee extra incentive to attack the new settlements. Warfare in the Bluegrass between the settlers and Native Americans was particularly violent in 1777, the year of "the terrible sevens," and many Euro-American settlements in Kentucky were abandoned.

The only archaeologically investigated Revolutionary War military site in Kentucky is George Rogers Clark's fort, Fort Jefferson, which was occupied from 1780 to 1781. Research on the general location of this fort on the Mississippi River in Ballard County has been underway since 1979 (Carstens 1986, 1991). The greatest and most enduring problem of the Fort Jefferson archaeological research is simply to find the fort's remains. Carstens knows only that it was buried in alluvium beneath the Mississippi River and Mayfield Creek floodplains. He is using a variety of search techniques, including remote sensing, environmental reconstruction, map scaling, standard archaeological survey, soil augering, and most recently, magnetometer survey, to locate this important site (Carstens 1984, 1986, 1987, 1991; Potter and Carstens 1986; Stein et al. 1983).

Post-Revolution Settlements and Plantations

Resettlement proceeded at a slow pace until after the end of the Revolutionary War in 1783. In 1782, there were only 8,000 Euro-Americans in Kentucky (Rohrbough 1978:25), but the postwar increase was dramatic, reaching 30,000 by 1784 (Rohrbough 1978:25). By this time settlers had also established farmsteads away from the stations and forts, and Georgetown, Danville, Stanford, and Lexington were becoming towns.

Settlement spread into the Pennyroyal, and the areas around Elizabethtown, Greensburg, and Russellville in particular became early population centers. Since raids by Native Americans continued in these newer and less densely populated areas, settlement was still somewhat clustered around forts or stations. Settlement reached as far as the mouth of the Cumberland River by 1791.

By the late 1780s and early 1790s, settlers also had begun moving into Appalachia. These mountain settlements tended to be off the main trails because Native American raids continued later in the Mountains than in the Bluegrass, at least in the latter's more settled regions (McClure 1933:88). The first Appalachian settlements or stations were Harmon's Station (1788) near the confluence of John's Creek and the Big Sandy River, and Vancouver's Station or Trading Post (1789) near the present site of Louisa. Other early settlements were Preston's Station, the Sellards Settlement on Buffalo Creek, the Leslie Settlements on Pond and, later, Sycamore Creek, and Paint Lick Station (Crowe-Carraco 1979; McClure 1933; Scalf 1966).

While most of these early settlers were of European ancestry, some successful early settlers established large agricultural plantations that incorporated African or African-American slave labor, first in the Bluegrass and later in portions of the Pennyroyal.

By 1790 there were over 12,000 slaves, who helped grow tobacco, hemp, and grains and raise livestock (Cotterill 1917:235). Tobacco was chosen as an important cash crop because it grew well in Kentucky, it had a favorable relationship between bulk and value, and it had a low rate of perishability (Earle and Hoffman 1976). These were important factors, given the limited Kentucky transportation routes of the late 1700s.

Archaeologists have not had the opportunity to conduct full-scale excavations at many early farm and plantations sites, although small-scale excavations are beginning to yield information about their organization. One of these sites is Locust Grove. In spite of its location in metropolitan Louisville, Locust Grove, the late eighteenth-century home of Major William Croghan, retains the central domestic complex and surrounding grounds of the plantation it once was. Excavations have exposed the stone foundation of what may have been a small cabin built in the eighteenth century before the construction of the main house (fig. 7.2). Bison bones and other early historic materials were found in this excavation (Philip DiBlasi, personal communication 1991; Joseph Granger, personal communication 1991). Archaeologists have also located remains of other cabins, which were most likely used to house slaves at the site (Amy Young, personal communication 1992).

Figure 7.2 Cabin excavation at Locust Grove Plantation in Louisville. Courtesy of the Program of Archaeology, University of Louisville.

Most plantations also contained a variety of outbuildings, as illustrated at Locust Grove by the remains of the original springhouse, in use between 1800 and 1840. Excavations at this building showed that it measured roughly 3 by 3 m and that its walls were about 45 cm thick. Sometime after 1840 it burned. Archaeologists found that its remains were used as a trash dump, and the springhouse well was turned into a dipping well or watering trough (Granger and Mocas 1970). The springhouse fill contained sherds of earthenware and stoneware storage vessels, many of which came from local potteries (McGraw 1971). Leather pieces were also found, preserved by the moist conditions of the ruined springhouse. Investigators found that glass marbles were used as bottle stoppers because the wet conditions of the springhouse caused mold to grow on corks (Granger and Mocas 1970).

Chaumière du Prairie, the eighteenth-century home of David Meade in Fayette County, offers another archaeological glimpse at early plantation life. Unlike Locust Grove in Louisville, the Chaumière du Prairie excavations were closer to the main house and reveal more of the household refuse (Livingston 1983). The excavations exposed a cellar and the foundation walls to several rooms. Interestingly, the size and placement of the foundation walls did not conform to the original plan of the house as shown in historic documents. This discovery suggests that the original plan had not been followed or had been modified (Livingston 1983). The wide assortment of decorated Chinese export porcelain and transfer-printed ceramics that were found in these excavations reflect the great wealth of the Meade family and provide insight into their reputation for lavish entertaining.

The Rise of Cities

By 1790, when the first U.S. census was taken, Kentucky had a population of 73,677. This included 61,133 Euro-Americans, 12,430 slaves, and 114 free African-Americans. Although most of Kentucky's population was rural and would remain so for many years, some cities had begun to develop. Lexington, for example, reached a population of 834 persons and had about 20 mercantile establishments in 1792 (Share 1982:9). Other larger late eighteenth-century towns were Washington (462 persons), Bardstown (216 persons), Louisville (200 persons), and Danville (150 persons) (Cotterill 1917:244).

One of the best-known urban home sites to be examined by archaeologists is Liberty Hall, the Frankfort residence of Senator John Brown (1757–1837). The main house and a few of the dependencies survive from the original 1796 construction. Archaeological excavations provided the data for the accurate restoration of the main house and outbuildings that visitors see today (Fay 1983, 1986:1). These excavations also uncovered three former cellar entrances, an early cellar drain (fig. 7.3), a cistern, and a brick privy

Figure 7.3 Interior cellar drain at Liberty Hall, Frankfort. Reproduced by permission of the William S. Webb Museum of Anthropology, University of Kentucky.

vault. Overall, the archaeological investigations provided invaluable architectural information about the house and kitchen ell.

Liberty Hall artifacts include ceramics, bottle glass, table glass, cutlery, toys (e.g., clay and stone marbles and porcelain doll parts), clothing, metal hardware, and such personal items as bone combs, smoking pipes, and bone toothbrush fragments. Expensive service items indicative of the Brown's social status include Chinese export porcelain, French wine bottles, and decorated wine glasses and water goblets. Analysis of animal bones found in the excavations indicate that the Browns preferred domestic meats, particularly beef, pork, and chicken, although turkey, lamb, and oysters were also popular. On a more personal level, an artifact which illustrates the activities of children is an engraved fragment of window glass. This pane fragment was engraved "Margaretta," which was the name of Senator Brown's granddaughter. Margaretta Mason Brown Barrett was born in 1839 and probably signed the glass in the 1840s or 1850s, when she was growing up at Liberty Hall (Fay 1983).

In downtown Lexington, archaeologists also recently excavated six urban residences occupied from the 1790s to the mid-twentieth century (McBride and McBride 1991a). Buried beneath the asphalt of a modern car lot were the remains of the homes of several local craftsmen and their families, a free

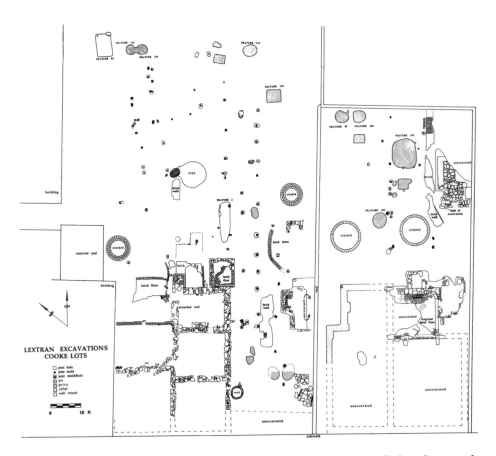

Figure 7.4 Site plan of LEXTRAN house lots, with foundations, well, fencelines, and other features. Reproduced by permission of the William S. Webb Museum of Anthropology, University of Kentucky.

African-American woman, and a physician. By the beginning of the twentieth century, these houses had become boarding houses and office buildings, and they were eventually destroyed.

Archaeological excavations exposed the house remains buried under as much as 2 m of gravel and dirt fill. A rich midden and many architectural features were exposed, including intact house foundations, an external kitchen and possible bake house, a stone cellar, a kitchen ell addition, several outbuildings and additions of unknown function, and stone walkways and patios (fig. 7.4). These occupations extended into later time periods discussed below, and produced nine privies that had been filled between 1865 and 1920, six cisterns filled in the early to mid-twentieth century, and many trash pits and postmolds. The discovery of old fence lines, represented by postmolds, helped the archaeologists to reestablish original property lines and divisions within the yards. Insurance maps provided information on the locations of privies and other outbuildings, and they showed how the houses changed through time as porches and additions were added or dismantled.

These excavations also yielded a large assemblage of late eighteenth- to nineteenth-century artifacts that provide a good picture of the kinds of china, bottles and other glassware, toys, and personal items used by residents of these houses. Faunal preservation at the sites was also extremely good. Close to one hundred French gunflints, commonly used in the late eighteenth and early nineteenth century, were found in one small area. Documentary research suggests that they belonged to a gunsmith who lived nearby, and who perhaps discarded them after the percussion cap replaced the flintlock.

ANTEBELLUM (1810–61)

Kentucky matured in the decades following the end of frontier conditions and before the Civil War, and its cities, institutions, and citizens grew more similar to those of the eastern states. As transportation and communication improved, such national and international developments as increased industrialization affected Kentuckians at a faster rate.

Regular steamboat traffic existed on the Ohio River by 1820, and it strengthened Kentucky's cultural and economic ties with the East Coast, the Deep South, and western Europe. The early part of the Antebellum decades was truly the age of the river town in Kentucky. Although the Bluegrass still had most of Kentucky's large towns, many river towns were growing fast. By 1830 Louisville had a population of over 10,000, far outdistancing its early rival, Lexington, which had only 6,087 inhabitants.

The prosperity of the late 1820s and 1830s and the success of the steamboat stimulated the demand for river improvements. Although many schemes were discussed, important improvements, often canals, were made to the Green, Barren, and Kentucky rivers and at the Falls of the Ohio. The most notable improvement was the construction of the Portland Canal around the Falls of the Ohio. The opening of the canal increased river trade, and as steamboats grew to be too large to fit into the canal and required unloading, Louisville's transshipment business was secure (Kramer 1986:441; Share 1982:36; Wade 1959).

Other important transportation improvements were the construction of new roads, especially to and from county seats, the widening and surfacing of some roads, and the construction of the first railways in Kentucky. After 1818 many major Kentucky roads or highways shifted from state to private control and became turnpikes or toll roads (Clark 1960:181).

Improved means of transportation and increased industrialization in the early Antebellum period improved Kentucky's general standard of living and further encouraged the growth of cities, county seats, and rural communities. These changes also fostered the commercialization of agriculture. Plantations expanded in the Bluegrass, parts of the Pennyroyal, and in the western Jackson Purchase. The number of Kentucky slaves increased to 165,213 in 1830, when they made up 25 percent of Kentucky's population. By the beginning of the Civil War, there were 225,483 slaves, comprising 20 percent of Kentucky's population.

Early Farms, Plantations, and Urban Residences

Archaeologists have conducted excavations on a number of sites from this time period. One example is Ashland, Henry Clay's antebellum plantation located within the present city limits of Lexington. Clay began this plantation around 1809, and on it he raised such crops as hemp and tobacco and bred a variety of livestock. The original main house was destroyed shortly after Henry Clay's death in 1852, and a nearly identical house was built on the same location in 1856–58. Archaeological investigations, which were directed toward assisting restoration activities, were clustered around this house and in the adjacent yard (McBride and McBride 1991b; W.S. McBride 1993).

Figure 7.5 Brick skirt from original Ashland mansion, Lexington, showing early-nineteenth-century land surface. Reproduced by permission of the William S. Webb Museum of Anthropology, University of Kentucky.

The excavations revealed evidence of the original house and of the rebuilding episode. Features associated with the original house included a herringbone pattern brick skirt at the front of the house (fig. 7.5) and a brick patio or skirt at its rear. Evidence of rebuilding included builder's trenches in the front and rear of the house, both of which contained post-1830 artifacts, and a zone of mortar at the top of the builder's trench. The presence of the builder's trenches suggested that the second house was placed on a new foundation rather than on the original foundation, as was commonly thought. The presence of the skirt and patio, however, confirms that the first and second houses were on the same spot.

The stratigraphy in the front and rear of the house showed evidence of excessive filling and two buried topsoil levels. This filling was probably done to correct drainage problems and for aesthetic reasons. Other discoveries during the Ashland excavation included a stone outbuilding foundation and a brick ornamental pond foundation. Early to middle nineteenth-century domestic refuse dumps were also found near the kitchen wing and smokehouse. These features yielded a dense quantity of architectural debris, suggesting that antebellum outbuildings may have been located behind the north wing of the house.

Archaeologists have conducted excavations at another antebellum plantation site, Waveland, the home of Joseph Bryan in Fayette County, which survives largely intact today as a Kentucky state historic site. Excavations around the slave/servants' quarters and the smokehouse have revealed well-preserved middle to late nineteenth-century archaeological remains (Hockensmith and Pollack 1985; Pollack and Hockensmith 1985). The uncovered archaeological features include a walkway from the main house to the smokehouse, a brick drainage system in front of the slave/servants' quarters, a fire pit or hearth area, and two trash pits. Many domestic artifacts were also found in these excavations (fig. 7.6).

Artifact comparisons between Waveland and Liberty Hall, the Frankfort home discussed in the preceding section, revealed that the Waveland deposits contain relatively little porcelain, an expensive ware. This difference suggests that the excavations at Waveland probably sampled wares that belonged to the slaves and servants rather than to the property owners (Henderson 1985).

Analysis of animal bones from the excavations suggests that pork was the most popular meat (Walters 1985). Most beef bones were found near the smokehouse; hardly any came from near the slave/servants' quarters. The remains near the smokehouse include teeth and other butchering debris. The faunal remains from the slave/servants' quarters, on the other hand, have a higher incidence of ribs and pig's knuckles, and were probably kitchen refuse (Walters 1985). The faunal assemblage from the slave/servants' quarters show that the diet of its occupants was dominated by lower quality cuts.

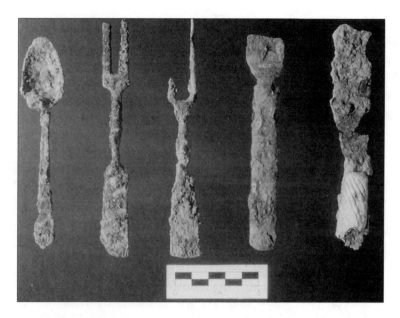

Figure 7.6   Metal tableware from Waveland. Reproduced by permission of the
William S. Webb Museum of Anthropology, University of Kentucky.

A significant study of an urban antebellum site was the architectural and
archaeological study of the 1811–12 house built for Senator John Pope in
Lexington. The Pope house is one of three remaining residences in the United
States designed by Benjamin Henry Latrobe, architect of the nation's capitol.
In 1987, after the house was severely damaged by fire, private donors
arranged for its purchase by the Blue Grass Trust for Historic Preservation,
which initiated a historical study of the house.

Archaeological investigations at the Pope House focused on architectural
changes (McBride and McBride 1991c; McBride 1992). Archaeologists excavated four brick piers that were associated with the original 1811–12 porch,
three pier holes possibly associated with an 1830s–1850s porch, and many
brick piers associated with the 1865 Italianate veranda. Excavations in the
interior of the house revealed large stone chimney bases in both the kitchen
and bake/wash oven rooms and, in the rear yard, the brick foundation of an
external kitchen.

All of the above discoveries helped determine how closely Latrobe's plans
were followed by Asa Wilgus, the builder, and how the house changed over
time. The presence of four brick piers, instead of the six shown on Latrobe's
plan, and the presence of a drip line beside the outer piers, suggesting a lack
of side steps on the porch as designed by Latrobe, indicate that Latrobe's
plans were significantly simplified by the local builder. The single rather

than double hearth found in the bake/wash oven room and the absence of Latrobe's stew pot structure in the kitchen room also reflect local simplifications of Latrobe's plan.

The conception of the external kitchen, which was probably built after 1830, and the roughly contemporaneous change in the porch, marked by the three pier holes, represent a change in the house from its unusual neoclassical design with an English basement first floor to a more typical Kentucky dwelling, probably with Greek Revival elements. The architect Patrick Snadon (personal communication 1993) suggests that Latrobe's picturesque interior pathways were altered in the 1840s, including the destruction of the bake/wash oven chimney, to create a more typical central hall plan on the first floor. The multiple veranda piers found in the front porch area were associated with an 1865 change in the house. At this time the architect Thomas Lewinski made the house into an Italianate villa.

By 1860, Louisville had become the twelfth-largest manufacturing center in the country and the largest in the South (Share 1982:33). It had a population of 68,033 people (Share 1982:37), which was rivaled only by "the Point" cities of Covington and Newport, with populations of 16,471 and 10,046, respectively. Other successful river towns were Frankfort, Henderson, Owensboro, Bowling Green, and Paducah.

Several excavations have been conducted at residential, commercial, and light industrial sites in Louisville. Recent excavations in the basement of the Cathedral of the Assumption in Louisville provide an unusual example of archaeological work, since the site was a religious one (Mansberger 1990). The cathedral was constructed in 1849–52 on the site of the much smaller St. Louis Church, which was demolished in 1850. The basement excavations exposed architectural remains of the Sisters of Charity building, two outbuildings, privies, and a variety of mid-nineteenth-century artifacts (Mansberger 1990). The artifacts, which include religious items, domestic refuse, and animal bones, provide a glimpse of the daily life of religious leaders during the nineteenth century. For instance, religious medals with French inscriptions and expensive French wine and oil bottles found in the excavation reflect both the continued French connections of the Sisters of Charity and the personal tastes of the sisters or priests.

Another unusual urban public site from this era is the original state jail, built in 1796 at the Old Capital Square in Frankfort (Deiss 1988). Excavation of the jail's foundation revealed that it had been partly converted to a privy in the mid-1800s. As such, it provides a nineteenth-century snapshot of everyday life around the square. The square's bureaucratic nature is reflected in the extraordinary frequency of coins (fig. 7.7), spittoons, ink wells, and pens found in the privy. Marbles, empty bottles, and campaign buttons, however, show that children and Old Capital Square political rallies also left their mark on the privy.

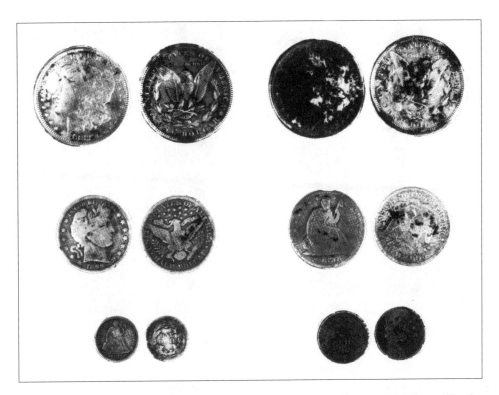

Figure 7.7 Coins from the state jail, Old Capital Square: top left, 1882 Liberty Head
dollar; top right, 1880 Liberty Head dollar; middle left, 1899 Liberty Head half-dollar;
middle right, 1876 Liberty Seated half-dollar; bottom left, 1875 Liberty Seated dime;
bottom right, 1867 Shield nickel. Courtesy of the Kentucky Historical Society.

Industry

Several kinds of industrial sites that began during the Antebellum period
have also been investigated archaeologically. The Shaker Mills on Shawnee
Run, a Kentucky River tributary in Mercer County, was part of the nineteenth-century religious community at Pleasant Hill, which has been
restored for visitors. The remains of the grist mill, which was in use in
1816–89, the stone-lined mill race, and the mill dam have been found and
excavated (Janzen 1981). The excavations shed light on the hydraulic engi-
neering system employed by the Shakers at the mill.

Recent excavations at Pleasant Hill have also exposed the remains of a
Shaker washhouse that was probably built in the 1830s or 1840s. The Shakers sold it in the 1880s and it was later converted to a residence. Buried
beneath gravel and earth fill inside the structure, archaeologists exposed
foundations of the original brick and stone masonry chambers used to heat

Figure 7.8 Foundation walls and lead pipe laid in limestone bedrock trough, West Lot Washhouse, Shakertown at Pleasant Hill. Reproduced by permission of the William S. Webb Museum of Anthropology, University of Kentucky.

the wash water. Excavations outside the house revealed that the Shakers laid lead pipes from a nearby spring to carry water into the washhouse. The pipes rested on limestone bedrock, which had been exposed and cut into a shallow trough at some points to protect the pipe (fig. 7.8). The findings inside the washhouse have been made into a permanent exhibit for public viewing.

The Shakers textile industry led them to construct fulling mills and a dye house. The dye house, which the Shakers built in the 1860s from the ruins of their initial 1808 log structure, has recently been excavated by the senior author. Here, archaeologists found not only the foundation of the building, but also tiny pieces of soil stained green, blue, red, and gold, providing information about the colors used by the Shakers in their textile industry.

The largest excavated antebellum industrial site is the Bromley Pottery in the Covington-Newport area of northern Kentucky. This factory, which produced yellowware, a semirefined earthenware, was in operation from 1859 to 1864. Archaeological discoveries show that the factory turned out such utilitarian vessels as chamber pots, pie plates, mugs, coffee pots, urinals,

Figure 7.9   Circular updraft type kiln at the Bromley Pottery at Covington. Courtesy of Bob Genheimer and the Beringer-Crawford Museum.

spittoons, pitchers, canning jars, and large bowls (Genheimer 1987:408). These vessels were fired in two circular updraft-type kilns with four fire boxes (fig. 7.9).

Antebellum nitre mining has been investigated in eastern and western Kentucky (Coy et al. 1984; Duncan 1993; Fig and Knudsen 1984; Webb and Funkhouser 1936). These studies have presented valuable information on the extraction and processing of nitre or saltpeter, and on the equipment used in these operations. Although it is seldom remembered today, Kentucky was the major United States producer of nitre during the War of 1812 and a major producer in the Civil War (Faust 1967). The remnants of hearths, troughs, hoppers, and leaching pits, which have sometime been extremely well preserved in the dry environment of caves and rockshelters, have been vital to reconstructing the nitre manufacturing processes and how they have changed over time (Fig and Knudsen 1984). For example, recent excavations and mapping in Saltpetre Cave of Carter Caves, in Carter County, suggest that at least 50,000 pounds and perhaps as much as 86,000 pounds of saltpeter were produced using a system of paired wooden leaching vats in this one cave, most of it for the War of 1812 (Duncan 1993).

CIVIL WAR (1861–65)

The recording and excavation of these nitre mining sites has been the major means for archaeologists to study Kentucky's role in the War of 1812. However, if we turn our attention to the Civil War, archaeologists in Kentucky find more numerous and more varied sites with which to address research topics.

When the Civil War began on April 12, 1861, Kentucky found itself in an awkward position. It was a slave state that did not support secession, and it was divided on whether to support military action against the seceding states. Initially, Kentucky's political leaders attempted to keep the state neutral, but by the end of 1861, Union troops occupied the northern half of the state and Confederate troops controlled the southern half. The first Confederate bases or forts in Kentucky were at Hickman and Columbus in the Jackson Purchase. Within a few months, other Confederate forts were established at Hopkinsville, Bowling Green, Glasgow, Monticello, and Somerset. These positions, along with Forts Henry and Donelson in Tennessee, formed the Confederacy's northern line of defense. By December 1861 there were 48,000 Confederate soldiers spread along this line (Harrison 1975:17).

A day or two after Columbus and Hickman were occupied, General Ulysses S. Grant established federal bases at Paducah, Smithland, Wickliffe (Fort Jefferson), and across the Ohio River from Cairo, Illinois (Fort Holt). Federal forts or camps were also soon established at Maysville and Covington, and Union Army headquarters for Kentucky were established at Louisville. With the fall of Forts Henry and Donelson in February 1862, the northern defenses of the Confederacy folded up and their positions across Kentucky were quickly abandoned (Harrison 1975:34; Mullen 1966:224).

The last major military campaign on Kentucky soil took place in the late summer and fall of 1862, when the Confederate forces again invaded the state under the commands of Generals Kirby Smith and Braxton Bragg. This campaign ended in early October, after Bragg's forces stumbled upon Buell's army of 60,000 at Perryville and fought an indecisive two-day battle. For the remainder of the war, the only engagements in Kentucky were raids and guerrilla actions.

The most extensive excavations at a Civil War site in Kentucky to date are those at Camp Nelson, a Jessamine County Union Army encampment and quartermaster depot. Camp Nelson was also an important recruitment center for African-American soldiers and a refugee camp for their families (Janzen 1987; Schock 1987). Archaeological investigations there have focused on the Owen's House, the post office complex, the headquarters complex, and the convalescent camp and hospital (Janzen 1987; McBride and Sharp 1991; Schock 1987).

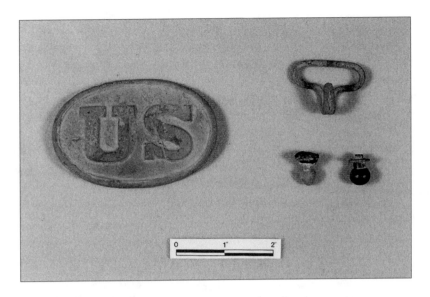

Figure 7.10   Military artifacts from Camp Nelson: left, U.S. belt buckle; right top, pack or belt buckle; right bottom, cap and cartridge box finials. Reproduced by permission of the William S. Webb Museum of Anthropology, University of Kentucky.

These Camp Nelson excavations yielded harness and wagon parts, ceramics, bottle glass, many nails, and ammunition (fig. 7.10) (McBride and Sharp 1991; Schock 1987). Analysis of these remains yields new information about the conditions and life of Union soldiers stationed in Kentucky during the latter half of the Civil War. For instance, the domestic dishes used at Camp Nelson were not as highly decorated as one finds in the remains of homes of the Civil War period. On the other hand, the animal bone and clothing remains show a pattern similar to that of contemporaneous civilian sites. The high percentage of pork remains and large numbers of decorative civilian coat and dress buttons shows a pattern different from most front-line military sites and reflects the rear echelon and more permanent nature of Camp Nelson, as well as the influence of local tastes. Local customs or supplies may have also been responsible for the great variety of nail sizes found during the excavations. These nails diverge from published army regulations. Stoneware pitchers, crocks, and jars were common vessels at the hospital and convalescent camp and may relate to storage and food preparation for the care of the sick and wounded (McBride and Sharp 1991). The excavations also suggest that camps like Nelson, which were far removed from the front lines, were sometimes sent out-of-date arms.

In Barren County, excavations at the site of Fort Williams, a Union Army fort at Glasgow, located the magazine and associated tunnel entrances, and provided construction information about the embankment walls and gun platforms (Schock 1978a, 1978b). Cut nails, lead bullets, a cartridge case, and a brass tack were found in these excavations. The embankment wall had been constructed by first setting posts along the intended line of the wall, nailing boards to the posts, and then stacking dirt against the boards. The boards that supported the wall had long since rotted away, but the cut nails that held them to the posts were still in place in the dirt.

In northern Kentucky, near Covington, at the Union Army fortification called Battery Bates, excavation exposed the earthen parapet and powder magazine, a rifle pit, and a gun platform (Harper et al. 1981). Lead sprue, cut nails, dark olive bottle glass, fused gunpowder, and a Flobert .22 caliber cartridge (patented 1848) were found in these trenches.

POSTWAR INDUSTRIALIZATION (1865–1915)

Compared to other southern states, Kentucky survived the Civil War in good shape. Since few major campaigns or battles took place within the state, physical devastation was not extensive (Harrison 1975:80). Nevertheless, Kentucky experienced profound social, economic, and political changes after the war. A large African-American population had to be integrated into the larger web of society; Kentucky's timber and coal industry developed; the tobacco market increased; there were fundamental changes in transportation; and toward the end of this era, the traditional agriculture system began to break down. Unlike the former Confederate states, Kentucky did not undergo Reconstruction, but it was included in the activities of the Freedmen's Bureau, the only non-Confederate state to receive such attention (Coulter 1966).

Kentucky's population increased from 1,648,690 in 1870 to 2,289,905 in 1910, an increase of 39 percent in 40 years. Many of these people settled in and around such large cities as Louisville and the Covington-Newport area. Initially, urban growth was influenced heavily by the migration of African-Americans to cities, but new job opportunities drew Euro-Americans to the cities as well.

Increased urbanization led to crowding and a decline in housing conditions in some cities. Tenement houses became more common as large, single-family structures were converted to rental units that often housed many families (Ellis 1981; Kemp 1909). Unsanitary and unpleasant conditions in these tenements and other structures soon led to legislative reforms, and cities began to establish municipal services. These new services had important ramifications for archaeologists. Once these services became regular and dependable, residents stopped constructing cisterns and privies, and often filled their old ones with domestic trash.

Despite the social and economic effects of the Civil War, Kentucky agriculture recovered rapidly. By 1900, the value of Kentucky farm products was $123,000,000, the highest in the South except for Texas (Tapp and Klotter 1977). Among the important cash crops, tobacco production increased more than 70 percent from 1870 to 1900, especially in the Bluegrass and parts of the Pennyroyal and Jackson Purchase (Tapp and Klotter 1977). However, soil depletion also followed the increased agricultural developments of the postwar years (Burroughs 1924, 1926; Davis 1923, 1927; Martin 1988; Sauer 1927).

Domestic Sites

Many of the trends mentioned above can be studied through the artifacts recovered during archaeological excavations. One example of the material frugality of many late nineteenth-century middle-class farmers can be seen at the Johnson-Bates farmstead in Jefferson County (O'Malley 1987a). Several areas around the two-story brick house were excavated, including a smokehouse, a frame barn, trash-filled sink-holes, and a log cabin that may have once been a slave's house. The results show that these farmers enjoyed moderate wealth during the Antebellum period but, not surprisingly, experienced hard times after the war. The artifacts recovered during the excavations are characterized by simplicity. This is especially true of the ceramics, which were primarily undecorated (O'Malley 1987a:578). Canning jar fragments were very common in the archaeological deposit, suggesting a high level of self-sufficiency, although commercially packaged foods were also represented by bottles and jars. Most maker's marks on ceramics and bottles dated from the early twentieth century and were from local Ohio Valley centers. The dominance of the Ohio Valley marks reflects this site's proximity to Louisville and also reflects the growth of the Ohio and West Virginia ceramic industry and the Ohio and Illinois glass industry in the early twentieth century.

The ceramics from the Prater farmstead in Floyd County and the "plain folk" farmstead in Meade County also illustrate rather frugal consumption of household goods (Esarey 1993b; Huser 1993; Otto and Gilbert 1982, 1984). This relatively frugal consumption pattern at these farmsteads illustrates a contrast in values between middle-class rural and middle-class urban residents. In the latter environment, the use of household goods as status reflectors appears to be much more important.

Another archaeologically investigated farm from the Postbellum era is that of John Luther Richards in Russell County (Fiegel 1989; Fiegel and Henderson 1987). This farm began in the late nineteenth century and was occupied until the late twentieth century. Archaeologists collected more than 17,000 artifacts at this site, including architectural hardware, bottle glass, ceramics, clothing, ammunition, farm equipment, and toys. These materials and the locations where they were found were studied to identify farm activity areas and the trade networks or markets from which the artifacts were purchased. Recreational areas, farm maintenance areas, and kitchen refuse areas were found by examining the distribution of toys, horseshoes and farm equipment, and ceramics, respectively. The maker's marks on glass and ammunition suggest that the main source of goods was the northeastern United States, followed by the Ohio Valley and the Southeast. The greater frequency of northeastern marks at the Luther site compared to the Johnson-Bates site reflects the Luther site's location away from the Ohio River and its rail connections with a wide geographical area.

Fiegel (1989) also found a close correlation between the layout and design of the farm structures that still stand at this site and the design types that were promoted in farm manuals of the period. The excavations suggest that the original farm house was of shed construction. Fiegel bases his inference on an innovative analysis of nails from the site, which correlated nail sizes and quantity from the excavations with building size and construction techniques.

A contrasting view of postbellum plantation and early university life in the Bluegrass was attained from the privy excavations at Ashland, in Lexington (W.S. McBride 1993). Many of these findings have been incorporated into a museum display within the former privy structure. Two test excavations in the privy floor revealed stratified deposits, with an upper layer of artifacts dating from about 1885–1920 and a lower layer of artifacts dating from around 1860–85. The earlier deposit was primarily associated with the time when Ashland was used as the campus for the A & M College and as the residence of its regent, John Bowman. The later layer of artifacts is associated with the occupation of the McDowell family, descendents of Henry Clay who purchased the estate and resumed the plantation agriculture on it.

The ceramic and table glass from both archaeological deposits show a pattern of great wealth, conspicuous consumption, and lavish entertaining (Esarey 1993a; W.S. McBride 1993). Expensive porcelains and ironstones in a great variety of consuming and serving forms were recovered. The presence of so many types of service vessels and the large quantity of pieces from individual matched sets is not unusual given upper-class patterns of purchasing, entertaining, and discarding. Table glass included many sizes and forms of pressed and cut stemmed ware, tumblers, dishes, bowls, and compotes. These again indicate large specialized vessels and individual place settings.

The bottles from the lower level included a very large proportion of French, and possibly Italian, wine bottles, which correlated well with upper-class tastes and lavish entertaining. The bottles from the later deposit did not display the high proportion of wine bottles, but the low proportion of beer bottles and high proportion of whiskey and medicine bottles from this deposit suggest an upper-class life-style.

Industry

Industrial and transportation systems in Kentucky changed and expanded tremendously in the decades immediately following the Civil War. Railroads and the construction of new lines were a high priority after the war, and improvements in rail transportation led to the relative neglect of Kentucky's roads and rivers. Such river towns as Smithland in Livingston County and Glasgow in Barren County declined with the river trade between 1870 and 1900 (Nourse 1934:340).

Despite the general decline in river traffic, the Ohio River continued to be a major transportation artery. Coal and timber from Appalachia were frequently shipped down the Ohio for local use, processing, or transshipment at Cincinnati or Louisville. Louisville, Covington-Newport, and other river cities continued to grow, both because of their role in transportation and their links to the developing coal industry.

The industrial archaeology of the Covington-Newport area of northern Kentucky offers an example of late nineteenth-century Ohio River city growth. The Hemingray Glass Factory, which produced bottles, jars, tableware, and insulators, began in 1853, but expanded in the Postbellum period

Figure 7.11   Wall remnants of the Hemingray Glass Company in the Covington area. There is a two-meter scale a little to the left of center in the photograph. Courtesy of Bob Genheimer and the Behringer-Crawford Museum.

(Genheimer 1987). Excavations of waster deposits shed light on changes in the production technology and the variety of glass products manufactured at this site. Remains of numerous bottle types, canning jars, and insulators, in many colors, were recovered archaeologically. The excavations also revealed the structural remains of the main factory building, a leer oven, two decorating ovens, other unidentified ovens, a large cistern, and the company privy (fig. 7.11). The number and type of furnaces excavated at this factory suggest that it was technologically advanced for its time (Genheimer 1987:449). The innovativeness of the company is illustrated by the 17 patents it received.

Timber and Coal Towns

Archaeological investigations in coal and timber camps also provide insights into the changes associated with industrialization during the late nineteenth and early twentieth centuries. Although timber had long been an important local resource in Kentucky, a full-scale timber industry began to develop in the mid-1870s, especially in Appalachia. The industry experienced a big boom from the mid-1880s to 1910. Simultaneously, Appalachian coal deposits attracted the attention of investors. By 1889 the tonnage of coal mined in Appalachia surpassed that of the Western Coalfield, which had developed earlier. By 1913 annual production in the Appalachian mines was nearly 11 million tons, and in the Western Coalfield it was over 8.5 million tons.

The growth of these industries spawned many "timber towns" (Eller 1982:122–23) and coal mining communities during this era. A dramatic example is the small town of Cumberland Gap. In the late 1880s, due to the infusion of English capital and the arrival of a Louisville and Nashville branch line, Cumberland Gap grew in several years from a small center of about 60 families and one store into the town of Middlesboro, complete with half a dozen churches, a public library, an opera house, a golf course, and a hotel. Unfortunately, the boom turned into a bust by October 1893. By 1900 its population, which some investors claimed had reached 17,000 (Share 1982), had declined to just over 4,000 persons.

Excavations at Onionville provide insight into this kind of community, which grew and died during the post-war industrialization era. Onionville existed for 20 years (1917–37), along the Green River in Henderson County in the Western Coalfield (Schenian 1988b). It was a small, local operation, transitional in its reliance upon water transportation (as opposed to rail) and technology (including mule-drawn cars) that had been surpassed in other areas.

The archaeological investigation of the site involved interviews, archival research, and archaeological fieldwork. Excavations were conducted at the mine owner's house site, a miner's house site, the company store and housing area, two garbage dumps, the tipple pile and track berm, and the coal loading area at the river's edge. These excavations revealed the company store foundation, a considerable quantity of domestic artifacts, tipple hardware, track remnants, and an entire coal car (Schenian 1988b).

Analysis of artifacts from the two garbage dumps, including bottles, ceramics, glassware, cans, and toys, provide much information about the subsistence patterns, economic status, and trade networks of the former residents of Onionville. Schenian (1988b) found that the Onionville residents relied heavily on purchased commodities, including canned and bottled foods and condiments. The animal bones from the dump were primarily cuts of beef or pork and were probably purchased from a store. The many canning jar fragments suggest that home canning was common.

To examine questions concerning economic status and consumption patterns, Schenian used Sears and Roebuck catalogs to construct a preliminary price index for the twentieth-century ceramics (i.e., dishes) from Onionville. She found that the miners purchased mostly middle- to lower-priced ceramics, which included banded and edge-decorated wares. Some higher-priced printed and painted wares and lower-priced undecorated ceramics were also found in the dumps, but in low quantities.

Maker's marks on sherds and bottles indicated that Onionville residents had access to regional, national, and international markets through mail-order catalogs and the company store. Identifiable ceramics came from the northeastern United States, the Ohio Valley, England, and Germany. The glass artifacts were produced in such areas as the Ohio Valley, the northeastern and southeastern United States, California, and Canada. One interesting component of Schenian's (1988b) investigation centered on the decorated glassware from Onionville. During her study, Schenian noted that most of the glassware vessels were not everyday tumblers or plates, but were decorative or entertaining pieces. She also found that the dates of manufacture for these dishes fell in two clusters, one around 1900 and the other around 1935. Schenian suggests that this temporal clustering may represent two generations of wedding gifts. In support of her claim, these dates conform to the wedding dates of some of the known residents of Onionville.

SUMMARY

Historical archaeologists in Kentucky have studied the remains of plantations, farms, urban dwellings, industrial sites, military camps, and frontier forts. Nevertheless, it should be clear from our review that Kentucky historical archaeology is still in its infancy. For example, much more is known archaeologically about the homes and plantations of a few wealthy early Kentuckians than about the homes and lifeways of ordinary citizens. Also, most of the studies completed to date have been primarily descriptive and have not addressed broader questions. This is a result of the history of historical archaeology in Kentucky. Most Kentucky historical archaeological projects in the 1960s and 1970s occurred on well-known upper-class urban residences, plantation houses, and other prominent structures or sites. These studies were oriented toward aiding architectural and landscape reconstruction or renovation. Because of these goals, broader historical and cultural questions were not addressed.

The prevalence of reconstruction-oriented studies in early Kentucky historical archaeology is not unique. This type of investigation dominated the first few decades of historical archaeology in most states and was undoubtedly influenced by the reconstruction and restoration of Williamsburg, Virginia, which began in the 1950s.

Beginning in the late 1970s and continuing to this day, most historical archaeological investigations, in Kentucky, as elsewhere, have been conducted as part of cultural resources management (CRM) projects, or what used to be called "salvage archaeology." Although many historic sites were recorded in archaeological surveys by the late 1970s, few were being excavated until the middle 1980s. The CRM reports were mostly descriptive, with little emphasis placed on examining and interpreting broader or even specific cultural historical questions.

Beginning in the mid-1980s, the number of CRM-sponsored excavations of historic sites increased in Kentucky. Grant-funded research on historic sites also increased. Research turned from a predominantly descriptive focus to one in which many anthropological questions were investigated, including socioeconomic variation, spatial organization, household formation, ethnicity, foodways, and economic development.

Historical archaeological sites are now more consistently recorded by archaeologists in the field, and the information gathered from surveys and excavations is used to answer many questions about the nature and process of the historical development of Kentucky. Possibly the greatest weakness of Kentucky historical archaeology is the small size of the existing database. Since historical archaeology is a comparative discipline, information on more sites and more different site types is needed from all regions of the state. Particularly neglected sites include middle- and lower-class rural and urban sites, nonAnglo-American sites, sites in eastern and southwestern Kentucky, and almost any nondomestic site.

As the Kentucky database grows, problem-oriented research will begin to achieve the interpretative potential of historical archaeology. Because of its position of combining documentary data and material culture, historical archaeology has a special ability to answer many questions. These questions include, for example, food consumption patterns and how various factors influence them; the process of assimilation or resistance of ethnic groups toward mainstream society and how this is materially reflected; the process of social and material adaptation to the frontier; the spatial organization of rural and urban lots and how this is influenced by cultural, economic, class, and environmental factors; and how the great industrial and transportation changes of the nineteenth and early twentieth centuries affected daily lives.

Recently, historic archaeological investigations of sites open for public visitation have increased. This trend should continue and include not only archaeology directed toward architectural reconstruction or renovation, but also archaeology directed toward and incorporated in the interpretation of the daily lives of a site's inhabitants.

THE FUTURE OF
KENTUCKY'S PAST

R. Barry Lewis and David Pollack

We have much to learn about the archaeology of Kentucky, but the rapid destruction of archaeological sites makes it increasingly hard to do. Unless archaeologists and the public work to preserve and protect significant sites, few will remain to be studied and appreciated by future generations. Unlike endangered plants and animals, which can sometimes be nursed back from the brink of extinction, the destruction of an archaeological site is irreversible. The loss of some sites is inevitable since we must plant fields, create water reservoirs, and build houses, roads, bridges, shopping malls, and do all of the other things that improve our lives—and incidentally destroy archaeological sites. Therefore, the best way to care for the past is to ensure that it is included in our planning for the future.

In this chapter we emphasize that the archaeological record is a complex, fragile, irreplaceable resource, and that everyone shares the responsibility of being stewards of the past. We first describe some important characteristics of the archaeological record and how scientists study it. This will help to clarify why archaeologists are so concerned about the future of the past. Second, we identify the major factors that threaten the archaeology of Kentucky. Third, we describe the major steps that can be taken to conserve Kentucky's archaeological resources. At the end of the chapter, suggestions are offered to the public about how it can help to conserve Kentucky's past.

THE ARCHAEOLOGICAL RECORD

Like oil and coal, the archaeological record is a finite resource. There is only so much of it, and once it is depleted, it is gone forever. No one is making any more 100-, 1,000-, or 10,000-year-old sites these days. Consequently, every time a site is vandalized, deep plowed, bulldozed off a bluff, or hauled away for fill dirt, another piece of Kentucky's heritage is lost.

Although it is the source of artifacts, the archaeological record is not simply an artifact mine. It is organized in a way that reflects the cultural behavior and beliefs of past peoples. For example, a house that burned down in A.D. 400 along the Mississippi River can be reconstructed fairly accurately, even to the extent of describing how the spaces inside the house were used, what the people who lived in the house ate, the tools they used and how they made them, and lots more. All of this is possible even if the site has been covered for 1,500 years by trees, underbrush, and spring floods; it's largely impossible if the site has been bulldozed up into a pile of earth. The remains of the house contain the contexts of artifacts and features and their associations, information archaeologists must have to reconstruct it. This information is irretrievably lost if the site is scraped up into a pile.

This brings up a related point—the most important thing that archaeologists study is a site, not an artifact. Archaeology's major concerns share nothing with those of the Hollywood archaeologist Indiana Jones. Likewise, although museum display cases full of artifacts effectively convey a sense of the past to the public, the aim of science is not merely to collect more artifacts. As discussed in chapter 1, the goal is to understand the beliefs, economies, and social organizations of the people who made the artifacts and to explain how and why these people lived and changed down through past millennia. To do this is ultimately to learn more about all civilizations, including our own.

In conclusion, the archaeological record is a complex, fragile, irreplaceable resource, and we must care for it just as we care for other resources. The rest of this chapter explores how to do this.

SITE DESTRUCTION FACTORS

The greatest threats to Kentucky's archaeological heritage are development projects, mining, urban expansion, farming, soil erosion, and other activities that change the face of the land. Scores of archaeological sites are destroyed unintentionally every day while producing food, excavating raw materials, and building houses. Most people are unaware that their activities destroy archaeological sites. Unfortunately, they also do not know that the preservation of Kentucky's archaeological heritage is compatible with development and progress.

Looting also destroys many sites. Looters have damaged and destroyed countless village sites and hundreds of mounds, cemeteries, and rockshelters throughout Kentucky. They range from the individual who digs big holes in mounds to find pots, skulls, and arrowheads for his or her collection, to the criminal who loots sites and sells what he or she finds to unscrupulous dealers and collectors. They know their activities destroy Kentucky's heritage and they don't care.

Let us take a closer look at each of these factors of site destruction.

Development Projects

Development is a broad term that includes the construction of residential subdivisions, industrial facilities, and many other large-scale projects. Every year, public and private development alters many large land tracts and destroys hundreds of archaeological sites in Kentucky. The destruction is unnecessary because development can be compatible with archaeological site preservation. Two common preservation measures are, first, to leave archaeological sites as green space within a development, and second, to have affected sites investigated by professional archaeologists prior to their destruction. The "green space" alternative is a cost-effective approach that requires little attention other than erosion control. The excavation alternative can be more costly to the developer, but it can also provide priceless goodwill and publicity. Furthermore, after the excavated materials are analyzed, described, and curated in a museum, and the report on the investigations is published, the information the site contained will be preserved although the location itself is destroyed.

Developers and planners have worked with archaeologists to protect many Kentucky archaeological sites. In 1990 a new industrial park was slated for development in Frankfort. As part of its planning, the city of Frankfort contracted for an archaeological survey, which examined two Fort Ancient sites in the proposed park. One of these, the Carpenter site, was preserved as green space. The other site, Capitol View, could not be avoided by the construction, so University of Kentucky archaeologists excavated it with support provided by the State Finance Cabinet.

In a similar case, in 1989 the Winchester–Clark County Industrial Authority decided to preserve the Clinkenbeard site as green space in the Winchester Industrial Park. This site, which is listed in the National Register of Historic Places, is the remains of an early frontier settlement. It was constructed by William Clinkenbeard in 1808 on property patented out of Strodes Station. The Winchester–Clark County Industrial Authority's decision ensures that the site will not be destroyed, and it did not hinder the development of the industrial park.

In Bourbon County, Columbia Gas worked with the landowner and archaeologists to investigate the Larkin site before building a gas transmission line across it. This large Fort Ancient village site contains hundreds of burials. Because of the cooperative efforts of Columbia Gas and the landowner, more than 10 protohistoric graves were investigated by professional archaeologists before the pipeline was laid. Columbia Gas reported on the results of this excavation in its company magazine, and both Columbia Gas and the landowner received preservation awards in recognition of their efforts.

With the construction of the LEXTRAN facility in Lexington in the late 1980s, the LEXTRAN Corporation and the Lexington-Fayette Urban-County Government encouraged local citizens and students to work with University of Kentucky archaeologists to excavate the remains of nineteenth-century residential households exposed by the construction (see the description of the LEXTRAN project in chapter 7). The sponsors have published articles on the excavations in transportation trade journals, and the new LEXTRAN facility will contain permanent exhibits that describe the results of the archaeological project.

Mining

The mining of coal and other minerals destroys hundreds of archaeological sites every year. Beginning in the 1980s, however, several mining companies began to hire professional archaeologists to find and evaluate archaeological sites in proposed mining areas. Today, proposed mining areas are routinely investigated by professional archaeologists. Because of these studies, important sites that would otherwise have been destroyed have been identified and preserved. Where the destruction of sites was unavoidable, some mining companies have paid to have the sites professionally excavated. The Andalex Village site, for example, a Mississippian village in Hopkins County, was investigated by professional archaeologists in 1989 prior to the area being mined (fig. 8.1). This project produced important new information about how people lived in this part of Kentucky during the thirteenth century A.D.

Urban Expansion

As cities and towns grow, archaeological sites are destroyed. Local governments are usually sensitive to the need to preserve the past, and they use several different tactics to achieve it. They have adopted preservation ordinances, prepared preservation plans, established green belts, and obtained development easements to protect important sites. The approaches that work are those in which possible effects on archaeological sites are considered when a development project is first proposed, not when it is under construction.

Boone County, for example, requires that developers consult the planning office to determine whether proposed projects will affect any of the recorded

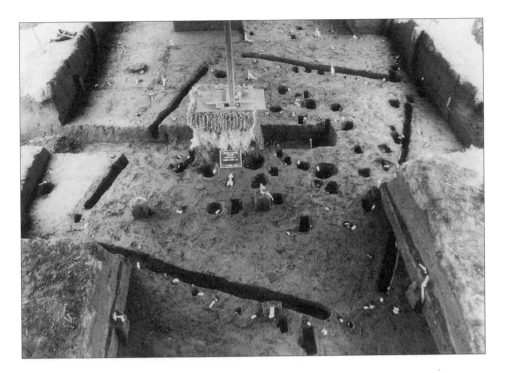

Figure 8.1 Wall trenches and postmolds of an Andalex Village submound structure. Photo courtesy of Cultural Resource Analysts, Lexington.

archaeological sites in the county. Elsewhere, some cities, especially those in the eastern states, have added archaeologists to their municipal staffs and draw on their expertise in city planning and educational projects.

Farming and Soil Erosion

Few farmers realize the extent to which farming destroys archaeological sites. Deep plowing, land leveling, and other farm-related factors destroy scores, if not hundreds of sites in Kentucky every year. Some of this destruction is unavoidable; in other cases, small changes can save sites.

Long ago, some farmers recognized the effects of farming on archaeological sites and changed the way in which they used their land so that the sites would be preserved and still be productive ground. In Greenup County, the owners of part of the Old Fort Earthwork recognized that if they continued to plow this site, it would eventually destroy the walls of the site's earthen enclosure. They put the site in permanent pasture and saved the prehistoric enclosure.

Figure 8.2   The Nelson Gay Mound in Clark County.

The Nelson Gay Mound (fig. 8.2) in Clark County also has been carefully tended by its owner. This mound is kept permanently in pasture. As a result, it is one of the best-preserved Woodland burial mounds in the Ohio River Valley.

Many archaeological sites are located along streams and river banks that are subject to erosion. Riprapping stream banks and planting vegetation are effective ways to stabilize areas that are eroding. In Livingston County, the Nashville District of the Army Corp of Engineers riprapped the river bank near the Whalen site, effectively preserving it.

Looting

Every year, hundreds of sites, among them some of Kentucky's most important archaeological resources, are damaged or destroyed by looting. Most rockshelter sites in the Daniel Boone National Forest, for example, have been vandalized. The looters usually take only a few artifacts from these sites, but to get these relics, they destroy the contexts and associations that hold the most important information about the people who lived in these shelters for thousands of years.

Figure 8.3   Looted Civil War grave
in Union County. Photo courtesy of
Kenny Barkley.

Besides rockshelters, other targets for looters in Kentucky are Woodland
burial mounds, Archaic shell middens, Mississippian and Fort Ancient villages, historic family cemeteries, Civil War cemeteries and battlefields (fig.
8.3), and early historic sites. The looters mostly take the grave goods buried
with the dead at these sites, but sometimes they want the human bones too.
Civil War battlefields and graves attract looters who want military artifacts.
Privy looters are usually after whole bottles.

One of the largest and most destructive looting episodes in the Ohio
River Valley happened in 1987 at the Slack Farm site near Uniontown in
Union County. Before they were arrested for grave robbing (the specific crime
is described in Kentucky law as "desecration of a venerated object") by the
Kentucky State Police, 10 men dug over 450 holes searching for artifacts and
bones (fig. 8.4). The State Medical Examiner's Office asked professional
archaeologists in Kentucky to help determine how many graves had been disturbed and to assess the nature and extent of the destruction caused by the
looters. Working with the Examiner's Office, the Kentucky Heritage Council
coordinated the archaeological effort and sought to learn as much as possible
about this site. More than 250 volunteers—amateur archaeologists, farmers,

Figure 8.4 Aerial photograph of the Slack Farm site in Union County showing hundreds of looters' holes. Kenny Barkley, Union County Advocate.

students, Girl Scouts, and concerned local citizens—helped the professional archaeologists. They discovered that the looters had disturbed more than 650 Mississippi period graves and destroyed a tremendous amount of information about the community in which those Native Americans lived.

The looting of the Slack Farm site attracted media attention. Stories about the looting and the voluntary efforts of professional archaeologists and citizens to assess and repair the damage appeared in most Ohio Valley newspapers, the major national dailies, television news shows, and even *National Geographic* magazine. The publicity and the following public outcry resulted in the Kentucky, Indiana, and Illinois state legislatures strengthening laws to protect prehistoric and historic cemeteries. Ironically, the individuals who looted the Slack Farm site were never prosecuted, and the charges against them were dropped in the spring of 1990.

CONSERVATION MEASURES

If our archaeological resources are assaulted from every side by vandals and the general effects of progress, what can be done to turn these trends around? How do we conserve this resource so that succeeding generations can profit from its existence? Our efforts are guided by education, identifying significant sites, planning, and legislation.

Education

Education promotes conservation by increasing our awareness of a resource, the factors that affect it, and how we can control those factors. It provides a basis for the definition of local, state, and national conservation issues. It is one of our most valuable tools for conserving Kentucky's archaeological heritage.

The primary responsibility for educating Kentucky's citizens about the conservation of our archaeological resources rests with archaeologists and several state agencies. Most of Kentucky's professional archaeologists work with local amateur archaeology groups and give talks to school classes, historical societies, environmental educators, Scout troops, and developers. The Kentucky Heritage Council also teaches the public about prehistoric lifeways by cosponsoring "archaeological weekends" with universities, museums, parks, and local governments. These programs feature artisans who make copies of aboriginal pottery, projectile points, and baskets, storytellers who know aboriginal myths and folklore, and archaeologists who describe Kentucky's rich prehistory and early history. Past cosponsors of archaeological weekends include the University of Kentucky, Murray State University, Behringer-Crawford Museum, Mammoth Cave National Park, and Jefferson County.

Other education programs include the University of Kentucky Museum of Anthropology traveling display cases that are loaned to public schools, and the Kentucky Historical Society's Junior Historian Program that provides high school students with an opportunity to participate in archaeological excavations. Most of Kentucky's universities also teach archaeology courses; advanced degree programs in archaeology exist at the University of Kentucky and the University of Louisville.

Although most education programs are aimed at the public, the Kentucky Heritage Council's Kentucky Archaeological Registry Program, which we describe in detail below, provides the owners of significant sites with archaeological information about their site. This is only one aspect of this program, which seeks to ensure the long-term preservation of significant sites by working closely with the landowners.

Kentucky does not have a state museum in which one can find comprehensive displays of the remains of our past. Several excellent small museums, such as the University of Kentucky Museum of Anthropology in Lexington, Behringer-Crawford Museum in Covington, and the Murray State University research center at Wickliffe, interpret Kentucky's archaeology to the public.

In spite of its rich archaeological heritage, Kentucky also lacks state-owned archaeological parks beyond Murray State University's Wickliffe facility in Ballard County on the Mississippi River. Although some of our state parks contain Civil War battlefields and other important archaeological sites, none of these parks was designed to interpret the archaeology. Well-known archaeological parks in adjacent states include Angel Mounds State Park in Indiana, Pinson Mounds State Park in Tennessee, and Fort Ancient State Park in Ohio. Such parks are good tourist attractions, preserve and protect archaeological sites, and interpret archaeology to the public.

The Identification of Significant Sites

The Office of State Archaeology at the University of Kentucky in Lexington maintains the official record of Kentucky archaeological sites. More than 15,000 sites have been reported to this office by professional and amateur archaeologists, state and federal agencies, and landowners. Several hundred new sites are recorded each year. This information is of crucial importance to archaeologists because nearly every research problem requires knowledge of where sites are (and where they are not), how old each site is, and what each was used for. But not every site is of equal importance, even to the archaeologist. Some sites are such significant places that they bear special consideration—for example, a well-preserved Adena "sacred circle" earthwork, a rockshelter site that has not yet been looted, a Mississippian town, the remains of an eighteenth–century farmstead, or a Civil War battlefield. At first glance, the identification of these significant sites would not appear to contribute much to preservation, but it does. It is difficult to protect a site if no one knows it exists. If a site's location is known, however, there are several federal and state programs that could protect it from thoughtless destruction.

The most important federal and state programs are linked to the National Register of Historic Places, a listing of United States historic structures and archaeological sites that are of special significance and are worthy of protection. Federal agencies are required to preserve National Register sites by avoiding them completely or by having professional archaeologists excavate part of them if avoidance is impractical. Many private developers also have come to recognize the national importance of these sites and willingly alter the design of their construction projects to avoid harming them.

Every state identifies and nominates sites for listing on the National Register, but some states are more aggressive than others in making use of this program. Among the 50 states, Kentucky ranks fourth in the number of National Register archaeological sites. Applications for nominating a site go through an extensive review procedure and must be approved by the Kentucky Historic Preservation Review Board, the director of the Kentucky

Heritage Council, who is also the State Historic Preservation Officer in Kentucky, and the Keeper of the National Register in Washington.

There is also the National Historic Landmark program, which is beginning to be used frequently and effectively as a preservation tool in Kentucky. This program was designed, in part, to identify properties for possible inclusion in the National Park system. National Historic Landmarks are monitored annually, and selected ones are inspected by the National Park Service. The federal government also offers such preservation assistance programs as the National Historic Landmark Fund and tax incentives to landmark owners. In addition, Congress can consider legislation to aid in the preservation of landmark sites. Nominations of prospective landmarks are primarily made by the National Park Service to the National Historic Landmark Review Board. By 1992, approximately 20 archaeological sites in Kentucky had been declared National Historic Landmarks and several others were under consideration.

At the state level, the Kentucky Heritage Council's Kentucky Archaeological Registry program protects important, privately owned sites by involving landowners in site preservation. The Kentucky Archaeological Registry Program is rooted in the belief that landowners have an interest in the resources they own, that they will not purposely destroy them, and that they will act as the resource's stewards. A site owner can participate in the registry by agreeing verbally or in writing to protect the site. Participants also are asked to notify the Kentucky Heritage Council if the site changes hands or if it is threatened by destruction. The Kentucky Heritage Council can assist the landowner in managing registry sites and, upon request, will advise landowners about the most appropriate tools for stronger site protection.

Planning

Section 106 of the National Historic Preservation Act of 1966 requires that all federal agencies consider what effect, if any, their proposed undertakings will have on archaeological resources that are listed in or are eligible for listing in the National Register of Historic Places. What this means is that, by law, each federal agency has to consider archaeological site preservation before building a dam, channeling a creek, constructing a new live-fire target range, and so on. As part of this process, the agency must consult the State Historic Preservation Officer. To comply with this law, the agency usually hires an archaeologist to identify and evaluate archaeological sites within the proposed project area. If this survey yields one or more sites determined to be eligible for listing in the National Register of Historic Places, the agency generally has two alternatives. The preferred alternative is to preserve the site, but if this is not possible or practical, the agency can contract with a professional archaeologist to investigate the site thoroughly before it is destroyed.

Legislation

Several laws protect sites on public land from damage or destruction. The most effective of these laws are the Archaeological Resources Protection Act of 1979, the Antiquities Act (KRS 164.705-735), Cave Legislation Statute (KRS 433), and Desecration of a Venerated Object (i.e., grave robbing) law (KRS 525.110). The Archaeological Resources Protection Act makes it unlawful to remove archaeological remains from federal property without the permission of the responsible federal agency. The Antiquities Act makes it unlawful to remove archaeological remains from state or municipal lands without a permit from the Department of Anthropology at the University of Kentucky. The Antiquities Act also requires that archaeological sites be reported to the Department of Anthropology. Within the Department of Anthropology, the Office of State Archaeology issues site permits and maintains the Kentucky archaeological site record file. The Cave Legislation statute makes it unlawful to remove archaeological remains from a Kentucky cave without a permit from the Department of Anthropology. The Desecration of a Venerated Object law, which figured prominently in the Slack Farm looting case, established grave looting as a felony act.

HOW YOU CAN HELP

What can you do to save the past for the future? First, do not set out on your own to dig holes in sites. We encourage you to report site vandalism and grave robbing to law enforcement officials. If you would like to participate in a dig or just learn more about archaeological fieldwork, volunteer on archaeological projects. Archaeology in the field and lab requires much hand work, and many archaeologists accept reliable, hardworking volunteers to help get the job done.

If you walk fields looking for arrowheads and other artifacts, keep a detailed record of what you find and precisely where it came from. As stressed in chapter 1, the context of a find is of critical importance, so always catalog your artifacts so that you and anyone who examines your collection can easily determine where each specimen was found. You should also report the sites you know about to the Office of State Archaeology in Lexington, to the Kentucky Heritage Council in Frankfort, or to an archaeologist who works for one of the regional Kentucky universities. In 1995 professional archaeologists were faculty or staff members at the University of Kentucky, University of Louisville, Murray State University, Western Kentucky University, and Northern Kentucky University.

If you own an archaeological site, do not allow people to dig on it unless they are qualified professional archaeologists who can produce valid university or state agency identification cards. Do not be deceived by someone who claims to represent a regional university and then proceeds to loot your property. If your site is vandalized, report it to local law enforcement personnel. You might also consider taking steps to ensure the long-term preservation of a significant site you own by putting it in pasture, by donating or selling the site to a public agency that will preserve it, or by drafting a management agreement or donating an easement to a public agency. The Kentucky Heritage Council staff can help you select an appropriate preservation approach for your site.

If you are interested in actively working to preserve archaeological sites, you might contact the Archaeological Conservancy, a national organization dedicated to protecting archaeological sites. The regional office of the Archaeological Conservancy is in Columbus, Ohio.

You might work with state and local preservation groups to promote new or stronger laws and regulations to protect, preserve, and manage archaeological sites. Kentucky also needs a state "Section 106" law that requires state agencies to consider the effects on archaeological sites of their proposed development projects, as well as local ordinances designed to protect archaeological sites. Encourage your local legislators to support interpretative displays at the state parks and the creation of archaeological parks or a Kentucky natural history museum.

If archaeologists and the public work together, we can foster a preservation ethic that will protect significant archaeological sites for future generations of Kentucky citizens to admire and study. Many of Kentucky's most significant sites can still be saved from destruction, but we must all act before it is too late.

WHERE TO WRITE FOR MORE INFORMATION

Kentucky Heritage Council
300 Washington Street
Frankfort, KY 40601

Eastern Regional Director
The Archaeological Conservancy
74 E. Jeffrey Place
Columbus, OH 43214-1702

Office of State Archaeology
Department of Anthropology
University of Kentucky
Lexington, KY 40506

Program for Cultural Resource
   Assessment
Department of Anthropology
University of Kentucky
Lexington, KY 40506

Archaeology Program
University of Louisville
Louisville, KY 40297

Department of Sociology and
   Anthropology
Western Kentucky University
Bowling Green, KY 42101

Department of Sociology and
   Anthropology
Northern Kentucky University
Highland Heights, KY 41076

U.S. Forest Service
Daniel Boone National Forest
1700 By Pass Road
Winchester, KY 40391

Department of Sociology and
   Anthropology
Murray State University
Murray, KY 42071

GLOSSARY

Adena: An Early Woodland and early Middle Woodland archaeological culture of the middle Ohio Valley.

Afro-American: A person of African-American descent.

Aplastic: *See* Temper.

Archaeological culture: The material remains of an extinct social group. Often the social group is assumed to have been comparable to a living society.

Archaic cultural tradition: Hunters and gatherers who inhabited the temperate forests of eastern North America after the end of the Pleistocene Epoch. By convention, the Archaic tradition (and the Late Archaic period) ends with the first appearance of pottery.

Assemblage: The artifacts found at a site; in multiple component sites, the material remains of a given component may be described as an assemblage, as in "the Medley phase assemblage at the Adams site."

Atlatl: A Nahuatl (central Mexico) word for a spear-thrower or throwing board, a notched stick that helps propel a spear with great force.

Barite/galena: The mineral form of lead.

Base camp: A campsite from which work parties leave to hunt and forage for food and other resources that are brought back to camp and eaten or used.

B.P.: Literally, *before present*. The "present" most archaeologists use is A.D. 1950, an arbitrary baseline agreed upon years ago for expressing the estimated ages of radiocarbon samples. *See also* Radiocarbon dating.

Bifacial tool (also Biface): A stone tool that shows convergent flaking on at least two surfaces. Most projectile points are bifacial tools.

Biota: The plant and animal life of a given environment.

Calibrated ages: Absolute age estimates that are corrected by reference to other instruments for measuring time. By necessity, radiocarbon age estimates, for example, assume that the atmospheric reservoir of C13, the radioactive carbon isotope, is constant over time. This reservoir is not constant, however, so all radiocarbon age estimates must be "calibrated" against dendrochronological master charts of high accuracy before they can be converted to calendar years.

Charnel house: A mortuary building.

Chiefdom: A small-scale society "ruled" by a chief or headman. However, social stratification, or true social classes, is not present in a chiefdom.

Chronological type: A named cluster of artifact characteristics (e.g., the pottery type Fayette Thick) selected because they are sensitive to temporal and, to a lesser extent, spatial changes.

Chronology: An archaeological chronology reconstructs the correct order of past human events in a unit of space, generally an archaeological region.

Component: A discrete episode of site use, typically one brief occupation of a site. Components are the building blocks of phases.

Copena: A Middle Woodland archaeological culture of northern Alabama.

227

CRM: *See* Cultural resources management.

Cross-dating: The process of dating sites on the basis of similar artifacts.

Cultural resources management (CRM): Archaeology done under contract for a sponsor who must comply with local, state, or federal historic preservation laws and regulations.

Culture (also Lifeways): The distinctively human nonbiological mechanism of adaptation. *See also* Archaeological culture.

Debitage: The waste by-products of stone toolmaking.

Demography: The science of the vital statistics of populations.

Dendrochronology: The method of dating sites by comparing the tree-rings of archaeological wood specimens with a master chart of tree-rings of known age.

Diagnostic artifact: An artifact that is distinctive for a given unit of time. A diagnostic artifact is also usually found in a spatially circumscribed region. For example, automobiles with wide tail fins are a diagnostic artifact of the late 1950s in the United States.

Egalitarian: A form of social organization in which there are as many positions of valued status as there are persons capable of filling them.

Euro-American: A person of European-American descent.

Fort Ancient culture: Late prehistoric villagers who inhabited northern and eastern Kentucky. These were the only major historically documented Native American groups in Kentucky.

Historic type: *See* Chronological type.

Historical archaeology: Archaeological research in which the material remains of a culture are supplemented by contemporaneous written records.

Holocene Epoch (also Recent Epoch): A geological time division of the Quaternary period between 10,000 B.P. and the present.

Hopewell: A Middle Woodland archaeological culture in the eastern United States.

Hopewell Interaction Sphere: A Middle Woodland complex of archaeological cultures that appear to have participated in a widespread network of trade and exchange of exotic raw materials and sumptuary goods.

Horizon: A grouping of archaeological artifacts that occurs over a large region during a brief interval of time. A modern example is the archaeological remains of World War II; these remains achieved a near worldwide distribution in less than a decade.

Hypsithermal climatic interval: The postglacial warming period between roughly 7,000 and 3,000 B.C. that may have affected Middle Archaic human populations in North America.

Ice Age: *See* Pleistocene Epoch.

Lifeways: *See* Culture.

Loess: Wind-blown silt deposit.

Mano: A stone used to grind meal or nuts on a metate, or grinding stone.

Megafauna: The big-game animals of the late Pleistocene Epoch.

Metate: A flat stone upon which seeds, grain, or nuts are ground into meal.

Midden: The accumulation of garbage and other living debris that marks the location of a former camp or village. A shell midden is one that contains many shells.

Mississippian tradition: Late prehistoric chiefdoms in western and southern Kentucky. These chiefdoms shared a strong riverine focus, were fully agricultural, and constructed planned villages and towns that were often fortified.

Native American: A descendent of the original inhabitants of the American continents; an American Indian.

Nutting stone (also Pitted anvil, Cupstone): A tabular stone, usually a sedimentary or granitic rock, that bears one or more large pits or depressions on its broad surfaces. These tools may have been used for nut cracking or as stone toolmaking anvils.

Occupation: A single episode of site use.

Open site: An archaeological site that is not covered by some terrain feature. For example, a rockshelter is not an open site because it has a natural roof; a village site in the forest next to a stream is an open site because no terrain feature protects it from the elements.

Paleoethnobotany: The study of the human use of plants and their by-products in the past.

Paleoindian: A nomadic big-game hunter and gatherer who inhabited North America near the end of the Pleistocene Epoch.

Period: A detailed description of contemporaneous phases viewed over many centuries, if not over several millennia. Unlike phases, periods span many regions.

Phase: A detailed description of the human communities of a region during a relatively short time interval, for instance one or two centuries.

Pleistocene Epoch: A geological time division of the Quaternary period between 1,700,000–10,000 B.P.

Pollen: Microscopic plant spores. Pollen grains preserve well in some contexts and can be readily identified by specialists. The study of fossil pollen samples reveals the gross vegetation pattern of a location and the changes in this pattern over time.

Prehistory: The archaeological record of human life prior to the advent of written documents.

Radiocarbon dating: A chronometric dating technique based on the known rate of decay of radioactive carbon atoms present in all living things.

Regional chronology: An archaeological reconstruction of the correct order of past human events in a region.

Rockshelter (also Rockhouse, Shelter): A sheltered overhang in the side of a bluff or cliff.

Sedentism: The condition of living in one place all the time. Sedentary, *adj.*

Seriation: A graphical or quantitative method designed to order archaeological materials on the basis of similarity, such that the most similar items are close together and the most different items are far apart.

Shell midden (also Shell mound): *See* Midden.

Stratigraphy: The superimposed levels or layers in an archaeological site.

Temper, Tempering (also Aplastic): Material added to potter's clay to control the expansion and contraction of a vessel when it is fired. Common temper in prehistoric Kentucky ceramics includes sand, rock grit, and crushed shells.

Terminal Archaic: The "late" Late Archaic period.

Tradition: A distinctive group of assemblages or artifacts that is found in a region during a long time interval (e.g., the Mississippian tradition).

Unifacial tool: A rock, usually a flake, that has been worked on only one side.

Village: A locus of settlement that is larger than a hamlet, generally more permanent than a camp, and smaller than a town.

Woodland tradition: Traditionally viewed as several archaeological periods in which mound ceremonialism, agriculture, and pottery-making were introduced into the East from other parts of the Americas.

REFERENCES

Ahler, Stephen R. 1987. Middle-Late Woodland Occupation at the Hansen Site, Greenup County, Kentucky. In *Current Archaeological Research in Kentucky: Volume One*, ed. David Pollack, pp. 44–77. Kentucky Heritage Council, Frankfort.

———. 1988. *Excavations at the Hansen Site (15Gp14) in Northeastern Kentucky*. Archaeological Report No. 173. Program for Cultural Resources Assessment, Department of Anthropology, University of Kentucky, Lexington.

Allen, Mark W. 1984. Preliminary Report on Human Skeletal Remains from the Adams Site (15Fu4). In *Late Prehistoric Research in Kentucky*, ed. David Pollack, Charles Hockensmith, and Thomas Sanders, pp. 181–85. Kentucky Heritage Council, Frankfort.

Allen, Roger C. 1976. Archaeological Investigations at Two Sites in the U.S. Interstate Highway 24 Right-of-Way in Marshall County, Kentucky. Ms. on file, Office of State Archaeology, University of Kentucky, Lexington.

———. 1977. The Page Phase: A Reexamination. Ms. on file, Office of State Archaeology, University of Kentucky, Lexington.

Allen, Roger C., and C. Wesley Cowan. 1976. *Test Excavations at American Smelting and Refining Corporation, Kentucky Refining Plant, Breckinridge County, Kentucky*. Ohio Valley Archaeological Research Associates, Lexington.

Allen, Roger C., and David Pollack. 1978. *Archaeological Survey and Testing at the Proposed Little Mountain Industrial Park, Mount Sterling, Montgomery County, Kentucky*. Archaeological Services, Lexington.

Alvord, Clarence W. 1920. The Illinois Country, 1673–1818. In *The Centennial History of Illinois* (Vol. 1, pt. 2), pp. 2–53. Illinois Centennial Commission, Springfield, Illinois.

Anderson, David G. 1990. The Paleoindian Colonization of Eastern North America: A View from the Southeastern United States. In *Early Paleoindian Economies of Eastern North America*, ed. Kenneth B. Tankersley and Barry L. Isaac, pp. 163–216. Research in Economic Anthropology, Supplement No. 5. JAI Press, Greenwich, Connecticut.

Asch, David L., and Nancy B. Asch. 1977. Chenopod as Cultigen: A Re-evaluation of some Prehistoric Collections from Eastern North America. *Midcontinental Journal of Archaeology* 2:3–45.

Aument, Bruce W. 1985. Results of the Boyd County Mounds Project and the Preliminary Interpretation of Prehistoric Mortuary Variability. In *Woodland Period Research in Kentucky*, ed. David Pollack, Thomas Sanders, and Charles Hockensmith, pp. 63–83. Kentucky Heritage Council, Frankfort.

———. 1986. *Archaeological Investigations of the Viney Branch, Brisbin, and Davis Sites, Boyd County, Kentucky*. Archaeological Report No. 122. Department of Anthropology, University of Kentucky, Lexington.

Barber, Paul. 1988. *Vampires, Burial, and Death*. Yale University Press, New Haven.

Bareis, Charles J., and James W. Porter (editors). 1984. *American Bottom Archaeology*. University of Illinois Press, Urbana.

Bell, Sir Charles. 1928. *The People of Tibet*. Oxford University Press, London.

Bense, Judith A. (editor). 1987. *The Midden Mound Project*. Report of Investigation No. 6. Office of Cultural and Archaeological Research, University of West Florida, Pensacola.

Black, Glenn A.. 1967. *Angel Site: An Archaeological, Historical, and Ethnological Study*. 2 vols. Indiana Historical Society, Indianapolis.

Bladen, Wilford A. 1973. The Mountains. In *Kentucky: A Regional Geography*, ed. Pradyumna P. Karan, pp. 23–51. Kendall/Hunt, Dubuque, Iowa.

Blakely, Robert L. 1971. Comparison of the Mortality Profiles of Archaic, Middle Woodland, and Middle Mississippian Skeletal Populations. *American Journal of Physical Anthropology* 34:43–53.

Boewe, Charles, Georges Reynaud, and Beverly Seaton (editors). 1987. *Précis ou Abrégé de Voyages, Travaux, et Recherches de C. S. Rafinesque (1833); The Original Version of A Life of Travels (1836)*. Verhandelingen der Koninklijke Nederlandse Akademie van Wetenschappen, Afd. Natuurkunde, Tweede Reeks, deel 86. North-Holland Publishing Company, Amsterdam and New York.

Boisvert, Richard A. 1982a. 1982 Excavations at Big Bone Lick, Kentucky. Paper presented at the Ohio Valley Archaeological Conference, Powdermill Nature Reserve, Carnegie Museum of Natural History, Ligionier, Pennsylvania.

———. 1982b. Late Archaic Occupations at Big Bone Lick, Kentucky: Evidence for a Focal Subsistence? Paper presented at the 39th Annual Meeting of the Southeastern Archaeological Conference, Memphis, Tennessee.

———. 1986. Late Archaic Settlement Models in the Middle Ohio Valley: A Perspective from Big Bone Lick, Kentucky. Ph.D. dissertation, Department of Anthropology, University of Kentucky, Lexington.

Brain, Jeffrey P. 1975. Artifacts of the Adelantado. *The Conference on Historic Site Archaeology Papers* 8:129–38.

Braley, Chad O. 1987. *The Battle of Gilgal Church: An Archaeological and Historical Study of Mid-Nineteenth Century Warfare in Georgia*. Southeastern Archaeological Services, Inc., Athens, Georgia.

Braun, David P. 1977. Middle Woodland–Early Late Woodland Social Change in the Prehistoric Central Midwestern United States. Ph.D. dissertation, Department of Anthropology, University of Michigan, Ann Arbor.

———. 1983. Pots as Tools. In *Archaeological Hammers and Theories*, ed. J.A. Moore and A.S. Keene, pp. 107–34. Academic Press, New York.

———. 1986. Midwestern Hopewellian Exchange and Supralocal Interaction. In *Peer Polity Interaction and Socio-Political Change*, ed. Colin Renfrew and John F. Cherry, pp. 117–26. Cambridge University Press, Cambridge.

Braun, David P., and Stephen Plog. 1982. Evolution of "Tribal" Social Networks: Theory and Prehistoric North American Evidence. *American Antiquity* 47:504–25.

Braun, E. Lucy. 1950. *Deciduous Forests of Eastern North America*. The Blakiston Company, Philadelphia.

Breitburg, Emanuel. 1982. Analysis of Area A Fauna. In *The Carrier Mills Archaeological Project: Human Adaptation in the Saline Valley, Illinois*, ed. Richard W. Jefferies and Brian M. Butler, pp. 863–957 Research Paper No. 33. Center for Archaeological Investigations, Southern Illinois University, Carbondale.

———. 1988. Faunal Remains. In *Muir: An Early Fort Ancient Site in the Inner Bluegrass*, ed. Christopher A. Turnbow and William E. Sharp, pp. 215–41. Reports of Investigations No. 165. Department of Anthropology, University of Kentucky, Lexington.

———. 1992. Vertebrate Faunal Remains. In *Fort Ancient Cultural Dynamics in the Middle Ohio Valley*, ed. A. Gwynn Henderson, pp. 209–42. Monographs in World Archaeology No. 8. Prehistory Press, Madison, Wis.

Brew, John O. 1968. Foreword. In *Bibliography of Salvage Archeology in the United States*, by Jerome E. Petsche, pp. 1–11. Smithsonian Institution, River Basin Surveys, Publications in Salvage Archeology No. 10. Lincoln, Nebraska.

Brisbin, Lansing G., Jr. 1976. The Stone Serpent Mound in Kentucky and Other Monuments. *The West Virginia Archaeologist* 25:26–36.

Broida, Mary O'Neal. 1983. Maize in Kentucky Fort Ancient Diets: An Analysis of Carbon Isotope Ratios in Human Bone. Master's thesis, Department of Anthropology, University of Kentucky, Lexington.

———. 1984. An Estimate of the Percents of Maize in the Diets of Two Kentucky Fort Ancient Villages. In *Late Prehistoric Research in Kentucky*, ed. David Pollack, Charles Hockensmith, and Tom Sanders, pp. 68–82. Kentucky Heritage Council, Frankfort.

Brooks, Pamela B., Robert L. Brooks, and Michael B. Collins. 1979. *The Bluestone Archaeological Project: Excavations at the 15Ro-35-36 Site Complex*. Special Report No. 1. Archaeological Services, Inc., Lexington, Kentucky.

Brose, David S., and N'omi Greber (editors). 1979. *Hopewell Archaeology: The Chillicothe Conference*. Kent State University Press, Kent, Ohio.

Brown, James A. 1979. Charnel Houses and Mortuary Crypts: Disposal of the Dead in the Middle Woodland Period. In *Hopewell Archaeology: The Chillicothe Conference*, ed. David S. Brose and N'omi Greber, pp. 211–19. Kent State University Press, Kent, Ohio.

———. 1985. The Mississippian Period. In *Ancient Art of the American Woodland Indians*, ed. David S. Brose, pp. 93–146. Detroit Institute of Arts, Detroit, Michigan.

———. 1986. Early Ceramics and Culture: A Review of Interpretations. In *Early Woodland Archeology*, ed. Kenneth B. Farnsworth and Thomas E. Emerson, pp. 598–608. Kampsville Seminars in Archaeology, Vol. 2. Center for American Archaeology, Kampsville, Illinois.

Brown, James A., and Robert K. Vierra. 1983. What Happened in the Middle Archaic? Introduction to the Ecological Approach to Koster Site Archaeology. In *Archaic Hunters and Gatherers in the American Midwest*, ed. James L. Phillips and James A. Brown, pp. 165–95. Academic Press, New York.

Broyles, Bettye J. 1971. *Second Preliminary Report: The St. Albans Site, Kanawha County, West Virginia, 1964–1968*. Report of Archaeological Investigations No. 3. West Virginia Geological and Economic Survey, Morgantown.

Burroughs, Wilbur G. 1924. *The Geography of the Western Kentucky Coal Field*. Kentucky Geological Survey, Series 6, Vol. 24. Lexington.

———. 1926. *Geography of the Kentucky Knobs*. Kentucky Geological Survey, Series 6, Vol. 19. Frankfort.

Butler, Brian M. 1991. Kincaid Revisited: The Mississippian Sequence in the Lower Ohio Valley. In *Cahokia and the Hinterlands*, ed. Thomas E. Emerson and R. Barry Lewis, pp. 264–73. University of Illinois Press, Urbana.

Butler, Brian M., and Richard W. Jefferies. 1986. Crab Orchard and Early Woodland Cultures in the Middle South. In *Early Woodland Archeology*, ed. Kenneth Farnsworth and Thomas E. Emerson, pp. 523–34. Kampsville Seminars in Archaeology, Vol. 2. Center for American Archaeology, Kampsville, Illinois.

Butler, Brian M., JoAnne M. Penney, and Cathy A. Robison. 1981. *Archaeological Survey and Evaluation for the Shawnee 200 MW A.F.B.C. Plant, McCracken County, Kentucky*. Research Papers No. 21. Center for Archaeological Investigations, Southern Illinois University, Carbondale.

Byers, Douglas S. 1954. Bull Brook–A Fluted Point Site in Ipswich, Massachusetts. *American Antiquity* 19:343–51.

Caldwell, Joseph R. 1964. Interaction Spheres in Prehistory. In *Hopewellian Studies*, ed. Joseph R. Caldwell and Robert L. Hall, pp. 133–43. Scientific Papers No. 12. Illinois State Museum, Springfield.

Caldwell, Joseph R., and Robert L. Hall (editors). 1964. *Hopewellian Studies*. Scientific Papers No. 12. Illinois State Museum, Springfield.

Call, Richard Ellsworth. 1895. *The Life and Writings of Rafinesque*. Filson Club Publication No. 10. J.P. Morton, Louisville.

Cambron, James W. 1974. Savage Cave. *Journal of Alabama Archaeology* 20:204–15.

Campbell, Joseph. 1959. *Primitive Mythology*. Penguin Books, New York.

Campbell, Julian J.N. 1985. The Land of Cane and Clover: Presettlement Vegetation in the So-Called Bluegrass Region of Kentucky. University of Kentucky Herbarium. Manuscript in possession of author.

Carr, Lucien, and Nathanial S. Shaler. 1876. On the Prehistoric Remains of Kentucky. *Memoirs of the Kentucky Geological Survey* 1(4). Frankfort.

Carstens, Kenneth C. 1980. Savage Cave: The Future of Its Prehistory. In *Western Kentucky Speleological Survey Annual Report 1980*, pp. 17–28. Murray State University, Murray.

———. 1982. *An Archaeological Reconnaissance of Two Areas Near Hickman (Fulton County), Kentucky*. Department of Anthropology and Sociology, Murray State University, Murray, Kentucky.

———. 1984. In Search of Fort Jefferson: Past, Present, and Future Studies. *Proceedings of the Symposium on Ohio Valley Urban and Historic Archaeology* 2:45–56.

———. 1986. In Pursuit of Fort Jefferson: A Summary of Investigations, 1980–1986. Paper presented at the 43rd Annual Meeting of the Southeastern Archaeological Conference, Nashville, Tennessee.

———. 1987. The William Clark Map of Fort Jefferson: An Exercise in 18th-Century Scaling. Paper presented to the 5th George Rogers Clark Trans-Appalachian Frontier History Conference, Vincennes, Indiana.

———. 1991. Current Field Strategies and Hypothesis Testing: The Fort Jefferson

Project Continues. *Proceedings of the Annual Archaeological Conference of the Kentucky Heritage Council*, ed. Charles D. Hockensmith, pp. 165–74. Kentucky Heritage Council, Frankfort.

Cassidy, Claire M. 1972. Comparison of Nutrition and Health in Pre-Agricultural and Agricultural Amerindian Skeletal Populations. Ph.D. dissertation, Department of Anthropology, University of Wisconsin, Madison.

———. 1980. Nutrition and Health in Agriculturalists and Hunter-Gatherers: A Case Study of Two Prehistoric Populations. In *Nutritional Anthropology: Contemporary Approaches to Diet and Culture*, ed. Norge W. Jerome, Randy F. Kandel, and Gretel H. Pelto, pp. 117–45. Redgrave, New York.

———. 1984. Skeletal Evidence for Prehistoric Subsistence Adaptation in the Central Ohio River Valley. In *Paleopathology at the Origins of Agriculture*, ed. Mark N. Cohen and George J. Armelagos, pp. 307–45. Academic Press, New York.

Chapman, Carl H. 1980. *The Archaeology of Missouri, II*. University of Missouri Press, Columbia.

Chapman, Jefferson C. 1975. *The Rose Island Site and the Bifurcate Point Tradition*. Report of Investigation No. 14. Department of Anthropology, University of Tennessee, Knoxville.

———. 1976. The Archaic Period in the Lower Little Tennessee River Valley: The Radiocarbon Dates. *Tennessee Anthropologist* 1:1–12.

———. 1977. *Archaic Period Research in the Lower Tennessee River Valley*. Report of Investigation No. 18. Department of Anthropology, University of Tennessee, Knoxville.

Chapman, Jefferson C., and Gary D. Crites. 1987. Evidence for Early Maize (*Zea mays*) from the Icehouse Bottom Site, Tennessee. *American Antiquity* 52:352–54.

Charles, Douglas K. 1985. Corporate Symbols: An Interpretive Prehistory of Indian Burial Mounds in West-Central Illinois. Ph.D. dissertation, Department of Anthropology, Northwestern University, Evanston, Illinois.

Charles, Douglas K., and Jane E. Buikstra. 1983. Archaic Mortuary Sites in the Central Mississippi Drainage: Distribution, Structure, and Behavioral Implications. In *Archaic Hunters and Gatherers in the American Midwest*, ed. James L. Phillips and James A. Brown, pp. 117–45. Academic Press, New York.

Chinn, George M. 1975. *Kentucky: Settlement and Statehood, 1750–1800*. Kentucky Historical Society, Frankfort.

Chomko, Stephen A., and Gary W. Crawford. 1978. Plant Husbandry in Prehistoric Eastern North America: New Evidence for its Development. *American Antiquity* 43:405–8.

Church, Flora. 1987. An Inquiry into the Transition from Late Woodland to Late Prehistoric Cultures in the Central Ohio Valley, Ohio Circa A.D. 500 to A.D. 1250. Ph.D. dissertation, Department of Anthropology, Ohio State University, Columbus.

Clark, Thomas C. 1960. *A History of Kentucky*. University Press of Kentucky, Lexington.

Clay, R. Berle. 1961. Excavations at the Tinsley Hill Village, 1960. Ms. on file, Office of State Archaeology, University of Kentucky, Lexington.

———. 1963a. Ceramic Complexes of the Tennessee-Cumberland Region in Western

Kentucky. Master's thesis, Department of Anthropology, University of Kentucky, Lexington.

————. 1963b. *The Tinsley Hill Mound*. University of Kentucky. Report submitted to the National Park Service, Region 1, Richmond, Virginia.

————. 1963c. *Tinsley Hill Village, 1962*. University of Kentucky. Report submitted to the National Park Service, Region 1, Richmond, Virginia.

————. 1979. A Mississippian Ceramic Sequence from Western Kentucky. *Tennessee Anthropologist* 4:111–28.

————. 1980. The Cultural Historical Placement of Fayette Thick Ceramics in Central Kentucky. *Tennessee Anthropologist* 5:166–78.

————. 1981. *Kentucky: An Introduction to State-Wide Research Design*. Office of State Archaeology, Lexington.

————. 1983. Pottery and Graveside Ritual in Kentucky Adena. *Midcontinental Journal of Archaeology* 8:109–26.

————. 1984. Styles of Stone Graves. In *Late Prehistoric Research in Kentucky*, ed. David Pollack, Charles Hockensmith, and Thomas Sanders, pp. 131–44. Kentucky Heritage Council, Frankfort.

————. 1985a. An Incident of Victorian Archaeology in Kentucky and its Historical and Regional Implications. In *Woodland Period Research in Kentucky*, ed. David Pollack, Thomas N. Sanders, and Charles D. Hockensmith, pp. 204–11. Kentucky Heritage Council, Frankfort.

————. 1985b. Peter Village 164 years later: 1983 excavations. In *Woodland Period Research in Kentucky*, ed. David Pollack, Thomas Sanders, and Charles Hockensmith, pp. 1–41. Kentucky Heritage Council, Frankfort.

————. 1986. Adena Ritual Spaces. In *Early Woodland Archeology*, ed. Kenneth B. Farnsworth and Thomas E. Emerson, pp. 581–95. Kampsville Seminars in Archaeology, Vol. 2. Center for American Archaeology, Kampsville, Illinois.

————. 1987. Circles and Ovals: Two Types of Adena Space. *Southeastern Archaeology* 6:46–56.

————. 1988a. The Ceramic Sequence at Peter Village and its Significance. In *New Deal Archaeology and Current Research in Kentucky*, ed. David Pollack and Mary L. Powell, pp. 105–13. Kentucky Heritage Council, Frankfort.

————. 1988b. Twenty Years of Preservation Archeology in Kentucky. Southeastern Archaeological Conference. *Special Publication* 6:25–29.

————. 1991. Chiefs, Big Men, or What? Economy, Settlement Patterns, and their Bearing on Adena Political Models. In *Cultural Variability in Context: Woodland Settlements of the Mid-Ohio Valley*, ed. Mark F. Seeman, pp. 77–80. Kent State University Press, Kent, Ohio.

Cobb, James E., and Charles H. Faulkner. 1978. The Owl Hollow Project: Middle Woodland Settlement and Subsistence Patterns in the Eastern Highland Rim of Tennessee. Ms. on file, National Science Foundation, Washington, D.C.

Coe, Joffre L. 1964. The Formative Cultures of the Carolina Piedmont. *Transactions of the American Philosophical Society*, new series, 54(5). Philadelphia.

Coe, Michael D., and F. William Fischer. 1959. Barkley Reservoir—Tennessee Portion, Archaeological Excavations 1959. Ms. on file, National Park Service, Regional Office, Richmond, Virginia.

COHMAP Members. 1988. Climatic Changes of the Last 18,000 Years: Observations and Model Simulations. *Science* 241:1043–52.

Cole, Fay-Cooper, Robert Bell, John Bennett, Joseph Caldwell, Norman Emerson, Richard MacNeish, Kenneth Orr, and Roger Willis. 1951. *Kincaid: A Prehistoric Illinois Metropolis.* University of Chicago Press, Chicago.

Collins, Michael B. 1979. The Longworth-Gick Site (15Jf243). In *Excavations at Four Archaic Sites in the Lower Ohio Valley, Jefferson County, Kentucky*, ed. Michael B. Collins. Occasional Papers in Anthropology No. 1, pp. 471–589. Department of Anthropology, University of Kentucky, Lexington.

————. 1980. Lithic Technology and Cultural Ecology in the Late Middle Woodland (Newtown) of Northwestern Kentucky. Paper presented at the 52d Annual Midwestern Archaeological Conference, Chicago.

Collins, Michael B., and Boyce N. Driskell. 1979. Summary and Conclusions. In *Excavations at Four Archaic Sites in the Lower Ohio Valley, Jefferson County Kentucky*, ed. Michael B. Collins. Occasional Papers in Anthropology No. 1, pp. 1023–42. Department of Anthropology, University of Kentucky, Lexington.

Conaty, Gerald T. 1985. *Middle and Late Archaic Mobility Strategies in Western Kentucky.* Ph.D. dissertation, Department of Archaeology, Simon Fraser University, Burnaby, British Columbia.

Cook, Thomas G. 1976. *Koster: An Artifact Analysis of Two Archaic Phases in West-Central Illinois.* Koster Research Reports No. 3. Northwestern University Archaeological Program Prehistoric Records, Evanston, Illinois.

Cotterill, Robert S. 1917. *History of Pioneer Kentucky.* Johnson and Hardin, Cincinnati.

Coulter, E. Merton. 1966. *The Civil War and Readjustment in Kentucky.* Peter Smith, Gloucester, Massachusetts. Originally published 1926.

Cowan, C. Wesley. 1975. *An Archaeological Survey and Assessment of the Proposed Red River Reservoir in Wolfe, Powell, and Menifee Counties, Kentucky.* Museum of Anthropology, University of Kentucky, Lexington. Report submitted to the National Park Service Interagency Archaeological Services Office, Atlanta.

————. 1976. *Test Excavations in the Proposed Red River Lake, Kentucky.* Museum of Anthropology, University of Kentucky, Lexington. Report submitted to the National Park Service, Atlanta.

————. 1978. Seasonal Nutritional Stress in a Late Woodland Population: Suggestions from Some Eastern Kentucky Coprolites. *Tennessee Anthropologist* 3:117–28.

————. 1979a. Excavations at the Haystack Rockshelters, Powell County, Kentucky. *Midcontinental Journal of Archaeology* 4:3–33.

————. 1979b. Prehistoric Plant Utilization at the Rogers Rockshelter, Powell County, Kentucky. Master's thesis, Department of Anthropology, University of Kentucky, Lexington.

————. 1985a. From Foraging to Incipient Food Production: Subsistence Change and Continuity on the Cumberland Plateau of Eastern Kentucky. Ph.D. dissertation, Department of Anthropology, University of Michigan, Ann Arbor.

————. 1985b. Understanding the Evolution of Plant Husbandry in Eastern North America: Lessons from Botany, Ethnography, and Archaeology. In *Prehistoric*

Food Production in North America, ed. Richard I. Ford, pp. 205–43. Anthropological Papers No. 75. Museum of Anthropology, University of Michigan, Ann Arbor.

———. 1987. *First Farmers of the Middle Ohio Valley: Fort Ancient Societies, A.D. 1000–1670.* Cincinnati Museum of Natural History, Cincinnati, Ohio.

———. 1990. Social Implications of Ohio Hopewell Art. Paper Presented at the 55th Annual Meetings of the Society for American Archaeology, Las Vegas, Nevada.

Cowan, C. Wesley, H. Edwin Jackson, Katherine Moore, Andrew Nickelhoff, and Tristine L. Smart. 1981. The Cloudsplitter Rockshelter, Menifee County, Kentucky: A Preliminary Report. *Southeastern Archaeological Conference Bulletin* 24:60–76.

Cowan, C. Wesley, and Frederick Wilson. 1977. *An Archaeological Survey of the Red River Gorge Area.* Kentucky Heritage Commission, Frankfort.

Coy, Fred E., Tom C. Fuller, Larry Meadows, Don Fig, J. Rosene, and G. Dever. 1984. Samuel Brown on Saltpeter from Sandstone Cliffs in Eastern Kentucky in 1806. *Tennessee Anthropologist* 9:48–65.

Crawford, Gary W. 1982. Late Archaic Plant Remains from West-Central Kentucky: A Summary. *Midcontinental Journal of Archaeology* 7:205–24.

Crowe-Carraco, Carol. 1979. *The Big Sandy.* University Press of Kentucky, Lexington.

Curran, Mary Lou. 1984. The Whipple Site and Paleoindian Tool Assemblage Variation: A Comparison of Intrasite Structuring. *Archaeology of Eastern North America* 12:5–40.

Dancey, William S. 1988. The Community Plan of an Early Late Woodland Village in the Middle Scioto River Valley. *Midcontinental Journal of Archaeology* 13:223–54.

Davis, Darrell H. 1923. *The Geography of the Jackson Purchase.* Kentucky Geological Survey, Series 6, Vol. 9. Lexington.

———. 1924. *The Geography of the Blue Grass Region of Kentucky.* Kentucky Geological Survey, Series 6, Vol. 23. Lexington.

———. 1927. *The Geography of the Mountains of Eastern Kentucky.* Kentucky Geological Survey, Series 6, Vol. 18. Lexington.

Deam, Charles C. 1940. *Flora of Indiana.* Department of Conservation, Division of Forestry, Indianapolis, Indiana.

Deiss, Ron W. 1988. *Test Excavations on Frankfort's Public Square: An Archaeological Investigation of Kentucky's Old State Capitol.* Kentucky Historical Society, Frankfort.

Deller, D. Brian, and Chris J. Ellis. 1988. Early Paleo-Indian Complexes in Southwestern Ontario. In Late Pleistocene and Early Holocene Paleoecology and Archaeology of the Eastern Great Lakes Region, ed. R. Laub, N. Miller, and D. Steadman, pp. 251–63. Bulletin of the Buffalo Society of Natural Sciences, Buffalo.

DiBlasi, Philip J. 1981. A New Assessment of the Archaeological Significance of the Ashworth Site (15Bu236): A Study in the Dynamics of Archaeological Investigation in Cultural Resource Management. Master's thesis, Interdisciplinary Studies, University of Louisville, Louisville, Kentucky.

Dickens, Roy S., Jr. 1976. *Cherokee Prehistory: The Pisgah Phase in the Appalachian Summit Region.* University of Tennessee Press, Knoxville.

Dorwin, John T., Edward Henson, Larry Meadows, and Donald T. Warholic. 1970. Archaeological Investigations of the Deep Shelter, Cave Run Reservoir Area, Rowan County, Kentucky. Ms. on file, University of Kentucky Museum of Anthropology, Lexington.

Dowell, Michael K. 1979. Archaeological Report of the Campbell and Watkins Mounds: Two Middle Woodland Burial Mounds in Southern Kentucky. Ms. on file, Department of Sociology and Anthropology, Western Kentucky University, Bowling Green.

Dragoo, Don W. 1963. *Mounds for the Dead: An Analysis of the Adena Culture*. Annals of Carnegie Museum No. 37, Pittsburgh.

———. 1976. Some Aspects of Eastern North American Prehistory: A Review 1975. *American Antiquity* 41:3–27.

Driskell, Boyce N. 1979. The Rosenberger Site (15Jf18). In *Excavations at Four Archaic Sites in the Lower Ohio Valley, Jefferson County, Kentucky*, ed. Michael B. Collins, pp. 697-803. Occasional Papers in Anthropology No. 1. Department of Anthropology, University of Kentucky, Lexington.

Driskell, Boyce N., and Roger C. Allen. 1976. *Excavations at the Cabin Creek Site, Mason County, Kentucky: Phase II*. Ohio Valley Archaeological Research Associates, Lexington.

Driskell, Boyce N., Cynthia Jobe, Christopher Turnbow, and Mary Dunn. 1984. *The Archaeology of Taylorsville Lake: Archaeological Data Recovery and Synthesis*. Archaeological Report No. 85. Department of Anthropology, University of Kentucky, Lexington.

Duffield, Lathel F. 1967. Preliminary Excavations at the Mont Corbin Site, Adair County, Kentucky. Ms. on file, Office of State Archaeology, University of Kentucky, Lexington.

———. 1974. Nonhuman Vertebrate Remains from Salts Cave Vestibule. In *Archaeology of the Mammoth Cave Area*, ed. Patty Jo Watson, pp. 123–33. Academic Press, New York.

———. 1979. Faunal Studies. In *Excavations at Four Archaic Sites in the Lower Ohio Valley, Jefferson County, Kentucky*, ed. Michael B. Collins, pp. 1006-19. Occasional Papers in Anthropology No. 1. Department of Anthropology, University of Kentucky, Lexington.

Duffield, Lathel F., and Richard A. Boisvert. 1983. The Adams Mastodon Site. Paper presented at the 48th Annual Meeting of the Society for American Archaeology, Pittsburgh.

Dunavan, Sandra L. 1985. Mississippian Ethnobotany at the Adams Site (15FU4). Undergraduate senior honors thesis, Department of Anthropology, University of Illinois, Urbana-Champaign.

Dunbar, James S., and Ben I. Waller. 1983. A Distribution of Clovis/Suwannee Paleoindian Sites of Florida: A Geographic Approach. *Florida Anthropologist* 36:18–30.

Duncan, Mary Susan. 1993. Kentucky's Saltpeter Caves: A Review and Comparison of an Early Nineteenth Century Industry. Master's thesis, Department of Anthropology, University of Kentucky, Lexington.

Dunnell, Robert C. 1961. A General Survey of Fort Ancient in the Kentucky-West Virginia Area. Ms. on file, Department of Anthropology, University of Kentucky, Lexington.

———. 1966. *1965 Excavations in the Fishtrap Reservoir, Pike County, Kentucky*. Museum of Anthropology, University of Kentucky, Lexington. Submitted to the National Park Service, Richmond, Virginia.

———. 1972. *The Prehistory of Fishtrap, Kentucky*. Publications in Anthropology No. 75. Yale University, New Haven.

———. 1983. Aspects of the Spatial Structure of the Mayo Site (15-JO-14), Johnson County, Kentucky. In *Lulu Linear Punctated: Essays in Honor of George Irving Quimby*, ed. Robert C. Dunnell and Donald K. Grayson, pp. 109–66. Anthropological Papers No. 7. Museum of Anthropology, University of Michigan, Ann Arbor.

Earle, Carville, and Ronald Hoffman. 1976. Staple Crops and Urban Development on the Eighteenth Century South. *Perspectives in American History* 10:7–80.

Earle, Timothy. 1991. Property Rights and the Evolution of Chiefdoms. In *Chiefdoms: Power, Economy, and Ideology*, ed. Timothy Earle, pp. 71–99. Cambridge University Press, Cambridge.

Edging, Richard. 1987. *Archaeological Investigations in the Gunpowder Creek Uplands, Boone County, Kentucky*. Archaeological Report No. 168. Program for Cultural Resource Assessment, University of Kentucky, Lexington.

——— (editor). 1985. *Archaeological Investigations at the Turk Site (15Ce6), Carlisle County, Kentucky*. Western Kentucky Project Report No. 3. Department of Anthropology, University of Illinois, Urbana-Champaign.

Eller, Ronald D. 1982. *Miners, Millhands, and Mountaineers: Industrialization of the Appalachian South, 1880–1930*. University of Tennessee Press, Knoxville.

Ellis, Chris J., and D. Brian Deller. 1988. Some Distinctive Paleo-Indian Tool Types from the Lower Great Lakes Region. *Midcontinental Journal of Archaeology* 13:111–58.

Ellis, William E. 1981. Tenement House Reform: Another Episode in Kentucky Progressivism. *Filson Club History Quarterly* 55:375–82.

Ellis, W. E., H. E. Everman, and Richard D. Sears. 1985. *Madison County: 200 Years in Retrospect*. Madison County Historical Society, Richmond, Kentucky.

Esarey, Duane, Kelvin Sampson, and Charles Suchy. 1984. The Carter Creek Site: A Weaver Phase Ring Midden in the Interior Uplands of West Central Illinois. *Wisconsin Archaeologist* 65:131–44.

Esarey, Mark E. 1993a. Ceramics from the Privy Vault. In *Archaeology at Henry Clay's Ashland Estate: Investigations of the Mansion, Yard, and Privy*, by W. Stephen McBride, pp. 61–89. Archaeological Report No. 281. Program for Cultural Resource Assessment, University of Kentucky, Lexington.

———. 1993b. Discussion and Interpretation. In *Phase III Archaeological Investigations at the Prater Historic Site (15Fd62) in Floyd County, Kentucky*, by William A. Huser, pp. 71–73. Archaeological Report No. 308. Program for Cultural Resource Assessment, University of Kentucky, Lexington.

Fagan, Brian M. 1987. *The Great Journey: The Peopling of Ancient America*. Thames and Hudson, London.

———. 1991. *In the Beginning: an Introduction to Archaeology*. 7th ed. HarperCollins, New York.

Fassler, Heidi. 1987. Guilfoil: A Middle Fort Ancient Village in Fayette County. In *Current Archaeological Research in Kentucky: Volume One*, ed. David Pollack, pp. 154–87. Kentucky Heritage Council, Frankfort.

Faust, Burton. 1967. The History of Saltpeter Mining in Mammoth Cave, Kentucky. *Filson Club History Quarterly* 41:5–20, 137–40, 227–62, 323–52.

Fay, Robert P. 1983. Restoration Archaeology at Liberty Hall, Frankfort, Kentucky: The 1987 and 1979 Seasons. *Proceedings of the Symposium on Ohio Valley Urban and Historic Archaeology* 1:29–35.

————. 1986. *Archaeological Investigations at Liberty Hall, Frankfort, Kentucky.* Kentucky Heritage Council, Frankfort.

Fenton, James P., and Richard W. Jefferies. 1989. The Camargo Earthworks and Mounds: An Adena-Hopewell Complex in the Kentucky Heartland. Paper presented at the 46th Annual Meeting of the Southeastern Archaeological Conference, Tampa, Florida.

Fiegel, Kurt H. 1989. *Stingy Ridge: An Archaeological and Historical Mitigation Report of the John Luther Richards Farm Complex, 15-Ru-12/15-Ru-43, Jamestown, Russell County.* Kentucky Transportation Cabinet, Division of Environmental Analysis, Frankfort.

Fiegel, Kurt H., and Jayne C. Henderson. 1987. *Archaeological and Cultural-Historic Report, 127 Improvement Project, Russell County, Kentucky.* Kentucky Transportation Cabinet, Division of Environmental Analysis, Frankfort.

Fig, Don, and Gary Knudsen. 1984. Niter Mining: An Incipient Industry of the Red River Gorge, Kentucky. *Proceedings of the Symposium on Ohio Valley Urban and Historic Archaeology* 2:67–73.

Fitting, James E., and Charles E. Cleland. 1969. Late Prehistoric Settlement Patterns in the Upper Great Lakes. *Ethnohistory* 16:289–302.

Ford, Richard I. 1974. Northeastern Archaeology: Past and Future Directions. *Annual Review of Anthropology* 3:385–413.

Fowler, Melvin L. 1957. *Rutherford Mound, Hardin County, Illinois.* Scientific Papers No. 1:1–44. Illinois State Museum, Springfield.

————. 1959. *Summary Report of Modoc Rock Shelter: 1952, 1953, 1955, 1956.* Reports of Investigations No. 8. Illinois State Museum, Springfield.

————. 1971. The Origin of Plant Cultivation in the Central Mississippi Valley: A Hypothesis. In *Prehistoric Agriculture*, ed. Stuart Struever, pp. 122–28. Natural History Press, Garden City, New York.

————. 1978. Cahokia and the American Bottom: Settlement Archaeology. In *Mississippian Settlement Patterns*, ed. Bruce D. Smith, pp. 455–78. Academic Press, New York.

————. 1989. *The Cahokia Atlas: A Historical Atlas of Cahokia Archaeology.* Studies in Illinois Archaeology No. 6. Illinois Historic Preservation Agency, Springfield.

Fried, Morton H. 1967. *The Evolution of Political Society.* Random House, New York.

Frison, George C. 1989. Experimental Use of Clovis Weaponry and Tools on African Elephants. *American Antiquity* 54:766–92.

Frison, George C., and Dennis J. Stanford. 1982. *The Agate Basin Site.* Academic Press, New York.

Fritz, Gayle J. 1986. Carbonized Plant Remains. In *The Calloway Site, A Transitional Early to Middle Woodland Camp in Martin County, Kentucky*, ed. Charles M. Niquette and Randall D. Boedy, pp. 90–102. Contract Publication Series 86-12. Cultural Resource Analysts, Lexington.

————. 1990. Multiple Pathways to Farming in Precontact Eastern North America. *Journal of World Prehistory* 4:387–435.

Fryman, Frank, Jr. 1968. The Corbin Site: A Possible Early Component of the Green River Phase of the Mississippian Tradition in Kentucky. Ms. on file, Office of State Archaeology, University of Kentucky, Lexington.

Funkhouser, William D., and William S. Webb . 1928. *Ancient Life in Kentucky*. Geologic Reports, Series 6, Vol. 34. Kentucky Geological Survey, Lexington.

————. 1929. *The So-called "Ash Caves" in Kentucky*. Reports in Archaeology and Anthropology No. 1(2):37–112. University of Kentucky, Lexington.

————. 1930. *Rock Shelters of Wolfe and Powell Counties*, Kentucky. Reports in Archaeology and Anthropology No. 1(4):239–306. University of Kentucky, Lexington.

————. 1931. *The Duncan Site on the Kentucky-Tennessee Line*. Reports in Archaeology and Anthropology, No. 1(6). University of Kentucky, Lexington.

————. 1935. *The Ricketts Site in Montgomery County, Kentucky*. Reports in Anthropology and Archaeology No. 3(3). University of Kentucky, Lexington.

————. 1937. *The Chilton Site in Henry County, Kentucky*. Reports in Anthropology and Archaeology No. 3:173–206. University of Kentucky, Lexington.

Genheimer, Robert A. 1987. *Archaeological Testing, Evaluation, and Final Mitigation Excavations at Covington's Riverfront Redevelopment Phase II Site, Kenton County, Kentucky*. R.G. Archaeological Services and Cultural Resource Analysts, Lexington.

Goad, Sharon I. 1980. Patterns of Late Archaic Exchange. *Tennessee Anthropologist* 5:1–16.

Goldstein, Lynne G. 1976. Spatial Structure and Social Organization: Regional Manifestations of Mississippian Society. Ph.D. dissertation, Department of Anthropology, Northwestern University, Evanston, Illinois.

Goodell, R.K. 1971. Fort Ancient in the Bluegrass of Kentucky. Ms. on file, Office of State Archaeology, University of Kentucky, Lexington.

Goodyear, Albert C. 1982. The Chronological Position of the Dalton Horizon in the Southeastern United States. *American Antiquity* 47:382–95.

Gramly, Richard M., and Carl Yahnig. 1991. The Adams Site (15Ch90) and the Little River, Christian County, Kentucky, Clovis Workshop Complex. *Southeastern Archaeology* 10:134–45.

Granger, Joseph E. 1984. David Ward's Mill: Entrepreneurism in a Semiperipheral "Ecotone" Between the Urban Core and Rural Periphery of Early Louisville. *Proceedings of the Symposium on Ohio Valley Urban and Historic Archaeology* 2:74–88.

————. 1986. Some Practical Paradigms for the Urban Archaeological Study of Nineteenth Century Development of Cities in the Ohio River Valley. *Proceedings of the Symposium on Ohio Valley Urban and Historic Archaeology* 4:24–39.

————. 1988. Late/Terminal Archaic Settlement in the Falls of the Ohio River Region of Kentucky: An Examination of Components, Phases, and Clusters. In *Paleoindian and Archaic Research in Kentucky*, ed. Charles D. Hockensmith, David Pollack, and Thomas N. Sanders, pp. 153–203. Kentucky Heritage Council, Frankfort.

Granger, Joseph E., Philip J. DeBlasi, and Jan Marie Hemberger. 1981. *Toward a Research and Management Design: Cultural Resources Studies in the Falls*

Region of Kentucky, Vol. III: The Search for a Research and Management Design Process. University of Louisville, Archaeological Survey. Submitted to the Kentucky Heritage Commission, Frankfort.

Granger, Joseph E., and Stephen T. Mocas. 1970. *Report of 1969–70 Excavations at the Locust Grove Restoration Area: The Springhouse*. University of Louisville Archaeological Survey, Louisville.

Graybill, Jeffrey R. 1981. The Eastern Periphery of Fort Ancient (A.D. 1050-1650): A Diachronic Approach to Settlement Variability. Ph.D. dissertation, Department of Anthropology, University of Washington.

Grayson, Donald K. 1987. An Analysis of the Chronology of Late Pleistocene Mammalian Extinctions in North America. *Quaternary Research* 28:281–89.

Green, Frank E. 1963. The Clovis Blades: An Important Addition to the Llano Complex. *American Antiquity* 29:145–65.

Green, Thomas J., and Cheryl A. Munson. 1978. Mississippian Settlement Patterns in Southwestern Indiana. In *Mississippian Settlement Patterns*, ed. Bruce Smith, pp. 293–330. Academic Press, New York.

Greenman, Emerson F. 1932. Excavation of the Coon Mound and an Analysis of the Adena Culture. *Ohio State Archaeological and Historical Quarterly* 41:366–523.

Griffin, James B. 1943. Adena Village Site Pottery from Fayette County, Kentucky. In *The Riley Mound, Site Be15 and the Landing Mound, Site Be17, Boone County, Kentucky with Additional Notes on the Mt. Horeb Site, Fa1 and Sites Fa14 and Fa15, Fayette County, Kentucky*, ed. William S. Webb, pp. 666–70. Reports in Archaeology and Anthropology No. 5. University of Kentucky, Lexington.

——. 1953. Comments on the Cultural Position of the Bintz Site, Campbell County, Kentucky. *American Antiquity* 18:262.

——. 1956. The Late Prehistoric Cultures of the Ohio Valley. *Ohio State Archaeological and Historical Quarterly* 61:186–95.

——. 1966. *The Fort Ancient Aspect: Its Cultural and Chronological Position in Mississippi Valley Archaeology*. Anthropological Papers No. 28. Museum of Anthropology, University of Michigan, Ann Arbor.

——. 1967. Eastern North American Archaeology: A Summary. *Science* 156:175–91.

——. 1974. Foreword to the New Edition. In *The Adena People*, by William S. Webb and Charles E. Snow, pp. v–xix. University of Tennessee Press, Knoxville.

——. 1976. A Commentary on Some Archaeological Activities in the Mid-Continent, 1925–1975. *Midcontinental Journal of Archaeology* 1:5–38.

——. 1978a. Eastern United States. In *Chronologies in New World Archaeology*, ed. by R.E. Taylor and C.W. Meighen, pp. 51–70. Academic Press, New York.

——. 1978b. Late Prehistory of the Ohio Valley. In *Northeast*, ed. Bruce G. Trigger, pp. 547–59. Handbook of North American Indians, Vol. 15, William G. Sturtevant, general editor. Smithsonian Institution, Washington, D.C.

——. 1985. Changing Concepts of the Prehistoric Mississippian Cultures of the Eastern United States. In *Alabama and the Borderlands: From Prehistory to Statehood*, ed. R. Reid Badger and Lawrence A. Clayton, pp. 40–63. University of Alabama Press, University, Alabama.

Guernsey, E.Y. 1939. Relationships among Various Clark County Sites. *Proceedings of the Indiana Academy of Science* 48:27–32. Indianapolis.

———. 1942. The Cultural Sequence of the Ohio Falls Sites. *Proceedings of the Indiana Academy of Science* 51:60–67. Indianapolis.

Guilday, John E. 1982. Appalachia 11,000–12,000 Years Ago: A Biological Review. *Archaeology of Eastern North America* 10:22–26.

Guilday, John, and Paul Parmalee. 1979. Pleistocene and Recent Vertebrate Remains from Savage Cave (15Lo11), Kentucky. *Western Kentucky Speleological Society Survey Annual Report 1979*, pp. 5–10. Murray State University, Murray.

Haag, William G. 1939. Pottery Type Descriptions. *Newsletter of the Southeastern Archaeological Conference* 1(3). Lexington, Kentucky.

———. 1940. A Description of the Wright Site Pottery. In *The Wright Mounds*, by William S. Webb, pp. 75–82. Reports in Anthropology and Archaeology No. 5. University of Kentucky, Lexington.

———. 1942a. Early Horizons in the Southeast. *American Antiquity* 7:209–22.

———. 1942b. *The Pottery from the C and O Mounds at Paintsville, Sites Jo2 and Jo9, Johnson County Kentucky*, by William S. Webb, pp. 341–49. Reports in Anthropology and Archaeology 5. University of Kentucky, Lexington.

———. 1965. William Snyder Webb, 1882–1964. *American Antiquity* 30:470–73.

———. 1985. Federal Aid to Archaeology in the Southeast, 1933–1942. *American Antiquity* 50:272–80.

Habenstein, Robert W., and William M. Lamers. 1963. *Funeral Customs the World Over*. National Funeral Directors Association of the United States, Milwaukee.

Hale, John R. 1981. *A Fort Ancient Village at Augusta, Kentucky*. Granger and Associates, Louisville.

Hall, Robert. 1979. In Search of the Ideology of the Adena-Hopewell Climax. In *Hopewell Archaeology: The Chillicothe Conference*, ed. David S. Brose and N'omi Greber. pp. 258–65. Kent State University Press, Kent, Ohio.

Hamilton, N.D., J.M. Adovasio, and J. Donahue. 1983. *An Archaeological Reconnaissance of the Main Stem of the Big Sandy River, Wayne County, West Virginia; Boyd and Lawrence Counties, Kentucky, and the Levisa Fork, Johnson County, Kentucky*. Cultural Resource Management Program, University of Pittsburgh, Pittsburgh.

Hanson, Lee H., Jr. 1960. The Analysis, Distribution, and Seriation of Pottery from the Green River Drainage as a Basis for an Archaeological Sequence of that Area. Ms. on file, Office of State Archaeology, University of Kentucky, Lexington.

———. 1966. *The Hardin Village Site*. Studies in Anthropology No. 4. University of Kentucky Press, Lexington.

———. 1970. *The Jewell Site, Bn-21, Barren County, Kentucky*. Tennessee Archaeological Society Miscellaneous Paper No. 8.

———. 1975. *The Buffalo Site—A Late 17th Century Indian Village Site (46Pu31) in Putnam County, West Virginia*. Report of Archaeological Investigations No. 5. West Virginia Geological Survey, Morgantown.

Hardesty, Donald L. 1964. The Biggs Site, a Hopewellian Complex in Greenup County, Kentucky. *Probes*, pp. 14–21. University of Kentucky, Lexington.

Harper, Gregory, J. Kreinbrink, and R. Reiter. 1981. *Battery Bates Civil War Gun Emplacement, Field Work Report*. Behringer Crawford Museum, Covington, Kentucky.

Harrison, Lowell H. 1975. *The Civil War in Kentucky*. University Press of Kentucky, Lexington.

Hart, T.B., and J.A. Hart. 1986. The Ecological Basis of Hunter-Gatherer Subsistence in African Rainforests: The Mbuti of Eastern Zaire. *Human Ecology* 14:29–56.

Haynes, C. Vance. 1966. Elephant Hunting in North America. *Scientific American* 241:104–12.

———. 1982. Were Clovis Progenitors in Beringia? In *Paleoecology of Beringia*, ed. D.M. Hopkins, J.V. Matthews, C.E. Schweger, and S.B. Young, pp. 383–98. Academic Press, New York.

———. 1990. The Antevs-Bryan Years and their Legacy for Paleoindian Geochronology. In *Establishment of a Geologic Framework for Paleoanthropology*, ed. L.F. Laporte, pp. 55–68. Special Paper No. 242. Geological Society of America, Boulder, Colorado.

Haynes, C. Vance, D. Jack Donahue, A. J. T. Jull, and T. H. Zabel. 1984. Application of Accelerator Dating to Fluted Point Paleo-Indian Sites. *Archaeology of Eastern North America* 12:184–91.

Heidenreich, Conrad E. 1978. Huron. In *Northeast*, edited by Bruce G. Trigger, pp. 368–88. Handbook of North American Indians, Vol. 15, William G. Sturtevant, general editor. Smithsonian Institution, Washington, D.C.

Hemberger, Jan Marie. 1985. Preliminary Findings at the Pit of the Skulls (15Bn51). In *Woodland Period Research in Kentucky*, ed. David Pollack, Thomas Sanders, and Charles Hockensmith, pp. 186–203. Kentucky Heritage Council, Frankfort.

Henderson, A. Gwynn. 1985. Kitchen Group. In *Archaeological Investigations at Waveland State Shrine, Fayette County, Kentucky*, by David Pollack and Charles D. Hockensmith, pp. 13–31. Kentucky Heritage Council, Frankfort.

Henderson, A. Gwynn, Cynthia E. Jobe, and Christopher A. Turnbow. 1986. Indian Occupation and Use in Northern and Eastern Kentucky During the Contact Period (1540–1795): An Initial Investigation. Ms. on file, the Kentucky Heritage Council, Frankfort.

Henderson, A. Gwynn, and David Pollack. 1985. The Late Woodland Occupation at the Bentley Site. In *Woodland Period Research in Kentucky*, ed. by David Pollack, Thomas Sanders, and Charles Hockensmith, pp. 140–64. Kentucky Heritage Council, Frankfort.

Henderson, A. Gwynn, David Pollack, and Dwight R. Cropper. 1988. The Old Fort Earthworks, Greenup County, Kentucky. In *New Deal Archaeology and Current Research in Kentucky*, ed. David Pollack and Mary L. Powell, pp. 64-81. Kentucky Heritage Council, Frankfort.

Henderson, A. Gwynn, David Pollack, and Christopher A. Turnbow. 1992. Chronology and Cultural Patterns. In *Fort Ancient Cultural Dynamics in the Middle Ohio Valley*, ed. A. Gwynn Henderson, pp. 253–79. Monographs in World Archaeology No. 8. Prehistory Press, Madison, Wis.

Henderson, A. Gwynn, and Christopher A. Turnbow. 1987. Fort Ancient Developments in Northeastern Kentucky. In *Current Archaeological Research in Kentucky: Volume One*, ed. David Pollack, pp. 205–24. Kentucky Heritage Council, Frankfort.

Hilgeman, Sherri L. 1992. Pottery and Chronology of the Angel Site, A Middle Missis-
    sippian Center in the Lower Ohio Valley. Ph.D. dissertation, Department of
    Anthropology, Indiana University, Bloomingon.

Hockensmith, Charles D., and David Pollack. 1985. Archaeological Investigations at
    Waveland: A Greek Revival Residence in Fayette County, Kentucky. *Proceed-
    ings of the Symposium on Ohio Valley Urban and Historic Archaeology*
    3:137–44.

Hockensmith, Charles D., Thomas N. Sanders, and David Pollack. 1985. The Green
    River Shell Middens of Kentucky. National Register of Historic Places the-
    matic nomination form on file, Kentucky Heritage Council, Frankfort.

Hodder, Ian. 1982. *The Present Past: An Introduction to Anthropology for Archaeolo-
    gists*. Pica Press, New York.

Hoffman, Michael A. 1965. The Ashby Site: A Late Woodland Occupation in the Lower
    Green River Valley. Ms. on file, Museum of Anthropology, University of Ken-
    tucky, Lexington.

———. 1966. *Archaeological Surveys of the Newburgh and Uniontown Lock and Dam
    Areas on the Kentucky Side of the Ohio River*. Report submitted to the
    Department of the Interior, National Park Service, Southeastern Region,
    Richmond, Virginia.

Holmes, William H. 1904. *Aboriginal Pottery of the Eastern United States*. Bureau of
    American Ethnology, Annual Report No. 20, pp. 1–200. Washington, D. C.

Honerkamp, Marjory W. 1975. The Angel Phase: An Analysis of a Middle Mississippi-
    an Occupation in Southwestern Indiana. Ph.D. dissertation, Department of
    Anthropology, Indiana University, Bloomington.

Hunter, William A. 1978. History of the Ohio Valley. In *Northeast*, ed. Bruce G. Trig-
    ger, pp. 588–93. Handbook of North American Indians, Vol. 15, William G.
    Sturtevant, general editor. Smithsonian Institution, Washington, D.C.

Huser, William A. 1993. *Phase III Archaeological Investigations at the Prater Historic
    Site (15Fd62) in Floyd County, Kentucky*. Archaeological Report No. 308. Pro-
    gram for Cultural Resource Assessment, Department of Anthropology, Uni-
    versity of Kentucky, Lexington.

Ison, Cecil R. 1988. The Cold Oak Shelter: Providing a Better Understanding of the
    Terminal Archaic. In *PaleoIndian and Archaic Research in Kentucky*, ed.
    Charles D. Hockensmith, David Pollack, and Tom Sanders, pp. 205–20. Ken-
    tucky Heritage Council, Frankfort.

———. 1989. Prehistoric Upland Farming Along the Cumberland Plateau. Paper pre-
    sented at the 6th Annual Kentucky Heritage Council Archaeological Confer-
    ence, Covington, Kentucky.

Jacobson, George L., and Eric C. Grimm. 1988. Synchrony of Rapid Change in Late-
    Glacial Vegetation South of the Laurentide Ice Sheet. In *Late Pleistocene and
    Early Holocene Paleoecology and Archaeology of the Eastern Great Lakes
    Region*, ed. R. Laub, N. Miller, and D. Steadman, pp. 31–38. Bulletin of the
    Buffalo Society of Natural Sciences, Buffalo.

Jacobson, George L., Thompson Webb, and Eric C. Grimm. 1987. Patterns and Rates of
    Vegetation Change During the Deglaciation of Eastern North America. In
    North America and Adjacent Oceans During the Last Deglaciation, ed. W.
    Ruddiman and H. Wright, pp. 277–88. Geological Society of America, Boulder.

Janzen, Donald E. 1977. An Examination of Late Archaic Development in the Falls of the Ohio River Area. In *For the Director: Research Essays in Honor of James B. Griffin*, ed. Charles E. Cleland, pp. 123–43. Anthropological Paper No. 61. University of Michigan Museum of Anthropology, Ann Arbor.

———. 1981. *The Shaker Mills on Shawnee Run: Historical Archaeology at Shakertown at Pleasant Hill, Mercer County, Kentucky*. Pleasant Hill Press, Harrodsburg.

———. 1987. *An Archaeological Survey of the Proposed Relocation of U.S. 27, Jessamine County, Kentucky*. Janzen, Inc., Danville.

Jefferies, Richard W. 1983. Middle Archaic-Late Archaic Transition in Southern Illinois: An Example from the Carrier Mills Archaeological District. *American Archaeology* 3:199–206.

———. 1988. The Archaic Period in Kentucky: Past Accomplishments and Future Directions. In *PaleoIndian and Archaic Research in Kentucky*, ed. Charles Hockensmith, David Pollack, and Thomas Sanders, pp. 85–126. Kentucky Heritage Council, Frankfort.

Jefferies, Richard W., and Brian M. Butler (editors). 1982. *The Carrier Mills Archaeological Project: Human Adaptation in the Saline Valley, Illinois*. 2 vols. Research Paper No. 33. Center for Archaeological Investigations, Southern Illinois University, Carbondale.

Jefferies, Richard W., and B. Mark Lynch. 1983. Dimensions of Middle Archaic Cultural Adaptation at the Black Earth Site, Saline County, Illinois. In *Archaic Hunters and Gatherers in the American Midwest*, ed. James L. Phillips and James A. Brown, pp. 299–322. Academic Press, New York.

Jelinek, Arthur J. 1967. Man's Role in the Extinction of Pleistocene Faunas. In *Pleistocene Extinctions*, ed. P.S. Martin and H.E. Wright, pp. 193–200. Yale University Press, New Haven.

———. 1971. Early Man in the New World: A Technological Perspective. *Arctic Anthropology* 8(2):15–21.

Jennings, Jesse D. 1985. River Basin Surveys: Origins, Operations, and Results, 1945–1969. *American Antiquity* 50:281–96.

———. 1989. *Prehistory of North America*. 3d edition. Mayfield Publishing Company, Mountain View, California.

Jillson, Williard R. 1923. *Geological Research in Kentucky*. Kentucky Geological Survey, Series 6, Vol. 15. Lexington.

———. 1936. *Big Bone Lick*. Big Bone Lick Association Publications No. 1. Louisville.

Johnson, Allen W., and Timothy Earle. 1987. *The Evolution of Human Society: From Foraging Group to Agrarian State*. Stanford University Press, Stanford, California.

Johnson, William C. 1982. Ceramics. In *The Prehistory of Paintsville Reservoir, Johnson and Morgan Counties, Kentucky*, compiled by James M. Adovasio, pp. 752–825. Ethnology Monographs No. 6. Department of Anthropology, University of Pittsburgh, Pittsburgh.

Johnston, Francis E., and Charles E. Snow. 1961. The Reassessment of the Age and Sex of the Indian Knoll Skeletal Population: Demographic and Methodological Aspects. *American Journal of Physical Anthropology* 19:237–44.

Jones, Volney H. 1936. The Vegetal Remains of Newt Kash Hollow Shelter. In *Rock Shelters in Menifee County, Kentucky*, by William S. Webb and William D.

Funkhouser, pp. 147–55. Reports in Anthropology and Archaeology No. 3. University of Kentucky, Lexington.

Judd, Neil M. 1967. *The Bureau of American Ethnology: A Partial History*. University of Oklahoma Press, Norman.

Justice, Noel D. 1987. *Stone Age Spear and Arrow Points of the Midcontinental and Eastern United States: A Modern Survey and Reference*. Indiana University Press, Bloomington.

Karan, Pradyumna P., and Cotton Mather. 1977. *Atlas of Kentucky*. University Press of Kentucky, Lexington.

Keel, Bennie C. 1976. *Cherokee Archaeology: A Study of the Appalachian Summit*. University of Tennessee, Knoxville.

Kellar, James H. 1960. *The C.L. Lewis Stone Mound and the Stone Mound Problem*. Prehistory Research Series No. 3. Indiana Historical Society, Indianapolis.

———. 1967. Material Remains. In *Angel Site: An Archaeological, Historical, Ethnological Study*, by Glenn A. Black, pp. 431–87. Indiana Historical Society. Indianapolis.

———. 1973. *An Introduction to the Prehistory of Indiana*. Indiana Historical Society, Indianapolis.

———. 1979. The Mann Site and "Hopewell" in the Lower Wabash-Ohio Valley. In *Hopewell Archaeology: The Chillicothe Conference*, ed. David Brose and N'omi Greber, pp. 100–107. Kent State University, Kent, Ohio.

Kemp, Janet E. 1909. *Report of the Tenement House Commission of Louisville*. Lousiville Tenement House Commission, Louisville.

Kent, Susan. 1989. And Justice for All: The Development of Political Centralization Among Newly Sedentary Foragers. *American Anthropologist* 91:703–12.

King, James E., and William H. Allen. 1977. A Holocene Vegetation Record from the Mississippi River Valley, Southeastern Missouri. *Quaternary Research* 8:307–23.

Kramer, Carl E. 1986. City with a Vision: Images of Louisville in the 1830s. *Filson Club History Quarterly* 60:427–52.

Kreisa, Paul P. 1987a. Late Prehistoric Settlement Patterns in the Big Bottoms of Fulton County, Kentucky. In *Current Archaeological Research in Kentucky, Volume One*, ed. David Pollack, pp. 78–99. The Kentucky Heritage Council, Frankfort, Kentucky.

———. 1987b. [Marshall Site] Faunal Remains. In *Archaeological Site Survey and Test Excavations in Carlisle, Hickman, and Fulton Counties, Kentucky: Site Survey and Excavations*, by Tom Sussenbach and R. Barry Lewis, pp. 67–68. Western Kentucky Project Report No. 4. Department of Anthropology, University of Illinois, Urbana-Champaign.

———. 1988. *Second-order Communities in Western Kentucky: Site Survey and Excavations at Late Woodland and Mississippi Period Sites*. Western Kentucky Project Report No. 7. Department of Anthropology, University of Illinois, Urbana-Champaign.

———. 1990. Organizational Aspects of Mississippian Settlement Systems in Western Kentucky. Ph.D. dissertation, Department of Anthropology, University of Illinois at Urbana-Champaign.

Kreisa, Paul P., and Charles Stout. 1991. Late Woodland Adaptations in the Mississippi and Ohio Rivers Confluence Region. In *Stability, Transformations, and Variation: The Late Woodland Southeast*, ed. Michael S. Nassaney and Charles R. Cobb, pp. 121–47. Plenum, New York.

Kruger, Robert P. 1985. The Faunal Remains. In *The Turk Site: A Mississippian Town of the Western Kentucky Border*, ed. Richard Edging, pp. 35–51. Western Kentucky Project Report No. 3. Department of Anthropology, University of Illinois, Urbana-Champaign.

Lafferty, Robert H., III. 1978. The Early Woodland Chronological and Cultural Affinities at Phipps Bend on the Holston River, Northeast Tennessee. *Journal of Alabama Archaeology* 24:132–50.

Lahren, L., and R. Bonnichsen. 1974. Bone Foreshafts from a Clovis Burial in Southwestern Montana. *Science* 186:147–50.

Lannie, Donna Dean. 1979. Ethnobotanical Analysis. In *Excavations at Four Archaic Sites in the Lower Ohio Valley, Jefferson County, Kentucky*, ed. Michael B. Collins, pp. 978–1006. Occasional Papers in Anthropology No. 1. Department of Anthropology, University of Kentucky, Lexington.

Ledbetter, R. Jerald, and Lisa D. O'Steen. 1992. The Grayson Site: Late Archaic and Late Woodland Occupations in the Little Sandy Drainage. In *Current Archaeological Research in Kentucky*, vol. 2, ed. David Pollack and A. Gwynn Henderson, pp. 13–42. Kentucky Heritage Council, Frankfort.

Lewellyn, Joe P. 1964. *Skeletal Analysis of Two Mississippian Sites in Kentucky*. Master's thesis, Department of Anthropology, University of Kentucky, Lexington.

Lewis, R. Barry. 1974. *Mississippian Exploitative Strategies: A Southeast Missouri Example*. Missouri Archaeological Society, Research Series No. 11. Columbia, Missouri.

———. 1985. The Ceramic Assemblage. In *Archaeological Investigations at the Turk Site (15Ce6), Carlisle County, Kentucky*, ed. Richard Edging, pp. 20–27. Western Kentucky Project Report No. 3. Department of Anthropology, University of Illinois, Urbana-Champaign.

———. 1986. Early Woodland Adaptations to the Illinois Prairie. In *Early Woodland Archeology*, ed. Kenneth B. Farnsworth and Thomas E. Emerson, pp. 171–78. Center for American Archaeology, Kampsville Seminars in Archaeology No. 2. Center for American Archeology Press, Kampsville, Illinois.

———. 1988a. New Deal Archaeology at Mississippian Sites in Kentucky. In *New Deal Era Archaeology in Kentucky*, ed. David Pollack and Mary Lucas Powell, pp. 26–45. Kentucky Heritage Council, Frankfort.

———. 1988b. Old World Dice in the Protohistoric Southern United States. *Current Anthropology* 29:759–68.

———. 1989. The Archaeology of the Western Kentucky Border and the Cairo Lowland. Paper presented at the 24th Annual Meeting of the Southern Anthropology Society, Memphis, Tennessee.

———. 1990a. The Late Prehistory of the Ohio-Mississippi Rivers Confluence Region, Kentucky and Missouri. In *Towns and Temples along the Mississippi River*, ed. David Dye and Cheryl A. Cox, pp. 38–58. University of Alabama Press, Tuscaloosa.

———. 1990b. The Mississippi Period. In *The Archaeology of Kentucky: Past Accomplishments and Future Directions*, ed. David Pollack, pp. 375–466. State Historic Preservation Comprehensive Plan Report No. 1. Kentucky Heritage Council, Frankfort.

———. 1990c. On Astragalus Dice and Culture Contact: Reply to Eisenberg. *Current Anthropology* 31:410–13.

———. 1991. The Early Mississippi Period in the Confluence Region and Its Northern Relationships. In *Cahokia and the Hinterlands*, ed. Thomas E. Emerson and R. Barry Lewis, pp. 274–94. University of Illinois Press, Urbana.

Lewis, R. Barry, and Charles B. Stout. 1992. On the Nature of Mississippian Towns in Kentucky. Paper presented at the 49th Southeastern Archaeological Conference Meetings, Little Rock, Arkansas.

Lewis, Thomas M.N., and Madeline K. Kneberg. 1946. *Hiwassee Island: An Archaeological Account of Four Tennessee Indian Peoples*. University of Tennessee Press, Knoxville.

Lewis, Thomas M.N., and Madeline K. Lewis. 1961. *Eva: An Archaic Site*. University of Tennessee Press, Knoxville.

Linney, William M. 1882. "Report on the Geology of Mercer County." *Geological Reports*, Series 2. Kentucky Geological Survey, Frankfort.

Livingston, G. Herbert. 1983. Chaumière de Prairie. *Proceedings of the Symposium on Ohio Valley Urban and Historic Archaeology* 1:36–43.

Long, Joseph K., III. 1961. The Hadden Site: To–1: A Transitional Woodland-Mississippian Village and Mound Site of Todd County, Western Kentucky. Ms. on file, Office of State Archaeology, University of Kentucky, Lexington.

———. 1974. The Hadden Site: A Transitional Woodland-Mississippian Village and Mound in Todd County, Kentucky. *Kentucky Archaeological Association Bulletin* 3:11–61.

Lopinot, Neal H. 1984. Archaeological Formation Processes and Human-Plant Interrelationships in the Midcontinental United States. Ph.D. dissertation, Department of Anthropology, Southern Illinois University, Carbondale.

———. 1988. Hansen Site (15Gp14) Archaeobotany. In *Excavations at the Hansen Site (15Gp14) in Northeastern Kentucky*, by Stephen R. Ahler, pp. 571–624. Archaeological Report No. 173. Program for Cultural Resources Assessment, University of Kentucky, Lexington

Loughridge, Robert H. 1888. *Report on the Geological and Economic Features of the Jackson Purchase Region*. Kentucky Geological Survey, Lexington.

Lundelius, Ernest L., Russell W. Graham, Ellaine Anderson, John Guilday, J. Alan Holman, David W. Steadman, and S. David Webb. 1983. Terrestrial Vertebrate Faunas. In *Late Quaternary Environments of the United States: Vol. 1, The Pleistocene*, ed. S.C. Porter, pp. 311–54. University of Minnesota Press, Minneapolis.

Lyon, Edwin A., II. 1982. New Deal Archaeology in the Southeast: WPA, TVA, NPS, 1934–1942. Ph.D. dissertation, Department of History, Louisiana State University, Baton Rouge.

Lyon, Sidney S. 1859. Account of Antiquities from Kentucky. *Annual Report for the Year 1858*, pp. 430–32. Smithsonian Institution, Washington, D.C.

———. 1871. Report of an Exploration of Ancient Mounds in Union County, Kentucky. *Annual Report of the Smithsonian Institution 1870*, pp. 392–405. Washington, D.C.

McBride, Kim A. 1991. *Preliminary Investigations at Shakertown at Pleasant Hill: The 1990 Field Season*. Archaeological Report No. 244. Program for Cultural Resource Assessment, Department of Anthropology, University of Kentucky, Lexington.

———. 1993. *A Background Archival and Oral Historical Study of the Barthell Coal Camp, McCreary County, Kentucky*. Archaeological Report No. 280. Program for Cultural Resource Assessment, Department of Anthropology, University of Kentucky, Lexington.

McBride, Kim A., and W. Stephen McBride. 1991a. The LEXTRAN Site: Explorations into Early Urban Life in Lexington, Kentucky. Paper presented to the William S. Webb Archaeological Society, Lexington, Kentucky.

———. 1991b. *Preliminary Archaeological Investigations at Ashland, 15Fa206, Lexington, Kentucky*. Archaeological Report No. 245. Program for Cultural Resource Assesesment, Department of Anthropology, University of Kentucky, Lexington.

———. 1991c. *Preliminary Archaeological Investigations at the Pope House, Lexington, Kentucky*. Archaeological Report No. 246. Program for Cultural Resource Assessment, Department of Anthropology, University of Kentucky, Lexington.

McBride, W. Stephen. 1992. *Continued Archaeological Investigations at the Pope House, 15Fa205, Lexington, Kentucky*. Archaeological Report No. 277. Program for Cultural Resource Assessment, Department of Anthropology, University of Kentucky, Lexington.

———. 1993. *Archaeology at Henry Clay's Ashland Estate: Investigations of the Mansion, Yard, and Privy*. Archaeological Report No. 281. Program for Cultural Resource Assessment, Department of Anthropology, University of Kentucky, Lexington.

McBride, Kim A., W. Stephen McBride, and Leslee F. Keys. 1988. *Cultural Resource Assessment of Fisher's Mill, 15JF551, Jefferson County, Kentucky*. Archaeological Report No. 183. Program for Cultural Resource Assessment, Department of Anthropology, University of Kentucky, Lexington.

McBride, W. Stephen, and William E. Sharp. 1991. *Archaeological Investigations at Camp Nelson: A Union Quartermaster Depot and Hospital in Jessamine County, Kentucky*. Archaeological Report No. 241. Program for Cultural Resource Assesesment, Department of Anthropology, University of Kentucky, Lexington.

McCartney, A.P. 1971. A Proposed Western Aleutian Phase in the Near Islands, Alaska. *Arctic Anthropology* 2:92–142.

McClure, Virginia Clay. 1933. *The Settlement of the Kentucky Appalachian Highlands*. Ph.D. dissertation, Department of History, University of Kentucky, Lexington.

MacCord, Howard A. 1953. The Bintz Site. *American Antiquity* 18:239–44.

MacDonald, William. 1986. Spatial and Temporal Variability at Helter Shelter, Madison County, Kentucky. Proposal to the National Science Foundation, Washington, D.C.

McGraw, Betty J. 1971. The Locust Grove Springhouse: A Case Study in the Functional Significance of Springhouses in Early Jefferson County, Kentucky. Ms. on file, University of Louisville Archaeological Survey, Louisville.

Mainfort, Robert C., Jr. 1989. Adena Chiefdoms? Evidence from the Wright Mound. *Midcontinental Journal of Archaeology* 14:164–78.

Mainfort, Robert C. Jr., and Kenneth C. Carstens. 1987. A Middle Woodland Embankment and Mound Complex in Western Kentucky. *Southeastern Archaeology* 6:57–61.

Mansberger, Floyd. 1990. *Archaeological Investigations at the Cathedral of the Assumption, Louisville, Kentucky*. Fever River Research, Springfield, Illinois.

Marquardt, William H. 1970. Archaeological Investigations in the Cave Run Reservoir, Kentucky: 1969 Season. Ms. on file, Department of Anthropology, University of Kentucky, Lexington.

———. 1971. Woodland Manifestations in the Western Coalfield. Ms. on file, Office of State Archaeology, Department of Anthropology, University of Kentucky, Lexington.

Marquardt, William H., and Patty Jo Watson. 1983. The Shellmound Archaic of Western Kentucky. In *Archaic Hunters and Gatherers in the American Midwest*, ed. James L. Phillips and James A. Brown, pp. 323–39. Academic Press, New York.

Martin, Charles E. 1988. The Pennyrile Cultural Landscape. Ms. on file, Kentucky Heritage Council, Frankfort.

Martin, Paul S., George I. Quimby, and Donald Collier. 1947. *Indians Before Columbus: Twenty Thousand Years of North American History Revealed by Archaeology*. University of Chicago Press, Chicago.

Maslowski, Robert F. 1984. Archaeological Survey and Evaluation of 15Bd42, A Woodland Hamlet on the Big Sandy River, Boyd County, Kentucky. Ms. on file, U. S. Army Corps of Engineers, Huntington District, West Virginia.

Mason, Ronald J. 1981. *Great Lakes Archaeology*. Academic Press, New York.

Maxwell, Moreau S. 1951. *The Woodland Cultures of Southern Illinois: Archaeological Excavation in the Carbondale Area*. Bulletin No. 7. Logan Museum Publications in Anthropology, Beloit University, Beloit, Wisconsin.

Mead, Jim I., and David J. Meltzer. 1984. North American Late Quaternary Extinctions and the Radiocarbon Record. In *Quaternary Extinctions: A Prehistoric Revolution*, ed. Paul S. Martin and R.G. Klein, pp. 440–50. University of Arizona Press, Tucson.

Meltzer, David J. 1985. North American Archaeology and Archaeologists, 1879–1934. *American Antiquity* 50:249–60.

Meltzer, David J., and Jim I. Mead. 1983. The Timing of Late Pleistocene Mammalian Extinctions in North America. *Quaternary Research* 19:130–35.

Miller, Rex K. 1941. McCain Site, Dubois County, Indiana. *Indiana Historical Society Prehistoric Research Series* 2(1). Indianapolis.

Mills, William C. 1902. Excavations of the Adena Mound. *Ohio Archaeological and Historical Society Publications* 10:451–79.

Milner, George R. 1980. Epidemic Disease in the Postcontact Southeast: A Reappraisal. *Midcontinental Journal of Archaeology* 5:39–56.

Milner, George L., and Richard W. Jefferies. 1987. A Re-examination of the W.P.A. Excavation of the Robbins Mound in Boone County, Kentucky. In *Current Archaeological Research in Kentucky, Volume One*, ed. David Pollack, pp. 33–42. Kentucky Heritage Council, Frankfort, Kentucky.

Milner, George L., and Virginia G. Smith. 1986. *New Deal Archaeology in Kentucky: Excavations, Collections, and Research*. Occasional Papers in Anthropology No. 5. Program for Cultural Resource Assessment, University of Kentucky, Lexington.

Milton, Katherine. 1984. Protein and Carbohydrate Resources of the Maku Indians of Northwestern Amazonia. *American Anthropologist* 86:7–27.

Mitchell, Samuel L. 1817. Notes on the Indian Mummy and Associated Artifacts Removed from Mammoth Cave in 1814. *The Medical Repository* 18 (n.s., Vol. 3): 187–88. New York.

Mocas, Stephen T. 1977. *Excavations at the Lawrence Site, 15Tr13, Trigg County, Kentucky*. University of Louisville Archaeological Survey Report, Louisville.

———. 1985. An Instance of Middle Archaic Mortuary Activity In Western Kentucky. *Tennessee Anthropologist* 10:76–91.

Moore, Clarence B. 1916. Some Aboriginal Sites on Green River, Kentucky; Certain Aboriginal Sites on Lower Ohio River; Additional Investigation on Mississippi River. *Journal of the Academy of Sciences of Philadelphia* 16.

Morse, Dan F. 1975. Paleo-Indian in the Land of Opportunity: Preliminary Report on the Excavations at the Sloan Site (3Ge94). In *The Cache River Archeological Project: An Experiment in Contract Archeology*, assembled by Michael B. Schiffer and John H. House, pp. 135–43. Arkansas Archeological Survey, Research Series No. 8. Fayetteville, Arkansas.

Morse, Phyllis A. 1981. *Parkin: The 1978–1979 Archeological Investigations of a Cross County, Arkansas, Site*. Arkansas Archeological Survey, Research Series No. 13. Fayetteville, Arkansas.

Mullen, Jay C. 1966. The Turning of Columbus. *Register of the Kentucky Historical Society* 64:209–25.

Muller, Jon D. 1978. The Kincaid System: Mississippian Settlement in the Environs of a Large Site. In *Mississippian Settlement Patterns*, ed. Bruce D. Smith, pp. 269–292. Academic Press, New York.

———. 1986. *Archaeology of the Lower Ohio River Valley*. Academic Press, New York.

Myers, Robin J. 1981. Archaeological Investigations at the Pleasant Point Site (15Oh50), Ohio County, Kentucky. Ms. on file, Resources Analysts, Bloomington, Indiana.

Nance, Jack D. 1977. Aspects of Late Archaic Culture in the Lower Tennessee/Cumberland River Valleys. *Tennessee Archaeologist* 33:1–15.

———. 1985. Lower Cumberland Archaeological Project: Test Excavation, 1984. Ms. on file, Simon Fraser University, Burnaby, British Columbia, Canada.

———. 1986a. The Archaic Prehistory of the Lower Tennessee-Cumberland Valleys. Paper presented at the Kentucky Heritage Council Conference on Paleoindian and Archaic Period Research in Kentucky, Louisville.

———. 1986b. The Morrisroe Site: Projectile Point Types and Radiocarbon Dates from the Lower Tennessee River Valley. *Midcontinental Journal of Archaeology* 11:11–50.

———. 1987. The Archaic Sequence in the Lower Tennessee-Cumberland-Ohio Region. *Southeastern Archaeology* 6:129–40.

Nelson, Nels C. 1917. *Contributions to the Archaeology of Mammoth Cave and Vicinity, Kentucky.* Anthropological Papers No. 22:1–73. American Museum of Natural History, New York.

Neumann, Georg K. 1942. Types of Artificial Cranial Deformation in the Eastern United States. *American Antiquity* 7:306–10.

Niquette, Charles M., and Randall D. Boedy. 1986. *The Calloway Site (15MT8): A Transitional Early to Middle Woodland Camp in Martin County, Kentucky.* Contract Publication Series 86-12. Cultural Resource Analysts, Lexington.

Niquette, Charles M., Randall D. Boedy, and Gayle J. Fritz. 1987. The Calloway Site (15MT8): A Woodland Camp in Martin County, Kentucky. *West Virginia Archaeologist* 39:21–56.

Niquette, Charles M., and Theresa K. Donham. 1985. *Prehistoric and Historic Sites Archaeology in the Proposed Yatesville Reservoir, Lawrence County, Kentucky.* Contract Publication Series 85-13. Cultural Resource Analysts, Lexington.

Niquette, Charles M., and A. Gwynn Henderson. 1984. *Background to the Historic and Prehistoric Resources of Eastern Kentucky.* Cultural Resource Series No. 1. Bureau of Land Management, Eastern State Office, Alexandria, Virginia.

Niquette, Charles M., and Myra A. Hughes. 1991. *Late Woodland Archeology at the Parkline Site (46PU99), Putnam County, West Virginia.* Cultural Resource Analysts, Contract Publication Series 90-93. Lexington, Kentucky.

Niquette, Charles M., and Jonathan P. Kerr (compilers). 1989. *Phase III Excavations at the Dow Cook Site (15La4) in the Proposed Yatesville Reservoir, Lawrence County, Kentucky.* Cultural Resource Analysts, Contract Publication Series 89-04. Lexington, Kentucky.

Nourse, Edwin G. (editor). 1934. *America's Capacity to Produce, Part 1: The Distribution of Income in Relation to Economic Progress.* Brookings Institute, Washington, D.C.

Nuttall, Thomas. 1821. *A Journal of Travels into the Arkansa Territory, During the Year 1819.* Thomas H. Palmer, Philadelphia.

O'Malley, Nancy. 1987a. *Middle Class Farmers on the Urban Periphery.* Archaeological Report No. 162. Program for Cultural Resource Assessment, Department of Anthropology, University of Kentucky, Lexington.

———. 1987b. *"Stockading Up:" A Study of Pioneer Stations in the Inner Bluegrass Region of Kentucky.* Archaeological Report No. 127. Program for Cultural Resource Assessment, Department of Anthropology, University of Kentucky, Lexington.

———. 1988. *"A New Village Called Washington": An Archaeological Study of Old Washington in Mason County, Kentucky.* McClanahan Printing Company, Maysville, Kentucky.

———. 1989. *Searching for Boonesborough.* Archaeological Report No. 198. Program for Cultural Resource Assessment, Department of Anthropology, University of Kentucky, Lexington.

Ottesen, Ann I. 1981. Report on a Preliminary Study of Prehistoric Settlement Patterns in Three Counties in Northwestern Kentucky. Ms on file, Kentucky Heritage Council, Frankfort.

Otto, John S., and Gerald D. Gilbert. 1982. The Plain Folk of the American South: An Archeological Perspective. *Pioneer America* 14:67–80.

———. 1984. Excavation of a "Plain Folk" Log Cabin Site, Meade County, Kentucky. *Filson Club History Quarterly* 58:40–53.

Parrington, Michael. 1980. Revolutionary War Archaeology at Valley Forge, Pennsylvania. *North American Archaeologist* 1:161–76.

Patterson, Thomas C. 1986. The Last Sixty Years: Toward a Social History of Americanist Archeology in the United States. *American Anthropologist* 88:7–27.

Peebles, Christopher S. 1974. *Moundville: The Organization of a Prehistoric Community and Culture.* Ph.D. dissertation, Department of Anthropology, University of California at Santa Barbara.

Pepper, George H. 1928. A Wooden Image from Kentucky. *Indian Notes and Monographs* 10:63–82.

Perzigian, Anthony Jo, Patricia A. Tench, and Donna J. Braun. 1984. Prehistoric Health in the Ohio Valley. In *Paleopathology at the Origins of Agriculture*, ed. Mark N. Cohen and George I. Armelagos, pp. 347–66. Academic Press, New York.

Peter, Robert. 1873. Ancient Mound Near Lexington, Kentucky. *Annual Report for the Year 1871*, pp. 420–23. Smithsonian Institution, Washington, D.C.

Peterson, Jean T. 1978. *The Ecology of Social Boundaries: Agta Foragers of the Philippines.* Illinois Studies in Anthropology No. 11. University of Illinois Press, Urbana.

Phillips, P. Lee. 1908. *"The First Map of Kentucky" by John Filson: A Bibliographical Account.* W.H. Lowdermilk, Washington, D.C.

Phillips, Philip, James A. Ford, and James B. Griffin. 1951. *Archaeological Survey in the Lower Mississippi Alluvial Valley, 1940–1947.* Papers of the Peabody Museum of American Archaeology and Ethnology No. 25. Cambridge.

Pickett, Thomas E. 1878. The Pre-Historic Inhabitants of Kentucky. In *History of Kentucky*, by Lewis Collins and Richard H. Collins. 2 vols. Collins, Covington, Kentucky.

Poirer, D.A. 1976. Camp Reading: Logistics of a Revolutionary War Winter Encampment. *Northeast Historical Archaeology* 5(1–2):40–52.

Pollack, David, 1990. *The Archaeology of Kentucky: Past Accomplishments and Future Directions.* State Historic Preservation Comprehensive Plan Report No. 1. Kentucky Heritage Council, Frankfort.

Pollack, David, and A. Gwynn Henderson. 1983. Contact Period Developments in the Middle Ohio Valley. Paper presented at the 48th Annual Meeting of the Society for American Archaeology, Pittsburgh, Pa.

———. 1984. A Mid-Eighteenth Century Historic Indian Occupation in Greenup County, Kentucky. In *Late Prehistoric Research in Kentucky*, ed. David Pollack, Charles Hockensmith, and Thomas Sanders, pp. 1–24. Kentucky Heritage Council, Frankfort.

Pollack, David. and Charles D. Hockensmith. 1985. *Archaeological Investigations at Waveland State Shrine, Fayette County, Kentucky.* Kentucky Heritage Council, Frankfort.

Pollack, David, and Cheryl A. Munson. 1989. Slack Farm, Union County, Kentucky: The Looting of a Late Mississippian Site. Ms. on file, Kentucky Heritage Council, Frankfort.

Pollack, David, Mary Lucas Powell, and Audrey Adkins. 1987. Preliminary Study of Mortuary Patterns at the Larkin Site, Bourbon County, Kentucky. In *Current Archaeological Research in Kentucky: Volume One*, ed. David Pollack, pp. 188–204. Kentucky Heritage Council, Frankfort.

Pollack, David, Thomas Sanders, and Charles Hockensmith (editors). 1985. *Woodland Period Research in Kentucky*. Kentucky Heritage Council, Frankfort.

Porter, Charlotte M. 1986. *The Eagle's Nest: Natural History and American Ideas, 1812–1842*. University of Alabama Press, University, Alabama.

Potter, William L., and Kenneth C. Carstens. 1986. Floral Reconstruction and Early Nineteenth Century Land Surveys in Western Kentucky: A Test Case From the Fort Jefferson Area. Paper presented at the 43d Annual Meeting of the Southeastern Archaeological Conference, Nashville, Tennessee.

Powell, John W. 1894. Report of the Director. *Annual Report of the Bureau of Ethnology* 12:xxi–xlviii. Washington, D.C.

Power, Marjory W. 1976. Delineation of the Angel Phase: A Middle Mississippian Occupation in Southwestern Indiana. *Southeastern Archaeological Conference Bulletin* 19:26–30.

Price, James E. 1978. The Settlement Pattern of the Powers Phase. In *Mississippian Settlement Patterns*, ed. Bruce D. Smith, pp. 201–31. Academic Press, New York.

Prufer, Olaf H. 1960. *Survey of Ohio Fluted Points, Nos. 1 and 3*. Cleveland Museum of Natural History, Cleveland.

———. 1964. The Hopewell Cult. *Scientific American* 211:90–102.

Prufer, Olaf H., and Orrin C. Shane. 1970. *Blain Village and the Fort Ancient Tradition in Ohio*. Kent State University Press, Kent, Ohio.

Purrington, Burton L. 1966. The Jones Mound, 15Hk11: Hopewellian Influence in Western Kentucky. Ms. on file, Museum of Anthropology, University of Kentucky, Lexington.

———. 1967. *Prehistoric Horizons and Traditions in the Eastern Mountains of Kentucky*. Master's thesis, Department of Anthropology, University of Kentucky, Lexington.

Rafferty, Janet E. 1974. The Development of the Ft. Ancient Tradition in Northern Kentucky. Ph.D. dissertation, University of Washington. University Microfilms, Ann Arbor.

Rafinesque, Constantine S. 1824. *Ancient History, or Annals of Kentucky; with a Survey of the Ancient Monuments of North America, and a Tabular View of the Principal Languages and Primitive Nations of the Whole Earth*. Privately printed, Frankfort.

———. 1836. *A Life of Travels and Researches in North America and South Europe*. F. Turner, Philadelphia.

Railey, Jimmy A. 1985a. The Gillespie Site (15Ms50). National Register of Historic Places Nomination Form on file at the Kentucky Heritage Council, Frankfort.

———. 1985b. Monterey Rockshelter (15On46). Kentucky Archaeological Site Survey Form on file, Office of State Archaeology, Department of Anthropology, University of Kentucky, Lexington.

———. 1991. Woodland Settlement Trends and Symbolic Architecture in the Kentucky Bluegrass. In *The Human Landscape in Kentucky's Past: Site Structure and Settlement Patterns*, ed. Charles Stout and Christine K. Hensley, pp. 56–77. Kentucky Heritage Council, Frankfort.

———. 1992. Chipped Stone Artifacts. In *Fort Ancient Cultural Dynamics in the Middle Ohio Valley*, ed. A. Gwynn Henderson, pp. 137–70. Monographs in World Archaeology No. 8. Prehistory Press, Madison, Wis.

———. (compiler). 1984. *The Pyles Site (15Ms28): A Newtown Village in Mason County, Kentucky*. Occasional Paper No. 1. William S. Webb Archaeological Society, Lexington.

Railey, Jimmy A., and Matthew M. Walters. 1985. *Archaeological Testing at Site 15Bd317 on the Kentucky Riverport Tract, Boyd County, Kentucky*. Archaeological Report No. 120. Program for Cultural Resource Assessment, University of Kentucky, Lexington.

Railey, Jimmy A., Teresa W. Tune, and Jack Rossen. 1989. The Conley-Greene Rockshelter (15El4): New Evidence for Early Woodland Occupation in the Eastern Kentucky Mountains. Paper presented at the 6th Annual Kentucky Heritage Council Archaeological Conference, Covington, Kentucky.

Ramenofsky, Ann F. 1987. *Vectors of Death: The Archaeology of European Contact*. University of New Mexico Press, Albuquerque.

Ray, H. Stan. 1967. Report on Archaeological Excavation of the Watkins Mound. Ms. on file, Department of Sociology and Anthropology, Western Kentucky University, Bowling Green.

Redmond, Brian G. 1990. The Yankeetown Phase: Emergent Mississippian adaptation in the Lower Ohio Valley. Ph.D. dissertation, Department of Anthropology, Indiana University, Bloomington.

Reid, Kenneth C. 1983. The Nebo Hill Phase: Late Archaic Prehistory in the Lower Missouri Valley. In *Archaic Hunters and Gatherers in the American Midwest*, ed. James L. Phillips and James A. Brown, pp. 11–39. Academic Press, New York.

———. 1984. Fire and Ice: New Evidence for the Production of Late Archaic Fiber-Tempered Pottery in the Middle Latitude Lowlands. *American Antiquity* 49:55–76.

Rennick, Robert M. 1984. *Kentucky Place Names*. University Press of Kentucky, Lexington.

Rice, Otis K. 1975. *Frontier Kentucky*. University Press of Kentucky, Lexington.

Ritchie, William A. 1932. *The Lamoka Lake Site*. Researches and Transactions of the New York State Archaeological Association, Vol. 7, No. 4. Rochester.

———. 1961. *A Typology and Nomenclature for New York Projectile Points*. Bulletin No. 384. New York State Museum and Science, Albany.

Robbins, Louise M. 1974. Prehistoric People of the Mammoth Cave Area. In *Archaeology of the Mammoth Cave Area*, ed. Patty Jo Watson, pp. 137–62. Academic Press, New York.

Robbins, Louise M., and Georg K. Neumann. 1972. *The Prehistoric People of the Fort Ancient Culture of the Central Ohio Valley*. Anthropological Papers No. 47. Museum of Anthropology, University of Michigan, Ann Arbor.

Robbins, Peggy. 1985. The Oddest of Characters. *American Heritage* 36:58–63.

Robinson, Kenneth W., and Steven D. Smith. 1979. The Villier Site (15JF110 Complex). In *Excavations at Four Archaic Sites in the Lower Ohio Valley Jefferson County, Kentucky*, ed. Michael B. Collins, pp. 590–696. Occasional Papers in

Anthropology No. 1. Department of Anthropology, University of Kentucky, Lexington.

Rohrbough, Malcom T. 1978. *The Trans-Appalachian Frontier*. Oxford University Press, New York.

Rolingson, Martha A. 1961. The Kirtley Site: A Mississippian Village in McLean County, Kentucky. *Transactions of the Kentucky Academy of Science* 22:21–59.

———. 1964. *Paleo-Indian Culture in Kentucky*. Studies in Anthropology No. 2. University of Kentucky, Lexington.

———. 1967. Temporal Perspective on the Archaic Cultures of the Middle Green River Region, Kentucky. Ph.D. dissertation, Department of Anthropology, University of Michigan. University Microfilms, Ann Arbor.

———. 1968. Preliminary Excavations in the Eagle Creek Reservoir, Grant and Owen Counties, Kentucky. Ms. on file, University of Kentucky, Lexington.

Rolingson, Martha A., and Michael J. Rodeffer. 1968. *Archaeological Excavations In Cave Run Reservoir, Kentucky: Progress Report*. University of Kentucky, Museum of Anthropology, Lexington.

Rolingson, Martha A., and Douglas W. Schwartz. 1966. *Late Paleo-Indian and Early Archaic Manifestations on Western Kentucky*. Studies in Anthropology No. 3. University of Kentucky, Lexington.

Rossen, Jack. 1985. *A Cultural Resource Assessment of a Proposed 204-Acre Surface Mine in Floyd County, Kentucky*. Archaeological Report No. 141. Department of Anthropology, University of Kentucky, Lexington.

———. 1987. [Guilfoil Site] Botanical Remains. In *Current Archaeological Research in Kentucky: Volume One*, ed. David Pollack, pp. 167–72. Kentucky Heritage Council, Frankfort.

———. 1988. Botanical Remains. In *Muir: An Early Fort Ancient Site in the Inner Bluegrass*, ed. Christopher A. Turnbow and William E. Sharp, pp. 243–62. Archaeological Report No. 165. Program for Cultural Resource Assessment, University of Kentucky, Lexington.

———. 1992. Botanical Remains. In *Fort Ancient Cultural Dynamics in the Middle Ohio Valley,* ed. A. Gwynn Henderson, pp. 189–208. Monographs in World Archaeology No. 8. Prehistory Press, Madison, Wis.

Rossen, Jack, and Richard Edging. 1987. East Meets West: Patterns in Kentucky Late Prehistoric Subsistence. In *Current Archaeological Research in Kentucky: Volume One*, ed. David Pollack, pp. 225–34. Kentucky Heritage Council, Frankfort.

Rothschild, Nan A. 1979. Mortuary Behavior and Social Organization at Indian Knoll and Dickson Mounds. *American Antiquity* 44:658–75.

Rutsch, Edward S., and K.M. Peters. 1977. Forty Years of Archaeological Research at Morristown National Historical Park, Morristown, New Jersey. *Historical Archaeology* 12:15–38.

Sanders, Thomas N. 1983. The Manufacturing of Chipped Stone Tools at a Paleo-Indian Site in Western Kentucky. Master's Thesis, Department of Anthropology, University of Kentucky, Lexington.

———. 1988. The Adams Site: A Paleoindian Manufacturing and Habitation Site in

Christian County, Kentucky. In *Paleoindian and Archaic Research in Kentucky*, ed. Charles Hockensmith, David Pollack, and Thomas Sanders, pp. 1–24. Kentucky Heritage Council, Frankfort.

———. 1990. *Adams: The Manufacturing of Flaked Stone Tools at a Paleoindian Site in Western Kentucky*. Persimmon Press, Buffalo.

Sanders, Thomas N., and David R. Maynard. 1979. *A Reconnaissance and Evaluation of Archaeological Sites in Christian County, Kentucky*. Archaeological Survey Reports No. 12. Kentucky Heritage Commission, Frankfort.

Sauer, Carl O. 1927. *Geography of the Pennyroyal*. Kentucky Geological Survey, Series 6, Vol. 25. Lexington.

Saunders, Jeffrey, George A. Agogino, Anthony T. Boldurian, and C. Vance Haynes. 1991. A Mammoth-Ivory Burnisher-Billet. *Plains Anthropologist* 36:359–63.

Saunders, Jeffrey, C. Vance Haynes, Dennis J. Stanford, and George A. Agogino. 1990. A Mammoth-Ivory Semifabricate from Blackwater Locality No. 1, New Mexico. *American Antiquity* 55:112–19.

Saxe, Arthur A. 1970. *Social Dimensions of Mortuary Practices*. Ph.D. dissertation, Department of Anthropology, University of Michigan, Ann Arbor.

Scalf, Henry P. 1966. *Kentucky's Last Frontier*. Published by the author, Prestonsburg, Kentucky.

Schebesta, Paul. 1933. *Among Congo Pygmies*. Hutchinson and Company, London.

Schenian, Pamela A. 1988a. An Overview of the Paleo-Indian and Archaic Occupations of the Savage Cave Site. In *Paleoindian and Archaic Research in Kentucky*, ed. Charles Hockensmith, David Pollack, and Thomas Sanders, pp. 67–83. Kentucky Heritage Council, Frankfort.

———. 1988b. *Report of the Archeological Mitigation of the Onionville Mine Complex, at Approximate Green River Mile 31.8, Henderson County, Kentucky*. Archaeology Service Center, Murray State University, Murray, Kentucky.

Schock, Jack M. 1977. Comments and Excavation Plan: Structures and Features at 15-Hl-304, A Pisgah Culture Site in Harlan County. Ms. on file, Office of State Archaeology, University of Kentucky, Lexington.

———. 1978a. *Archaeological Excavations at Fort Williams, Glasgow, Kentucky, Phase I*. Western Kentucky University, Bowling Green.

———. 1978b. *Supplement to Phase I Archaeological Excavations at Fort Williams, Glasgow, Kentucky*. Western Kentucky University, Bowling Green.

———. 1987. *Archaeological Testing of Civil War Sites 15JS96, 15JS97: A Supplement to The Original Survey Report for the Relocation of Highway 27 South of Nicholasville in Jessamine County, Kentucky*. Arrow Enterprises, Bowling Green.

Schoenwetter, James. 1974. Pollen Analysis of Human Paleofeces from Upper Salts Cave. In *Archaeology of the Mammoth Cave Area*, ed. Patty Jo Watson, pp. 49–58. Academic Press, New York.

Schultz, C. Bertrand, L.G. Tanner, F.C. Whitmore, L.L. Ray, and E.C. Crawford. 1963. Paleontological Investigations at Big Bone Lick State Park, Kentucky. *Science* 142:1167–69.

———. 1967. Big Bone Lick, Kentucky. *Museum Notes, University of Nebraska News* 33(3):1–12.

Schwartz, Douglas W. 1961. *The Tinsley Hill Site: A Late Prehistoric Stone Grave Cemetery in Lyon County, Kentucky.* Studies in Anthropology No. 1. University of Kentucky Press, Lexington.

———. 1967. *Conceptions of Kentucky Prehistory: A Case Study in the History of Archaeology.* Studies in Anthropology No. 6. University of Kentucky Press, Lexington.

Schwartz, Douglas W., and Tacoma G. Sloan. 1958. Archaeological Excavation in the Barkley Basin–1958. Ms. on file, Office of State Archaeology, University of Kentucky, Lexington.

Scott, Douglas D., and Richard A. Fox, Jr. 1987. *Archaeological Insights into the Custer Battle: An Assessment of the 1984 Field Season.* University of Oklahoma Press, Norman.

Seeman, Mark F. 1977. Stylistic Variation in Middle Woodland Pipe Styles: The Chronological Implications. *Midcontinental Journal of Archaeology* 2:47–66.

———. 1979a. Feasting with the Dead: Ohio Hopewell Charnel House Ritual as a Context for Redistribution. In *Hopewell Archaeology*, ed. David S. Brose and N'omi Greber, pp. 39–46. Kent State University Press, Kent, Ohio.

———. 1979b. *The Hopewell Interaction Sphere: The Evidence for Interregional Trade and Structural Complexity.* Prehistory Research Series 5(2). Indiana Historical Society, Indianapolis.

———. 1980. A Taxonomic Review of Southern Ohio Late Woodland. Paper presented at the 52d Midwestern Archaeological Conference, Chicago.

———. 1986. Adena "Houses" and Their Implications for Early Woodland Settlement Models in the Ohio Valley. In *Early Woodland Archeology*, ed. Kenneth B. Farnsworth and Thomas E. Emerson, pp. 564–80. Kampsville Seminars in Archaeology No. 2. Center for American Archaeology, Kampsville, Illinois.

———. 1992. The Bow and Arrow, the Intrusive Mound Complex, and a Late Woodland Jack's Reef Horizon in the Mid-Ohio Valley. In *Cultural Variability in Context: Woodland Settlements of the Mid-Ohio Valley*, ed. Mark F. Seeman, pp. 41–51. Kent State University Press, Kent, Ohio.

Seeman, Mark F., and Cheryl A. Munson. 1980. Determining the Cultural Affiliation of Terminal Late Woodland-Mississippian Hunting Stations: A Lower Ohio Valley Example. *North American Archaeologist* 2:53–65.

Semenov, S.A. 1964. *Prehistoric Technology: An Experimental Study of the Oldest Tools and Artefacts from Traces of Manufacture and Wear.* Cory, Adams, and MacKay Press, London.

Semken, Holmes A. 1983. Holocene Mammalian Biogeography and Climatic Change in the Eastern and Central United States. In *Late Quaternary Environment of the United States, Vol. 2, The Holocene*, ed. Henry E. Wright, pp. 182–207. University of Minnesota Press, Minneapolis.

———. 1988. Environmental Interpretations of the "Disharmonious" Late Wisconsinan Biome of Southeastern North America. In *Late Pleistocene and Early Holocene Paleoecology and Archaeology of the Eastern Great Lakes Region*, ed. R. Laub, N. Miller, and D. Steadman, pp. 185–94. Bulletin of the Buffalo Society of Natural Sciences No. 33.

Service, Elman R. 1971. *Primitive Social Organization.* 2d ed. Random House, New York.

Shaler, Nathaniel S., and A. R. Crandall. 1876. *Report on the Forests of Greenup, Carter, Boyd and Lawrence Counties, in Eastern Kentucky*. Geological Survey of Kentucky, Series 2, Vol. 1. Frankfort.

Share, Allen J. 1982. *Cities in the Commonwealth: Two Centuries of Urban Life in Kentucky*. University Press of Kentucky, Lexington.

Sharp, William E. 1984. The Dry Run Site: An Early Fort Ancient Site in the Bluegrass. In *Late Prehistoric Research in Kentucky*, ed. David Pollack, Charles Hockensmith, and Thomas Sanders, pp. 105–29. Kentucky Heritage Council, Frankfort.

———. 1990. Fort Ancient Period. In *The Archaeology of Kentucky: Past Accomplishments and Future Directions*, ed. David Pollack, pp. 467–557. State Historic Preservation Comprehensive Plan Report No. 1. Kentucky Heritage Council, Frankfort.

Shott, Michael J. 1989. *Childers and Woods: Two Late Woodland Sites in the Upper Ohio Valley, Mason County, West Virginia*. Archaeological Report No. 200. Program for Cultural Resources Assessment, University of Kentucky, Lexington.

Shyrock, Andrew J. 1987. The Wright Mound Reexamined: Generative Structures and the Political Economy of a Simple Chiefdom. *Midcontinental Journal of Archaeology* 12:243–69.

Silverberg, Robert. 1968. *Mound Builders of Ancient America: The Archaeology of a Myth*. New York Graphic Society, Greenwich, Connecticut.

Simmons, Donald B., Michael J. Shott, and Henry T. Wright. 1984. The Gainey Site: Variability in a Great Lakes Paleo-Indian Assemblage. *Archaeology of Eastern North America* 12:266–79.

Smith, Bruce D. 1984. Mississippian Expansion: Tracing the Historical Development of an Explanatory Model. *Southeastern Archaeology* 3:13–32.

———. 1986. A Comparison of the Exploitation of Animal Species by Middle Mississippi and Fort Ancient Groups. *Southeastern Archaeological Conference Newsletter* 28(2):19–22.

———. 1989. Origins of Agriculture in Eastern North America. *Science* 246:1566–71.

——— (editor). 1978. *Mississippian Settlement Patterns*. Academic Press, New York.

Smith, Edward E., and Andrea K.L. Freeman. 1991. The Archaeological Investigation of a Series of Early Paleoindian (Clovis) Sites in the Little River Region of Christian County, Kentucky. *Current Research in the Pleistocene* 8:41–43.

Sorensen, Jerrel H., Michael B. Collins, Thomas W. Gatus, Susan Grant, Richard Levy, Charles R. Norville, Nancy O'Malley, Julie Riesenweber, and Malinda Stafford. 1980. *Final Report: Taylorsville Lake, Kentucky Archaeological Resources Survey and Evaluation, Season II*. Archaeological Report No. 24. Department of Anthropology, University of Kentucky, Lexington.

Squier, Ephraim G., and E.H. Davis. 1848. *The Ancient Monuments of the Mississippi Valley*. Smithsonian Contributions to Knowledge No. 1. Washington, D.C.

Stein, Julie K., Kenneth C. Carstens, and Kit W. Wesler. 1983. Geoarchaeology and Historic Archaeology: An Example from Fort Jefferson, Kentucky. *Southeastern Archaeology* 2:132–144.

Stelle, Len J. 1985. The Lithic Assemblage. In *The Turk Site: A Mississippian Town of the Western Kentucky Border*, ed. Richard Edging, pp. 28–34. Western Kentucky Project Report No. 3. Department of Anthropology, University of Illinois, Urbana-Champaign.

Sterling, Keir B. 1978. Introduction. In *Rafinesque: Autobiography and Lives*, assembled by Keir B. Sterling, pp. i–xiv. Arno Press, New York.

Stoltman, James B. 1973. The Southeastern United States. In *The Development of North American Archaeology*, ed. James E. Fitting, pp. 116–50. Anchor Press, Garden City, New York.

———. 1978. Temporal Models in Prehistory: An Example from Eastern North America. *Current Anthropology* 19:703–46.

Storck, Peter L., and John Tomenchuk. 1990. An Early Paleoindian Cache of Informal Tools at the Udora Site, Ontario. In *Early Paleoindian Economies of Eastern North America*, ed. Kenneth B. Tankersley and Barry L. Isaac, pp. 45–94. Research in Economic Anthropology, Supplement No. 5. JAI Press, Greenwich, Connecticut.

Stout, Charles B. 1985. *The Adams Site: A Spatial Analysis—Preliminary Report.* Western Kentucky Project Report No. 2. Department of Anthropology, University of Illinois, Urbana-Champaign.

———. 1989. The Spatial Patterning of the Adams Site: A Mississippian Town in Western Kentucky. Ph.D. dissertation, University of Illinois at Urbana-Champaign. University Microfilms, Ann Arbor.

Stout, Charles B., and R. Barry Lewis. 1993. Toward a Functional Grammar of Mississippian Town Composition in Kentucky. Paper presented at the 58th Annual Meeting of the Society for American Archaeology, St. Louis, Missouri.

Struever, Stuart. 1964. The Hopewell Interaction Sphere in Riverine-Western Great Lakes Culture History. In *Hopewellian Studies*, ed. Joseph R. Caldwell and Robert L. Hall, pp. 85–106. Scientific Papers No. 12. Illinois State Museum, Springfield.

———. 1968. A Re-Examination of Hopewell in Eastern North America. Ph.D. dissertation, Department of Anthropology, University of Chicago, Chicago.

Struever, Stuart, and Gail L. Houart. 1972. An Analysis of the Hopewell Interaction Sphere. In *Social Exchange and Interaction*, ed. E. Wilmsen, pp. 47–79. Anthropological Papers No. 46. Museum of Anthropology, University of Michigan, Ann Arbor.

Styles, Bonnie W., Steven R. Ahler, and Melvin L. Fowler. 1983. Modoc Rock Shelter Revisited. In *Archaic Hunters and Gatherers in the American Midwest*, ed. James L. Phillips and James A. Brown, pp. 261–97. Academic Press, New York.

Sussenbach, Tom. 1986. *Cultural Resource Assessment of a 450 Acre Tract at the Cincinnati International Airport, Boone County, Kentucky.* Archaeological Report No. 151. Program for Cultural Resource Assessment, University of Kentucky, Lexington.

———. 1992. The Yankeetown Occupation at the Foster Site in Daviess County, Kentucky. In *Current Archaeological Research in Kentucky, Volume II*, ed. David Pollack and A. Gwynn Henderson, pp. 103–17. Kentucky Heritage Council, Frankfort.

———. 1993. Agricultural Intensification and Mississippian Developments in the Confluence Region of the Mississippi River Valley. Ph.D. dissertation, University of Illinois at Urbana-Champaign. University Microfilms, Ann Arbor.

Sussenbach, Tom, and R. Barry Lewis. 1987. *Archaeological Investigations in Carlisle, Hickman, and Fulton Counties, Kentucky: Site Survey and Excavations*. Western Kentucky Project Report No. 4. Department of Anthropology, University of Illinois, Urbana-Champaign.

Tainter, Joseph A. 1977. Woodland Social Change in West-Central Illinois. *Midcontinental Journal of Archaeology* 2:67–98.

Tankersley, Kenneth B. 1985. The Potential for Early-Man Sites at Big Bone Lick, Kentucky. *Tennessee Anthropologist* 10:27–49.

———. 1987. Big Bone Lick, A Clovis Site in Northcentral Kentucky. *Current Research in the Pleistocene* 4:36–37.

———. 1989a. A Close Look at the Big Picture: Early Paleoindian Lithic Procurement in the Midwestern United States. In *Paleoindian Lithic Resource Use*, ed. Christopher Ellis and Jonathan Lathrop, pp. 259–92. Westview Press, Boulder.

———. 1989b. Late Pleistocene Lithic Exploitation and Human Settlement in the Midwestern United States. Ph.D. Dissertation, Department of Anthropology, Indiana University, Bloomington.

———. 1990. Late Pleistocene Lithic Exploitation in the Midwest and Midsouth: Indiana, Ohio, and Kentucky. In *Early Paleoindian Economies of Eastern North America*, ed. Kenneth B. Tankersley and Barry L. Isaac, pp. 259–99. Research in Economic Anthropology, Supplement No. 5. JAI Press, Greenwich, Connecticut.

Tankersley, Kenneth B., Brad Koldehoff, and Edwin R. Hajic. 1993. The Bostrom Site: A Paleo-Indian Habitation in Southwestern Illinois. *North American Archaeologist* 14:43–69.

Tapp, Hambleton, and James C. Klotter. 1977. *Kentucky: Decades of Discord, 1865–1900*. Kentucky Historical Society, Frankfort.

Taylor, Walter W. 1967. *A Study of Archaeology*. Southern Illinois University Press, Carbondale.

Thiel, Barbara. 1972. The Distribution of Grave Goods with Infants and Children at Indian Knoll. Ms. on file, Office of State Archaeology, Lexington.

Thomas, Cyrus. 1894. *Report on Mound Explorationn of the Bureau of Ethnology*. Bureau of American Ethnology, Annual Report No. 12. Washington, D.C.

Thompson, Raymond H. 1954. Archaic Culture in Kentucky. *Southern Indian Studies* 6:7–8.

Tippitt, Ann V., and William H. Marquardt. 1984. *Archaeological Investigations at Gregg Shoals, A Deeply Stratified Site on the Savannah River*. Atlanta Interagency Archaeological Services Division, National Park Service, Russell Papers.

Tune, Teresa W. 1987. [Guilfoil Site] Vertebrate Fauna. In *Current Archaeological Research in Kentucky: Volume One*, ed. David Pollack, pp. 173–84. Kentucky Heritage Council, Frankfort.

Turnbow, Christopher A. 1992. Fox Farm. In *Fort Ancient Cultural Dynamics in the Middle Ohio Valley*, ed. A. Gwynn Henderson, pp. 51-68. Monographs in World Archaeology No. 8. Prehistory Press, Madison, Wis.

Turnbow, Christopher A., and Cynthia E. Jobe. 1981. *Cultural Resource Investigations of the J.K. Smith Power Station, Clark County, Kentucky*. Archaeological

Report No. 60. Department of Anthropology, University of Kentucky, Lexington.

———. 1984. The Goolman Site: A Late Fort Ancient Winter Encampment in Clark County, Kentucky. In *Late Prehistoric Research in Kentucky*, ed. David Pollack, Charles Hockensmith, and Thomas Sanders, pp. 25–48. Kentucky Heritage Council, Frankfort.

Turnbow, Christopher A., Cynthia E. Jobe, Nancy O'Malley, Dee Ann Wymer, Michelle Seme, and Irwin Rovner. 1983. *Archaeological Excavations of the Goolman, DeVary, and Stone Sites in Clark County, Kentucky*. Archaeological Report No. 78. Department of Anthropology, University of Kentucky, Lexington.

Turnbow, Christopher A., Malinda Stafford, Richard Boisvert, and Julie Riesenweber. 1980. *A Cultural Resource Assessment of Two Alternate Locations of the Hancock Power Plant, Hancock and Breckinridge Counties, Kentucky*. Archaeological Report No. 30. Program for Cultural Resource Assessment, University of Kentucky, Lexington.

Turnbow, Christopher A., and William E. Sharp. 1988. *Muir: An Early Fort Ancient Site in the Inner Bluegrass*. Archaeological Report No. 165. Program for Cultural Resource Assessment, University of Kentucky, Lexington.

Turner, Frederick Jackson. 1920. *The Frontier in American History*. H. Holt and Co., New York.

Tuzin, Donald. 1976. *The Ilahita Arapesh: Dimensions of Unity*. University of California Press, Berkeley.

———. 1980. *The Voice of the Tambaran: Truth and Illusion in Ilahita Arapesh Religion*. University of California Press, Berkeley.

Vesper, Dennis, and Ray Tanner. 1984. Man and Mammoth in Kentucky. *Ohio Archaeologist* 34(3):18–19.

Vickery, Kent D. 1980. Preliminary Definitions of Archaic "Study Unit" in Southwestern Ohio. Unpublished manuscript prepared for the State Archaeological Preservation Plan Meeting held on April 25, 1980, Columbus, Ohio.

Wade, Richard C. 1959. *The Urban Frontier: Pioneer Life in Early Pittsburg, Cincinnati, Lexington, Louisville, and St. Louis*. University of Chicago Press, Chicago.

Wagner, Gail E. 1983. Fort Ancient Subsistence: The Botanical Record. *West Virginia Archaeologist* 35:27–39.

———. 1984. Fort Ancient Plant Remains from Northern Kentucky. In *Late Prehistoric Research in Kentucky*, ed. David Pollack, Charles D. Hockensmith, and Thomas N. Sanders, pp. 50–66. Kentucky Heritage Council, Frankfort.

———. 1987. Uses of Plants by the Fort Ancient Indians. Ph.D. dissertation, Department of Anthropology, Washington University, St. Louis.

Walker, John W. 1975. *Assessment of Archeological Resources of Cumberland Gap National Historic Park*. Southeast Archaeological Center, National Park Service, Tallahassee, Florida.

Walters, Matthew M. 1985. Faunal Remains at Waveland (15FA177), Fayette County, Kentucky. *Proceedings of the Symposium on Ohio Valley Urban and Historic Archaeology* 3:145–50.

Walthall, John A., and Ned Jenkins. 1976. The Gulf Formational Stage in Southeastern Prehistory. *Southeastern Archaeological Conference Bulletin* 19:43–49.

Watson, Patty Jo. 1969. *The Prehistory of Salts Cave, Kentucky*. Reports of Investigations No. 16. Illinois State Museum, Springfield.

———. 1985. The Impact of Early Horticulture in the Upland Drainages of the Midwest and Midsouth. In *Prehistoric Food Production in North America*, ed. Richard I. Ford, pp. 99–147. Anthropological Papers No. 75. Museum of Anthropology, University of Michigan, Ann Arbor.

———. 1989. Early Plant Cultivation in the Eastern Woodlands of North America. In *Foraging and Farming: The Evolution of Plant Exploitation*, ed. David R. Harris and G. C. Hillman, pp. 555–71. Unwin Hyman, London.

———. (editor). 1974. *Archaeology of the Mammoth Cave Area*. Academic Press, New York.

Webb, Thompson. 1987. The Appearance and Disappearance of Major Vegetational Assemblages: Long-Term Vegetational Dynamics in Eastern North America. *Vegetatio* 69:177–87.

———. 1988. Eastern North America. In *Vegetation History*, ed. B. Huntley and T. Webb, pp. 383–414. Kluwer Academic Publishers, Boston.

Webb, Thompson, Patrick J. Bartlein, and John E. Kutzbach. 1987. Climatic Changes in Eastern North America During the Past 18,000 years; Comparisons of Pollen Data with Model Results. In *North America and Adjacent Oceans During the Last Deglaciation*, ed. by W. Ruddiman and H. Wright, pp. 447-62. Geological Society of America, Boulder.

Webb, William S. 1940. *The Wright Mounds, Sites 6 and 7, Montgomery County, Kentucky*. Reports in Anthropology and Archaeology No. 5:6–134. University of Kentucky, Lexington.

———. 1941a. *The Morgan Stone Mound, Site 15, Bath County, Kentucky*. Reports in Anthropology and Archaeology No. 5(3):233–91. University of Kentucky, Lexington.

———. 1941b. *The Mt. Horeb Site Earthworks, Site 1, and the Drake Mound, Site 11, Fayette County, Kentucky*. Reports in Anthropology and Archaeology No. 5(2): 139–218. University of Kentucky, Lexington.

———. 1942. *The C and O Mounds at Paintsville, Sites Jo2 and Jo9, Johnson County,. Kentucky*. Reports in Anthropology and Archaeology No. 5:297–372. University of Kentucky, Lexington.

———. 1943. *The Riley Mound, Site Be15, and the Landing Mound, Site Be17, Boone County, Kentucky with Additional Notes on the Mt. Horeb Site, Fa1 and Sites Fa14 and Fa15, Fayette County, Kentucky*. Reports in Anthropology and Archaeology No. 5:582–672. University of Kentucky, Lexington.

———. 1946. *Indian Knoll Site Oh 2 Ohio County, Kentucky*. Reports in Anthropology and Archaeology No. 4(3), part 1:113–365. University of Kentucky, Lexington.

———. 1950a. *The Carlson Annis Mound, Site 5, Butler County, Kentucky*. Reports in Anthropology No. 7:267–354. University of Kentucky, Lexington.

———. 1950b. *The Read Shell Midden, Site 10, Butler County, Kentucky*. Reports in Anthropology No. 7(5). University of Kentucky, Lexington.

———. 1951. *The Parrish Village Site, Site 45, Hopkins County, Kentucky*. Reports in Anthropology No. 7(6):406–61. University of Kentucky, Lexington.

———. 1952. *The Jonathan Creek Village*. Reports in Anthropology and Archaeology No. 8(1). University of Kentucky, Lexington.

———. 1974. *Indian Knoll*. University of Tennessee Press, Knoxville. Originally published in 1946.

———. 1981. *The Development of the Spearthrower*. Occasional Papers in Anthropology No. 2. Department of Anthropology, University of Kentucky, Lexington.

Webb, William S., and Raymond S. Baby. 1957. *The Adena People No. 2*. Ohio Historical Society, Columbus.

Webb, William S., and John B. Elliott. 1942. *The Robbins Mounds, Site Be3 and Be14, Boone County, Kentucky*. Reports in Anthropology and Archaeology No. 5(5):377–499. University of Kentucky, Lexington.

Webb, William S., and William D. Funkhouser. 1929. *The Williams Site in Christian County, Kentucky*. Reports in Archaeology and Anthropology No. 1(1). University of Kentucky, Lexington.

———. 1930. *The Page Site in Logan County, Kentucky*. Reports in Archaeology and Anthropology No. 1(3). University of Kentucky, Lexington.

———. 1931. *The Tolu Site in Crittenden County, Kentucky*. Reports in Archaeology and Anthropology No. 1(5). University of Kentucky, Lexington.

———. 1932. *Archeological Survey of Kentucky*. Reports in Anthropology and Archaeology No. 2. University of Kentucky, Lexington.

———. 1933. *The McLeod Bluff Site*. Reports in Archaeology and Anthropology No. 3(1). University of Kentucky, Lexington.

———. 1936. *Rock Shelters in Menifee County, Kentucky*. Reports in Anthropology and Archaeology No. 3(4):105–67. University of Kentucky, Lexington.

———. 1940. *Ricketts Site Revisited, Site 3, Montgomery County, Kentucky*. Reports in Anthropology and Archaeology No. 3:211–69. University of Kentucky, Lexington.

Webb, William S., and William G. Haag. 1939. *The Chiggerville Site, Site 1, Ohio County, Kentucky*. Reports in Anthropology No. 4(1):1–62. University of Kentucky, Lexington.

———. 1940. *Cypress Creek Villages, Sites 11 and 12, McLean County, Kentucky*. Reports in Anthropology No. 4(2):67–110. University of Kentucky, Lexington.

———. 1947a. *Archaic Sites in McLean County, Kentucky*. Reports in Anthropology No. 7:1–48. University of Kentucky, Lexington.

———. 1947b. *The Fisher Site, Fayette County, Kentucky*. Reports in Anthropology No. 7:49–104. University of Kentucky, Lexington.

Webb, William S., and Charles E. Snow. 1943. *The Crigler Mounds, Sites Be20 and Be27, and the Hartman Mound Site, Be32, Boone County, Kentucky*. Reports in Anthropology and Archaeology No. 5:505–79. University of Kentucky, Lexington.

———. 1945. *The Adena People*. Reports in Anthropology No. 6. University of Kentucky, Lexington.

———. 1959. *The Dover Mound*. University of Kentucky Press, Lexington.

Weinland, Marcia K. 1980. The Rowena Site, Russell County, Kentucky. *Kentucky Archaeological Association Bulletins* 16–17:1–150.

Wesler, Kit W. 1985. *Archaeological Excavations at Wickliffe Mounds, 15BA4: Mound A, 1984*. Report No. 1. Wickliffe Mounds Research Center, Wickliffe, Kentucky.

————. 1989. *Archaeological Excavations at Wickliffe Mounds, 15BA4: Mound D, 1987*. Report No. 3. Wickliffe Mounds Research Center, Wickliffe, Kentucky.

————. 1991. *Archaeological Excavations at Wickliffe Mounds, 15BA4: North Village and Cemetery, 1988–1989*. Report No. 4. Wickliffe Mounds Research Center, Wickliffe, Kentucky.

Wesler, Kit W., and Sarah W. Neusius. 1987. *Archaeological Excavations at Wickliffe Mounds, 15BA4: Mound F, Mound A Addendum, and Mitigation for the Great River Road Project, 1985 and 1986*. Report No. 2. Wickliffe Mounds Research Center, Wickliffe, Kentucky.

West, Frederick Hadleigh. 1983. The Antiquity of Man in America. In *Late Quaternary Environments of the United States, Vol. 2, The Holocene*, ed. H.E. Wright, pp. 364–82. University of Minnesota Press, Minneapolis.

Wilkins, Gary R. 1977. Cultural Ecology of Prehistoric Mountaintop Sites in the Kanawha Basin, West Virginia. Master's thesis, University of Arkansas, Fayetteville, Arkansas.

Willey, Gordon R. 1966. *An Introduction to American Archaeology: Volume 1, North and Middle America*. Prentice-Hall, Englewood Cliffs, New Jersey.

————. 1985. Some Continuing Problems in New World Culture History. *American Antiquity* 50:351–63.

Willey, Gordon R., and Philip Phillips. 1958. *Method and Theory in American Archaeology*. University of Chicago Press, Chicago.

Willey, Gordon R., and Jeremy A. Sabloff. 1980. *A History of American Archaeology*. 2d ed. W.H. Freeman, San Francisco.

Williams, Stephen. 1980. Armorel: A Very Late Phase in the Lower Mississippi Valley. *Southeastern Archaeological Conference Bulletin* 22:105–10.

Winters, Howard D. 1967. *An Archaeological Survey of the Wabash Valley in Illinois*. Report of Investigations No. 10. Illinois State Museum, Springfield.

————. 1968. Value Systems and Trade Cycles of the Late Archaic in the Midwest. In *New Perspectives in Archaeology*, ed. Sally R. Binford and Lewis R. Binford, pp. 175–221. Aldine, Chicago.

————. 1969. *The Riverton Culture: A Second Millennium Occupation in the Central Wabash Valley*. Reports of Investigations No. 13. Illinois State Museum, Springfield.

————. 1974. Introduction to the New Edition. In *Indian Knoll*, by William S. Webb, pp. iii–xxvii. University of Tennessee Press, Knoxville. Originally published in 1946.

Witthoft, John. 1952. A Paleo-Indian Site in Eastern Pennsylvania: An Early Hunting Culture. *Proceedings of the Philadelphia Academy of Natural Sciences* 87:299–303.

Woodard, Justine. 1987. [Marshall Site] Botanical Remains. In *Archaeological Investigations in Carlisle, Hickman, and Fulton Counties, Kentucky*, by Tom Sussenbach and R. Barry Lewis, pp. 67–72. Western Kentucky Project Report No. 4. University of Illinois, Department of Anthropology, Urbana-Champaign.

Wright, William C. 1982. *The Confederate Magazine at Fort Wade, Grand Gulf, Mississippi: Excavations, 1980–1981*. Archaeological Report No. 8. Mississippi Department of Archives and History, Jackson.

Wymer, Dee Ann. 1987. The Paleoethnobotanical Record of the Lower Tennessee Cumberland Region. *Southeastern Archaeology* 6:124–29.

———. 1989. Paleoethnobotanical Analysis. In *Phase III Excavations at the Dow Cook Site (15La4) in the Proposed Yatesville Reservoir, Lawrence County, Kentucky*, compiled by Charles M. Niquette and Jonathan P. Kerr, pp. 126–65. Cultural Resource Analysts, Contract Publication Series 89-04. Lexington, Kentucky.

Yarnell, Richard A. 1974. Plant Food and Cultivation of the Salts Cave. In *Archaeology of the Mammoth Cave Area*, ed. Patty Jo Watson, pp. 113–22. Academic Press, New York.

Yarnell, Richard A., and M. Jean Black. 1985. Temporal Trends Indicated by a Survey of Archaic and Woodland Plant Food Remains from Southeastern North America. *Southeastern Archaeology* 4:93–106.

Young, Bennett H. 1910. *The Prehistoric Men of Kentucky*. Filson Club Publications No. 25. Louisville, Kentucky.

Young, Jon N. 1962. Annis Mound: A Late Prehistoric Site on the Green River. Master's thesis, Department of Anthropology, University of Kentucky, Lexington.

CONTRIBUTORS

RICHARD W. JEFFERIES, assistant professor of anthropology at the University of Kentucky, has studied the Archaic cultures of the Ohio Valley for more than fifteen years. He has published many articles on the subject, as well as written, *The Archaeology of Carrier Mills: 10,000 Years in the Saline Valley of Illinois*, which focuses on the important Middle Archaic occupation at the Black Earth site. He is currently studying the development of Middle Archaic trade networks in the lower Ohio and middle Mississippi River Valleys.

R. BARRY LEWIS, associate professor of anthropology at the University of Illinois at Urbana-Champaign, has published many articles and several edited books about the archaeology of the midwestern and southeastern United States. He has worked on Mississippi period sites in western Kentucky and southeastern Missouri since the mid-1960s. His most recent book, coedited with Thomas E. Emerson, is *Cahokia and the Hinterlands*. Working with his colleague Charles B. Stout, he is now editing a new book on the archaeology and architecture of Mississippian towns and central places.

KIM A. MCBRIDE is a historical archaeologist specializing in the nineteenth- to twentieth-century United States. She received her B.A. from Beloit College and her M.A. and Ph.D. from Michigan State University. She is a staff archaeologist with the Kentucky Archaeological Survey and an adjunct assistant professor in the Department of Anthropology. Her research background includes historical demography of the southern United States, and her recent archaeological work has included four years of excavations at the restored Shaker village at Pleasant Hill in Mercer County.

W. STEPHEN MCBRIDE is a historical archaeologist focusing on the eighteenth- to nineteenth-century United States. He received his B.A. from Beloit College and his M.A. and Ph.D. from Michigan State University. He is a staff archaeologist with Wilbur Smith Associates in Lexington, Kentucky. His recent work in Kentucky includes several years of excavations at Camp Nelson, a Civil War quartermaster station and recruitment center in Jessamine County; as well as other excavations at sites such as Farmington, the John Speed estate in Louisville; Ashland, the Henry Clay estate in Lexington; and Benjamin Latrobe's Pope House in Lexington. He has also pursued eighteenth-century frontier fort research in southeastern West Virginia.

DAVID L. MORGAN is director of the Kentucky Heritage Council and Kentucky's State Historic Preservation Officer. He is a 1975 graduate of Centre College and received a Master of Science degree in historic preservation from Columbia University in New York City. Recently he received the National Park Service's 1994 Southeast Regional Preservation Award for his efforts to preserve and protect Kentucky's rich historic and archaeological heritage. During his tenure as director of the Kentucky Heritage Council, the agency has initiated an annual archaeological conference, published several books on Kentucky archaeology, supported archaeological research in all areas of the state, and cosponsored Native American exhibits at the Kentucky State Fair. In the late 1980s the Heritage Council also initiated the Kentucky Archaeological Registry Program, which works with private landowners to preserve important archaeological sites.

DAVID POLLACK is an archaeologist on the Kentucky Heritage Council staff and a Ph.D. candidate in anthropology at the University of Kentucky. He has edited Kentucky's Comprehensive State Plan, *The Archaeology of Kentucky: Past Accomplishments and Future Directions*, and has edited or coedited several collections of papers on Kentucky archaeology, including *Current Research in Kentucky*, volumes 1 and 2, and *Late Prehistoric Research in Kentucky*. He is coauthor of *Chambers: An Upland Mississippian Village in Western Kentucky* and has published several articles on the Woodland and Fort Ancient cultures of the Ohio Valley. With Cheryl Munson of Indiana University he is currently working on a monograph and a well-illustrated book for the general public on the late Mississippian Caborn-Welborn phase of the lower Ohio Valley. The primary focus of this research is the materials and records from the Slack Farm Site in Union County, Kentucky.

JIMMY A. RAILEY is a Ph.D. candidate in the Department of Anthropology at Washington University in St. Louis. He has contributed several publications on the Woodland periods and late prehistoric archaeology in Kentucky and surrounding areas. He edited *The Pyles Site: A Newtown Village in Mason County, Kentucky*, coauthored *Chambers: A Upland Mississippian Village in Western Kentucky*, and contributed a chapter to *Fort Ancient Cultural Dynamics in the Middle Ohio Valley*. His current research focuses on settlement and social trends in the central Ohio Valley and prestate developments in China.

DOUGLAS W. SCHWARTZ is president of the School of American Research in Santa Fe, New Mexico. He is the author of *Conceptions of Kentucky Prehistory: A Case Study in the History of Archaeology* and many articles, monographs, and research reports about Kentucky archaeology. His most recent monograph is *On the Edge of Splendor: Exploring the Grand Canyon's Human Past*. In recognition of his many contributions to American anthropology, the Society for American Archaeology and the American Anthropological Association have awarded him their Distinguished Service Awards.

WILLIAM E. SHARP, an archaeologist for the U.S. Forest Service on the Daniel Boone National Forest, is a native Kentuckian with a keen interest in Kentucky prehistory. He has written a number of short articles on Kentucky Fort Ancient archaeology and has had the privilege of working with some of the real pioneers in this field—A. Gwynn Henderson, Cynthia E. Jobe, David Pollack, Jimmy A. Railey, Jack Rossen, and Christopher A. Turnbow.

KENNETH B. TANKERSLEY, assistant professor of anthropology at State University of New York-Brockport, has written many journal articles and book chapters on the Clovis complex and Paleoindian tradition in North America. He also coedited *Early Paleoindian Economies of Eastern North America*. His current research concentrates on human adaptations to late Pleistocene environmental change.

INDEX

Page numbers in *italics* refer to figures. Page numbers in **boldface** indicate glossary entries.

Abraders, 131, 134, 145, 170
Acorns, 60, 64, 69, 70, 77
Adair County: Early Mississippi period occupation of, 139-40
Adams Mastodon site (Harrison County), 27, 37
Adams site (Christian County), 28, 37
Adams site (Fulton County), 142-45, 154, 156
Adena culture: Webb's contribution to understanding of, 11, 18, 79, 91-94, 97; definition of, 18, 79, **227;** cranial deformation in, 88; chronology of, 91, 98-100, 108; settlement patterns of, 91-94; burial mounds and earthworks of, 94-96; technology (tools) of, 96-97; social complexity (interaction) in, 97-98; demise of, 100-101
Adena-like projectile points, 70
Adena Plain pottery, 97, 99, 100, 107
Adena Stemmed projectile points, 81, 85, 87, 88, 90, 97, 99, 100, 104
Adzes, 66, 131, 135, 145
Afro-Americans: on plantations, 189-91; as Civil War soldiers, 202; definition of, **227**
Age, and status, 61, 74, 154
Agriculture: introduction of, 2, 18, 19, 120-21; and evidence of plant domestication, 18; in Mississippian tradition, 127, 152, 157; in Fort Ancient tradition, 161, 166, 170, 177, 178-79, 181; archaeology about, 184-85; site destruction due to, 217-18. *See also* Horticulture; Maize; Plantation (and farmstead) archaeology
Alexander Series pottery, 85
Allen, Mark W., 154
Allen, Roger C., 139
Amaranth, 84
American lotus, 129
Ancient Buried City site (Ballard County), 132
Ancient History, or Annals of Kentucky . . . (Rafinesque), xi, 7
Ancient Monuments of the Mississippi Valley (Squier and Davis), 8
Andalex Village site (Hopkins County), 216
Andrew's Run (Baker) site, 58
Angel Mounds State Park (Indiana), 222

Angel phase (Early Mississippi period), 134, 147
Angel site (Indiana), 133-34, 147, 154, 222
Animal teeth, 46, 54, *59,* 177
Annis Village and Mounds site (Butler County), 134, 135-37, 149
Antebellum lifeways (Historic period), 194-201
Antelope, 26
Anthropology, development of, 9-10
Antler tools: of Early Paleoindian period, 24, 26, 36; of Early Archaic period, 46; of Middle Archaic period, *52,* 54; of Middle Woodland period, 110; of Fort Ancient culture, 171, 177
Anvils, 48, 140, 149, 172
Aplastic. *See* Temper
Archaeological Conservancy, 225
Archaeological cultures, 36, 47, **227**
Archaeological record, characteristics of, 213-14
Archaeological Resources Protection Act of 1979, 224
Archaeological sites: destruction of, 213, 214-20; identification of, 222-23
Archaeology: speculative period in, 6-7; classificatory-descriptive period of, 7-9; classificatory-historical period of, 9-11; explanatory period of, 11-13
Archaic cultural tradition (periods): hunters and gatherers of, 2, 18, 66-67; Webb's contribution to understanding of, 11, 18, 57-58, 60; definition of, 18, 39, **227;** technology (tools) of, 18, 40, 47-48, 54-55, 75-76; climate of, 39, 45, 47, 50, 54, 72, 73, 77; horticulture in, 39, 57, 60, 73-74, 76, 77; settlement patterns of, 39, 41-46, 50-54, 57-61, 72-73, 76-77; subsistence of, 39, 40, 49-50, 56-57, 58-60, 73-74, 75-76, 77; social complexity (interaction) in, 48, 54, 58, 61, 74, 77; population trends in, 72; sedentism in, 72-73, 76, 77; diet in, 73-74; exchange in, 74-75. *See also* Early Archaic period; Late Archaic period; Middle Archaic period
Arrasmith site, 167
Arrowhead Farm site (near Louisville), 88
Arrowheads. *See* Projectile points
Arthritis, 62
Artifacts. *See* Technology (tools)

Jonathan Creek phase (Early Mississippi period), 132, 146
Jonathan Creek site (Marshall County), 132, 145, 155
Jones Mound (Hopkins County), 103, 104
Junior Historian Program, Kentucky Historical Society, 221
Justice, Noel D., 40, 81

Kanawha Bifurcate Base projectile points, 43
Karst, 4, 104
Kenton, Simon, 183, 187
Kentucky: geography of, 3-6, 19; history of archaeology in, 6; first published list of sites in, 7; mound distribution in, 8; record of site locations in, 12, 13; numbers of professional archaeologists in, 12-13; regional chronology of, *17*, 17-19
Kentucky Antiquities Act (KRS 164.705-735), 224
Kentucky Archaeological Registry Program, 221, 223
Kentucky Cave Legislation Statute (KRS 433), 224
Kentucky Department of Transportation (DOT), 13
Kentucky Desecration of a Venerated Object law (KRS 525.110), 224
Kentucky Geological Survey, 8, 20
Kentucky Heritage Council, 13, 219, 221, 222-23, 224, 225
Kentucky Historical Society, 221
Kentucky Historic Preservation Review Board, 222
Kentucky Office of State Archaeology, 13, 222, 224, 225
Kentucky Organization of Professional Archaeologists, 13
Kerr, Jonathan P., 118
Kill sites, burial and exposure of, 26-27
Kincaid site (Illinois), 155
King, Blanche, 132
King, Fain, 132
Kirkland site, 61
Kirk-like projectile points, 45, 46
Kirk projectile points, 40, 42, 45, 46
Kirk Serrated projectile points, 45
Kirk Stemmed projectile points, 45
Kirtley site (McLean County), 134-35, 137
Knives: of Early Paleoindian period, 24; of Middle Paleoindian period, 33; of Late Paleoindian period, 34, 35, 36; of Late Archaic period, 67; of Early Mississippi period, 134, 135, 140; of Late Mississippi period, 149
Knobs (hills), 5

Knotweed, 57, 60, 69, 74, 84, 115, 118, 129. *See also* Erect knotweed
Koster site (Illinois), 40
Kramer projectile points, 81
Kreisa, Paul P., 156
KYANG site (Jefferson County), 54, 65

Lamoka Lake site (New York State), 39
Lanceolate or triangular projectile points, 105
Lanceolate Plano projectile points, 33, *34*
Land Between the Lakes National Recreation Area, 70
Larkin site (Bourbon County), 171, 180, 215-16
Late Archaic period: definition of, 18, 54; subsistence of, 39, 56-57, 58-60, 63, 67, 69, 70, 73-74, 76, 77; exchange in, 54, 55, 58, 61, 62, 74, 75, 77; settlement patterns of, 54, 57-61, 73, 77; technology (tools) of, 54-55, 60-71, 73, 76; mortuary practices of, 58, 60, 61-71; biota of, 62; health of population in, 62
Late Mississippi period: in Mississippi River Valley, 142-45; technology (tools) of, 143, 145, 146, 148, 149, 158; population trends in, 145, 146, 152-53, 159; in Pennyroyal region, 145-47, 149-50; in Tennessee-Cumberland River valleys, 145-47; in Western Coal Field, 147-49; mortuary practices of, 148-49
Late Paleoindian period: definition of, 22; technology (tools) of, 33-34, 38; subsistence and settlement patterns of, 35-36, 37, 38; mortuary practices of, 37
Late Prehistoric (Fort Ancient) period, 19. *See also* Fort Ancient culture
Late Woodland period: definition of, 19, 79, 110; technology (tools) of, 19, 89, 110-11, 113, 114, 115, 117, 119, 124; subsistence of, 111, 113, 114, 115, 118, 120-21, 124; settlement patterns of, 111-19, 125; population density in, 112, 124; social complexity (interaction) in, 115, 121, 122
Latrobe, Benjamin Henry, 197-98
Lawrence County: Late Woodland period occupation of, 117-19; industrial archaeology in, 185
Lawrence site (Trigg County), 46, 85
Lean-tos, 62
LeBus Circle (Bourbon County), 96
LeCroy Bifurcate Base projectile points, 45
LeCroy projectile points, 40, 43, 45
Ledbetter-Pickwick projectile points, 70
Lee County: Late Archaic period occupation of, 68-69

102, 103-5, 122-23; of Early Mississippi period, 137-38; of Late Mississippi period, 148-49; of Fort Ancient culture, 164, 168, 170, 177, 179-80, 215-16
Mound Builders, myth of, 6-7, 8, 19
Mound building: introduction of, 2, 18; speculative interest in, 6-7; BAE exploration of, 8; in Early Woodland period, 87; in Middle Woodland period, 90-91, 94-96, 101, 109; in Late Woodland period, 113; in Early Mississippi period, 135, 139; in Late Mississippi period, 148-49, 150
Mountains ("Eastern Mountains") region: geography of, 5-6; Late Paleoindian period occupation of, 22, 35; Early Archaic period occupation of, 41-46; Late Archaic period occupation of, 65-69; Early Woodland period occupation of, 81, 86-88; Middle Woodland period occupation of, 106-10; Late Woodland period occupation of, 117-19; Mississippi period occupation of, 150-52; Fort Ancient culture in, 177-78; Euro-American settlement of, 189
Mt. Horeb site (Fayette County), 96
Muhlenberg County: Middle Woodland period occupation of, 103-4
Muir site (Jessamine County), 162-64, 178, 179
Mulberry Creek Cordmarked pottery, 129, 131
Muller, Jon, 102, 110, 113
Mummy, from Salts Cave, 84
Murray, John (4th earl of Dunmore), 187
Murray State University, 12, 221, 226
Musk ox, 21, 26
Mussels, 40, 50, 56, 69, 70, 129, 164. *See also* Shell middens

National Historic Landmark program, 223
National Historic Preservation Act of 1966, 12, 13, 223
National Register of Historic Places, 215, 222, 223
National Research Council, 10
Native Americans, definition of, **229**
Needles, 24, 46
Negative-painted pottery, 134, 148, 149
Nelson, Nels C., xii
Nelson Gay Mound (Clark County), 218
Net weights, 64
New Deal, 11
Newport: development of, 198, 204, 207; urban archaeology near, 200-201; industrial archaeology near, 207-8
Newt Kash Hollow Rockshelter (Menifee County), 81, 87

Newtown complex, 115-17, 124
New York State: Archaic cultural tradition in, 39
Nickelhoff, Andrew, 43
Niquette, Charles M., 118
Nitre (saltpeter) mining, 185, 201, 202
"Nodena" projectile points, 145, 148
Nolichucky projectile points, 81
North Carolina: Early Archaic period occupation of, 40; Middle Archaic period occupation of, 47
Northern Kentucky University, 12, 226
Northern red oak, 6
Nucleated villages. *See* Settlements
Nuts: Early Woodland period exploitation of, 84, 85; Late Woodland exploitation of, 118. *See also* Acorns; Chestnuts; Hickory nuts; Walnuts
Nuttall, Thomas, 6
Nutting stones: of Late Archaic period, 67; of Early Woodland period, 88; definition of, **229**

Oak-chestnut forests, 5
Oak-hickory-chestnut forests, 67
Oak-hickory forests, 4, 5
Oak trees, 4, 5, 6, 67. *See also* Acorns
O'Byam Incised var. Stewart pottery, 146
O'Byam's Fort site (Fulton County), 101-2
Occupations, definition of, **229**
Office of State Archaeology, 13, 222, 224, 225
Ohio: Late Archaic period occupation of, 63; Middle Woodland period occupation of, 106; Late Woodland period occupation of, 116; Fort Ancient culture in, 161
Ohio County. *See* Indian Knoll site (Ohio County)
Ohio River Valley: Early Archaic period occupation of, 41-42; Middle Archaic period occupation of, 53; Late Archaic period occupation of, 63-65; Early Woodland period occupation of, 85-86; Middle Woodland period occupation of, 100, 103; Late Woodland period occupation of, 112-15; Euro-Americans in, 127, 181, 186, 194, 207; Early Mississippi period occupation of, 132; Fort Ancient culture in, 161, 162, 170-76
Old Clarkesville phase (Middle Archaic period), 54
Old Field Swamp peat deposit (Missouri), 47
Old Fort Earthwork (Greenup County), 107-8, 217
Old Town Red pottery, 140
O'Malley, Nancy, 184, 188
Onionville site (Henderson County), 185, 208-9

occupation of, 205-6
Russellville, settlement of, 189
Rutherford Mound (Illinois), 103

Sabloff, Jeremy A., 6, 7
Sacred sites, 84. *See also* Mortuary practices;
    Mound building
St. Albans Side Notched projectile points, 45
St. Albans site (West Virginia), 40
Salt-glazed stoneware, 188
Saltpans: of Early Mississippi period, 129,
    131; of Fort Ancient culture, 171, 177
Saltpeter. *See* Nitre (saltpeter) mining
Saltpetre Cave (Carter County), 201
Salts Cave (Hart County), 82, *83,* 84, 88
Salvage archaeology, 11, 210
Sanders, Thomas N., 50
Sandstone-tempered pottery, 97
Sand-tempered pottery, 100
Saratoga Type Cluster projectile points, 71
Sassafras Ridge site, 145
Sauer, Carl, 4
Savage Cave site (Logan County), 30, 37
Savannah River projectile points, 81
Schenian, Pamela A., 185, 209
Schwartz, Douglas W., 6, 10, 12, 20, 45
Scrapers: of Early Paleoindian period, 24, 28;
    of Middle Paleoindian period, 31; of Late
    Paleoindian period, 33, 34, 35, 36; of
    Early Archaic period, 46; of Late Archaic
    period, 60, 62, 63; of Early Mississippi
    period, 129, 134, 140; of Late Mississippi
    period, 148, 149; of Fort Ancient culture,
    171, 172
Second Geological Survey (1873), 8
Sedentism: in Archaic periods, 72-73, 76, 77;
    in Mississippi period, 127-28, 141-42,
    147-48, 150, 156-57; in Fort Ancient tra-
    dition, 166; definition of, **229**
Seeman, Mark F., 86, 87, 100
Sellards Settlement, 189
Seriation, 14, **229**
Settlement patterns: of Early Paleoindian
    period, 24, 26-30, 36, 38; of Middle Pale-
    oindian period, 32-33, 37, 38; of Late
    Paleoindian period, 35-36, 37, 38; of Early
    Archaic period, 41-46, 72-73, 76; of Mid-
    dle Archaic period, 50-54, 73, 76-77; of
    Late Archaic period, 54, 57-61, 73, 77; of
    Early Woodland period, 81-82, 84-88, 121;
    of Middle Woodland period, 90-110, 124;
    of Late Woodland period, 111-19, 125; of
    Mississippi period, 127-28, 141-42,
    147-48, 150, 156-57, 179; of Fort Ancient
    culture, 161, 162-76, 179, 181-82; of His-
    toric period, 186-209

Settlements: of Mississippi period, 2, 127-28,
    130, 156-57; of Late Archaic period,
    60-61; definition of, 61; of Middle Wood-
    land period, 91, 100-101, 109, 124; of Late
    Woodland period, 111-12, 115, 118-19,
    121-22, 156
Sewing needles. *See* Needles
Shaker Mills at Pleasant Hill (Mercer Coun-
    ty), 185, 199-200
Shaler, Nathaniel S., 6
Shane, Orrin C., 166
Sharp, William E., 128, 186
Shawnee (ethnic group), 175, 181, 188
Sheep House Shelter (Madison County), 116
Shell beads: of Late Archaic period, *59,* 61; of
    Middle Woodland period, 90; of Fort
    Ancient culture, 170, 172, 177, 180
Shellfish, 40, 50, 56, 69, 70, 164
Shell gorgets and pendants: of Late Archaic
    period, *59,* 61; of Middle Woodland peri-
    od, 104; of Late Mississippi period, *146;* of
    Fort Ancient culture, 171, 172-73, 177,
    180-81, 182
Shell masks, 180, 182
Shell middens, 58. *See also* Green River shell
    mounds
"Shell Mound Archaic." *See* Green River shell
    mounds
Shell mounds. *See* Shell middens
Shell-tempered pottery: of Early Mississippi
    period, 129, 133, 134, 135-36, 140; of Late
    Mississippi period, 143, 149; of Fort
    Ancient culture, 164, 169, 171, 177, 182
Shelter: of Early Paleoindian period, 24; of
    Late Archaic period, 62. *See also* Houses;
    Lean-tos; Rockshelters
Shoop site (Pennsylvania), 36
Siderite (ironstone) flaked stone tools, 67
Side scrapers, 31, 33, 35
Silverberg, Robert, 7
Simon Fraser University, 12, 45
Simple stamped pottery, 89, 97, 103, 104, 105,
    106
Sim's Creek phase (Woodland period), 67, 117
Sim's Creek site (Pike County), 117
Site 15Bl10 (Bell County), 152
Site 15Br9, 177
Site 15Gp183 (Greenup County), 115
Site 15He13 (Henderson County), 103
Site 15Hl304 (Harlan County), 151
Site 15McN20 (McCracken County), 71
Site 15Pi7 (Pike County), 177
Site 15Pi12 (Pike County), 117
Site 15Pi13 (Pike County), 177
Skidmore phase (Late Archaic period), 66-67
Skidmore site (Powell County), 66-67

Taylor, Walter W., 11
Technology (tools): of Archaic periods, 18, 75-76; of Early Woodland period, 18, 81-82, 85, 87, 88, 90, 97, 99, 100, 104, 124; of Late Woodland period, 19, 89, 110-11, 113, 114, 115, 117, 119; of Early Paleoindian period, 22-28, 36; of Middle Paleoindian period, 31, 33; of Late Paleoindian period, 33-34, 38; of Early Archaic period, 40, 42-43, 45, 46, 75; of Middle Archaic period, 47-48, 53, 54, 73, 74, 75-76, 124; of Late Archaic period, 54-55, 60-71, 73; of Middle Woodland period, 89-90, 96-97, 98, 100, 101, 103, 104, 105, 106, 108, 109, 110, 124; of Early Mississippi period, 129, 131, 133, 134, 135-36, 139, 140, 158; of Mississippi period, 129, 157-58; of Late Mississippi period, 143, 145, 146, 148, 149, 158; of Fort Ancient culture, 161, 164, 170
Teeth (human), wear on, 62, 159
Temper, definition of, **229**. *See also names of specific tempers*
Tempering. *See* Temper
Tennessee: Early Archaic period occupation of, 40; Middle Archaic period occupation of, 47, 49-50; Late Archaic period occupation of, 70
Tennessee-Cumberland River Valleys: Middle Archaic period occupation of, 53; Late Archaic period occupation of, 69-71; Early Woodland period occupation of, 85; Early Mississippi period occupation of, 132; Late Mississippi period occupation of, 145-47; continuity between Kentucky and Tennessee cultures in, 155
Tennessee Valley Authority, 10
Terminal Archaic period, definition of, **230**
Territorialism, 84, 87, 112
Textiles, 81-82, 97
Thacker phase (Woodland period), 67, 87-88, 117
Thacker site (Pike County), 87
Thompson, Raymond H., 30
Thompson site (Greenup County), 162, 164-66
Timber industry, 204, 207, 208-9
Time. *See* Chronology; Regional chronologies
Tinsley Hill phase (Late Mississippi period), 145-47
Tinsley Hill site (Lyon County), 145-47, 158-59
Tobacco farming, 190, 204, 205
Todd County: Early Mississippi period occupation of, 139, 140

Toolmaking. *See* Chert; Debitage; Flintknapping tools
Tools. *See* Bifacial tools (bifaces); Technology (tools); Unifacial tools
Trade. *See* Exchange
Traditions, definition of, **230**
Trait-list approach, 11
Transient camps, 60-61
Transportation systems, development of, 194, 204, 207
Triangular projectile points: Type 2, 164, 166; Type 3, 170; Type 4, 171, 177; Type 5, 170, 171, 175, 177; Type 6, 171, 175, 177
Trigg County: Late Paleoindian period occupation of, 35, 37; Early Archaic period occupation of, 46
Trimble Side Notched projectile points, 63, 64, 65, 67, 71
Tuliptrees. *See* Beech-yellow poplar forests
Turkey digit pendants, 177
Turkeys, 35, 49, 64, 69, 131, 132, 134, 143, 157, 164, 170, 178
Turkeytail projectile points, 81, 85
Turk site (Carlisle County), 129, 130-31
Turner, Frederick Jackson, 154
Turtles, 45, 53, 69, 129, 143, 157
Turtle shell cups and rattles, 61
Twined fabrics, 81-82
Twin Mounds site, 145

Unifacial tools: of Early Paleoindian period, 28; of Late Paleoindian period, 33, 36; of Middle Paleoindian period, 33; definition of, **230**. *See also* Knives; Scrapers
Union County: Early Woodland period occupation of, 85; Late Woodland period occupation of, 114; Early Mississippi period occupation of, 148; looting of sites in, 219-20
University of Illinois at Urbana-Champaign (UIUC), 12
University of Kentucky: Department of Anthropology and Archaeology established at, 10; excavations supervised by, 10, 12, 215, 216; archaeological research (recent) at, 12, 225; Museum of Anthropology collections at, 12; Office of State Archaeology at, 13, 222, 224, 225; public education programs at, 221
University of Kentucky Museum of Anthropology, 221
University of Kentucky Reports in Anthropology and Archaeology, 10, 12
University of Kentucky Studies in Anthropology, 12